THE IDEOLOGIES OF THE DEVELOPING NATIONS

The IDEOLOGIES of the
DEVELOPING NATIONS

Second Revised Edition

Edited by
PAUL E. SIGMUND

PRAEGER PUBLISHERS
New York · Washington · London

PRAEGER PUBLISHERS
111 Fourth Avenue, New York, N.Y. 10003, U.S.A.
5, Cromwell Place, London SW7 2JL, England

Published in the United States of America in 1972
by Praeger Publishers, Inc.

Second printing, 1972

This is the second revised and enlarged edition of the book published
in the United States of America in 1963 by Frederick A. Praeger, Inc.
The first revised and enlarged edition was published in 1967.

Library of Congress Catalog Card Number: 71–150706

Printed in the United States of America

Contents

v

THE IDEOLOGIES OF THE DEVELOPING NATIONS

INTRODUCTION
TO THE FIRST EDITION *

The dictionary defines "ideology" as "a systematic scheme or co-ordinated body of ideas about human life or culture"—a definition that seems to equate ideology with philosophy or social theory. In common usage, however, the word has additional connotations —of commitment (both emotional and intellectual), of action-orientation (the maintenance of the *status quo*, which may be the goal of conservative ideologies, is itself an action), and even of conscious or unconscious distortion of the facts to fit a pre-estab-lished doctrine.[1] The period from the seventeenth century to the nineteenth century in Europe has been described as the "age of ideology," for it saw an extraordinary outpouring of theories about the nature of man in relation to the present or future state of society. It was also a period of political, economic, and social revo-lution, in which the traditional order of medieval Europe gave way to a modern industrial society and men became conscious of the variety of alternative paths open to them in their own personal lives, in their religious, philosophical, and political creeds, and in the ordering of society.

This crisis of modernization has now affected large areas of Asia, Africa, the Middle East, and Latin America. What is often described as the "anticolonial revolution" is more than an attempt to assert political autonomy and to end European domination. It is also a social and economic revolution brought about by the attempt of the members of a Westernized elite to bring their coun-tries into the modern world, to create modern states and indus-trialized economies where traditional cultures and subsistence pro-duction had predominated.

The fact that, in addition to its anticolonial character, this is a revolution of modernization makes it possible to consider Latin

---

*A few minor revisions have been made to bring this introduction up to date.

[1] This is the sense in which it is used by Karl Mannheim when he defines ideologies as "more or less conscious disguises of the real nature of the situa-tion." (*Ideology and Utopia* [New York: Harcourt, Brace & Co., 1954], p. 49.)

3

4

INTRODUCTION TO THE FIRST EDITION

America, which has been politically independent for 130 years, in the same category as nations that have only recently received their independence. The leaders of the old nations of Latin America and of the new nations in other parts of the world are experiencing similar problems of economic development and social change, and are often developing similar solutions to them.

To explain to themselves and to others the nature and justification of the changes they wish to induce, the nationalist leaders have been compelled to give more specific content to the general goal of development to which they all subscribe. In doing this, they have been able to draw upon ideologies developed earlier in Europe. Especially in Latin America, the ideologies of the period of early industrialism in Europe have been adapted to fit an analogous situation in nations now experiencing the problems associated with modern development. Yet, if one takes a broader view of the developing areas as a whole, there is a notable absence of the conflict of ideologies that has characterized European political life during the last century. As recent debates in the United Nations have demonstrated, the leaders of the group of nations variously described as "new," "uncommitted," "emerging," or "developing" share many political, economic, and social ideas as to the type of society they are building. Although they may differ regarding the appropriate methods for reaching their goals, these leaders (with the exception of those in the most backward and tradition-bound areas) are united by a group of beliefs that give expression to common feelings about the past, present, and future.

These beliefs correspond to our definition of ideology in that they elicit an emotional commitment by the leadership and their followers and are directed toward action—the development of a new society in a certain direction, in conformity with certain goals. However, the doctrines of modernizing nationalism do not have the all-encompassing quality of the great ideological world-systems of Marxism, Christianity, or utilitarian liberalism, although they may coincide in some respects with one or another element in these ideologies. They are held by leaders with a wide variety of religious and philosophical outlooks, or with no particular metaphysical presuppositions. The particular problems of individual states also vary in accordance with their special situations. Yet, all the developing nations are undergoing the same general experience, and their reactions to it are similar in theoretical content and practical application. To determine whether these goals, aspirations, and doctrines—given their eclectic character and practical orientation—can be systematically organized in a way that would qualify them as an alternative ideology to current political creeds, it is necessary to give more detailed consideration to the specific content of the doctrines of modernizing nationalism.

National Independence and Freedom

A basic principle of the nationalist leaders has already been mentioned—the absolute primacy of the goal of national development. Since development takes place within the framework of the nation-state, whether it is in existence or in the process of being created, national independence is the first step on the road to development. As the inscription on Kwame Nkrumah's statue in Accra read, "Seek ye first the political kingdom and all other things shall be added unto it." It is as a prerequisite to development that the nationalist leaders demand freedom. However, this freedom refers to *national* rather than individual liberty. It is the assertion of the right of the nation to self-direction and independence of foreign domination. Freedom is demanded for "the people," not for the individual.[2]

It is sometimes difficult to determine exactly what constitutes the nation that ought to be free. In Africa, and to some extent in the Middle East, where movements for regional unification are strong, there has been some ambivalence about national boundaries as they were imposed by the Europeans. However, on the whole, the existing divisions seem to be accepted as the basis from which to work. Except where the alteration of the frontier involves the elimination of a colonial enclave, as in Goa or Dutch New Guinea, the existing boundaries are accepted, and it is felt that they may only be changed by the free consent of the governments involved.

The meaning of the term "the people" is also in need of clarification. Independence, freedom, and development are asserted as goals in the name of the people. It is the authority of the people that gives legitimacy to anticolonial revolutions and post-independence governments. Yet, there is always a certain amount of

---

[2] "We have chosen the freedom, the right, the power, the sovereignty of the people, and not of the individual. Before this people you should have no individual personality. Our personality becomes part of the personality of the nation." (Sékou Touré, quoted in *West Africa*, July 22, 1961, p. 799.)

elitism mixed with the "populism" of the nationalist leadership.[8] Before independence, it was assumed without any need of proof that the people desired to be liberated from colonialism. Yet, after independence, a massive political education program often must be carried on to assure that the popular will actually corresponds to the conception of it in the theory of the nationalist leadership.

The Creation of Modern Nationalism

There are difficulties in determining what constitutes "the nation" or "the people" because in many cases neither entity really exists. A sense of nationhood and loyalty to the people as a collective entity must first be created to replace or supplement other allegiances based on traditional or hierarchical status differentiations. In Max Weber's terms, the transition must be made from a "traditional" to a "rational-legal" order.[4]

Westerners are familiar with the organic process by which European society was transformed from a largely traditional and agrarian, even tribal, social organization into the modern, rationalized, and institutionalized nation-state. European economic development, new organizational and scientific techniques, and the new political ideas drawn from the classical and Christian heritage of the late Middle Ages resulted in the radical change of ways of living and ways of thinking about life associated with the emergence of modern industrial civilization. Powerful ideological justifications for status differentiation, hereditary privilege, and hierarchical social organization were developed in Europe between the twelfth and the nineteenth century, and enclaves of traditionalism still remain. However, the overwhelming power of the nationalist and equalitarian ideology has either overcome other loyalties in the West or, alternatively, achieved a kind of coexistence with them which has permitted the integration of diverse ethnic, religious, and social groupings within a pluralistic consensus in the modern

---

[8] "He [the intellectual] looks up to the people and down on the masses." (Mary Matossian, "Ideologies of Delayed Industrialization," in John Kautsky [ed.], Political Change in Underdeveloped Countries [New York: John Wiley & Sons, 1962], p. 262.) On the "populism" of the nationalist leaders in relation to similar phenomena in Germany, Russia, and America, see the discussion by Edward Shils in the same collection (especially pp. 214–15).

[4] David Apter has used these categories in his analysis of the creation of a new nation, in The Gold Coast in Transition (Princeton, N.J.: Princeton University Press, 1955).

nation-state. In most Western countries, the organic development of national unity over the centuries has created a sense of common purpose and civic responsibility, and led to a rationalization and legalization of the structure of authority.[5]

The creation of loyalty to the nation and the emergence of the nation as a functional community is now under way in many of the new states. Differences of caste, tribe, clan, or religion must be integrated into the political process, and it is precisely because they loom so large as an obstacle to the creation of the modern nation-state that the leaders place great emphasis on the primacy of "the nation" and the elimination of traditional status differentiations.[6] In nationalist thinking, there is a recognition of the need for the creation of a broader community on a regional and international level, but the first requirement is the implementation of the common ideal of universal participation in the nation. The recent experience of the Congo, India's continuing problem with communalism, earlier difficulties with Ashanti regionalism in Ghana, and differences between the various regions of Nigeria are all examples of the fissiparous tendencies against which the new nation-builders must work.

In dealing with the problem of the creation of a new society and a new center of loyalty and faith, the leaders of Asia, Africa, Latin America, and the Middle East have taken three different positions. First, there remain the traditionalists or conservatives like King Saud of Saudi Arabia, the tribal leaders of Africa, or dictators like Stroessner of Paraguay. Such leaders try to preserve the existing oligarchic order, and view the disruptive forces of modernization as a threat to their maintenance of power (as indeed they are). Yet, they cannot avoid being drawn into the world-wide

[5] The divisions, traditional-modern or traditional-rational-legal, are not absolute. There are no completely "modern" systems, and, conversely, modern elements can be perceived in many traditional political cultures. (Cf. discussion in Gabriel Almond and James S. Coleman, The Politics of the Developing Areas [Princeton, N.J.: Princeton University Press, 1960], p. 11.)

[6] "In three or four years, no one will remember the tribal, ethnic, and religious differences which have caused so much difficulty to the country and people in the recent past. . . . We are for a united people, a unitary state at the service of an indivisible nation." (Sékou Touré, La Lutte du Parti Démocratique de Guinée pour l'Emancipation Africaine [Conakry: Imprimerie Nationale, 1959], pp. 58, 149.) Cf. Thomas Hodgkin, "A Note on the Language of African Nationalism," African Affairs (Carbondale, Ill.), No. 1 (1961), pp. 22–40.

technological revolution, with all its subversive social and political consequences. In order to justify their positions, these leaders may appeal to religious beliefs, custom, or the requirements of order and stability but the attraction of modernization to the educated elite makes it difficult for their regimes to compete for support. The second category of leaders comprises those who wish to strike a balance between the maintenance of traditional structures and the radical transformation of society as a whole. One thinks of such diverse figures as Gandhi, Ayub Khan, Léopold Senghor, or Joseph Kasavubu as typical of the reforming elite who wish to integrate and utilize the traditional loyalties and hierarchical groupings in the formation of a new nation, creating a synthesis of the old and the new. Finally, there is the third group, which, while not necessarily aiming at the destruction of traditional groups, wishes to eliminate them from political influence and power as obstacles to the process of social and political transformation.[7] The radical modernizers see no rational basis for status differentiations not based on political or economic function, and they are willing to use persuasion, propaganda, monolithic political parties, and sometimes force as well to bring about the new community.

While the first does no more than pay occasional lip service to the ideals of modernization, the other two types of ruling elite accept them completely. Neither the reformers nor the radicals wish to wait for organic development to bring their societies into the modern world. However, the two groups differ significantly on methods. And this particular difference has already made its impact in Africa in the divisions in the Organization of African Unity; in Latin America in the profound division between Fidelist movements and reformist leaders like Frei, Figueres, and Haya de la Torre; and in Asia, where the Chinese revolution provides a Communist model of forced economic development that contrasts with the more gradual and democratic approach of India.

This is not to assert that there are not profound differences

---

[7] A similar but somewhat misleading distinction between "revolutionary" and "radical-reformist" Pan-Africanists is made by Colin Legum, in *Pan-Africanism* (rev. ed.; New York: Frederick A. Praeger, 1965), pp. 62–64. Cf. also David Apter's distinction between "mobilization" and "consociational" regimes, in *The Political Kingdom of Uganda* (Princeton, N.J.: Princeton University Press, 1961), pp. 4–5; and the division into neotraditional, transitional, and actively modernizing oligarchies, in Max F. Millikan and Donald L. M. Blackmer, *The Emerging Nations* (Boston: Little, Brown, 1961), pp. 79–88.

among the various representatives of both the radical and the reformist wings of the modernizing elite. To identify Sékou Touré's approach to social change with that of Fidel Castro, or Nehru's with that of Houphouet-Boigny or Haya de la Torre, is to ignore the diversity of national situations and of the solutions proposed. The division into traditionalists, reformers, and radicals is based on general similarities of attitude toward social, political, and economic change, within which there are considerable differences. However, it provides a more useful analytical tool than classifications reflecting European ideological categories or distinctions derived from the East-West conflict which are not related to the problems of modernization and development.

A National System of Education

Both the radicals and the reformers recognize the key role of education in nation-building. They criticize the unrealistic content and limited scope of the colonial educational systems, which reflected the standards and the needs of the metropoles and were often unrelated to local conditions and requirements. A system geared solely to the training of a few civil servants, teachers, and lawyers is not considered adequate for a nation undergoing an economic and social revolution. One of the first steps after independence, therefore, has been an increase in the number of primary and secondary schools and of universities and technical schools, as well as a reform of the content of education to meet the need for skilled and semiskilled personnel.

On a basic level, the problem of illiteracy is being attacked by massive programs of primary education, often with considerable political content. The literacy campaigns carried out by Fidel Castro in Cuba and by Sékou Touré in Guinea have demonstrated that an organized program can virtually eradicate this problem in a short time and can also be useful in building political loyalty. The illiterate masses who have had little or no relation to national politics are educated to read the party literature and to become aware of national and international problems from the party point of view.

It is not only the radical or revolutionary regimes that put a high priority on basic education and political indoctrination. All the modernizing nationalists recognize that the educational system can be used to develop loyalty to the nation—and to the party, often considered to be synonymous with the nation. The line between education for citizenship and political indoctrination is a thin one (as indeed it often is in the developed countries) but the modernizing nationalists universally accept the need for a high political content in education.

Because of both the political significance of education and its importance in developing the various levels of trained cadres required for economic development, the nationalist program usually calls for centrally planned control and development of the school system. Since education in many of the new nations had been carried out by missionary groups or under private auspices, there is a potential (and, in a few cases, actual) conflict between these groups and the nationalist leaders, who desire a "national" educational system. These tensions are aggravated by the accusation of radical nationalists (often themselves the products of mission schools) that missionary education is an instrument of colonial domination aimed at producing a subservient colonial mentality among the students. In some cases, this may lead to conflicts recalling the church-state struggles of Europe in the nineteenth and early twentieth centuries, while in others, a working adjustment may be worked out with a mutual recognition of the rights of private groups and the requirements of the new nations.

With national control of education, the curriculum is being altered to emphasize national history, culture, and politics. In Africa, where the Pan-African ideology is strong, there is also an increasing emphasis on the cultural heritage of the African peoples and their distinctive contributions to civilization (see discussion below of the "African personality").

Another aspect of the nationalist revolution as it affects education is the desire to develop a native teaching staff and reduce dependence on foreign teaching personnel. A number of African countries, for instance, are drawing up long-range programs of "Africanization" of education, but the expansion of education and the opening of other career opportunities for educated Africans make it likely that there will be a continued teacher shortage, despite the increase in teacher-training programs that has followed independence.

At the university level, a rapid development of educational facilities is also taking place, along with a shift of emphasis away from the humanistic bias of the colonial university and in the direction of technical subjects. The new University of Nsukka in Nigeria, sponsored by an American land-grant state university, is attempting to carry out this reorientation of the curriculum with emphasis on agriculture and technology rather than the classical subjects of the British university. In Guinea, a planned program for the development of technicians involves sending large numbers of students abroad to study technical subjects in both Eastern and Western countries. These efforts are aimed at producing native cadres who can carry out programs of national development, for education is a means to nation-building, not only in the sense of the creation of nationhood but also as a prerequisite of economic progress.

Economic Development Through "Socialist" Methods

When the nationalist leaders speak of the "development" of the nation, they are speaking primarily of *economic* development. The leadership and members of nationalist movements are acutely aware of the galling contrast between the poverty, illiteracy, and disease of their own countries and the affluence of the economically developed areas. For them, the crucial division in the world is not between the rival political faiths of Communism and liberal democracy, but between the rich and the poor, the economically developed and the underdeveloped, the technically competent and the technologically "backward" areas of the world. The key to the eradication of this difference in living standards lies in economic development, and more particularly in industrialization. With development and industrialization, it will be possible to achieve social equality, educational opportunity, and minimum standards of health and sanitation—in short, the modern welfare state. Without it, population growth and the "revolution of rising expectations" will bring about increasing suffering, political frustration, and social discontent.

Nationalist thinking has given less attention to the need for agricultural development than to the requirements of industrialization, although the present agricultural difficulties of the Soviet Union and China are an indication of the importance of the balanced development of the agricultural sector of the economy. A steel mill is a more dramatic symbol of economic development and national prestige than is a bag of fertilizer, and it seems to promise a much more immediate effect on economic growth. Moreover, agriculture is involved too closely with their former colonial status as a source of primary products to engender much enthusiasm among nationalist leaders.

In their drive toward industrialization, the modernizing nationalists are not prepared to follow the model of the United States, the European nations, or Japan, each of which achieved economic development under private auspices. The nationalist leaders, with the exception of some Latin Americans, are in agreement in rejecting the capitalist method of development as slow, inefficient, and unsuited to their conditions. It is their view that rapid economic growth can only be attained by "socialist" methods, although the precise meaning of this socialism is rarely defined in detail.

Capitalism is rejected and socialism preferred for moral as well as economic reasons. The socialism of the developing nations is said to be directed at the establishment of a society based on justice rather than profit, rational planning rather than the blind operation of the market, and forced economic growth and industrialization as opposed to the orientation of the economy to the production of raw materials for the profit of foreign enterprises. These goals are accepted by nearly all the leaders of Asia, Africa, Latin America, and the Middle East, although their implementation is not as commonly agreed upon or even understood.

Since the Soviet bloc describes itself as the "camp of socialism" or the "socialist countries,"[8] there is the appearance of similarity between Communist goals and methods and those of the emerging nations. Yet, while there is no denying the appeal of the Soviet example of economic development, to equate the two positions is to ignore a fundamental and recurring feature in the ideology of modernizing nationalism—its attempt to establish a separate identity in an intermediate position between East and West. The nationalist leaders insist that they are forging a new approach to economic development that avoids the errors of both capitalism and Communism. Whether it is the "communitarian society" of Frei, the "African socialism" of Senghor, "ujamaa" of Nyerere, the "communocracy" of Sékou Touré, or the "democratic, socialist, cooperative democracy" of Nasser, there is a common commitment to a new form of development that will allow planning and central control of the economy while continuing to permit some measure of private initiative. At the same time that these theories denounce a stereotyped capitalism for its excessive

[8] Even Julius Nyerere speaks of the Communist countries as the "socialist bloc" in "Nationalism and Pan-Africanism" (see below, p. 283).

individualism, its lack of concern with human and social values, and its fostering of the spirit of ruthless competition, they also criticize a stereotyped Communism for its excessive collectivism, its suppression of the individual, its materialism, and its narrow commitment to the national interest of a single country or group of countries.

Because of the intimate involvement of capitalism in the colonial enterprise, the criticisms of capitalism often seem considerably harsher than those of Communism. Even native capitalists are linked to the colonial rulers in nationalist theory. Capitalists are concerned only with profit, the argument goes, and they are willing to collaborate with those who have financial control—in the case of the colonial countries, with the foreign rulers. They are not concerned with the welfare of the people, with national independence, or with economic development—but only with the maximization of their profits (usually lodged in foreign banks).

This is an accurate description of the conduct of certain business leaders in the underdeveloped countries, but it ignores the contributions—financial, intellectual, and political—that others have made to the nationalist cause. In addition, even if the businessman is acting merely out of his own economic interest, independence may be more to his immediate benefit than foreign rule. It can give him a protected market, a government subsidy, and restrictions against foreign competition. Some of the strongest support for economic nationalism and "anti-imperialism" in Latin America, for instance, comes from the domestic business interests, and the Congress Party in India received heavy financial assistance from Indian business leaders throughout its long struggle with the British. In Africa as well, native businessmen have been deeply involved with nationalist parties.

Capitalism also suffers from its association with the evils of colonialism, described in the Leninist theory of imperialism. The theory of imperialism that has achieved the status of "conventional wisdom" among the nationalist leaders does not emphasize, as did Lenin, the importance of finance monopoly and finance capital in generating the need for overseas investment opportunities. The nationalists accept the more general Marxist theory that, because of increased production costs and their inability to dispose of consumption goods, the colonial countries seek a cheap source of raw materials and a market for their products.[9] It is the nature of capitalism to seek to maximize profits, the argument goes, and colonial domination assures the capitalists of a protected market from which all competition is excluded, and it maintains the colony in a permanent state of underdevelopment, so that wages will remain low and raw materials cheap.[10]

The part of the Leninist theory with the greatest appeal to nationalist thinking is Lenin's argument that the continued success of capitalism in advanced countries is based on capitalist bribes to the workers from the fruits of colonial exploitation. In nationalist thinking, Lenin's theory is transformed from an ideological justification of Marxist predictions into a burning indictment of the evils of colonial oppression. If the prosperity of the advanced nations is grounded on the exploitation of colonies, then foreign aid, for instance, is not an act of generosity or of mutual interest. It is either an attempt to maintain continued economic control or, alternatively, a meager effort to restore to Africa (or Latin America or the Middle East) the riches stolen during centuries of imperialist exploitation.[11] (The fact that countries such as Sweden have attained a high level of prosperity without colonies—demonstrating that the prosperity of the advanced nations depends on something more than colonies and cheap raw materials—is not considered, for the theory is not so much an argument as a rationalization or ideological justification for needed economic assistance from the West.)

The nationalists' suspicion of the economic influence of the

[9] The Senegalese nationalist leader Abdoulaye Ly attributes this theory to Rosa Luxemburg; quoted in Hodgkin, *op. cit.*, p. 32. However, the link between overproduction and the need for foreign markets is a commonplace of Marxist theory.

[10] "The economy of European nations consists fundamentally of selling manufactured products to underdeveloped countries at high prices and buying raw materials from them at the lowest possible cost." (Léopold Sédar Senghor, *African Socialism*; see below, p. 244.)

"Human greed . . . stimulated a search for territories from which raw materials could be obtained cheaply and plentifully. After the raw materials had been processed into manufactured goods, it became necessary again to look for markets which would be under their control, so that the manufactured goods could be sold at prices to suit them." (U Nu, *Toward a Socialist State* [Rangoon, 1958], p. 4.)

[11] "The states with a colonialist past are, more than others, compelled to offer to the nations aspiring to development part of the national wealth they sapped when that wealth was a booty for all looters." (Nasser, "Arab Socialism"; see below, p. 162.)

West is expressed in their theory of "neocolonialism." As developed by the radical nationalists, but also given wide credence among the more moderate group, this theory asserts that although political independence has been achieved, there are still links of economic dependence that vitiate the apparent autonomy of the new nations. The wealthy nations wish to exploit the proletarian nations in order to keep them poor and underdeveloped, as well as politically favorable to the policies of the "neocolonialist" powers. Proponents of the theory cite the powerful influence of the United States in Latin America, politically independent since the early nineteenth century, demonstrated by the unanimity with which (before the rise of Castro) the Latin American nations followed U.S. policy in the United Nations. They note that the new states of French-speaking Africa that are most dependent economically on France consistently supported the French position on the Algerian question in the United Nations, despite the unanimity of African support for the rebel nationalists. The division of Africa into two general groupings—and more particularly into many small and economically nonviable states (described as "Balkanization")—is seen as an effort both to maintain political influence and to assure economic domination and the maintenance of profits.[12] Above all, the events following the independence of the Congo, the secession of Katanga and the murder of Lumumba have appeared to confirm the belief in the sinister machinations of international capitalist interests.

The extent to which these events are attributed exclusively to economic factors is a measure of the impact of Marxist theories of causation on the thinking of many of the leaders of emergent nationalism. To explain colonialism and the politics of the post-colonial era solely in terms of economic domination is simple and intellectually satisfying; moreover, it often seems to fit the facts. On this basis, colonial domination and imperialism are the result of capitalism, and the Western "capitalist" nations are necessarily imperialistic, while the Communist states, lacking an economic motive for imperialist expansion, are exempt from this criticism.[13]

[12] See, for example, the resolutions on neocolonialism adopted at the All-African Peoples' Conference, Cairo, March 23–31, 1961, in Legum, *op. cit.*, pp. 272–75.

[13] See, for example, Kofi Baako, "Nkrumaism," *The Party* (Accra), Nos. 4–7 (April–July, 1961). Baako states that "imperialism and its twin sister, capitalism, are by their very nature and content the main causes of wars."

Yet, many nationalist leaders recognize that the Leninist theory is inadequate. They perceive that colonial domination and post-colonial attempts to retain control and influence are the products of the rivalries of powerful nations, which will inevitably attempt to draw weak nations into their spheres of influence.[14] While the economic motive is a factor in the assessment of the conduct of the "capitalist" West, *all* powerful nations, whatever their economic system, are regarded as potentially imperialistic. This alternative theory of imperialism is quite compatible with the neutralist orientation of the nationalists. It applies to the Soviet Union as much as to the West—and, taking into account the lack of restraints on power in the U.S.S.R., with an even greater validity. Yet, those who give greater emphasis to power politics as an explanation of imperialism have experienced only Western imperialism and hence are likely to continue to direct their criticisms principally at the West. Imperialism usually means Western "capitalist" imperialism, and Soviet imperialism is only rarely criticized.[15]

In the stereotype of the nationalist ideology, both the domestic capitalists and the "international imperialists" are associated in their common desire to control the political process so as to assure that it does not interfere with their economic interests. The domestic capitalists are the "stooges" of the international exploiters. Together with the feudal aristocracy and traditional ruling classes, they form the controlling "oligarchy" whose power, supported by foreign interests, must be broken by the nationalist leaders.[16]

14 Nyerere speaks of the two "power blocs" using the slogans of anti-Communism and anti-imperialism in a "second scramble for Africa." ("Nationalism and Pan-Africanism"; see below, p. 283.) Nasser also warns that both sides in the Cold War are trying to draw the U.A.R. into a "zone of influence." (*President Nasser's Speeches, 1959* [Cairo, 1960], pp. 469–70.) See also Reinhold Niebuhr, "The Relation of Strength to Weakness in the World Community," in Laurence W. Martin (ed.), *Neutralism and Nonalignment* (New York: Praeger Publishers, 1962), pp. 196–98.

15 Archbishop Makarios of Cyprus was the only leader at the Belgrade Conference in September, 1961, to take a strong stand on Berlin and on the Soviet resumption of nuclear tests.

16 Cf. Nasser, "Principles of Socialist, Cooperative Democracy," *Egyptian Economic and Political Review*, September–October, 1961, p. 23, in which he denounces "the inherited social system dominated by the imperialists and their stooges, feudalists, and capitalists." On the role of the "oligarchy" in Latin America, see Rómulo Betancourt, *Trayectoria Democrática de una Revolución* (Caracas: Imprenta Nacional, 1948). In Africa, the terms, "Uncle Tom" and "Quisling" are used to the same effect. (Cf. Hodgkin, *op. cit.*, p. 29.)

Here economic and political objectives join with the equalitarianism of nationalist social thought in the demand for the elimination of economic differences in the new "socialist" society being built. The prejudice against both domestic and foreign capitalism is not only based on the narrow concern of the capitalists with the maximization of profits and their supposed opposition to economic development in the emerging nations. It is also derived from a view of capitalist society as one that is essentially based on social and economic inequality. Contrasted with the passionate concern of the nationalist leaders to eliminate inequality and to develop economically, the wealthy nations are seen as conspiring with the wealthy classes in the poor nations to maintain poverty, illiteracy, and underdevelopment.

The "socialism" of the new nations is thus fed by antiforeign feelings, by a passion for social equality, and by a desire for rapid economic development. It is influenced by the Marxist analysis of capitalism and the Leninist description of imperialism, but it does not accept the entire Marxist-Leninist theory as the basis of action. It is a *nationalist* socialism, and therefore it rejects the Marxist-Leninist theory of the class struggle, at least as applied to internal economic relations. The working men (and, more important, the peasants) *do* have a country—despite Marx's assertion to the contrary—and the unity of the people in building the nation requires that the nationalist leader play down the special interests of any one class, including the proletariat. The African leaders who are most influenced by Marxism assert that Africa is *now* a classless society and therefore is not subject to the contradictions of the Marxist class struggle.[17]

In addition, it is a *humanist* socialism and therefore opposed to Marxist materialism. The nationalist leaders—whether Nasser, Nkrumah, or Senghor—insist that there is no opposition between their socialism and spiritual or religious values.[18] In fact, they

[17] "[The African] rejects the class struggle because of African social groups' identity of living conditions and lack of differentiation into antagonistic classes." (Sékou Touré, quoted in Legum, *op. cit.*, pp. 129–30.) Nasser, in his speech to the National Congress of Popular Forces, on May 21, 1962, specifically ruled out the class struggle as part of "Arab socialism" (see below, p. 157).

[18] "Islam in its early days was the first socialist state." (Nasser, "Principles of Socialist, Cooperative Democracy,". p. 27.)

"Today I am a nondenominational Christian and a Marxist socialist, and assert that their socialism is more in accord with religious and moral norms than the *laissez-faire* capitalism they reject.

It is also a socialism *planned by an elite*. If socialism means participation by the worker in the process of economic planning, there seems to be little evidence of thinking in this direction in the writings or speeches of these nationalists. Although Nasser speaks of his socialism as "cooperative," and although there may be admiration and imitation of the Yugoslav system of workers' councils, there does not seem to be any real intention in the new nations (any more than there is in Yugoslavia) of allowing important economic decisions to be made democratically or as the result of any but the most superficial public discussion. Even in the developed countries, only the general lines of economic policy are decided on by popular consultation. Still more in the case of the developing nations, economists of a wide variety of political and economic beliefs accept the need for a rationalized development through expert planning.[19] When the Kennedy Administration reorganized the U.S. foreign-aid program in the Agency for International Development (AID) in 1961, it indicated that greater U.S. assistance would be forthcoming to those countries presenting an integrated program or plan of economic development. It recognized that in countries where the per capita income is under $100 a year (and this applies to areas containing 50 per cent of the world's population),[20] the transition from traditional and subsistence economies to an expanding and developing dynamic economic system must be made by government planning, whether it is described as socialism or not.

The socialism of the modernizing nationalists often involves

I have not found any contradiction between the two." (Nkrumah, *Ghana: The Autobiography of Kwame Nkrumah* [New York: Thomas Nelson and Sons, 1957], p. 13.)

"We stand for a middle course, for a *democratic socialism* which goes so far as to integrate spiritual values, a socialism which ties in with the old ethical current of the French socialists." (Senghor, *African Socialism*; see below, p. 246.)

[19] Latin American criticisms of development through state planning are the exception. (Summarized in Albert O. Hirschman, "Ideologies of Economic Development in Latin America," in Albert O. Hirschman [ed.], *Latin American Issues, Essays and Comments* [New York: The Twentieth Century Fund, 1961], pp. 23 ff.)

[20] See Millikan and Blackmer, *op. cit.*, pp. 149–59.

some measure of nationalization. The ideology of the nationalist leaders leads them to regard nationalization as a preferred means of assuring national control and direction of economic development. In addition—as was made clear in Nasser's speech of July 22, 1961, when he nationalized major industries and confiscated the holdings of the wealthiest Egyptians—nationalization is considered useful as a measure to bring about social equality and eliminate hostile foreign influences (the alliance of domestic capitalists with former colonial rulers or foreign capitalist interests). Problems may be created, however, if ideological preconceptions interfere with a realistic assessment of the best method to achieve the goal of maximum economic growth. Guinea, for instance, has been forced to dismantle its State Trading Commission, through which it attempted to nationalize all import and export activity and to control most of the distribution of goods. The Guineans learned that it was difficult, if not impossible, to centralize in a government bureau in Conakry all the countless decisions involved in distribution; while retaining a centralized development plan, they have now substantially decentralized decision-making in this area.

The difficulty with the nationalist ideology of economic development is that it does not distinguish between the new-style economically productive business innovators and the old-style nonproductive absentee landlords and moneylenders. There is still a lingering suspicion of the businessman's role as essentially exploitative and a hesitancy to recognize his contribution to national development.

Yet, recently, the doctrinaire espousal of nationalization has given way to a search for new forms of economic life, combining over-all government promotion and direction of economic development with a measure of individual initiative and private ownership. Nasser followed his large-scale nationalizations with measures to promote private ownership of land (up to 100 acres) and of small enterprises. Fourteen years of economic planning in India have also shown that nationalization is not always the appropriate way to economic development. Despite his espousal of socialism, Prime Minister Nehru was frank to admit that nationalization would not assure the rationalized development of the economy that India seeks. The Indian experience seems to demonstrate that as an economy expands, an entrepreneurial class of "innovators" emerges which can invest and utilize the new surpluses more efficiently than government planners.[21]

In Africa, there is little evidence of impending large-scale nationalization even among the more radical nations. Both the radicals and the more moderate governments agree that controls on private business are needed, and both recognize that it has a place in the national economy. However, the radicals tend to prefer a mixture that leans more heavily in the direction of state control.

The same pattern emerges in attitudes toward investment by foreign private capital. The moderate reformers are more eager to encourage private companies and investors to engage in economic development, but they are also aware of the need for appropriate government regulation to assure that this investment is directed toward the development of the country. The radicals, while eager to have foreign capital, often prefer to secure it through direct government-to-government relations, and the restrictions they place on foreign private investment may discourage the additional flow of such capital in their direction, particularly when there are other countries that can offer better terms.[22]

This does not mean, however, as the Marxist analysis would have it, that the individual nation (like the individual worker in the days before the advent of trade unionism) is always at the mercy of international monopoly capitalism because of its weak competitive bargaining position. Larger nations and federal group-

21 See Nasser's speech "Arab Socialism" (below, pp. 156–64), delivered on May 21, 1962. Nehru discusses nationalization in "Indian Socialism" (below, pp. 139–40).   On the role of entrepreneurs in the economies of the developing nations, see Barbara Ward, *India and the West* (New York: W. W. Norton & Company, 1961), Chap. xv; Millikan and Blackmer, *op. cit.*, Chap. v; W. W. Rostow, *The Stages of Economic Growth* (New York: Cambridge University Press, 1960), pp. 50 ff.; Edward Shils, "The Concentration and Dispersion of Charisma," *World Politics*, XI, No. 1 (October, 1958), 1–19.

22 Examples of the two approaches would include the moderate policies toward foreign and domestic capital adopted by Nigeria and Senegal, and the more stringent controls by the governments of Guinea, Ceylon, and Indonesia. Ghana under Nkrumah invited foreign investment, but its official position favored government loans as a preferable method of development. (Cf. Kofi Baako, "Nkrumaism," *The Party* [Accra], No. 6 [June, 1961]: "The Nkrumaist prefers loan capital to investment capital. . . . Loan capital allows the receiver . . . say, the government—to use its loan to set up any state enterprises within the framework of its socioeconomic plan.")

ings are often in a better position to assert control over economic activity by foreign investors (and this is one of the numerous reasons for the movements for a common market in Latin America, and for regional federation in Africa and the Middle East), but even the smaller nations, if they are politically independent, can gain certain advantages from the current competition by foreign investors for investment opportunities in developing countries. The increase in the percentage of profits allocated to Iran and other countries by an Italian oil company from the standard 50–50 arrangement to a 75–25 division is an example of the possibilities to be derived from such competition.

That similar advantages can also come from competition among the governmental sources of capital is clear to all the leaders of the developing nations. The reformists and radicals among the modernizing elite agree on the virtues of "aid without strings" from both East and West. The examples of Nasser's success in playing off the rival blocs in the Cold War and of the construction of steel mills in India by rival teams from the Soviet Union and West Germany have not been lost on other national-ist leaders. It should not be surprising, therefore, that increasing numbers of nations in Asia, Africa, Latin America, and the Middle East turn to the Soviet Union, Eastern Europe, and China for economic assistance, since this policy conforms both to their own urgent need for additional foreign capital and to their ideological position of neutralism or nonalignment in international affairs.

If the developing nations are internally strong, if by maintaining economic links with the West as well as the East they avoid becoming dependent on the Soviet bloc, and if they are themselves committed to democratic methods, aid from the East may strengthen democracy and weaken internal pressures for the more drastic methods of totalitarian control. This is the case already in India, where aid from the Soviet bloc has helped the Congress Party in its struggle to develop the country in the face of both the external example of China and the internal threat of the Indian Communist Party.[23]

When it is a question of *military* aid from the Soviet Union, the situation becomes more complicated. Nasser does not seem to

[23] See Paul Sigmund, "The Uses of Neutralism," *Commonweal*, LXXIII, No. 21 (February 17, 1961), 523–26. Reprinted in David K. Marvin, *Emerging Africa* (San Francisco: Chandler Publishing Company, 1965), pp. 223–31.

have compromised his independent policy by accepting Soviet and Czech weapons, but it would appear that, if only because of the need for ammunition and replacement parts, a certain dependence may result. In addition, the military advisers who accompany this aid may also influence government policy. In apparent recognition of the difference between the two types of aid, the nations of the uncommitted world have so far been much less eager to secure military assistance than economic aid from the Soviet bloc, although India, Indonesia, Guinea, and Mali, in addition to Egypt, have received such military assistance.

Strong Government Under a Single or Dominant Party

All the nationalist leaders see the need for a strong government to achieve the goals of modernization and development. To carry out a social and economic revolution in addition to a political transfer of power requires a government that can act vigorously to educate the people in the new nationalism and to initiate a program of forced economic development. Development requires foreign assistance, whether private or governmental, and a strong government is also considered necessary to direct and control the use of this capital in accordance with national objectives.

The failure of parliamentary regimes to provide this type of effective leadership has meant that a reforming military elite has taken control in a number of the new states. Unlike the old military oligarchies of Latin America and the Iberian peninsula, these new military rulers are committed to the goals of modernization and development. They reject as inapplicable and even fraudulent the party systems borrowed from European parliamentary practice. However, they may retain, in an altered form, the representative assembly and periodic elections by universal suffrage, which are needed to demonstrate that political power comes from the people, the sole source of legitimacy in the modern state.[24]

The modernizing military oligarchies usually justify their authoritarianism as temporary in character, preparing for the introduction of democracy when economic and social progress permit. In the past, the model for this type of transitional authoritarianism

---

[24] Nasser established a modified parliamentarism in the United Arab Republic, which had some importance in legitimizing the succession after his death.

has been the modernizing rule of Kemal Atatürk in Turkey, which prepared the way for what appeared to be an orderly transition to democracy (although recent events in Turkey have called into question the success of that transition).

A similar transitional role may be played by the popular leader with quasi-charismatic qualities derived from his part in the nationalist effort to gain independence. This is frequently the case in Africa, as well as in countries like India, where the tradition of subordination of the military to the civilian authority is strong. The nationalist leaders have developed an effective instrument of modernization in the single or dominant nationalist party reaching down into every level of national life. Military reformers like Nasser have recognized its effectiveness and have attempted to develop their own nationalist parties to organize the people, to control and to respond to public opinion, and to give legitimacy to the government.

Both the moderate and radical wings of the nationalist elite favor the single or dominant national party, and such parties exist in many of the new nations of Africa, in several countries in Asia, and, in the case of Mexico, in Latin America as well.[25] However, the structure of a dominant moderate or reformist party is usually different from that of a radical one. Where the radicals create an entirely new structure from the basic unit (or "cell") to the leadership, the reformists often make use of existing groups and traditional loyalties to build their parties. In the latter instance, the dynamic of social change is considerably diminished since groups with an interest in the present arrangement of society often form an important segment of the party.[26]

Similarly, the more moderate parties are less eager to mobilize and control the various voluntary groups in the society as auxiliaries of the party. The radical leaders argue that the task of nation-building requires that student, youth, labor, and women's groups

[25] Senghor has defended the existence of an opposition party (see below, p. 249), but Senegal now has, in effect, a one-party system.

[26] This distinction based on attitudes toward other groups in the society differs from the mass-party, elite-party dichotomy based on internal structure, which is utilized by Thomas Hodgkins, in *African Political Parties* (Baltimore, Md.: Penguin Books, 1961), pp. 68–75, and by Ruth Schachter, in "Single Party Systems in West Africa," *American Political Science Review*, LV, No. 2 (June, 1961), 294–307. Houphouet-Boigny's PDCI, for example, is a mass party with a moderate reformist program.

be organized and directed toward national goals by the party, rather than being left to their own parochial concerns. In the more extreme versions of this theory, every such group organized in the colonial period is viewed as an instrument of colonialist and imperialist attempts to influence the thinking of the colonized peoples. Whether it is the Boy Scouts or the Young Men's Christian Association, or international affiliation with groups like the World Assembly of Youth or the International Confederation of Free Trade Unions, all are suspect as organizations that either divert the energies of the interest group in question from the task of nation-building or are actively used by an external enemy to subvert national independence. (In Africa, some of the more moderate regimes have also borrowed the radicals' techniques and decreed the dissolution of student, youth, and labor groups or their integration into the party, particularly when they are opposed to the government.)

The nationalist leaders admit to a degree of elitism in their views on the relation of party and government to the people. Whether in the "guided democracy" of Sukarno, the "basic democracy" of Ayub Khan, or the "democratic dictatorship" of Sékou Touré, the popular will from which a government or ruling party must derive its legitimacy in a democratic age seems to consist as much in what the people *should* desire as in what they *do* desire. That there should be some confusion on this point is not surprising since democratic theory has always been ambiguous in this respect. The classical democratic assumption of the automatic coincidence of the subjective will of the majority and the objective standard of natural law or the greatest good of the greatest number has not always been realized in fact. Rousseau himself admitted that a "legislator" was required to prepare the people to exercise their responsibilities as participants in the general will.[27] In a sense, the nationalist leaders see themselves as the "lawgivers" of the new dispensation, involving the entire population, and imposing modernization, economic development, and "democracy."

As in the case of the reformist military regimes, the single party is defended as a transitional stage necessary to establish the essential preconditions of liberal democracy. The new nations are

[27] Jean Jacques Rousseau, *The Social Contract*, Chap. vii. The "legislator" also appears in Greek thought and in Machiavelli's *Discourses*.

said to lack a minimum national unity and consensus on basic values, the economic basis for a middle class to give stability to the system, a sufficiently high literacy rate to make political discussion and choice meaningful, and a tradition of self-restraint on the part of both majority and minority necessary for the give and take between those in power and the loyal opposition that is characteristic of a democratic system.[28] Yet, despite the admitted authoritarian elements, the single party is said to be democratic in structure and purpose. It is a mass organization open to all the citizenry—and this is an important difference from the Leninist conception of the party as an elite group.[29] It is the energizing force that carries out the program of development, but it is also in touch with the people and communicates their feelings to the leadership. In some defenses of the single party by leaders of Africa, Asia, and the Middle East (and by Cuba's Castro as well), it is even argued that a new and superior form of democracy is being developed in the single party.

The single or dominant party system is said to be more democratic than a system of two or more parties, since the Western parties usually represent narrow class, religious, or ethnic interests rather than the nation as a whole. Even in the two-party system, rule is exercised by a majority that may be as small as 50 per cent plus one, instead of by the whole people.[30] Those most influenced by the Marxist analysis argue that in the case of the United States, for instance, both parties are under the control of the same oligarchy of wealthy business interests. To an even greater extent, the multiparty systems of the colonial or semicolonial period are viewed as a facade for control by foreign or capitalist interests. Outside influences use the divisions and rivalries of the multiparty system and play upon the selfishness of petty politicians who are concerned only with playing the parliamentary game,

[28] For a typical expression of the view that under present conditions there is no alternative to one-party rule in Africa, see Immanuel Wallerstein, *Africa, The Politics of Independence* (New York: Random House, 1961), p. 163. An opposing view, which denounces the Western paternalism implied in this attitude, appears in Obafemi Awolowo's autobiography, *Awo* (Cambridge and New York: Cambridge University Press, 1960), pp. 300–305.

[29] Fidel Castro has adopted the Leninist conception of the party as an elite "vanguard of the proletariat." (See below, p 353.)

[30] Sukarno criticizes "free-fight liberalism, where half plus one is **always** right" (see below, p. 111). Cf. Julius Nyerere, "Democracy and the Party System" (below, pp. 305–13).

rather than working for reform and development. In a new nation where, except for "the agents of imperialism," there is no sharp differentiation of economic interest, the single party is more appropriate to the economic and social development of society, and more necessary in order to resist outside pressures and pursue the interest of the nation as a whole.[31] The requirements of democracy are observed, say the defenders of the single-party system, *within* the parties rather than between them. There is no need for more than one party if there is freedom of discussion, democratic election of party leaders, and responsiveness of those in power to a mass membership that is broadly representative of the whole population. Multipartyism encourages disunity and factionalism, even subversion, at a time when there is the greatest need for national unity.

If this argument sounds suspiciously like the Soviet defense of "democratic centralism," this is no accident. Sékou Touré, the leading apologist for the single party, is frank to acknowledge the influence of the Leninist theory. However, while not ignoring Lenin's insistence on rigid party discipline, Touré emphasizes the importance of the maintenance of democratic procedures within the party and sees it as a mass movement rather than a conspiratorial elite.[32] Not only the Marxists defend the single party for nations undergoing the revolution of modernization. Leaders as diverse as Nyerere of Tanganyika and former President Sukarno of Indonesia assert that it is in keeping with the traditional methods of decision-making in their societies, which tend to operate on the basis of consensus rather than dialectical opposition. Democracy is "talking until you agree," says Nyerere, not opposition for opposition's sake.[33]

The analogy in the one-party theory is more with Rousseau than with Lenin. The single party is "democratic" not because it is a vanguard that has an insight into the real meaning of economics and history, but because all participate and there is a continual

[31] See Sékou Touré on Africa as a classless society (p. 17, n. 17); Gamal Abdel Nasser's defense of the National Union Party (see *President Nasser's Speeches*, 1959); and Fidel Castro's description of the bourgeois party as "a gang of politicians, a conglomeration of individuals who defend class interests" (below, p 353).

[32] Below, pp. 238 ff. Use of the term "democratic centralism" to describe the party structure is characteristic of the radical wing of African nationalism, but it is not used by other nationalist parties.

[33] "Democracy and the Party System" (below, pp. 305–13).

dialogue among leader, leading party, and the masses. The am-
biguity in Rousseau's "general will" and its potential for tyranny,
whether by the leader or by the majority, is shared by the theory
of the single party, which often tends to minimize the possibility
of a conflict between the individual and the group, party, or
nation.

Yet, in his classic defense of the single party, Madeira Keita,
ex-Minister of Justice of the Republic of Mali, recognized that
there are real dangers in this system. Keita emphasized the great
demands that the absence of an organized opposition places upon
the leadership of the single party. (Keita also noted that he favored the term "unified party," emphasizing the variety of tendencies within the movement.) Perhaps in anticipation of subsequent
developments, the French-speaking African intellectual Cheikh
Anta Diop, commenting on Keita's speech, expressed the fear that
unless the African territories formed a larger federation, the single-
party systems in each country would become the instrumentalities
of "petty ephemeral dictatorships" of the Latin American type.[34]

In the absence of institutional safeguards for the expression of
dissenting opinions, there is a danger that the charismatic leader,
convinced of his mission to reform society, may suppress even
legitimate criticism of those in power. Some observers see in the
auxiliary organizations of youths, students, labor, etc., the means
of institutional expression of criticism, but Roberto Michels' "iron
law of oligarchy," a sociological generalization from the experience
of the concentration of power at the top of any institutional
hierarchy, suggests that this might not often take place.[35] Particularly when nationalist leaders are enjoying the perquisites of power
after a revolt against existing laws, it may be difficult to develop
respect for the sharing of power in accordance with legal and institutional norms.

The danger is all the more real, since the single-party ideology,
while allowing and encouraging mass affiliation and freedom of

[34] See Madeira Keita, "Le Parti Unique en Afrique," *Présence Africaine*
(Paris). No. 30 (Feb.-March, 1960).

[35] Michels, *Political Parties, A Sociological Study of Oligarchical Tendencies of Modern Democracy* (Glencoe, Ill.: The Free Press, 1958). The argument concerning auxiliary organizations is made by Clement Moore, in "The
National Party: A Tentative Model," in C. J. Friedrich and Seymour Harris
(eds.), *Public Policy*, X (1960), 262 ff. See also Douglas Ashford, "Labor
Politics in a New Nation," *Western Political Quarterly*, XIII, No. 2 (June,
1960), 312–31.

discussion for differing points of view, is often unwilling to accord these rights to the representatives of the traditional order, the "feudal classes," or to those who are considered to be or to have been collaborators with foreigners. Loose charges of "reactionary feudalist" or "imperialist stooge" can be used to stifle legitimate dissent, and the prisons can contain both loyal and disloyal oppositionists. The theory of the single party can result in the revolutionary transformation of society by means of persuasion and democratic discussion, or it can be used to justify the imposition of the will of an oligarchic elite by coercion, propaganda, and Rousseauan mysticism about the will of the people.

An optimistic view is that once the single party has initiated economic development and succeeded in replacing local, tribal, caste, and religious loyalties with a sense of involvement in the nation, it will develop a healthy pluralism of parties or interest groups. Within the national consensus, there will thus be an institutionalized opportunity for the expression of differences as to the method or pace of social change, or even simply of the opposition of the "outs" to the "ins."[36] The Congress Party of India, for instance, once contained within its ranks the leaders of the present Communist and Praja Socialist parties, and recently the supporters of the right-wing Swatantra (Freedom) Party have split off from it.

On the other hand, a more pessimistic critic might doubt whether those who hold power are not more likely to label legitimate economic and social grievances as the product of foreign intrigue and domestic reaction, and thus to step up the pace of repressive measures as the opposition becomes less able to pose a threat to those in control.

Regional Cooperation or Federation

A development which could counteract the single party is the possibility that movements toward federation may promote politi-

[36] Tom Mboya has said that opposition parties will develop "in ten or more years . . . as a normal and natural process of the individual freedom of speech and freedom to criticize the government." (Quoted in Legum, *op. cit.*, p. 124.) Characteristically, Sékou Touré links the existence of the opposition party to the state of economic development. In developed countries, he says, political opposition "by its presence and action, increases the dynamism of the party in power." (Quoted in Immanuel Wallerstein, "Political Theory in an African Context," paper presented to the African Studies Association, September, 1960, p. 13.)

cal pluralism. States of differing political persuasion in geographical proximity may hesitate to suppress political groups in a position to retaliate in a neighboring state of the same federal grouping. Yet, thus far, the two unsuccessful examples of such federation—the union of Syria, and Egypt in the United Arab Republic, and that of Senegal and the Sudan (now the Mali Republic) in the Federation of Mali—seem to indicate that organic federation between states of differing ideologies and social systems is very difficult.

The movement toward regional federation or confederation is not an important one in Asia (although the Bandung Conference of 1955 gave a symbolic expression to the solidarity of Asians and Africans). But in Africa, the Middle East, and Latin America, the desire to create regional structures is strong enough to be a major factor in the ideological appeal of certain nationalist leaders, such as Nasser and Nkrumah, both within and outside their own territorial limits. Nasser has used Pan-Arab feeling to increase Egyptian influence elsewhere in the Middle East; and at one point after the Suez crisis, he seemed close to realizing the dream of Arab unity. In Africa, the movement toward closer cooperation on a Pan-African level receives the support of all groups, but there is disagreement as to the methods and rate by which the goal of a united African continent is to be attained. The radicals call for political union and measures such as the establishment of an African Military High Command, while the moderates support the establishment of functional links (customs, a common currency, etc.) that can form the basis of closer cooperation in the future. The moderates accuse the radicals of fomenting subversion and attempting to alter existing national boundaries, while the radicals view the moderates as tools of "neocolonialism."[37] Yet, both groups agree on the danger of the balkanization of the continent, and both urge a Pan-African regional grouping. Despite the schism in Africa, the appeal of the Pan-African ideal is so great that the present divisions may only be temporary, and a broader form of Pan-African cooperation may be developed in the future.

[37] In the first edition of this book, the radicals and the moderates were described, respectively, as the "Casablanca" and the "Monrovia" powers. With the formation of the Organization of African Unity, this terminology became outmoded, but the differences described above still persist.

In Latin America and the Middle East, efforts at regional co-operation have had little success. The mystique of regional cooperation or unification is not enough, it seems, to overcome personal antagonisms and nationalistic rivalries. Territorial expansion by a strong power is one classic way in which unification has taken place, but the new nations thus far lack the military power to engage in this form of unification, and the great powers, their relationship delicately stabilized in a balance of mutual terror, seem reluctant to involve themselves in a major way in the rivalries of the new nations.

Another possible means to union is a joint effort against a common enemy. The African threat of a crusade to liberate Angola and the Republic of South Africa may someday result in the realization of the projected African army repeatedly discussed during the Congo crisis.[38] Fidel Castro has attempted to use hostility to "Yankee imperialism" in a similar way in Latin America, and the Suez crisis was one of the few occasions in which the Arab world was united.

The remaining alternative, that of a gradual evolution of regional cooperation, is not an appealing one to the impatient nationalists, but it is possible that closer ties will come about through the development of further economic and cultural links rather than by political means. The United Nations Economic Commission for Latin America (ECLA), with headquarters in Santiago de Chile, has already influenced Latin American economic thinking along regional lines, and preliminary efforts have been made to create common organs of regional economic cooperation in Latin America. The Economic Commission for Africa is also exerting a similar influence, and the obvious mutual interdependence of many of the African states has already led to the lowering of some of the economic barriers raised at the time of national independence. The African states continue to meet together, and the tentative gropings of youth, student, and trade-union organizations in Latin America and Africa for regional cooperation either within or out-

---

[38] An African army was proposed by President Nkrumah in his speech to the United Nations on September 23, 1960, and by Julius Nyerere speaking to the Pan-African Seminar of the World Assembly of Youth (WAY) at Dar-es-Salaam on August 6, 1961. The Organization of African Unity has established a Liberation Committee with headquarters in Dar-es-Salaam but it has no armed forces at its disposal.

side existing international organizations are a further reassertion of the federalist ideal.[39]

The Revival of Traditional Culture

Part of the impetus to regional cooperation comes from the awareness of a common heritage of values. Again, this is not true of Asia as a whole, although the consciousness of an underlying unity among the diverse cultures of India is an important element in Indian nationalism. However, the common background of Islamic culture and Arab language in the Middle East, Latin America's belief in a community of values derived from the Iberian peninsula but given a different content by its fusion with Indian and Negro elements, and (especially) the rediscovery or creation of an African culture symbolized by Senghor's Negritude and Nkrumah's "African personality"—all serve in varying degrees to strengthen the common bonds in their respective regions.

Despite their desire for modernization, the nationalist leaders feel a need to maintain elements of their traditional cultures and the moral values they represent. Nehru has alluded to the "spiritual loneliness" of the Westernized elite, which both needs and rejects the values of traditional civilization. The description in Nasser's *Philosophy of the Revolution* of an Egyptian family in

[39] The relation of the voluntary organizations of students, youth, labor unions, etc., to the movements for regional federation lies outside the scope of this book. Relevant regional groups include the All-African Trade Union Federation formed in Casablanca in May, 1961, the African Trade Union Conference established in Lagos in 1962, the Pan-African Youth Movement (MJP), the Latin American Student Congress, the Organización Regional Interamericana de Trabajadores (ORIT), and the African Regional Organization (AFRO). Only ORIT and AFRO are associated with an international organization, the International Confederation of Free Trade Unions. In recent years, both the Communist front organizations (e.g., the World Federation of Democratic Youth, the International Union of Students, the World Federation of Trade Unions, and the International Federation of Teachers' Unions) and the non-Communist groupings (e.g., the International Student Conference, the World Assembly of Youth, the International Confederation of Free Trade Unions, and the World Confederation of Organizations of the Teaching Profession) have greatly increased their regional programing in Asia, Africa, the Middle East, and Latin America. For examples on the Communist side, see Robert H. Bass, "Communist Fronts," *Problems of Communism,* IX, No. 5 (September–October, 1960), 8–17. A detailed account of the political struggle over the establishment of the All-African Trade Union Federation appears in Legum, *op. cit.,* pp. 81–92.

which one son is English-educated, a daughter French-educated, the father comes from an Egyptian peasant family, and the mother has a Turkish background is typical of the cultural confusion produced by the disorganizing impact of the West.

The reassertion of certain features of traditional culture is psychologically necessary to balance the overwhelming technical, economic, and military superiority of the West. Characteristically, the nationalist leaders stress the moral, religious, or spiritual superiority of their culture in contrast to the materialism, utilitarianism, and technocracy of the West (and not only of the West, since these qualities can be attributed with even greater validity to the Communist world).[40] They hail the distinctive contributions of native music, literature, art, and poetry, and warn against the "mental colonialism" that has separated the intellectuals from their cultural heritage and subjected them to the alien values of the dominant European civilization.[41] The cultural renaissance in the developing nations is thus a partial rejection of the Western culture, which was held up previously as a model. It is an effort to establish national pride and self-respect—integral factors in the building of new nations.

Indian nationalism had a rich culture to draw on, but the interest in African culture and history that now forms an important part of the ideology of African nationalism stemmed from the work of English anthropologists and French-speaking African in-

[40] "Among Indian and African civilizations, which are essentially spiritualistic, the idea of economic utility is appreciated otherwise than in the old or young materialistic civilizations, or civilizations issuing from formative processes where, in spite of spiritual factors, the materialistic element dominates." (Mamadou Dia, The African Nations and World Solidarity [New York: Praeger Publishers, 1961], pp. 89–90.)

"The tendency of Indian civilization is to elevate the moral being, that of the Western civilization is to propagate immorality." (Gandhi, Indian Home Rule; see below, p. 114).

"Between the ideology of Communism and the materialist conceptions of the West, Islam is the only point of view that can prevent the spirit of humanity from being destroyed." (Ayub Khan, "Islam in Pakistan"; in the first edition (1963) of this book, p. 110.

"A third revolution is taking place, as a reaction against capitalistic and Communistic materialism—one that will integrate moral, if not religious, values with the political and economic contributions of the two great revolutions [French and Russian]." (Senghor, African Socialism; see below, p. 248.)

[41] The term "mental colonialism" is used by Haya de la Torre (see below, p. 345). See also Sékou Touré's discussion of the French attempt to "depersonalize and Westernize" the African intellectual elite (below, p. 227).

tellectuals in Paris. The very names Ghana and Mali are a conscious attempt to recall the glories of the medieval empires under those names, and the governments of Senegal, Mali, Guinea, and Ghana have subsidized and popularized the work of African and European scholars on these subjects. To the charge that there is a racist element in the glorification of the past accomplishment of the African, Léopold Senghor replies that a period of self-assertion of African values is necessary to correct the distortions of African culture and history produced by the inevitable bias of European historians. In righting the balance to emphasize the positive achievements and values of the "African personality," a dialogue between the two views will be created that can contribute to universal culture. A national and regional cultural revival thus precedes a higher and truer internationalism that will include African culture and civilization on an equal basis with that of other parts of the world.[42]

Nonalignment in International Affairs

With some exceptions dictated by special circumstances, most of the new nations in Asia, Africa, and the Middle East (but not in Latin America) have adopted a policy of nonalignment with either East or West in the Cold War. While remaining outside alliances and power groupings, they have not hesitated to pass judgment on the actions of the great powers, seeing themselves as specially fitted for this role because of their nonaligned position. Since each of the new nations has a vote in the U.N. General Assembly, they have an international forum in which, particularly in recent years, they exert a voting strength far out of proportion to their power in international affairs. They are thus encouraged, if not compelled, to take positions on a wide range of problems and to pursue an active international policy.

Since the General Assembly is dominated by their votes, the representatives of the developing nations view it as an instrument to defend the small and weak nations against the large and powerful. Conscious of their own weakness in physical power, they have resisted attempts to dilute the effectiveness of the U.N., since it

---

[42] Senghor, "What Is 'Negritude'?" (see below, pp 250–53). See also the interview with Ayo Ogunshaye in Melvin Lasky, "Africa for Beginners," *Encounter*, XVII, No. 1 (July, 1961), 44–46.

remains the best forum for the exercise of moral pressure by them upon the great powers.

To Western critics, the nationalist leaders seem to overemphasize the virtues of moral suasion and to underestimate the importance of a military balance in maintaining the present uneasy peace—and even in maintaining their own national independence. Yet, the nonaligned nations are not willing to leave to the stronger nations the problems of international war and peace because their entire effort to develop would be destroyed by a war between the great powers.

At the same time, they also insist that they be left to regulate their internal and regional affairs among themselves. As the example of the Congo demonstrates, the major powers may not be willing to comply with this demand, particularly when it is put forward by countries with ambitions of their own in the area. Moreover, the nationalists' principle of nonintervention is not an absolute. The Latin Americans condemn the United States for not taking action against authoritarian dictatorships in Central and South America, and the Africans have pressed us to take drastic action against our allies who still hold colonial territories. Nonintervention is a doctrine to be applied to legitimate regimes, but not to colonial or reactionary governments.

The claim of the uncommitted nations to represent the "unbiased conscience of humanity,"[43] is somewhat tarnished by what appears to Western eyes to be a greater readiness to condemn Western misdeeds than those of the Soviet Union, as well as by the neutrals' support of the use of violence in the case of Goa. Examples like India's attitude on Kashmir or Morocco's claim to Mauritania indicate that on questions affecting what are considered to be their vital interests, the uncommitted nations are no more likely to defer to international morality and opinion than do the more powerful nations whom they upbraid for their immoral behavior. Yet, despite the fact that no nation is ready to abjure the use or threat of violence, the very military weakness of the new nations which leads them to adopt a moralistic attitude also makes armed conflict among them less likely, provided the great powers

[43] Statement by Premier Saeb Salaan of Lebanon to the United Nations General Assembly; quoted by Ernest W. Lefever, in "Nehru, Nasser, and Nkrumah on Neutralism," in Martin, *op. cit.*, p. 103.

restrain themselves or are restrained from becoming deeply involved in their rivalries.

In addition to their role as the moral conscience of humanity, the uncommitted nations also view themselves as a balance or intermediary between the two power blocs. Nationalist thinking has added the theory of the "third area" countries to the older bipolar view of world politics. Like the bipolar theory, this view of international relations overlooks the pluralistic elements in the West and (especially since the recent Sino-Soviet ideological division) in the East as well, but it serves the purpose of establishing a separate identity and special role in international affairs for the new nations. Yet, the two roles—that of the independent moral conscience exercising an unbiased judgment on each case, and that of the balance wheel located precisely midway between the positions of East and West—need not lead to the same conclusions. The conception of themselves as the mean between the extremes, typical of the thinking of emergent nationalists, leads to an automatic assumption of a middle ground on East-West questions, with quite different results from the attempt to make an independent assessment of the moral worth of the claims of the two antagonists.[44]

However, one might question whether the third area can also be described as a third bloc. Many of the speakers at the Belgrade Conference denied that it was their intention to act as a bloc, and the divisions among the nations of Asia, Africa, and Latin America are such that the probability is slight that they will be able to act together on any regular basis. Moreover, with the exception of Cuba, Latin America has so far not been considered a member of the uncommitted group. However, a common concern with development, a similar suspicion of strong and wealthy nations, and parallel problems of social and economic reform make it likely that closer links will be developed among the developing nations,

[44] "Neither side has won us and we are determined that neither side will." (Statement by an African diplomat at the United Nations; quoted by Henry Kissinger, in *The Necessity for Choice* [New York: Harper & Brothers, 1961], p. 330.) This should be compared with Modibo Keita's statement: "[Nonalignment] must not be compared with *équilibrisme*, with a balancing act which takes up no fundamental position and which aligns itself now with one, now with the other, of the two blocs." (Quoted in Legum, *op. cit.*, pp. 113–14.) Neutralism is criticized by Chief Awolowo (*op. cit.*, pp. 309–11) and (in certain forms) by Mamadou Dia (*op. cit.*, pp. 84–85).

particularly on issues such as colonialism and underdevelopment, on which there is a large measure of agreement.[45]

The most powerful motivating force determining the policy of the uncommitted nations is neither neutralism nor the urge to sit in judgment upon their fellows, but nationalism and the desire for national independence and prestige. A neutral or nonaligned position, meetings of the uncommitted nations, and a moralistic attitude toward world politics help to create an international climate in which the weak nations can better defend and develop themselves economically and politically. The East-West question and the ideological conflict surrounding it, while they may indirectly benefit the new nations, are more often viewed as obstacles to the goal of national independence, economic development, and social change. To divide the new nations into pro-Western and pro-Eastern is to be ignorant of this primary concern and of the frequently expressed disinterest of the new nations in becoming involved in the ideological struggles of the great powers.

Modernizing Nationalism and Communism

If, as the preceding discussion seems to indicate, there is a belief system that can be classified as the ideology of modernizing nationalism, if what the French call the *Tiers-Monde* has a world view of its own, then a terminology of international politics derived from the Cold War is inadequate. Different questions must be asked and a different classification utilized. At the outset, the question was posed as to whether the common ideas of modernizing nationalism could be described as an ideology, similar to but different from the ideological systems of Europe. This review of the ideas of the nationalist leaders has suggested that, if we omit the leaders of traditional and conservative oligarchies, the two other general types of nationalist leaders, the radicals and the reformers, share a body of political and economic theory, distinct from both Western liberalism and Soviet collectivism. It is a suffi-

[45] The denials by Nasser, Nkrumah, and others at the Belgrade Conference are quoted in Legum, *op. cit.*, p. 115. A typical expression of the three-bloc conception appears in Sukarno's "Lecture to the Students of Hasanuddin University": "These three groupings I regard as a phenomenon of the twentieth century: the group of Thomas Jefferson, the group adhering to the Communist Manifesto, and the group of Asian and African nationalism." (See below, pp. 106–7.) Note that Sukarno appears to consider Latin America part of the Western group.

ciently coherent body of ideas to be called an ideology—the ideology of modernizing nationalism. The goal of national development elicits an emotional response and commitment on the part of the members of the nationalist movement. It is accompanied by a set of doctrines about the proper methods to attain economic progress, the nature of world politics, and the special contribution of the new nations to world culture and world peace. The ideology has a function—to carry the nation through the period of modernization of traditional society and to justify the ensuing sacrifices and dislocations. For its content, it draws upon the political ideas of both East and West.

This is not to ignore the real dangers in the appeals of Communism to the developing nations. The examples of China, of Cuba since late 1959, or even of Russia itself demonstrate that the ideology of Marxism-Leninism has a particular appeal for a nation undergoing the upheavals and dislocations associated with modernization and development.[46] It is only to assert that Marxism-Leninism is not the only ideology appropriate to this process, and that, in fact, the modernizing nationalists have developed an alternative set of ideological assumptions and propositions that shares some elements of the Marxist-Leninist model, but differs significantly from it in other respects. Moreover, this ideology is in many ways superior to Marxism-Leninism, since it is more pragmatic and more related to the problem of modernization than are the simplistic dogmas derived from the experience of nineteenth- and early twentieth-century Europe which comprise the Marxist-Leninist solution.[47]

From the Marxist analysis, the modernizing nationalists have accepted certain elements and rejected others. While recognizing the central importance of economic motivation, they do not accept

[46] Cf. Adam B. Ulam, "The Historical Role of Marxism and the Soviet System," *World Politics*, VIII, No. 1 (October, 1955), 20–45.

[47] The inapplicability of classical Marxism to the problems of an agrarian society was recognized by Mao Tse-tung in his *On New Democracy* (see below, pp. 71–77) which describes "the joint dictatorship of several revolutionary classes," including the peasants and intelligentsia. The European derivation of Marxism-Leninism is also the basis of the criticism of Communism by Haya de la Torre of Peru (see below, p 390), and by a group of African Marxists who, at the Second Conference of Negro Writers and Artists in Rome, March 25–April 1, 1959, adopted a resolution calling for a revision of Marxism to make it less Western and more universal in its application. (The resolution is printed in Legum, *op. cit.*, p. 238.)

Marxist economic determinism. In nationalist thinking, political forces are capable of subduing and controlling economic forces, and the state is not destined to wither away. Moreover, Marxist materialism is specifically rejected in favor of the recognition of the importance of the spiritual aspects of life. Marxist class analysis is also regarded as inadequate. History involves more than the struggle of the proletariat and bourgeoisie. Other groups in society are also significant, among them the rural elements, the intellectuals, and perhaps the military men as well. The nation as a whole is the primary unit of loyalty, not the class, and in the case of the African nationalists, it is denied that class divisions even exist in the new nations.[48]

In the case of Lenin's additions to Marxist theory, there is the same pattern of partial incorporation and partial rejection. On the one hand, the Leninist theory of imperialism is widely accepted, but on the other, the Leninist association of Western capitalism with imperialism does not prevent the developing nations from inviting Western investment and accepting Western aid. In addition, there remains a healthy suspicion of Soviet intentions which, while perhaps not as strong as the suspicion of the West, demonstrates the nationalists' assumption that tendencies toward domination are not a capitalist monopoly. The Leninist conception of the role of the party and auxiliary organizations in mobilizing the society has been accepted by the radical wing of modernizing nationalism, but thus far even the radical parties have been more open and less rigidly authoritarian in character than was Lenin's elite "vanguard of the proletariat." The same regimes also use Leninist vocabulary—"democratic centralism," "Young Pioneers," "Politbureau," etc.—but this does not necessarily mean that the centralized totalitarianism of the Soviet Party is reproduced wherever the same terms are used.

Undoubtedly, there are strong authoritarian tendencies in the desire of the nationalist leaders to remold their societies by government action, but thus far there is little evidence of the characteristic totalitarian attempts at thought control, absolute unanimity, and the establishment of the infallibility of leader and party. The

---

[48] Soviet writers have criticized African leaders for their refusal to apply the Marxist class analysis to the West African scene. See David L. Morison, "Communism in Africa: Moscow's First Steps," *Problems of Communism*, X, No. 6 (November–December, 1961), 8–15.

emphasis is on persuasion, negotiation, and conciliation, while the threat or use of violence that has typically accompanied the totalitarian attempts to transform society is largely absent.[49] Moreover, with the exception perhaps of Nkrumah's version of Pan-Africanism, the ideology itself is limited in its goals to national independence and development and does not have the universality or inherent expansionism of the totalitarian doctrines.

Marxism-Leninism also provides a model of forced economic development by state action—a goal that the modernizing nationalists share. However, the lack of success of the Soviet and Chinese regimes in developing the agricultural sector of the economy should be a warning that their method is not without failings. The nationalists are not willing, thus far, to carry out a ruthless program of collectivization of rural producers, although the establishment of rural cooperatives is often part of their program. Similarly, except in Cuba, Algeria, and the U.A.R., there has been little actual large-scale nationalization or confiscation of private business and native industry, as called for by Marxist-Leninist dogma.

With the exception of Cuba, even the nationalists most heavily influenced by Marxism have criticized Soviet policy and taken measures against domestic Communist subversion. Sékou Touré, who has borrowed Soviet organizational techniques and accepted considerable amounts of Soviet aid, has twice publicly indicated his opposition to Soviet interference in the affairs of other countries—in his 1960 speech to the United Nations and during the "teachers' plot" in 1961, which led to the departure of the Soviet Ambassador from Guinea. While they are willing to use the Soviet Union for their own purposes, as Nasser did in 1955 in order to reduce his dependence on the West for military and economic aid, the nationalist leaders have no desire to substitute one form of domination for another, or to adopt what is to them an alien ideology.

The modernizing regimes need an ideology because they are engaged in a social and economic revolution and they must dramatize the changes they wish to bring about. But it is an ideology resembling that of Atatürk more than that of Marx—an ideology of development and industrialization based in national culture

[49] The lack of violence in African politics is emphasized in Herbert J. Spiro, *Politics in Africa, Prospects South of the Sahara* (Englewood Cliffs, N.J.: Prentice-Hall, 1962).

and tradition and related to local conditions.[50] As the Cuban example demonstrates, it is necessary to have an organization as well as a specific program; if not, the local Communist Party's superior organizational techniques and tactical skill may enable it to take over the social and economic revolution that the nationalist leader is attempting to bring about. But with a strong party organization, a popular leader, and some progress in meeting the desire for modernization and development, a nation can pursue its own course without resort to Communist ideology or affiliation with the Soviet bloc.

These are the goals of modernizing nationalism: national independence; rapid economic development; the creation of a nation-state governed by a regime based on a populist identification of leader, party, and people; regional federation; and nonalignment in international affairs. There is no mention of liberal pluralistic democracy in the Western sense, because—except for countries like Israel and India, where the leadership, experience, and internal balance of forces favor political development along Western lines—the theory and practice of constitutional democracy as it is known in Europe or North America is not much in evidence. What has emerged in the developing nations is a reasonably coherent set of ideas about society and government which constitutes the ideology of modernizing nationalism. It is in the hope of achieving a better understanding of these ideas that the selections from the speeches and writings of a wide range of nationalist leaders are presented in this volume.

[50] For an earlier version of modernizing nationalism, see the program of "Kemalism," published by Atatürk's party in 1935. (Printed as Appendix E to Donald E. Webster, *The Turkey of Atatürk* [Philadelphia: The American Academy of Political and Social Science, 1939], pp. 307–18; note particularly the economic and cultural sections.) The Turkish example poses the question of the capacity of modernizing nationalism to maintain its dynamism when it is in power for an extended period.

INTRODUCTION
TO THE SECOND REVISED EDITION

The gratifying response to earlier editions of this collection and the new writings by leaders and intellectuals in the developing nations have made it desirable to prepare a third expanded version. Changes have been made in this edition on the basis of my own judgment as to what theories and ideas are either of intrinsic importance or widely influential today in Asia, Africa, and Latin America. I have been assisted by many helpful suggestions by specialists in the areas concerned, but the ultimate decisions have necessarily been my own.

The introduction to the first edition has been retained, with a few minor changes to bring it up to date. While there have been important political developments in the nine years since the first edition was published, it continues to be a reasonably accurate summary of the main themes in the thinking of the nationalist leaders. The significant developments since the first edition have been three. First, a number of important new statements of ideological principles have been published, some of which have been included in this edition. Second, the course of national and international politics has in fact served to test and to apply some of the ideas and programs contained in the ideologies set forth in the earlier editions. Third, there is now a considerable literature outside the developing areas which is devoted to a critical analysis of the theory and practice of the policy-makers in the developing nations. This new introduction will attempt to review these developments and to relate them to the themes discussed in the previous section.

Ideology and Modernization

The tentative definition of ideology given in the first introduction seems still valid, although there is no doubt that the term is an exceedingly difficult one to define with precision. Most recent discussions of ideology have emphasized function rather than content —the importance of an action-oriented belief system in explaining the world, justifying action, limiting policy choices, and creating social solidarity. The origins of the term have been traced to the French philosopher Destutt de Tracy, who at the end of the eighteenth century attempted to establish an empirically based science of ideas—an attempt which provoked the opposition of Napoleon to the "ideologues" who were subverting morality and religion.[1] It was with Marx, however, in such works as *The German Ideology*, that the term received its present-day connotation of distortion, the attempt to conceal one's real motives behind a cloak of ideational rationalizations. But whereas for Marx ideology was based on the relations of the forces of production, for later writers it has meant any attempt to justify or rationalize a situation or a needed change through a systematic body of value-laden ideas.

Ideology, then, can be used in two principal senses—as a body of ideas that serves as a guide and impulse to action, and as a systematic distortion, exaggeration, or simplification which has other bases besides the attempt to understand and evaluate the world of experience and action. In the case of the political leader, this implies a difference between a sincere attempt to translate values into a systematic guide to action, and the devious and manipulative use of rational and emotional symbols to attain or retain power or to further some other interest. This is not to say that one can make this kind of assessment in every individual case, but only to indicate that the term can be used either descriptively or pejoratively. The discussion in this book tends to the first interpretation, although, as the earlier introduction has indicated, the need to persuade the people to participate in modernization and nation-building is an inducement to the development of ideological justifications which are inevitably somewhat exaggerated and simplified.

Nationalism has been criticized as a contentless ideology that

---

[1] For discussions of the function and meaning of ideology, see Robert E. Lane, *Political Ideology* (New York: Free Press, 1962); David Apter (ed.), *Ideology and Discontent* (New York: Free Press, 1964); Daniel Bell, *The End of Ideology* (rev. ed.; New York: Free Press, 1965); Judith N. Shklar (ed.), *Political Theory and Ideology* (New York: Macmillan, 1966); George Lichtheim, *The Concept of Ideology* (New York: Random House, 1967); Richard H. Cox, *Ideology, Politics, and Political Theory* (Belmont, Cal.: Wadsworth, 1967); William E. Connolly, *Political Science and Ideology* (New York: Atherton, 1967); and Reo M. Christenson *et al.*, *Ideologies and Modern Politics* (New York: Dodd, Mead, 1971).

merely defines the political frame of reference and goes no further.[2] Yet nationalists in the developing countries are concerned with more than simple geographic boundaries. It is a *modernizing* nationalism that is being analyzed here—and the adjective helps to explain the goals, if not the methods.

The literature on modernization and development has expanded considerably since the first edition of this book was published. It is generally agreed that *political* modernization describes the phenomena of centralization, integration, rationalization, and specialization of function which modern states exhibit. There remains a lively controversy as to whether democratization is also a characteristic of the modern politically developed state.[3] In *economic* terms, industrialization and self-sustained growth are two indices of development, while the size of per capita income and gross national product measure the relative position of various nations.[4] *Psychologically*, the development of an open and flexible attitude to change and to human relations is said to mark the citizen of the modern state. *Socially*, the breakdown of traditional and ascriptive distinctions and their replacement by standards based on universalistic norms and achievement are characteristic of modern social life.[5]

[2] Nationalism is "inherently a subjective sentiment from which nothing further may be logically derived." Leonard Binder, "The Ideological Foundations of Egyptian Arab Nationalism," in Apter, *Ideology and Discontent*, p. 129.

[3] On political development and modernization, see A. F. K. Organski, *The Stages of Political Development* (New York: Alfred A. Knopf, 1965); Samuel Huntington, "Political Development and Political Decay," *World Politics*, XVII, No. 3 (April, 1965), 386–430; Lucian Pye, *Aspects of Political Development* (Boston: Little, Brown, 1965); J. Roland Pennock, "Political Development, Political Systems, and Political Goods," *World Politics*, XVIII, No. 3 (April, 1966), 415–34; Cyril E. Black, *The Dynamics of Modernization* (New York: Harper & Row, 1966); Samuel Huntington, *Political Order in Changing Societies* (New Haven: Yale University Press, 1968); Gabriel Almond, *Political Development* (Boston: Little, Brown, 1970); and especially Samuel Huntington, "The Change to Change: Modernization, Development and Politics," *Comparative Politics*, III, No. 3 (April, 1971), 283–322.

[4] Cf. W. W. Rostow, *The Stages of Economic Growth* (Cambridge and New York: Cambridge University Press, 1960); and Max F. Millikan and Donald L. M. Blackmer (eds.), *The Emerging Nations* (Boston: Little, Brown, 1961).

[5] Cf. Daniel Lerner, *The Passing of Traditional Society* (Glencoe, Ill.: The Free Press, 1958); and Lucian Pye, *Politics, Personality, and Nation-Building* (New Haven, Conn.: Yale University Press, 1962).

But modernization is a highly general goal, and the argument of the preceding section has been that there is also a very large consensus on means among the leaders of Africa, Asia, and the Middle East, if not of Latin America. It may be useful, therefore, to re-examine some of these means as well as the goals at which they are directed, both to determine whether there is, in fact, such a consensus and to evaluate the attempt to achieve those goals.

National Independence and Revolution

In their attitude toward the question of national independence, the nationalist leaders and intellectuals continue to be divided along the radical and reformist lines sketched out earlier. The most radical position has now been taken by the Chinese, who urge that less developed countries achieve their independence by waging guerrilla war against the developed powers of the world. Despite differences on other matters, China and Cuba are in fundamental agreement on this point and, since his death in 1967, Che Guevara has become an international symbol for the partisans of guerrilla warfare.[6] The Algerians, due to their history, also tend to endorse revolutionary violence as the way to achieve political independence, and one writer influenced by their experience has even praised violence for its liberating and elevating effects. The African leaders, most of whom came to power without violence, are less certain of its utility, though in looking at the situation in the southern part of the continent it is hard for them to see any other solution.[7] Moreover, despite the relatively rare instances of its success, the attraction of the belief in violent revolutionary transformation of society to the young and alienated in the developing (and developed) areas means there will be no scarcity of revolutionary ideologies in the future.

A second area of differentiation between radicals and reformists

[6] See Lin Piao, "The Victory of the People's War," and Che Guevara, "Two, Three . . . Many Vietnams" (below, pp. 88–95, 379–81).

[7] See Frantz Fanon, "Concerning Violence," in *The Wretched of the Earth* (New York: Grove Press; London: McGibbon and Kee, 1965), pp. 27–84, and the extract below, pp. 202–13. See also Kwame Nkrumah, *Consciencism* (London: Heinemann Educational Books; New York: Monthly Review Press, 1964), p. 74 (on reform and revolution in Africa); and Tom Mboya, *Freedom and After* (Boston: Little, Brown, 1963), where he states, "Even those who accept Gandhi's philosophy find there are limitations to its use in Africa" (p. 52).

appeal. Yet when the former revolutionary is in power he is com-
is that of neocolonialism. While both groups are opposed in principle to the continuation of colonial control through other
means, the radicals' definition of the term is much broader, including almost any relationship with an economically or politically
stronger developed country, particularly if that country is the
former colonial power.[8] The moderates are less likely to use the
term and less reluctant to make defense or economic agreements
with the former metropole. Yet even in these cases there is an
inevitable tendency to loosen the ties established in the colonial
period and to develop alternative economic and political relationships so as to lessen "dependence" on the former colonial power.

An exploitative relationship is not the only one possible between
a newly independent country and its former colonial master. A reverse exploitation is also possible when a former colonial power
pays an artificially high price for the tropical products of its ex-
colonies. Through the United Nations Conference on Trade and
Development (UNCTAD) the developing countries have been
pressing for similar special arrangements on a worldwide basis in the
form of tariff preferences by the developed countries for the products of the less developed areas.[9] In 1971 the European Common
Market announced it would establish such preferences, and in the
United States the Nixon administration indicated it would ask
Congress to adopt similar legislation.

In the view of the radical left and the Communists of the
Fidelist or Maoist variety, revolutionary violence is the only solution to the continuation of neocolonialism. Nothing has really
been changed by the transfer of political power, it is said, and
only by a radical and violent transformation of social and economic
structures can the society be modernized and developed. In a
political universe which has seen examples of sham democracy,
the falsification of electoral procedures, and the corruption of

[8] See the lengthy list of "manifestations" and "agents" of neocolonialism
(defined as "the survival of the colonial system in spite of the formal recognition of political independence") in the resolution adopted at the Third
All-African Peoples' Conference in Cairo in March, 1961, printed in Colin
Legum, *Pan-Africanism* (rev. ed.; New York: Praeger Publishers, 1965),
pp. 272–75. Kwame Nkrumah defines neocolonialism as "any oblique attempt
of a foreign power to thwart, balk, corrupt, or otherwise pervert the true
independence of a sovereign people" (below, p. 262).

[9] See the report by Raúl Prebisch, its Secretary General (below, pp. 423 ff.).

parties, the argument against a more moderate policy has great appeal. Yet when the former revolutionary is in power he is compelled to see that it is no easy matter to transform an entire society and culture. He may blame imperialists and neocolonialists, but he soon finds his real enemies are underdevelopment, ignorance, apathy, and corruption.

Revival of Traditional Culture

One of the ways for a nation to assert its independence is to turn to its traditional culture for inspiration. This is also a means of re-establishing links between the new leaders and the majority of the population which has not been uprooted, modernized, and secularized. Examples of this have occurred in the Middle East, where leaders such as Bourguiba and Nasser struggle to demonstrate that their reforms are in keeping with the spirit, if not the letter, of the Koran.[10] The political vitality of traditional religion has also been demonstrated in Turkey, where the secularizing efforts of Ataturk have not prevented religious appeals by politicians in recent elections. Islamic elements were also principal supporters of the bloody Indonesian reaction against the Communist Party in the fall of 1965.

It is not always the case that traditional elements will block modernization. They sometimes serve as the basis for more typically modern interest groups or political parties, as is the case with the caste associations in India and the Northern Peoples Congress in Nigeria, which until the military coup of January, 1966, was using traditional lines of authority and association to create a modern political party.[11] In other cases, however, such as the communal parties of India, the insistence that a religious or ethnic group be given preference undermines the equality and unity which is required for the creation of a modern state.

Of the modernized versions of traditional culture in Africa, Senghor's notion of "Negritude" continues to be a source of dis-

[10] See Bourguiba, "The Fast of Ramadan" (below, pp. 188–93); and Kamil al-Shinnawi, "Against Ramadan Reform," in Benjamin Rivlin and Joseph Szyliowicz (eds.), The Contemporary Middle East (New York: Random House, 1965), pp. 174–78. The Islamic element in the Algerian revolution has become more evident since the overthrow of Ben Bella in June, 1965.

[11] See Lloyd I. Rudolph and Susanne Hoeber Rudolph, The Modernity of Tradition (Chicago: University of Chicago Press, 1967).

agreement, especially between English-speaking and French-speaking Africans. The controversy was given renewed emphasis in the spring of 1966 at the Festival of Negro Arts, sponsored by the Government of Senegal, at which Negritude was attacked by some as a form of reverse racism.[12] Regardless of the evaluation of the underlying philosophic conception which inspired it, the festival demonstrated that African independence has stimulated wide interest in native art, literature, music, and sculpture.

In Latin America, in addition to Haya de la Torre's theory of "Indo-America," mention should be made of the Mexican Government's effort to glorify the accomplishments of the pre-Columbian Indian civilizations, and to integrate the Indian and the mestizo into the national culture and life. More recently, the Peruvian military junta, which seized power in 1968, has made a special effort to relate its reforms to the communal aspects of the Inca civilization in Peru.

Rapid Economic Development through "Socialist" Methods

Once national independence has been established, how is economic development to be achieved and neocolonialist dependence avoided? A majority of the leaders of Africa, the Middle East, and Asia (but not of Latin America) would reply, "through socialism." (The exceptions would include Haile Selassie of Ethiopia, the leaders of the Philippines, Turkey, Lebanon, Jordan, and Saudi Arabia, Felix Houphouet-Boigny of the Ivory Coast, as well as some of the military rulers in Africa and Asia.) This surprising agreement on the rejection of a stereotyped capitalism and acceptance of an undefined socialism was noted in the earlier edition, but a critical examination of this unanimity has revealed that the use of the term does not necessarily imply the adoption of the same measures, or even a common understanding of its meaning. Thus the excerpts in this book reveal an important difference of emphasis among the various versions of African socialism put for-

---

[12] Newell Flather, "Impressions of the Dakar Festival," *Africa Report*, XI, No. 5 (May, 1966), 57–60; and Ellen Kennedy and Paulette J. Trout, "The Roots of African Negritude," *Africa Report*, XI, No. 5 (May, 1966), 61–62. Criticism of Negritude as a "romantic" concept not concerned with economic and political liberation was also voiced at the Pan-African Cultural Festival held in Algiers in July, 1969. See the report in the *New York Times*, July 28, 1969.

ward by Nkrumah, Sékou Touré, Senghor, Nyerere, and the Kenya
cabinet, as well as the different types of socialism in other areas
represented by the Destourian socialism of Bourguiba, the Ba'thist
Party in Syria, the Arab socialism of Nasser, and Sukarno's now
discredited Indonesian socialism. On the theoretical level, the
emphasis may be on a Marxist-influenced state control and central
direction (Nkrumah and Touré's writings), on a type of humanism
and social concern (Senghor and Nyerere), or on increased economic equality and freedom from exploitation (Nasser). On the
practical level there is also great diversity. Nkrumah had put so
little of his theory into practice that it was relatively easy for the
military regime which succeeded him to dismantle the state enterprises he had set up. Touré has been careful not to touch his greatest source of foreign exchange, the foreign-owned Fria bauxite
plant, and has returned trade and distribution to private enterprise. The Kenya Government Sessional Paper's discussion of nationalization makes it clear that this would only be a last resort
while Algeria, Tanzania, Zambia, and the United Arab Republic
have nationalized large sections of their industry, although not
their agriculture. When we look to the former French colonies in
West and Central Africa, other than Guinea and Mali, we find
that their theoretical preference for socialism has meant in practice a limited amount of government planning and a small number of welfare programs which are often beyond their economic
means to support.[13] Thus to say that many of the leaders of the

---

[13] On the meaning of African socialism, see the special issue of *Africa Report* of May, 1963; A. Fenner Brockway, *African Socialism* (London: Bodley
Head; Chester, Springs, Pa.: Dufour Editions, 1963); and William H. Fried-
land and Carl G. Rosberg, Jr. (eds.), *African Socialism* (Stanford, Calif.:
Stanford University Press, 1964). The latter has an article comparing the
thought of Touré and Senghor by Charles F. Andrain, who has also written
similar analyses in Apter, *Ideology and Discontent*, Chap. v (under the title
"Democracy and Socialism: Ideologies of African Leaders"), and in *African
Forum*, I, No. 3 (Winter, 1966), 41–60 (entitled "Patterns of African
Socialist Thought"). Another useful source of African views is contained in
the proceedings of the Colloquium on African Socialism held at Dakar in
December, 1962, and published by *Présence Africaine* in Paris in 1963 under
the title *Colloque sur les Politiques de Développement et les Diverses Voies
Africaines vers le Socialisme*. For the genesis of Nasser's Arab Socialism, see
Leonard Binder, "Nasserism: The Protest Movement in the Middle East," in
Morton A. Kaplan (ed.), *The Revolution in World Politics* (New York:
John Wiley, 1962), pp. 152–74, as well as Binder's *The Ideological Revolu-
tion in the Middle East* (New York: John Wiley, 1964).

Third World are socialists is not to reveal much about their ideas or their policies. It is also to ignore the numerous exceptions to this generalization, as well as the whole of Latin America, where comparatively few leaders are avowed socialists even when pursuing policies similar to those seen as socialist elsewhere.[14]

Yet there are some common themes in the discussion of socialism in the developing countries. There is a belief in the necessity of government action to stimulate economic development and a corresponding rejection of laissez-faire liberalism. There is an increasing tendency to nationalization or divestment on a fixed schedule.[15] There is a denunciation of selfishness, exploitation, and class conflict, and a hope that by government appeals and political education the people can be persuaded to cooperate for the good of the nation. There is, most important, a belief that rational planning can result in the elimination of waste, inefficiency, and selfishness, both domestically and in international economic relations.

A general preference for the interests of society over those of the individual and for government over private action may be said to characterize governments which call themselves socialist, but these preferences will be implemented in a variety of ways. In Guinea the government tries to harness idle manpower through *investissement humain*. In Senegal, it is *animation rural*. In Tanzania it is self-help, "villagization," and the substitution of leaseholding for freehold titles. A number of these programs have been de-emphasized in recent years or replaced with more direct appeals to self-interest, but, if they have not had the hoped-for economic results, they have probably contributed to the political mobilization of the population.[16]

[14] The government of Salvador Allende in Chile is avowedly socialist (see below, pp. 000). The military government in Peru has embarked on a similar program but refuses to apply the term to itself (see General Juan Velasco, "The Industrial Law,' below, pp 407–10). Cf. also discussion in Charles W. Anderson, *et al.*, Issues of Political Development (Englewood Cliffs, N.J.: Prentice-Hall, 1967), Chap. 10.

[15] Between 1965 and 1970 the formula of government purchase of 51% control of the major national extractive industry and compensation out of future profits was adopted by Chile (copper), Tanzania (sisal and oil refining), Zambia (copper), Sierra Leone (diamonds), and Guyana (bauxite) and proposed by Algeria (oil). Divestment was written into the Foreign Investment Code of the Andean Group and the Industrial Law in Peru.

[16] For a pessimistic evaluation of the Guinean and Senegalese programs, see

Little criticism has been leveled at the various doctrines of socialism in the developing areas. It has been observed that the term itself is vague, and that those who appeal to it in theory do not always apply it in practice.[17] At least one American economist, however, has written a scathing attack on African socialism as "the wrong ideology in the wrong place at the wrong time," arguing that the lack of trained bureaucrats and the existence of a largely agricultural and subsistence economy make socialism in the sense of government-directed and controlled economic development unworkable in Africa at the present time.[18] He cites the failure of the state trading corporations and other centralized economic measures in Guinea. Experiences in Ghana, Mali, Nigeria, and Indonesia could also be cited to show that state-owned enterprises do not eliminate, and may encourage, waste, corruption, and inefficiency. They may even produce exploitation, the cardinal sin of capitalism, when the profits of the government-controlled sector of the economy are used to purchase luxurious homes, cars, and yachts for the new ruling class of politicians.

A further problem which has emerged in the discussion of socialism in the developing areas has been the relation between agriculture and industry. Much of the writing on socialism in African,

---

David Hapgood, *Africa: From Independence to Tomorrow* (New York: Atheneum, 1965). On those in Tanzania, see Fred G. Burke, "Tanganyika: The Search for Ujamaa," in Friedland and Rosberg, *op. cit.*, pp. 194–219.

[17] After his term as Vice Chancellor of the University of Ghana, Conor Cruise O'Brien spoke critically of the Ghanaian politicians under Nkrumah with "socialist slogans in their mouths and contractors' money in their pockets." The revelation after his overthrow of Nkrumah's use of his position to develop a large personal fortune did much to discredit his version of African socialism. Jeanne Mintz says of Indonesian socialism, "Although its slogans lay great stress on socialist doctrines, although its supporters reiterate its militant anti-capitalism and its unqualified rejection of political and economic liberalism, it can hardly be called a socialist system" (*Mohammed, Marx, and Marhaen: The Roots of Indonesian Socialism* [New York: Praeger Publishers, 1965], p. 224).

[18] Elliott J. Berg, "Socialism and Economic Development in Tropical Africa," *The Quarterly Journal of Economics*, LXXVIII, No. 4 (November, 1964), 571. A reply to Berg by Giovanni Arrighi and John Saul ("Socialism and Economic Development in Tropical Africa," *The Journal of Modern African Studies*, VI, No. 2 [Dec., 1968], 141–69) only confirms him by showing that state intervention has principally benefited the new African bureaucratic elite. For a case study on Mali's unsuccessful effort to introduce socialism see William I. Jones, "The Keita Decade: The Economics of the Coup," Africa Report, XIV, Nos. 3–4 (Mar.-Apr., 1969), 23–26, 51–53.

Asian, and Latin American countries has emphasized the need for industrialization as the way to economic growth. Yet recent criticism has demonstrated that the first requirement is to feed the people and to develop exports so that they can earn sufficient revenue to purchase capital goods and build a domestic industry. Here the primary emphasis should be placed on getting farmers out of subsistence agriculture and into producing for the market, and on research and assistance in better farming techniques and the improved use of fertilizers. The problem has been underscored by recent indications that the United States stock of surplus food, which has been supplying food deficits in many parts of the world under Public Law 480, is rapidly dwindling, and methods must be found to enable the developing nations to feed themselves.[19]

What appeared to be an impending crisis in food production has been averted by the so-called green revolution—the development under the auspices of the Ford and Rockefeller Foundations of highly productive "miracle rice" in the Philippines, "miracle wheat" in Mexico, and "miracle corn" in Kenya. However, the fact that they require capital and technology to which only the wealthier farmers have access has created additional economic and social problems in areas where the new strains have been successfully applied.[20]

Agricultural problems are different in different parts of the developing areas. In many Latin American countries and parts of Asia, the problem is one of inefficient farming methods and the concentration of landholdings in the hands of the few. In Africa, except for Kenya, land ownership is widespread and the problem is to get the small farmer to produce more. The partisans of African socialism often see cooperative farming as both an application of their ideology and a remedy for problems of food production, but so far, with the exception of the Gezira scheme in the Sudan, the cooperative schemes have not been notably successful. Even less successful have been the state farms in Ghana and Cuba.[21]

---

[19] On the food problem in developing countries see the breezily written but pessimistic *Hungry Nations*, by William and Paul Paddock (Boston: Little, Brown, 1964). The failure of West African leaders to deal adequately with the food problem is discussed in Hapgood, *op. cit.*, pp. 90 ff.

[20] See Francine R. Frankel, *India's Green Revolution* (Princeton: Princeton University Press, 1971).

[21] On Cuba, see Jacques Chonchol, "Análisis Crítico de la Reforma Agraria Cubana," *El Trimestre Económico*, XXX, No. 1 (January–March, 1963), 69–143.

Much of the socialism versus capitalism debate deals with stereotypes rather than real systems of economics and politics. All governments today engage in planning, are concerned about the welfare of their citizens, and have placed some limits on private economic activity. And all, except for Communist governments, allow private investment, small business, and private landholding and agriculture. There are important differences in practice, but they are often differences of emphasis; on the other hand, two governments may be remarkably similar in practice while they describe what they are doing in very different ways.[22]

There is a difference, however, in value-preferences, terminology, and choices in a marginal situation. Given a choice, an American may opt for freedom of economic activity while an Asian, Latin American, or African may call for controls or nationalization. In the event of a failure in economic development, the American is likely to blame the government while the African will place the blame on foreign capitalism, imperialism, or the structure of international trade. The American will describe his system as capitalist when the state controls 20 per cent of the GNP, while the African or Asian will call his government socialist when far less is state owned or controlled. Both Kenya and Tanzania describe themselves as socialist, but in Kenya foreign investment is welcome, politicians are actively engaged in private business, and land speculation is rife; in Tanzania foreign investment is seen as a threat to independence (Arusha Declaration, 1967), civil servants and politicians are forbidden to own shares in business or rent a second house, and land is held on leaseholding tenure.

There is still discussion of imperialist exploitation in the Leninist sense, but a new ideology of exploitation on the international level recently has been propagated in the developing areas. As a result of the Conference on Trade and Development held in Geneva from March to June, 1964, the focus has shifted to the exploitation which results from the terms of trade—the declining prices paid for raw materials and primary products in the international market as compared with the long-run rise in the price of manufactured goods. The conclusion drawn by many of the leaders of Asia, Africa, and Latin America, even those who do not call themselves socialists, is that there must be some kind of intergov-

[22] See Ralph K. White, " 'Socialism' and 'Capitalism', an International Misunderstanding," *Foreign Affairs*, XLIV, No. 2 (January, 1966), 216–28.

ernmental control mechanism to maintain raw material prices through commodity price agreements. Meanwhile, the developed countries, especially the United States, have been reluctant to participate in what they see as an international cartel agreement which encourages inefficiency and taxes the consumer as a disguised form of foreign aid. Yet it can be argued that in nearly every developed country a program of farm price supports has been in effect that cushions the farmer from the same problems in the domestic market that the developing countries are experiencing internationally. The difference, of course, is that the domestic producers of primary products have elected representatives and pressure groups to defend their interests, while the developing countries have no such constituency.[23]

The Single or Dominant Nationalist Party

One of the most striking characteristics of the recent thinking of the leaders and intellectuals in the developing areas has been their disillusionment with the one-party political system. The first edition of this book included critical remarks by one Nigerian leader (who subsequently changed his mind). We now have adverse comments by writers of a variety of political views as well as the experience of a series of military coups aimed at corrupt and exploitative one-party governments in a number of African countries.[24]

Radicals criticize the single party because it enables conservatives and opportunists to repress those who wish to improve the lot of the people and end dependency on the metropole.[25] Libertarians argue that the single party leads to repression and stifles initiative, criticism, and free expression.[26] An intermediate position

[23] See selections below by Raúl Prebisch (pp. 423–38), as well as the discussions in Albert O. Hirschman (ed.), *Latin American Issues: Essays and Comments* (New York: The Twentieth Century Fund, 1961); and Harry G. Johnson, *Economic Policies toward Less Developed Countries* (Washington, D.C.: The Brookings Institution, 1967).

[24] Single-party governments have been overthrown in Algeria, Dahomey, the Central African Republic, Ghana, Mali, the Congo (Brazzaville), and Uganda. Economic stagnation and the corporate self-interest of the military were also motivating factors in many cases.

[25] See the selection below by Frantz Fanon (pp. 202–13).

[26] See the selection below by Munif al-Razzaz (pp. 183–88), and William McCord, *The Springtime of Freedom* (London and New York: Oxford University Press, 1965), Part III.

is taken by one writer who believes that while the single party is necessary during the first years of independence it becomes increasingly reactionary and oppressive with the passage of time.[27] The supposed advantages of the one-party system in terms of stability, mobilization of talent for economic development, overcoming ethnic and other divisions, and its suitability to a communal society have also been challenged on both theoretical and factual grounds.[28]

The most telling criticism has been the actual conduct of many of the single-party regimes. Lacking a critical opposition, they have been able to engage in large-scale corruption and high living that make a mockery of the doctrines they profess. The golden bed purchased by the wife of one of Kwame Nkrumah's ministers was something of a symbol of this until Nkrumah's overthrow revealed that what one writer has called "kleptocracy" was the prevailing form of government in Ghana.

It should be noted that this problem is by no means restricted to the more radical regimes. Moderate leaders have often been just as lavish in their spending, without receiving as much publicity. The temptations of unchecked power are great, and it demands the self-denial and devotion of a saint to resist the impulse to self-enrichment, although certain regimes (usually the more radical, e.g., Guinea and Tanzania) have been notable for the puritanism and self-sacrifice of their elites.

The single-party system has assumed many different forms and it is difficult to evaluate it as a single phenomenon. In some cases, it has remained relatively open, and internal criticism has induced policy changes by the leadership. In others, the party itself seems largely to have disappeared after coming to power as its leaders

[27] See the article below by Bechir Ben Yahmed (pp. 199–201), and the debate on the single party from which it is drawn in the issues of *Jeune Afrique*, between November, 1963, and January, 1964. Earlier (October 7–13, 1961), its predecessor, *Afrique Action*, had published an article entitled "Pouvoir Personnel" (Personal Power), which was one of the first attacks on the charismatic leader and the single party.

[28] See the lectures by the West Indian economist Arthur Lewis, *Politics in West Africa* (London and New York: Oxford University Press, 1965), who proposes coalition government as the solution for African ethnic pluralism; Edward Shils, "The Role of the Opposition in the New States of Africa and Asia," *Government and Opposition*, I, No. 2 (January, 1966), 175–204; and Igor Kopytoff, "Socialism and Traditional Societies," in Friedland and Rosberg, *op. cit.*, pp. 53–62.

take positions with the government, and a "no-party state" dominated by politicians and bureaucrats replaces the one-party state.[29] An interesting experiment in providing a real choice and opportunity for criticism to the voter has been successfully carried out in Tanzania, where the party nominated two candidates for nearly every office in the elections of 1965 and 1970 (the presidency was a significant exception)—a direct result of Nyerere's thinking on "Democracy and the Party System" (excerpted below). What does not seem to have happened is the development of quasi-totalitarian "mobilization regimes" of the type feared not too long ago by Western observers. Whether because of institutional and personnel difficulties or internal beliefs and inhibitions, it is difficult to find a state among the developing nations (with the exception of Cuba) which approaches the totalitarian model in propaganda, thought control, and police repression. Some of the writings and speeches of the more radical leaders may make it appear that this will or should be the case, but investigation reveals that they are a long way from the German, Soviet, or Chinese models of totalitarianism.[30]

[29] On the no-party state, see James S. Coleman and Carl G. Rosberg, Jr. (eds.), *Political Parties and National Integration in Tropical Africa* (Berkeley, Calif.: University of California Press, 1964), pp. 676–78; and Immanuel Wallerstein, "The Decline of the Party in Single-Party African States," in J. LaPalombara and M. Weiner (eds.), *Political Parties and Political Development* (Princeton: Princeton University Press, 1966), 201–14. The Coleman and Rosberg volume and Gwendolyn Carter (ed.), *African One-Party States* (Ithaca, N.Y.: Cornell University Press, 1962), provide useful insights into the various forms taken by the one-party state in Africa. An analysis of the specifics of the operation of the Tunisian single party may be found in Charles A. Micaud, Leon Carl Brown and Clement H. Moore, *Tunisia: The Politics of Modernization* (New York: Praeger Publishers, 1964); and Clement H. Moore, *Tunisia Since Independence: The Dynamics of One-Party Government* (Berkeley, Calif.: University of California Press, 1965) and *Politics in North Africa* (Boston: Little, Brown, 1970).

[30] See the discussion on this point in Clement H. Moore, "Mass Party Regimes in Africa," in Herbert J. Spiro (ed.), *Africa: The Primacy of Politics* (New York: Random House, 1966), pp. 85–115, which criticizes Robert C. Tucker's "Toward a Comparative Politics of Movement-Regimes," *American Political Science Review*, LV, No. 2 (June, 1961), 281–89. For specific case studies see Henry Bienen, *Tanzania: Party Transformation and Economic Development* (Princeton: Princeton University Press, expanded edition, 1970) and Samuel P. Huntington and Clement H. Moore (eds.), *Authoritarian Politics in Modern Society: The Dynamics of Established One-Party Systems* (New York: Basic Books, 1970).

It is also an error to believe that all the states of Africa, the Middle East, and Asia which are not under military control have adopted the single-party form.[31] Sierra Leone and Zambia still have competitive party politics, although the opposition is suffering increasing difficulties, while Ghana returned to the parliamentary system with competitive elections in 1969. India is the largest democracy in the world, and, in 1971, it conducted multi-party general elections for the fifth time since independence. Opposition parties control the governments of many Indian states. Other countries with several active parties include Gambia, Morocco, Lebanon, Turkey, Israel, Malaysia, Ceylon, Indonesia, and the Philippines.

Yet the most common form of government in Africa is still the single party, often headed by a leader with charismatic appeal. For all its drawbacks, the single party has, in cases like Guinea, Tanzania, and Senegal, normally been able to overcome ethnic and tribal divisions, forge national unity, and constitute an effective instrument of communication between the government and the people. So far, however, there has not been the evolution in the direction of party pluralism or the development of independent interest groups that was hoped for by early observers. It is true that trade unions had important roles in the overthrow of the governments of Upper Volta (1965) and the Congo-Brazzaville (1964) and have occasionally played a critical role in Nigeria. However, the result has been either a more radically authoritarian government (the Congo-Brazzaville) or military control.

The Role of the Military

The emergence of the military in the developing areas should come as no surprise to anyone familiar with the history of Latin American politics since independence in the early nineteenth century. In the face of the "revolution of rising frustrations" under civilian rule, the military, citing the corruption and inefficiency around them, step in to reform the government and administer it in the hierarchical fashion in which their own military establishment is organized. Little attempt is made to justify military control on ideological grounds except as a negative reaction to the excesses of the civilian governments which preceded them. A spirit

---

[31] This seems to be the assumption in the discussion "Party Charisma in the Afro-Asian Bloc," in Irving Louis Horowitz, *Three Worlds of Development* (London and New York: Oxford University Press, 1966), Chap. VIII.

of puritanism and sacrifice is urged upon the people and administrative and economic reforms are promised. In the case of Nasser, over a period of almost ten years a more complete ideology was developed, but most military men are content to rely on nationalism and promises of reform to gain the support of the people. The lack of a single military ideology is illustrated in the contrast between the two coups in Nigeria and Ghana in early 1966. In Nigeria, the military leaders promised increased centralization, and attempted to modify the Nigerian federal system; in Ghana, the National Liberation Council appointed a commission to draw up a constitution based on the separation of powers so as to prevent the concentration of power in the hands of a single individual.[32] It cannot even be said that the military are more likely to be pro-Western in their orientation. Nasser was not the only military leader prepared to use Communist assistance to weaken his enemies. Ayub Khan's British military training did not prevent him from effecting rapprochement with China when he saw this as useful in Pakistan's dispute with India. Perón in Argentina was also strongly anti-American by the end of his regime.

What can be said is that the military are likely to have a technocratic orientation, an inclination to use government resources to mobilize the country by the use or threat of coercion, and a deep distrust of civilian politicians. Conversely, military rulers often lack the ability to respond to the people's needs and desires as effectively as the civilian politician. And like his civilian counterpart, the military ruler often finds it difficult to resist the temptation to use his position to secure privileges for members of his profession.[33]

If it is difficult to discern a single pattern among the military of the new nations, a distinction can at least be made between

[32] See J. A. Ankrah, "Broadcast to the Nation" in the second edition of this book, pp. 263–68.

[33] On the role of the military, see John J. Johnson (ed.), *The Role of the Military in Underdeveloped Countries* (Princeton, N.J.: Princeton University Press, 1962); William Gutteridge, *Armed Forces in the New States* (London and New York: Oxford University Press, 1962); and Morris Janowitz, *The Military in the Political Development of New Nations* (Chicago: University of Chicago Press, 1964). On the military in specific regions, see Sydney N. Fisher (ed.), *The Military in Middle Eastern Society and Politics* (Columbus, Ohio: Ohio State University Press, 1963); Edwin Lieuwen, *Generals vs. Presidents* (New York: Praeger Publishers, 1964); and J. M. Lee, *African Armies and Civil Order* (New York: Praeger Publishers, 1969).

conservatives and reformers in attitudes toward social change. Perón in Argentina, Nasser in the United Arab Republic, Ayub Khan in Pakistan, and Kemal Ataturk in Turkey are examples of military reformers who have worked with varying degrees of success to achieve modernization and social progress in their countries. Many others (especially until recently in Latin America) could be cited who did not succeed or did not wish to succeed in making any changes in the traditional order of their societies. As the above examples indicate, however, there is no necessary connection between a military background and conservatism.

What does seem almost inevitable is a lack of sensitivity to political pressures which, necessary at times, may at other times lead to disaster. Nasser recognized the need to supplement military rule by a mass party which would establish a two-way communication between the government and the people, and repeatedly attempted to establish a single official party; the latest and most successful is the Arab Socialist Union, created in 1962. The incapacity of the Sudanese military rulers to deal with the two problems of the revolt in the south and the dissatisfaction of the university students in Khartoum led to the resignation of the military in that country in 1964 and a return to democratic government, which was overthrown again in 1969. In Latin America, the alternation of military and civilian governments has become an established pattern in Argentina, Ecuador, and Guatemala.

In Africa, a similar but not identical pattern of alternation between civilian single-party governments and rule by military reformers may be emerging. Alternatively, the military or civilian leader may develop the necessary combination of sensitivity, demagogy, and ruthlessness which will enable him to remain in power for a considerable time. Recent events have demonstrated that there is no necessary connection, however, between a single party or a military regime and stability in government.

Regionalism

The relationship between stability and development, a delicate one in internal politics, is even more difficult in international and regional relations. In Africa, the emphasis in regional affairs has moved more and more in the direction of assuring stability even if this favors the more conservative nations. In Latin America, which has seen a long period of relative stability in its own regional relations, the pressures are building for a greater effort for political and economic development. The same kind of dichotomy, in the form of a choice between regional unity and opposition of the moderate and radical states, characterizes regional relations in the Middle East; in Asia the disparity of interests, ideology, and power have made any kind of regional organization impractical.

The most important change in regional relationships in Africa since the first edition of this book was published was the establishment of the Organization of African Unity at Addis Ababa in May, 1963. For a time, at least, this obscured the division between the radical Casablanca and the moderate Monrovia groups in African politics. It also established an instrument through which some important efforts at conciliation of disputes have been made (e.g., between Mauritania and Morocco, Algeria and Morocco, and Somalia, Kenya, and Ethiopia), and created a Liberation Committee to coordinate efforts to free the territories remaining under European domination.

Yet important differences remained, and were expressed in the organization in maneuvering for influence and policy. The Congo rebellion of 1964 and the accession of Moise Tshombe as Premier of the central government exacerbated the differences between those who wished to adhere to the OAU Charter's insistence on noninterference in the affairs of others and those who felt that the first requirement was to liberate Africa from neocolonialist and imperialist-dominated regimes. The result was the re-emergence, not of the entire Monrovia group, but of the French-speaking moderates in the African and Malagasy Common Organization (OCAM) in February, 1965, to provide an instrument for the closer cooperation of like-minded moderates in politics, economics, and international relations.[34]

In the ideology of Pan-Africanism, the aims of regional unity are to present a united front to outside powers, to regulate internal disputes, and to prevent Balkanization of the continent. All-African pressure has been brought to bear on issues relating to colonialism and white domination, although even on this question there

[34] The Charter of the Organization of African Unity is reproduced below (pp. 218–22). It appears to represent a victory for the moderates, who were in a majority at Addis Ababa. However, a Guinean, Diallo Telli, was elected Secretary General, and the Cairo meeting of 1964, from which Tshombe was excluded, seemed to convince the moderates that they should recreate their own organization. See selection no. 16, pp. 224–25 below, and Wallerstein, *Africa, The Politics of Unity* (New York: Random House, 1967).

was serious division in early 1966 on the forcefulness of the measures to be taken against Rhodesia. Some disputes have been successfully mediated, although the OAU, despite its efforts, had
no effect on the outcome of the 1964 Congo rebellion or the
Nigerian civil war. The issue of subversion became another
source of division in 1965, when the OCAM powers accused Ghana
of harboring revolutionaries working for their overthrow. With
the military coup against Nkrumah this has no longer been a
serious problem.

Other smaller regional associations are likely to develop in the
future, within or outside of the OAU. The East African Economic Community, the Customs Union of Central African States
(UDEAC), and the Organization of Senegal River States (OERS)
have all promoted economic integration. The Entente, an association of French-speaking West African states under the leadership
of the Ivory Coast, continues to function. Other efforts are likely
to be made to secure the advantages of closer association, particularly in the economic field. And the African caucus, with some
thirty-six members, will continue to exert an important influence
in the United Nations General Assembly.

When one turns to the Middle East, the differences between
radicals and moderates emerge with even greater intensity. The
Middle East is divided between the United Arab Republic, Libya,
Syria, and Iraq on the one hand, and Saudi Arabia, Jordan,
and, to at least some extent, Lebanon on the other. A similar
division exists in North Africa between Algeria and the more moderate states of Tunisia and Morocco. At one time the only bond
between these states was a common opposition to the state of
Israel, but even here the ranks have been broken by Bourguiba,
who has advocated a compromise settlement. The emergence of
smaller groups, such as a closer union of the North African
(Maghreb) countries, and the projected Union of Arab Republics,
is likely in the future.

In Latin America, the situation is complicated by the existence
of the Organization of American States, which unites the Latin
American countries and the United States. Proposals continue to
be made for a closer political union of the Latin American states
without the participation of the United States (and even as a
counterweight to it), but the fact that the OAS performs many
of the functions of such a regional organization has limited initiatives in this direction. In 1964, a Latin American Parliament was

formed which held its first meeting in Lima in 1965, but the most important new structure outside the OAS is the Latin American Special Coordinating Commission (CECLA) which first met in Chile in early 1969 and drew up the *Consensus of Vina del Mar* on the subject of Latin America's economic relations with the United States. CECLA continues to meet and develop common approaches to Latin American economic relations.

In the area of economic integration, the most significant new development has been the emergence of the Andean Group on the west coast of South America.[35] The Latin American Free Trade Association is still a very loose arrangement for mutual agreement on the reduction of tariffs on specific items, and relatively little progress has been made in creating a free trade area—principally because of difference in degree of industrialization among its members. An additional very important area of regional economic cooperation has been the Central American Common Market; in the few years of its existence it has promoted a great economic expansion in that area, and may provide a model for similar sub-regional associations in other parts of Latin America.[36] As in the political area, much of the important regional economic activity is carried on through the Organization of American States and the Alliance for Progress, which is associated with it although still largely under American control. (Though the Alliance is simply the Latin American section of the Agency for International Development [AID], the advisory Inter-American Committee for the Alliance for Progress includes Latin Americans among its members; proposals have also been made to vest control of the Alliance in an OAS body such as the Economic and Social Control.)[37]

The division between radicals concerned with continental liberation and moderates who favor nonintervention also exists in Latin

[35] The Andean Group, which was established by the Cartagena Agreement of 1969, is composed of five Latin American countries: Colombia, Ecuador, Peru, Bolivia, and Chile.

[36] See Miguel S. Wionczek, *Latin American Economic Integration* (New York: Praeger Publishers, 1966); and Sydney Dell, *A Latin American Common Market?* (London and New York: Oxford University Press, 1966). The latter includes a letter by Eduardo Frei proposing a Latin American Common Market similar to that endorsed at the Punta del Este Presidents' meeting in April, 1967.

[37] See the speech by the Chilean Foreign Minister Gabriel Valdes at the OAS Foreign Ministers Conference in Rio de Janeiro in November, 1965, printed by the Chilean foreign ministry.

America. The single advocate of the export of revolution to all parts of Latin America, Castro's Cuba, has been excluded from all organs of the Organization of American States. However, there still remain differences between those who wish the organization to take a more active role in the extension of democracy and human rights in the hemisphere and those who see the organization as committed to nonintervention. The conflict became even more confused in the wake of the Dominican intervention of 1965 when some of those most committed to democracy, such as Chile and Mexico, actively opposed the establishment of an OAS Inter-American Peace Force on the grounds that this was a violation of the principle of nonintervention. (Their real grounds seem to have been the fear of establishing a precedent for similar antirevolutionary forays by the OAS in the future.)

On a broader scale, the notion of a unity of interest and action among the Afro-Asians which was propagated at the Bandung Conference of 1955 has not prevented Africans and Asians from conducting their foreign policies in terms of what they conceive to be their national interests. The Belgrade Conference of Non-Aligned Nations has been followed by meetings at Cairo and Lusaka but they have resulted in nothing more than a series of declarations and resolutions. More important in terms of practical results has been the creation of a permanent organization by the United Nations Conference on Trade and Development which first met in Geneva in 1964. The UNCTAD secretariat has acted as a lobby to secure trade concessions for the less developed nations and in 1971 the EEC agreed to grant the tariff preferences urged by UNCTAD. Some success in combining to extract concessions from the more developed consumer countries has also been experienced by the organization of oil-producing countries (OPEC).

Nonalignment in International Relations

Various international developments are making the concept of nonalignment increasingly obsolete. The division between the developed and the developing countries is beginning to overshadow the East-West division on which earlier concepts of nonalignment were based. The increasing intensity of the Sino-Soviet split and the divisions in the West make it difficult to analyze international relations in terms of a bipolar model. In addition, the less active role of the Soviet Union in the developing areas since the overthrow of Khrushchev, and disillusionment in the United States with foreign aid, have meant that there is less opportunity for less developed countries to exploit their nonaligned position. The Chinese attack on India in 1962 resulted in the shift of a leading exponent of nonalignment to a somewhat more favorable attitude to the West—although India continues to get considerable assistance from the Soviet Union.

Yet most countries in Africa and Asia (but not in Latin America) continue to favor nonalignment, although there are various conceptions of what that position implies. For the radicals, it means the termination of all military relations with the former colonial power. For those who have agreements for military assistance (as do many of the former French colonies), it simply means nonmembership in an Eastern or Western bloc.[38] For both groups, however, nonalignment offers a way of opting out of the East-West struggle, and making an independent assessment of the individual questions related to it.

In Latin America also one can see an increase in neutralist sentiment. Chile's Marxist president, Salvador Allende, has opened relations with China, North Korea, North Vietnam, and East Germany. The term, "the third-world," which is used increasingly to describe the less developed nations that are not affiliated with either East or West, usually includes Latin America. Yet Latin American governments still find the Rio Treaty of 1947 a useful guarantee of their security, and the OAS an appropriate mechanism for settlement of their disputes.

The leaders of the developing countries have indicated their opposition to revolutionary or subversive activity by a major power of either bloc. Yet here, too, there is a difference between the attitudes of the radicals and the moderates. The Chinese lost support throughout Africa when their foreign minister announced that the continent was "ripe for revolution," but the Chinese attitude was

[38] On the definition of nonalignment, see Cecil V. Crabb, Jr., *The Elephants and the Grass* (New York: Praeger Publishers, 1965); and Doudou Thiam, *The Foreign Policy of African States* (London: Phoenix House; New York: Praeger Publishers, 1965). In addition to the discussions below by Nehru, Sukarno, Nyerere, Nasser, and others, see the documents on the subject collected in Paul Power (ed.), *Neutralism and Disengagement* (New York: Charles Scribner's, 1964). For a criticism of the excessively ideological character of Nkrumah's foreign policy, see W. Scott Thompson, *Ghana's Foreign Policy, 1957–1966* (Princeton: Princeton University Press, 1969).

denounced with particular vehemence by Houphouet-Boigny, the leader of the moderate French-speaking group. Western attempts at subversion tend to be the objects of attacks by the radicals, and it was as a Western plot that the overthrow of Nkrumah was seen by the more radical Africans. The distinction which has been made between "Western-oriented" and "pro-Eastern" leaders may be exaggerated, but it has some basis in fact, even though both groups claim to be objectively neutral.[39]

Modernizing Nationalism and Communism

The distinction between Communism and modernizing nationalism made in the earlier editions of this book has become still clearer in the intervening years. No state in the developing areas has joined the Communist world since Castro's decision to do so in 1960–61. It is true that Indonesia was working closely with China until September, 1965, and that Communist-oriented leadership has had considerable influence in the Congo (Brazzaville) and in Zanzibar (before it joined Tanganyika to form the Republic of Tanzania). The same is true of some, although not all, of the leaders of the rebellion in the Congo in 1964. Yet it is only in Vietnam that an early and clear identification of nationalism with Communism has enabled the Communist leadership to channel the appeal of modernization and nationalism in the direction of Communism. Elsewhere, nationalist leaders have been careful to develop their own ideologies and to maintain their independence, even when working closely with the Soviet Union or China or receiving considerable assistance from them.

Yet this does not exclude the possibility of a nationalist-Communist synthesis in other areas. As it becomes evident that not all of the promises of the nationalist leaders can be implemented, it is possible that Castroite or Maoist revolutionary movements may become more important in the developing areas. Such movements, whether rural (Guatemala, Peru, Venezuela, the Congo, Bolivia, or Ceylon) or urban (Uruguay or Brazil) have not been successful in overturning established governments and as the Venezuelan ex-

[39] Thus the military leaders who overthrew Nkrumah in Ghana in February, 1966, did so in the name of nonalignment. (See General Ankrah's statement above, n. 32.) Similar considerations were voiced in the reversal of Sukarno's pro-Chinese policy in Indonesia in 1965 and 1966. Both countries have taken steps to improve their relations with the West.

ample indicates, a government which is reformist, nationalist, democratic, and decisive can overcome the revolutionary movement with time, effort, and public support. There is therefore no inevitability about a series of violent revolutions in the developing countries, although the Chinese strategists are counting on this for the future.

On the Soviet side, the hope has been that the "national democracies" described in the Moscow Declaration of eighty-one Communist Parties in 1960 will prepare the way for a gradual transition to "socialism" of the Soviet variety. The difficulty of both supporting such governments and preparing the way for their overthrow was illustrated at a meeting of the Communist Party of the Soviet Union, where the delegation of the National Liberation Front of Algeria walked out when it saw that the outlawed Algerian Communist Party had been seated in a place of honor. While there are similarities between the views and policies of the more radical states in the developing areas and those of the Communist world, there are still important differences between them, especially on the question of who is to control the government.

Yet Marxism continues to exert an appeal in the developing areas, especially upon intellectuals and students. The people may have replaced the proletariat as the agents of revolution; imperialism may have been substituted for the class struggle as the moving force in history; the principal impetus and support for revolution may come from nationalism; and the workers may, in fact, be a "labor aristocracy," while the peasants are traditional or apathetic (particularly if there is no shortage of land). Nonetheless, wherever revolution appears to be the only way to achieve "real" national independence (as defined by the revolutionaries), Marxism provides a rationale, a *mystique*, an organization, and the promise of external support.

Yet organizational rivalries and disputes over timing and tactics have now deeply divided the Marxist left. Maoists, Trotskyites, orthodox Communists, adherents of the New Left, and followers of Fidel Castro or Che Guevara engage in mutual recrimination while the leaders of modernizing nationalism for the most part succeed in maintaining mass support and holding and consolidating their power—and when they do not, they surrender it not to the Marxists but to the military.[40]

[40] See Richard Lowenthal, " 'National Democracy' and the Post-Colonial Revolution," in Kurt London (ed.), *New Nations in a Divided World* (New York: Praeger Publishers, 1964) and John H. Kautsky, *Communism and the*

Conclusion

In the decade that has elapsed since the first edition of this book appeared, the visions of the future it contained have been put to the test. The dreams and hopes that the new nations could create a different society characterized by equality, solidarity, unity, and economic and social progress have given way in many cases to the harsh realities of corruption, compromise, instability, and apathy. Yet perhaps just because the millennium has not arrived as quickly as was hoped, the appeal of the ideologies of the modernizing nations is still strong. If anything, these have become more radical in the intervening period.

As the governments in Asia, Africa, and Latin America become increasingly capable of putting down revolutionary efforts (at least those attempted by civilians), the call for violent revolution contained in the writings of Fanon, Guevara, or Mao finds an increasingly receptive audience among intellectuals and students. Although the nationalist single-party regime has revealed that it is in many ways less capable than alternative systems of dealing with the problems of national development, it is still the most prevalent system of government on the African continent. And, while governments that call themselves socialist have produced economic stagnation, bureaucratic inefficiency, or megalomaniacal leadership, the demand for socialism—in terms of a drastic redistribution of income, a centralized planned economy, and nationalization (especially of foreign holdings)—is stronger than ever. (Since the first edition of this book, foreign companies have been nationalized in Peru, Bolivia, and Chile, in Algeria, Libya, Syria, and the Sudan, in Tanzania, Uganda, the Congo, Zambia, Mali, and Sierra Leone, and in Indonesia and Ceylon.) Increasing divergences have emerged within and among the developing nations, and ethnic, tribal, and

---

Politics of Development (New York: John Wiley, 1968). The division in the Marxist left and an inability to appeal to Bolivian nationalism contributed to Che Guevara's defeat in Bolivia in 1967. See Paul E. Sigmund (ed.), *Models of Political Change in Latin America* (New York: Praeger Publishers, 1970), Chap. 2. The author has been attacked as a "bourgeois ideologist" for asserting that modernizing nationalism is more appropriate than Marxism-Leninism for the problems of the developing nations (see p. 37, above) in A. Letnev, "Neocolonialists in the Role of Interpreters of Socialism," *Internationalism, National Liberation Movement, and Our Epoch* (Moscow: Novosti Press, 1967), p. 163.

regional differences threaten to break them apart; yet, the belief in the unity of the third world has spread and now includes those in the developed world whose ancestors came from Africa or Latin America years or even centuries ago, so that Eldridge Cleaver can find asylum in Algeria and Palestinian guerrillas can secure support from among American blacks. And despite repeated demonstrations by the Soviet Union and China that a "socialist" system can also be power-hungry and imperialistic, imperialism (and its Latin American equivalent, *dependencia*) is still associated principally with Western capitalism.

Yet the experience of countries like India, Ghana, and Venezuela has demonstrated that the Western model of constitutionalism, competitive elections, individual freedom, and a mixed economy, which was so vigorously rejected by many of the leaders of the developing nations a decade ago, is still able to hold its own against the claims made by the advocates of collectivism or authoritarianism.[41] The ideologies of the developing nations have produced such genuinely creative innovations as the Industrial Law of Peru, which provides for the gradual transfer of ownership to the workers, or Tanzania's system of competitive elections within its single party, or the 51 per cent formula for asserting national control of mineral resources without losing the expertise and capital of the foreign companies. But they have also often been used as a mask for self-aggrandizement, greed, and oppression. The attempt to find new ways to resolve the competing claims of modernity and tradition, of strong government and individual liberty, of national unity and group autonomy, and of social justice and economic development will continue in the developing areas, and new systems and ideologies will emerge. But they will still have in common the goals that are shared today by the emerging nations: modernization, development, self-determination, and—above all—nationalism.

[41] See Reinhold Niebuhr and Paul Sigmund, *The Democratic Experience: Past and Prospects* (New York: Praeger Publishers, 1969).

PART I

ASIA

It is far more difficult to generalize about ideology and politics in an area as vast and diverse as Asia than in the case of the other areas under consideration. Asians have much less in common with one another, and national traditions and cultures are stronger than in Africa, the Middle East, and Latin America. Moreover, the travail of securing and consolidating national independence is largely past in most Asian countries. Reasonably stable and permanent regimes to which the populace is loyal are in control in most Asian countries, making ideological appeals less necessary. In one instance, Japan, the rate of economic development has progressed to such a point that the nation can no longer be considered underdeveloped.

Yet, there are some common elements in Asian political psychology and ideology. Asian philosophy and political practice emphasize conciliation in the resolution of conflict, and this is expressed in the speeches and writings of Asian political leaders by the attempt to stress common elements in conflicting views and to achieve a consensus as a basis for policy. This consensus is often to be found or typified in a single leader, endowed with quasi-religious charismatic qualities.

The attempt to find agreement and to gloss over differences also characterizes the approach of Asian leaders to the East-West conflict. It is no accident that the philosophy of neutralism was first formulated by Nehru and Sukarno, although it should be noted that this philosophy is not operative in Asian countries where there is an immediate Communist threat to national integrity.

In economic development, a mixed economy predominates in

practice, although Marxist anticapitalism has strongly influenced the theories of the intellectuals and the speeches of political leaders. Today, two models of economic and political development, those of China and of India, are in competition for Asian allegiance, symbolizing the choice between democratic planning in an open society and forced growth under a totalitarian regime.

This competition is also one of cultural influence. India and China have old and deeply rooted cultural traditions, and both have been subjected to heavy Western influence, but they have reacted in different ways. The urbane and civilized synthesis of East and West typified by the character and personality of Nehru contrasts with the crusading aggressiveness of the Chinese transformation of an ancient culture into a modern nation, on the basis of rigid adherence to the thinking of Mao Tse-tung.

Since the Bandung Conference in 1955, China has attempted to develop its relations with other underdeveloped countries. More recently, it has embarked upon a program of trade, aid, and propaganda in Asia and Africa that has capitalized on the desire of the new nations to establish new contacts and learn from all national experiences. Yet, thus far, the uncommitted nations, while accepting Chinese assistance, have been careful to maintain their neutrality, and they continue to view China with suspicion. In its competition with the Soviet Union for influence in the developing nations, Chinese ideology has stressed the continuing necessity for violent revolution to achieve needed social change—and for frequent internal upheavals like the Great Proletarian Cultural Revolution, in order to maintain revolutionary fervor.

1. Mao Tse-tung

Mao Tse-tung, the Chairman of the Politbureau of the Chinese Communist Party, was born in 1893 in a village in northern China. The son of a peasant landowner, Mao wished to become a scholar. After his mother's death in 1918, he went to Peking University, where he worked as assistant librarian and came under the influence of two professors who were among the founders of the Chinese Communist Party. In 1921, he attended the first Congress of the Chinese Communist Party and then began work in party organizing. After the split between Chiang Kai-shek and the Communists, he established himself as political commissar of the Red Army, and by 1935 he had achieved supremacy in the Party. At this time, he led the Long March of the Communists from southeast to northwest China. Starting from a base in Yenan and gaining peasant support through a program of agrarian reform, he expanded his control of China. Finally, in 1949, Chiang Kai-shek was driven off the Chinese mainland. From then until 1959, Mao Tse-tung was President of the Chinese People's Republic. He resigned from this post, but continues to serve as Party Chairman.

In his On New Democracy, written in 1940, Mao saw the significance of the anticolonial revolution and tried to identify Communism with the desires of traditional societies for national independence and economic development. He also developed a theory of "joint dictatorship of all anti-imperialist classes" that departs from the classical Marxist belief in the dictatorship of the proletariat as the stage that follows capitalism. Although this dictatorship must be under the leadership of the proletariat, the peasants have a prominent place and a section of the bourgeoisie, as well as the revolutionary intellectuals, also is admitted. In 1957, Mao permitted a limited period of free criticism in the "Hundred Flowers" campaign. The campaign was soon terminated, but Mao-

*ist ideology continues to distinguish between "antagonistic" con-
tradictions, which can only be resolved by force, and "nonantagonistic" contradictions, which will continue to exist under socialism
and will be resolved by discussion and persuasion. How powerful
those methods can be was illustrated in the Great Proletarian Cultural Revolution (1966–68) when the entire country devoted itself
to the study of Quotations from Chairman Mao Tse-tung, which
contained excerpts from Mao's earlier writings warning against the
dangers of bureaucratization, revisionism, and dogmatism. The
Quotations combined Mao's belief in the possibilities of the "re-
education" of the intellectuals and bureaucrats with his insistence
that "political power grows out of the barrel of a gun" and "imperialism and all reactionaries are paper tigers." But, whether using
force or persuasion, the important thing for a true revolutionary was
to dedicate himself to the teachings of Chairman Mao, and to "dare
to struggle, dare to win." **

ON NEW DEMOCRACY (1940)†

The Chinese Revolution as Part of the World Revolution

The historical feature of the Chinese revolution consists in two
steps, democracy and socialism; the first step is no longer democracy in a general sense, but democracy of the Chinese type, a new
and special type—New Democracy. How, then, has this historical
feature come into existence? Has it been in existence for the past
hundred years, or is it of only recent birth?

If we make a study of the development of China and of the
world, we shall see that this historical feature did not emerge as
a consequence of the Opium War, but began to take shape only
after the first imperialist world war and the October Revolution
in Russia. Let us now study the process of its formation.

Evidently, the colonial, semicolonial, and semifeudal character
of present-day Chinese society requires two steps in the Chinese
revolution. The first step is to change a colonial, semicolonial, and

---

* On the relation of Mao's writings to Marxism-Leninism, see Arthur
Cohen, "How Original is 'Maoism'?," *Problems of Communism*, X, No. 6
(November–December, 1961), 34–42.

† Excerpts from Mao Tse-tung, *On New Democracy* (Peking: Foreign
Languages Press, 1960).

semifeudal society into an independent, democratic society. The second is to push the revolution further and build a socialist society. The Chinese revolution at present is taking the first step....

The Revolution of 1911 was the beginning of that revolution in a fuller sense. In its social character that revolution is bourgeois-democratic and not proletarian-socialist. It is not yet completed, and great efforts are still required because its enemies remain very powerful. When Dr. Sun Yat-sen said, "The revolution is not yet completed; all my comrades must strive on," he was referring to the bourgeois-democratic revolution.

A change, however, occurred in the Chinese bourgeois-democratic revolution after the outbreak of the first imperialist World War in 1914 and the founding of a socialist state on one-sixth of the globe in consequence of the October Revolution in Russia in 1917. Before these events, the Chinese bourgeois-democratic revolution belonged to the category of the old bourgeois-democratic world revolution, and was part of it. After these events, the Chinese bourgeois-democratic revolution changes its character and comes within the category of the new bourgeois-democratic revolution and, so far as the revolutionary front is concerned, forms part of the proletarian-socialist world revolution.

Why? Because the first imperialist World War and the first victorious socialist revolution, the October Revolution, have changed the course of world history and marked a new historical era. This is an era in which the capitalist front has collapsed in one part—one-sixth—of the world and fully revealed its decadence in other parts; those parts still under capitalism cannot get along without depending more than ever on the colonies and semicolonies; a socialist state has come into being and has declared itself willing to help the liberation movement of all colonies and semicolonies; the proletariat of the capitalist countries is increasingly freeing itself from the social-imperialist influence of the social-democratic parties and has also declared itself in support of the liberation movement of the colonies and semicolonies. In this era, any revolution that takes place in a colony or semicolony against imperialism—that is, against the international bourgeoisie and international capitalism—belongs no longer to the old category of bourgeois-democratic world revolution. . . . Such revolutionary colonies and semicolonies should no longer be regarded as allies of the counterrevolutionary front of world capitalism: They have become allies of the revolutionary front of world socialism.

Although in its social character the first stage or step of such a revolution in a colonial and semicolonial country is still basically bourgeois-democratic, and although the task imposed on it by objective conditions is to clear the path for the development of capitalism, it is no longer a revolution of the old type led by the bourgeoisie and aimed at establishing a capitalist society and a state under bourgeois dictatorship, but one of the new type led by the proletariat and aimed at establishing in the first stage a New Democratic society and a state under the joint dictatorship of all revolutionary classes. Thus, this revolution will clear an even wider path for the development of socialism. In the course of its progress, such a revolution, owing to changes in the situation of its enemies and to changes of alignment within its own front, passes through several further stages; but its basic character remains unchanged.

This revolution attacks the very foundation of imperialism, and for this reason is disapproved and opposed by imperialism. But it is approved by socialism and supported by a socialist state and the international socialist proletariat. Therefore, such a revolution inevitably becomes part of the proletarian-socialist world revolution.

The correct formulation that the Chinese revolution is part of the world revolution was made as long ago as 1924-27, during China's first great revolution. It was made by the Chinese Communists and approved by all those taking part in the anti-imperialist and antifeudal struggle of the time. However, the theoretical implication of this formulation was not then fully expounded, and consequently the whole question was only vaguely understood.

The "world revolution" referred to here is no longer the old world revolution or the old bourgeois world revolution, for that ended long ago, but a new world revolution, the socialist world revolution. Similarly, the "part" is not a part of the old bourgeois revolution but of the new socialist revolution. This is a tremendous change unparalleled in the history of China and of the world.

This correct formulation made by the Chinese Communists is based on Stalin's theory. As early as 1918, Stalin wrote in an article commemorating the first anniversary of the October Revolution:

The great world-wide significance of the October Revolution chiefly consists in the fact that:

1. It has widened the scope of the national question and con-

verted it from the particular question of combating national oppression in Europe into the general question of emancipating the oppressed peoples, colonies, and semicolonies from imperialism.

2. It has opened up wide possibilities for their emancipation and the right paths toward it, has thereby greatly facilitated the cause of the emancipation of the oppressed peoples of the West and the East, and has drawn them into the common current of the victorious struggle against imperialism.

3. It has thereby erected a bridge between the socialist West and the enslaved East, having created a new front of revolutions against world imperialism, extending from the proletarians of the West, through the Russian Revolution, to the oppressed peoples of the East.*

Thus it can be seen that there are two kinds of world revolution, the first belonging to the bourgeois and capitalist category. The era of this kind of world revolution is long past, having come to an end as early as 1914, when the first imperialist World War broke out, and especially in 1917, when the October Revolution occurred in Russia. Since then, the second kind—namely, the proletarian-socialist world revolution—has started. The main force in this revolution is the proletariat of the capitalist countries, and it has as its allies the oppressed peoples of the colonies and semicolonies. No matter what classes, parties, or individuals in the oppressed nations join the revolution, and no matter whether or not they are conscious of this fact and fully understand it, so long as they oppose imperialism, their revolution becomes part of the proletarian-socialist world revolution, and they themselves become allies of this revolution.

Today, the Chinese revolution assumes an even greater significance. This is a time when the world is being plunged more and more deeply into the Second World War by the economic and political crises of capitalism; when the Soviet Union has reached the period of transition from socialism to Communism and is now capable of leading and helping the proletariat and oppressed nations of the world in their fight against imperialist war and capitalist reaction; when the proletariat of the capitalist countries is preparing to overthrow capitalism and establish socialism; and when China's proletariat, peasantry, intelligentsia, and other sec-

* Stalin, Works (Eng. ed.; Moscow, 1953), IV, 169–70.

tions of the petty bourgeoisie have become a mighty independent political force under the leadership of the Chinese Communist Party. At such a juncture, are we not right in claiming that the Chinese revolution has assumed a greater significance in the world? I think we are. . . .

The first stage of the Chinese revolution, which contains many subdivisions, belongs, so far as its social character is concerned, to a new type of bourgeois-democratic revolution which is not yet a proletarian-socialist revolution in itself, but it has long been part of the proletarian-socialist world revolution and is now even an important part of it and a powerful ally. The first step or stage of this revolution is certainly not, and cannot be, the establishment of a capitalist society under the dictatorship of the Chinese bourgeoisie, but will be the establishment of a New Democratic society under the joint dictatorship of all Chinese revolutionary classes headed by the Chinese proletariat. Then the revolution will develop into the second stage to establish a socialist society in China. . . .

New Democratic Politics

The Chinese national bourgeoisie, because it belongs to a colonial and semicolonial country and lives under imperialist oppression, retains, even in the era of imperialism, at certain periods and to a certain degree, a revolutionary quality as expressed in its opposition to foreign imperialism and the home governments of bureaucrats and war lords (instances of the latter can be found in the Revolution of 1911 and in the Northern Expedition), and can ally itself with the proletariat and the petty bourgeoisie to oppose those enemies whom it wants to oppose. This is the difference between the Chinese bourgeoisie and the bourgeoisie of old Czarist Russia. Since Czarist Russia was already a militarist and feudalist imperialist power which carried on aggression against other countries, her bourgeoisie was in no way revolutionary. In Czarist Russia, the task of the proletariat was to oppose the bourgeoisie, not to unite with it. On the other hand, because China is a colony and a semicolony suffering from aggression by others, her national bourgeoisie has at certain periods and to a certain degree a revolutionary quality. Thus, in China, the task of the proletariat is to take into account the revolutionary quality of the national bourgeoisie and form with it a united front against imperialism and the bureaucratic and war-lord regime. . . .

It is quite evident that whoever in China can lead the people to overthrow the imperialist and feudal forces will win the people's confidence, because these forces, especially imperialism, are the mortal enemies of the people. Today, whoever can lead the people to drive out Japanese imperialism and carry out democratic policies will be the savior of the people. History has proved that the Chinese bourgeoisie is incapable of fulfilling this responsibility, which consequently falls upon the shoulders of the proletariat.

Therefore, in all circumstances, the proletariat, the peasantry, the intelligentsia, and other sections of the petty bourgeoisie in China are the basic forces which decide China's fate. These classes, some already awakened and others on the point of awakening, will necessarily become the basic components of the state structure. The democratic republic of China, which we now want to establish, can only be a democratic republic under the joint dictatorship of all anti-imperialist and antifeudal people, led by the proletariat—that is, a New Democratic republic. . . .

While different from the old European-American form of capitalist republic under bourgeois dictatorship, which is now out of date, this New Democratic republic is also different from the socialist republic of the type of the U.S.S.R., the republic of the dictatorship of the proletariat. The socialist republic is already flourishing in the Soviet Union, and will be established in all the capitalist countries and undoubtedly become the dominant form in the structure of state and political power in all industrially advanced countries, but, during a given historical period, it is not yet suitable for revolutions in colonial and semicolonial countries. Therefore, a third form of state must be adopted . . . namely, the New Democratic republic. This is the form for a given historical period and therefore a transitional form, but it is the necessary form to which there is no alternative.

The multifarious types of state system in the world can be reduced to three basic kinds, according to the class character of their political power: (1) republics under bourgeois dictatorships; (2) republics under the dictatorship of the proletariat; and (3) republics under the joint dictatorship of several revolutionary classes.

The first kind includes the old democratic states. Today, after the outbreak of the second imperialist war, there is no longer even a trace of democracy in many of the capitalist countries, which have come under, or are coming under, the bloody militarist dictatorship of the bourgeoisie. Certain countries under the joint dictatorship of the landlords and the bourgeoisie can be classed with this kind.

The second kind exists in the Soviet Union, and conditions for its birth are ripening in all capitalist countries. In the future, it will become the dominant form throughout the world for a certain period.

The third kind is the transitional form of state to be adopted in revolutions in colonial and semicolonial countries. Of course, revolutions in different colonial and semicolonial countries necessarily have certain different characteristics, but these are only minor differences within a general framework of uniformity. So long as they are revolutions in colonies or semicolonies, the form of state and political power will of necessity be basically the same, a New Democratic state under the joint dictatorship of several anti-imperialist classes. . . .

As to the question of political structure, it concerns the structural form of political power, the form adopted by certain social classes in organizing their political power to protect themselves against their enemies. Without a suitable organ of political power, there would be nothing to represent the state. In China, we can adopt a system of people's congresses—the national people's congress, the provincial people's congress, the county people's congress, the district people's congress, down to the township people's congress, and let these congresses at various levels elect the organs of government. But a system of really universal and equal suffrage—irrespective of sex, creed, property, or education—must be introduced so that each revolutionary class can be equitably represented according to its status in the state, the people's will properly expressed, the revolutionary struggles properly directed, and the spirit of New Democracy properly embodied. This is the system of democratic centralism. Only a government of democratic centralism can fully express the will of all the revolutionary people and most effectively fight the enemies of the revolution. The spirit of the phrase "not to be monopolized by a few" must be embodied in the government and the army apparatus; without a genuinely democratic system, this aim can never be attained, and there will be a discrepancy between the political structure and the state system.

The state system—joint dictatorship of all revolutionary classes. The political structure—democratic centralism. This is New Democratic government; this is a republic of New Democracy. . . .

QUOTATIONS FROM
CHAIRMAN MAO TSE-TUNG *

III. *Socialism and Communism*

The people's democratic dictatorship is based on the alliance of the working class, the peasantry, and the urban petty bourgeoisie, and mainly on the alliance of the workers and the peasants, because these two classes comprise 80 to 90 per cent of China's population. These two classes are the main force in overthrowing imperialism and the Kuomintang reactionaries. The transition from New Democracy to socialism also depends mainly upon their alliance.†

Class struggle, the struggle for production, and scientific experiment are the three great revolutionary movements for building a mighty socialist country. These movements are a sure guarantee that Communists will be free from bureaucracy and immune against revisionism and dogmatism, and will forever remain invincible. They are a reliable guarantee that the proletariat will be able to unite with the broad working masses and realize a democratic dictatorship. If, in the absence of these movements, the landlords, rich peasants, counterrevolutionaries, bad elements, and ogres of all kinds were allowed to crawl out, while our cadres were to shut their eyes to all this and in many cases fail even to differentiate between the enemy and ourselves but were to collaborate with the enemy and were corrupted, divided, and demoralized by him, if our cadres were thus pulled out or the enemy were able to sneak in, and if many of our workers, peasants, and intellectuals were left defenseless against both the soft and the hard tactics of the enemy, then it would not take long, perhaps only several years or a decade, or several decades at most, before a counterrevolutionary restoration

---

* From the official English translation, Peking, 1967. (Spelling has been altered to conform to American usage).

† "On the People's Democratic Dictatorship" (June 30, 1949), *Selected Works*, Vol. IV, p. 421.

on a national scale inevitably occurred, the Marxist-Leninist party would undoubtedly become a revisionist party or a fascist party, and the whole of China would change its color.*

The people's democratic dictatorship uses two methods. Toward the enemy, it uses the method of dictatorship, that is, for as long a period of time as is necessary it does not let them take part in political activities and compels them to obey the law of the People's Government and to engage in labor and, through labor, transform themselves into new men. Toward the people, on the contrary, it uses the method not of compulsion but of democracy, that is, it must necessarily let them take part in political activities and does not compel them to do this or that, but uses the method of democracy in educating and persuading them.†

Under the leadership of the Communist Party, the Chinese people are carrying out a vigorous rectification movement ‡ in order to bring about the rapid development of socialism in China on a firmer basis. It is a movement for carrying out a nation-wide debate which is both guided and free, a debate in the city and the countryside on such questions as the socialist road versus the capitalist road, the basic system of the state and its major policies, the working style of Party and government functionaries, and the question of the welfare of the people, a debate which is conducted by setting forth facts and reasoning things out, so as correctly to resolve those actual contradictions among the people which demand immediate solution. This is a socialist movement for the self-education and self-remolding of the people.**

* Note on "The Seven Well-Written Documents of Chekiang Province Concerning Cadres' Participation in Physical Labour" (May 9, 1963), quoted in *On Khrushchev's Phoney Communism and Its Historical Lessons for the World*, pp. 71–72.

† Closing speech at the Second Session of the First National Committee of the Chinese People's Political Consultative Conference (June 23, 1950).

‡ A reference to the "Hundred Flowers" Campaign.—ED.

** "Speech at the Meeting of the Supreme Soviet of the U.S.S.R. in Celebration of the 40th Anniversary of the Great October Socialist Revolution" (November 6, 1957).

The Correct Handling of Contradictions Among the People

In the conditions prevailing in China today, the contradictions among the people comprise the contradictions within the working class, the contradictions within the peasantry, the contradictions within the intelligentsia, the contradictions between the working class and the peasantry, the contradictions between the workers and peasants on the one hand and the intellectuals on the other, the contradictions between the working class and other sections of the working people on the one hand and the national bourgeoisie on the other, the contradictions within the national bourgeoisie, and so on. Our People's Government is one that genuinely represents the people's interests, it is a government that serves the people. Nevertheless, there are still certain contradictions between the government and the people. These include contradictions among the interests of the state, the interests of the collective and the interests of the individual; between democracy and centralism; between the leadership and the led; and the contradiction arising from the bureaucratic style of work of certain government workers in their relations with the masses. All these are also contradictions among the people. Generally speaking, the people's basic identity of interests underlies the contradictions among the people.*

We are confronted by two types of social contradictions—those between ourselves and the enemy and those among the people themselves. The two are totally different in their nature.†

To understand these two different types of contradictions correctly, we must first be clear on what is meant by "the people" and what is meant by "the enemy." . . . At the present stage, the period of building socialism, the classes, strata, and social groups which favor, support, and work for the cause of socialist construction all come within the category of the people, while the social forces and groups which resist the socialist revolution and are hostile to or sabotage socialist construction are all enemies of the people.‡

* *Ibid.*, pp. 3–4.
† *On the Correct Handling of Contradictions Among the People* (February 27, 1957), 1st pocket ed., p. 2.
‡ *Ibid.*, pp. 2–3.

The contradictions between ourselves and the enemy are antagonistic contradictions. Within the ranks of the people, the contradictions among the working people are nonantagonistic, while those between the exploited and the exploiting classes have a nonantagonistic aspect in addition to an antagonistic aspect.*

The question of suppressing counterrevolutionaries is one of a struggle between ourselves and the enemy, a contradiction between ourselves and the enemy. Among the people, there are some who see this question in a somewhat different light. Two kinds of persons hold views different from ours. Those with a Rightist way of thinking make no distinction between ourselves and the enemy and take the enemy for our own people. They regard as friends the very persons whom the broad masses regard as enemies. Those with a "Left" way of thinking magnify contradictions between ourselves and the enemy to such an extent that they take certain contradictions among the people for contradictions with the enemy and regard as counterrevolutionaries persons who are not really counterrevolutionaries. Both these views are wrong. Neither can lead to the correct handling of the question of suppressing counterrevolutionaries or to a correct assessment of this work.†

Qualitatively different contradictions can only be resolved by qualitatively different methods. For instance, the contradiction between the proletariat and the bourgeoisie is resolved by the method of socialist revolution; the contradiction between the great masses of the people and the feudal system is resolved by the method of democratic revolution; the contradiction between the colonies and imperialism is resolved by the method of national revolutionary war; the contradiction between the working class and the peasant class in socialist society is resolved by the method of collectivization and mechanization in agriculture; contradiction within the Communist Party is resolved by the method of criticism and self-criticism; the contradiction between society and nature is resolved by the method of developing the productive forces. . . . The principle of using different methods to resolve different contradictions is one which Marxist-Leninists must strictly observe.‡

* *Ibid.*, p. 3.
† *Ibid.*, p. 25.
‡ "On Contradiction" (August 1937), *Selected Works*, Vol. I, pp. 321–22.

Contradiction and struggle are universal and absolute, but the methods of resolving contradictions, that is, the forms of struggle, differ according to the differences in the nature of the contradictions. Some contradictions are characterized by open antagonism, others are not. In accordance with the concrete development of things, some contradictions which were originally nonantagonistic develop into antagonistic ones, while others which were originally antagonistic develop into nonantagonistic ones.*

In ordinary circumstances, contradictions among the people are not antagonistic. But if they are not handled properly, or if we relax our vigilance and lower our guard, antagonism may arise. In a socialist country, a development of this kind is usually only a localized and temporary phenomenon. The reason is that the system of exploitation of man by man has been abolished and the interests of the people are basically the same.†

In our country, the contradiction between the working class and the national bourgeoisie belongs to the category of contradictions among the people. By and large, the class struggle between the two is a class struggle within the ranks of the people, because the Chinese national bourgeoisie has a dual character. In the period of the bourgeois-democratic revolution, it had both a revolutionary and a conciliationist side to its character. In the period of the socialist revolution, exploitation of the working class for profit constitutes one side of the character of the national bourgeoisie, while its support of the Constitution and its willingness to accept socialist transformation constitute the other. The national bourgeoisie differs from the imperialists, the landlords, and the bureaucratic-capitalists. The contradiction between the national bourgeoisie and the working class is one between the exploiter and the exploited, and is by nature antagonistic. But in the concrete conditions of China, this antagonistic class contradiction can, if properly handled, be transformed into a nonantagonistic one and be resolved by peaceful methods. However, it will change into a contradiction between

* "On Contradiction" (August, 1937), *Selected Works*, Vol. I, p. 344.
† *On the Correct Handling of Contradictions Among the People* (Febru-

ourselves and the enemy if we do not handle it properly and do not follow the policy of uniting with, criticizing, and educating the national bourgeoisie, or if the national bourgeoisie does not accept this policy of ours.*

It [the counterrevolutionary rebellion in Hungary in 1956] was a case of reactionaries inside a socialist country, in league with the imperialists, attempting to achieve their conspiratorial aims by taking advantage of contradictions among the people to foment dissension and stir up disorder. This lesson of the Hungarian events merits attention.†

War and Peace

War is the highest form of struggle for resolving contradictions, when they have developed to a certain stage, between classes, nations, states, or political groups, and it has existed ever since the emergence of private property and of classes.‡

"War is the continuation of politics." In this sense war is politics and war itself is a political action; since ancient times there has never been a war that did not have a political character. . . .

But war has its own particular characteristics and in this sense it cannot be equated with politics in general. "War is the continuation of politics by other . . . means." When politics develops to a certain stage beyond which it cannot proceed by the usual means, war breaks out to sweep the obstacles from the way. . . . When the obstacle is removed and our political aim attained, the war will stop. But if the obstacle is not completely swept away, the war will have to continue till the aim is fully accomplished. . . . It can therefore be said that politics is war without bloodshed while war is politics with bloodshed.**

* *Ibid.,* pp. 4–5.
† *Ibid.,* p. 15.
‡ "Problems of Strategy in China's Revolutionary War" (December, 1936), *Selected Works,* Vol. 1, p. 180.
** "On Protracted War" (May, 1936), *Selected Works,* Vol. II, pp. 152–53.

History shows that wars are divided into two kinds, just and unjust. All wars that are progressive are just, and all wars that impede progress are unjust. We Communists oppose all unjust wars that impede progress, but we do not oppose progressive, just wars. Not only do we Communists not oppose just wars, we actively participate in them. As for unjust wars, World War I is an instance in which both sides fought for imperialist interests; therefore the Communists of the whole world firmly opposed that war. The way to oppose a war of this kind is to do everything possible to prevent it before it breaks out and, once it breaks out, to oppose war with war, to oppose unjust war with just war, whenever possible.*

Revolutions and revolutionary wars are inevitable in class society and without them it is impossible to accomplish any leap in social development and to overthrow the reactionary ruling classes and therefore impossible for the people to win political power.†

Revolutionary war is an antitoxin which not only eliminates the enemy's poison but also purges us of our own filth. Every just, revolutionary war is endowed with tremendous power and can transform many things or clear the way for their transformation. The Sino-Japanese war will transform both China and Japan; provided China perseveres in the War of Resistance and in the united front, the old Japan will surely be transformed into a new Japan and the old China into a new China, and people and everything else in both China and Japan will be transformed during and after the war.‡

Every Communist must grasp the truth, "Political power grows out of the barrel of a gun." **

The seizure of power by armed force, the settlement of the issue by war, is the central task and the highest form of revolution. This

---

* *Ibid.*, p. 150.
† "On Contradiction" (August, 1937), *Selected Works*, Vol. I, p. 344.
‡ "On Protracted War" (May, 1938), *Selected Works*, Vol. II, p. 131.
** "Problems of War and Strategy" (November 6, 1938), *Selected Works*, Vol. II, p. 224.

Marxist-Leninist principle of revolution holds good universally, for China and for all other countries.*

Without armed struggle neither the proletariat, nor the people, nor the Communist Party would have any standing at all in China and it would be impossible for the revolution to triumph. In these years [the eighteen years since the founding of the Party] the development, consolidation, and bolshevization of our Party have proceeded in the midst of revolutionary wars; without armed struggle the Communist Party would assuredly not be what it is today. Comrades throughout the Party must never forget this experience for which we have paid in blood.†

According to the Marxist theory of the state, the army is the chief component of state power. Whoever wants to seize and retain state power must have a strong army. Some people ridicule us as advocates of the "omnipotence of war." Yes, we are advocates of the omnipotence of revolutionary war; that is good, not bad, it is Marxist. The guns of the Russian Communist Party created socialism. We shall create a democratic republic. Experience in the class struggle in the era of imperialism teaches us that it is only by the power of the gun that the working class and the laboring masses can defeat the armed bourgeoisie and landlords; in this sense we may say that only with guns can the whole world be transformed.‡

Imperialism and All Reactionaries Are Paper Tigers

All reactionaries are paper tigers. In appearance, the reactionaries are terrifying, but in reality they are not so powerful. From a long-term point of view, it is not the reactionaries but the people who are really powerful.**

*† *Ibid.*, p. 219.
† "Introducing *The Communist*" (October 4, 1939), *Selected Works,* Vol. II. p. 292.
‡ "Problems of War and Strategy" (November 6, 1938), *Selected Works,* Vol. II, p. 225.
** "Talk with the American Correspondent Anna Louise Strong" (August, 1946), *Selected Works*, Vol. IV, p. 100.

Just as there is not a single thing in the world without a dual nature (this is the law of the unity of opposites), so imperialism and all reactionaries have a dual nature—they are real tigers and paper tigers at the same time. In past history, before they won state power and for some time afterwards, the slave-owning class, the feudal landloard class, and the bourgeoisie were vigorous, revolutionary, and progressive; they were real tigers. But with the lapse of time, because their opposites—the slave class, the peasant class and the proletariat—grew in strength step by step, struggled against them more and more fiercely, these ruling classes changed step by step into the reverse, changed into reactionaries, changed into backward people, changed into paper tigers. And eventually they were overthrown, or will be overthrown, by the people. The reactionary, backward, decaying classes retained this dual nature even in their last life-and-death struggles against the people. On the one hand, they were real tigers; they devoured people, devoured people by the millions and tens of millions. The cause of the people's struggle went through a period of difficulties and hardships, and along the path there were many twists and turns. To destroy the rule of imperialism, feudalism and bureaucrat-capitalism in China took the Chinese people more than a hundred years and cost them tens of millions of lives before the victory in 1949. Look! Were these not living tigers, iron tigers, real tigers? But in the end they changed into paper tigers, dead tigers, bean-curd tigers. These are historical facts. Have people not seen or heard about these facts? There have indeed been thousands and tens of thousands of them! Thousands and tens of thousands! Hence, imperialism and all reactionaries, looked at in essence, from a long-term point of view, from a strategic point of view, must be seen for what they are—paper tigers. On this we should build our strategic thinking. On the other hand, they are also living tigers, iron tigers, real tigers which can devour people. On this we should build our tactical thinking.*

It is my opinion that the international situation has now reached a new turning point. There are two winds in the world today, the East Wind and the West Wind. There is a Chinese saying, "Either

* Speech at the Wuchang Meeting of the Political Bureau of the Central Committee of the Communist Party of China (December 1, 1958), quoted in the explanatory note to "Talk with the American Correspondent Anna Louise Strong," *Selected Works*, Vol. IV, pp. 98–99.

the East Wind prevails over the West Wind or the West Wind prevails over the East Wind." I believe it is characteristic of the situation today that the East Wind is prevailing over the West Wind. That is to say, the forces of socialism have become overwhelmingly superior to the forces of imperialism.*

2. Lin Piao

Marshal Lin Piao, born in northern China in 1907 into a lower middle-class family, studied for a year at the Whampoa Military Academy where one of his teachers was Chou En-lai, and, in 1926, joined the Communist Youth; two years later, he led a military uprising that resulted in the formation of the Red Army. In 1934– 35, he led the advance section of the Long March in which 100,000 troops marched 8,000 miles to northern China. In 1937 he went to Moscow, returning in 1942 to participate actively in the war against Japan and, later, against the Nationalist forces under Chiang Kai-shek. After the Communist victory, he became Vice Premier of the People's Republic of China (1954), Vice Chairman of the Central Committee and a member of the Politburo of the Chinese Communist Party (1958), and Minister of National Defense (1959). In the early 1960's he initiated a program of political indoctrination in the armed forces using quotations from Mao Tsetung's writings; since the Cultural Revolution, especially as the People's Liberation Army took a more important role in early 1967, he has been the most important Chinese leader after Mao. In 1969, the Ninth Congress of the Chinese Communist Party adopted a new constitution which states in its sixth paragraph, "Comrade Lin Piao is the close comrade-in-arms and successor of Comrade Mao Tse-tung." By 1971, he had fallen from favor.

Marshal Lin's rise to power was first signaled by the publication in all major Chinese newspapers on September 3, 1965, of a major ideological statement attributed to him and entitled Long Live the Victory of the People's War. *Just as the Chinese Communist armies, based in the countryside and supported by the peasantry,*

* Speech at the Moscow Meeting of Communist and Workers' Parties (November 18, 1957).

were able to overcome Chiang Kai-shek, who controlled the principal urban centers, so, Lin writes, "the countryside of the world"—Asia, Africa, and Latin America—will ultimately defeat "the cities" —North America and Europe. The article attacks the Soviet "revisionists" for advocating peaceful coexistence, and promises Chinese support for "people's wars" in which Lin predicts that guerrilla forces will ultimately defeat "U.S. imperialism and its lackeys."

The important role of Marshal Lin and the People's Liberation Army in the Great Proletarian Cultural Revolution was demonstrated in his report to the 1969 Congress of the Chinese Communist Party, in which he described the development of the Revolution, attacked demoted President Liu Shao-chi, and praised the army for taking control of the movement in early 1967 through the Revolutionary Three-in-One Committees (comprising representatives of the army, the Red Guards, and what was left of the state and party bureaucracy after the upheavals of the last part of 1966). Like Mao, whom he quotes frequently, Lin wishes to maintain the revolutionary fervor of the Liberation Army during the long years of struggle, and like him he fears that, unless the revolution is continued after the seizure of power, bureaucratization and opportunism in the party and government or among the intellectuals will lead China to follow what he considers to be the "bourgeois" path of the Soviet Union.

THE VICTORY OF THE PEOPLE'S WAR*

. . . It was on the basis of the lessons derived from the people's wars in China that Comrade Mao Tse-tung, using the simplest and the most vivid language, advanced the famous thesis that "political power grows out of the barrel of a gun."

He clearly pointed out: The seizure of power by armed force, the settlement of the issue by war, is the central task and the highest form of revolution. This Marxist-Leninist principle of revolution holds good universally, for China and for all other countries.

War is the product of imperialism and the system of exploita-

* Excerpts from Lin Piao's article "Long Live the Victory of the People's War!"; text released by the New China News Agency, September, 1965.

tion of man by man. Lenin said that "war is always and everywhere begun by the exploiters themselves, by the ruling and oppressing classes." So long as imperialism and the system of exploitation of man by man exist, the imperialists and reactionaries will invariably rely on armed force to maintain their reactionary rule and impose war on the oppressed nations and peoples. This is an objective law independent of man's will. . . .

In the last analysis, whether one dares to wage a tit-for-tat struggle against armed aggression and suppression by the imperialists and their lackeys, whether one dares to fight a people's war against them means whether one dares to embark on revolution. This is the most effective touchstone for distinguishing genuine from fake revolutionaries and Marxist-Leninists.

In view of the fact that some people were afflicted with the fear of the imperialists and reactionaries, Comrade Mao Tse-tung put forward his famous thesis that "the imperialists and all reactionaries are paper tigers. . . . In appearance the reactionaries are terrifying, but in reality they are not so powerful. From a long-term point of view, it is not the reactionaries but the people who are really powerful."

The history of people's war in China and other countries provides conclusive evidence that the growth of the people's revolutionary forces from weak and small beginnings into strong and large forces is a universal law of development of class struggle, a universal law of development of people's war. A people's war inevitably meets with many difficulties, with ups and downs and setbacks in the course of its development, but no force can alter its general trend toward inevitable triumph.

Comrade Mao Tse-tung points out that we must despise the enemy strategically and take full account of him tactically. To despise the enemy strategically is an elementary requirement for a revolutionary. Without the courage to despise the enemy and without daring to win, it will be simply impossible to make revolution and wage a people's war, let alone to achieve victory. . . .

The imperialists are extremely afraid of Comrade Mao Tse-tung's thesis that "imperialism and the reactionaries are paper tigers," and the revisionists are extremely hostile to it. They all oppose and attack this thesis and the Philistines follow suit by ridiculing it. But all this cannot in the least diminish its importance. The light of truth cannot be dimmed by anybody.

Comrade Mao Tse-tung's theory of people's war solves not only the problem of daring to fight a people's war, but also that of how to wage it.

Comrade Mao Tse-tung is a great statesman and military scientist, proficient at directing war in accordance with its laws. By the line and policies, the strategy and tactics he formulated for the people's war, he led the Chinese people in steering the ship of the people's war past all hidden reefs to the shores of victory in most complicated and difficult conditions.

It must be emphasized that Comrade Mao Tse-tung's theory of the establishment of rural revolutionary base areas and the encirclement of the cities from the countryside is of outstanding and universal practical importance for the present revolutionary struggles of all the oppressed nations and peoples in Asia, Africa, and Latin America against imperialism and its lackeys.

Many countries and peoples in Asia, Africa, and Latin America are now being subjected to aggression and enslavement on a serious scale by the imperialists headed by the United States and their lackeys. The basic political and economic conditions in many of these countries have many similarities to those that prevailed in old China. As in China, the peasant question is extremely important in these regions. The peasants constitute the main force of the national-democratic revolution against the imperialists and their lackeys.

In committing aggression against these countries, the imperialists usually begin by seizing the big cities and the main lines of communication, but they are unable to bring the vast countryside completely under their control. The countryside, and the countryside alone, can provide the broad areas in which the revolutionaries can maneuver freely. The countryside, and the countryside alone, can provide the revolutionary bases from which the revolutionaries can go forward to final victory. Precisely for this reason, Comrade Mao Tse-tung's theory of establishing revolutionary base areas in the rural districts and encircling the cities from the countryside is attracting more and more attention among the people in these regions.

Taking the entire globe, if North America and Western Europe can be called "the cities of the world," then Asia, Africa, and Latin America constitute "the rural areas of the world." Since World War II, the proletarian revolutionary movement has for various reasons been temporarily held back in the North American and Western European capitalist countries, while the people's revolutionary movement in Asia, Africa, and Latin America has been growing vigorously. In a sense, the contemporary world revolution also presents a picture of the encirclement of cities by the rural areas. . . .

The October Revolution opened up a new era in the revolution of the oppressed nations. The victory of the October Revolution built a bridge between the socialist revolution of the proletariat of the West and the national-democratic revolution of the colonial and semicolonial countries of the East. The Chinese revolution has successfully solved the problem of how to link up the national-democratic with the socialist revolution in the colonial and semicolonial countries.

Comrade Mao Tse-tung has pointed out that, in the epoch since the October Revolution, anti-imperialist revolution in any colonial or semicolonial country is no longer part of the old bourgeois, or capitalist, world revolution, but is part of the new world revolution, the proletarian-socialist world revolution.

Comrade Mao Tse-tung has formulated a complete theory of the new democratic revolution. He indicated that this revolution, which is different from all others, can only be, nay must be, a revolution against imperialism, feudalism, and bureaucratic capitalism waged by the broad masses of the people under the leadership of the proletariat.

This means that the revolution can only be, nay must be, led by the proletariat and the genuinely revolutionary party armed with Marxism-Leninism, and by no other class or party.

This means that the revolution embraces in its ranks not only the workers, peasants, and the urban petty bourgeoisie, but also the national bourgeoisie and other patriotic and anti-imperialist democrats.

This means, finally, that the revolution is directed against imperialism, feudalism, and bureaucratic capitalism.

The new democratic revolution leads to socialism, and not to capitalism.

Comrade Mao Tse-tung's theory of the new democratic revolution is the Marxist-Leninist theory of uninterrupted revolution.

Comrade Mao Tse-tung made a correct distinction between the two revolutionary stages, that is, the national-democratic and the socialist revolutions; at the same time, he correctly and closely linked the two. The national-democratic revolution is the necessary preparation for the socialist revolution, and the socialist revolution is the inevitable sequel to the national-democratic revolution. There is no great wall between the two revolutionary stages. But the socialist revolution is only possible after the completion of the national-democratic revolution. The more thorough the national-democratic revolution, the better the conditions for the socialist revolution.

The experience of the Chinese revolution shows that the tasks of the national-democratic revolution can be fulfilled only through long and tortuous struggles. In this stage of revolution, imperialism and its lackeys are the principal enemy. In the struggle against imperialism and its lackeys, it is necessary to rally all anti-imperialist patriotic forces, including the national bourgeoisie and all patriotic persons. All those patriotic persons from among the bourgeoisie and other exploiting classes who join the anti-imperialist struggle play a progressive historical role: they are not tolerated by imperialism but welcomed by the proletariat.

It is very harmful to confuse the two stages, that is, the national-democratic and the socialist revolutions. Comrade Mao Tse-tung criticized the wrong idea of "accomplishing both at one stroke," and pointed out that this utopian idea could only weaken the struggle against imperialism and its lackeys, the most urgent task at the time. The Kuomintang reactionaries and the Trotskyites they hired during the War of Resistance deliberately confused these two stages of the Chinese revolution, proclaiming the "theory of a single revolution" and preaching so-called socialism without any Communist Party. With this preposterous theory they attempted to swallow up the Communist Party, wipe out any revolution, and prevent the advance of the national-democratic revolution, and they used it as a pretext for their nonresistance and capitulation to imperialism. This reactionary theory was buried long ago by the history of the Chinese revolution.

The Khrushchev revisionists are now actively preaching that socialism can be built without the proletariat and without a genuinely revolutionary party armed with the advanced proletarian ideology, and they have cast the fundamental tenets of Marxism-Leninism to the four winds. The revisionists' purpose is solely to divert the oppressed nations from their struggle against imperialism and to sabotage their national-democratic solution, all in the service of imperialism.

The Chinese revolution provides a successful lesson for making a thoroughgoing national-democratic revolution under the leadership of the proletariat; it likewise provides a successful lesson for the timely transition from the national-democratic revolution to the socialist revolution under the leadership of the proletariat. . . .

Ours is the epoch in which world capitalism and imperialism are heading for their doom, and socialism and Communism are marching to victory. Comrade Mao Tse-tung's theory of people's war is not only a product of the Chinese revolution, but has also characteristics of our epoch. The new experience gained in the people's revolutionary struggles in various countries since World War II has provided continuous evidence that Mao Tse-tung's thought is a common asset of the revolutionary people of the whole world. This is the great international significance of the thought of Mao Tse-tung. . . .

The contradiction between the revolutionary peoples of Asia, Africa, and Latin America and the imperialists headed by the United States is the principal contradiction in the contemporary world. The development of this contradiction is promoting the struggle of the whole world against U.S. imperialism and its lackeys. . . .

The struggles waged by the different peoples against U.S. imperialism reinforce each other and merge into a torrential world-wide tide of opposition to U.S. imperialism. The more successful the development of people's war in a given region, the larger the number of U.S. imperialist forces that can be pinned down and depleted there. When the U.S. aggressors are hard pressed in one place, they have no alternative but to loosen their grip on others. Therefore, the conditions become more favorable for the people elsewhere to wage struggles against U.S. imperialism and its lackeys. . . .

However highly developed modern weapons and technical equipment may be and however complicated the methods of modern warfare, in the final analysis the outcome of a war will be decided by the sustained fighting of the ground forces, by the fighting at close quarters on battlefields, by the political consciousness of the men, by their courage and spirit of sacrifice. Here the weak points of U.S. imperialism will be completely laid bare, while the superiority of the revolutionary people will be brought into full play. The reactionary troops of U.S. imperialism cannot possibly be endowed with the courage and the spirit of sacrifice possessed by the revolutionary people. The spiritual atom bomb that the revolutionary people possess is a far more powerful and useful weapon than the physical atom bomb. . . .

Ever since Lenin led the great October Revolution to victory, the experience of innumerable revolutionary wars has borne out the truth that a revolutionary people who rise up with only their bare hands at the outset finally succeed in defeating the ruling classes who are armed to the teeth. The poorly armed have defeated the better armed. People's armed forces, beginning with only primitive swords, spears, rifles, hand-grenades, have in the end defeated the imperialist forces armed with modern airplanes, tanks, heavy artillery, and atom bombs. Guerrilla forces have ultimately defeated regular armies. "Amateurs" who were never trained in any military schools have eventually defeated "professionals" graduated from military academies. And so on and so forth. Things stubbornly develop in a way that runs counter to the assertions of the revisionists, and facts are slapping them in the face. . . .

We know that war brings destruction, sacrifice, and suffering on the people. But the destruction, sacrifice, and suffering will be much greater if no resistance is offered to imperialist armed aggression and the people become willing slaves. The sacrifice of a small number of people in revolutionary wars is repaid by security for whole nations, whole countries, and even the whole of mankind; temporary suffering is repaid by lasting or even perpetual peace and happiness. War can temper the people and push history forward. In this sense, war is a great school. . . .

In diametrical opposition to the Khrushchev revisionists, the Marxist-Leninists and revolutionary people never take a gloomy view of war. Our attitude toward imperialist wars of aggression has always been clear-cut. First, we are against them, and secondly, we are not afraid of them. We will destroy whoever attacks us. As for revolutionary wars waged by the oppressed nations and peoples, so far from opposing them, we invariably give them firm support and active aid. It has been so in the past, it remains so in the present and, when we grow in strength as time goes on, we will give them still more support and aid in the future. . . .

The peoples of the world now have the lessons of the October Revolution, the antifascist war, the Chinese people's war of resistance and war of liberation, the Korean people's war of resistance to U.S. aggression, the Vietnamese people's war of liberation and their war of resistance to U.S. aggression, and the people's revolutionary armed struggles in many other countries. Provided each people studies these lessons well and creatively integrates them with the concrete practice of revolution in their own country, there is no doubt that the revolutionary peoples of the world will stage still more powerful and splendid dramas in the theater of people's war in their countries and that they will wipe off the earth once and for all the common enemy of all the peoples, U.S. imperialism and its lackeys. . . .

THE GREAT PROLETARIAN CULTURAL REVOLUTION *

I. ON THE PREPARATION FOR THE GREAT PROLETARIAN CULTURAL REVOLUTION

The Great Proletarian Cultural Revolution of our country is a genuine proletarian revolution on an immense scale.

Chairman Mao has explained the necessity of the current great revolution in concise terms, "The current Great Proletarian Revolution is absolutely necessary and most timely for consolidating the dictatorship of the proletariat, preventing capitalist restoration, and building socialism." In order to comprehend this scientific thesis of Chairman Mao's fully, we should have a deep understanding of his theory of continuing the revolution under the dictatorship of the proletariat.

In 1957, shortly after the conclusion of the Party's Eighth National Congress, Chairman Mao published his great work *On the Correct Handling of Contradictions Among the People,* in which, following his Report to the Second Plenary Session of the Seventh Central Committee of the Communist Party of China, he comprehensively set forth the existence of contradictions, classes, and class struggle under the conditions of the dictatorship of the proletariat, set forth the thesis of the existence of two different types of contradictions in socialist society, those between ourselves and the enemy and those among the people, and set forth the great theory of continuing the revolution under the dictatorship of the proletariat. Like a radiant beacon, this great work illuminates the course of China's socialist revolution and socialist construction and has laid

* From Lin Piao, "Report to the Ninth National Congress of the Communist Party of China," *Peking Review,* No. 18, April 30, 1969.

the theoretical foundation for the Great Proletarian Cultural Revolution. Chairman Mao has comprehensively summed up the historical experience of the dictatorship of the proletariat both in its positive and negative aspects and, in order to prevent the restoration of capitalism, has put forward the theory of continuing the revolution under the dictatorship of the proletariat.

As early as March, 1949, on the eve of the transition of the Chinese revolution from the new-democratic revolution to the socialist revolution, Chairman Mao explicitly pointed out in his report to the Second Plenary Session of the Seventh Central Committee of the Party: After the country-wide seizure of power by the proletariat, the principal internal contradiction is "the contradiction between the working class and the bourgeoisie." The heart of the struggle is still the question of state power. Chairman Mao especially reminded us: "After the enemies with guns have been wiped out, there will still be enemies without guns; they are bound to struggle desperately against us, and we must never regard these enemies lightly. If we do not now raise and understand the problem in this way, we shall commit the gravest mistakes."

Having foreseen the protracted and complex nature of the class struggle between the proletariat and the bourgeoisie after the establishment of the dictatorship of the proletariat, Chairman Mao set the whole Party the militant task of fighting imperialism, the Kuomintang, and the bourgeoisie in the political, ideological, economic, cultural, and diplomatic spheres.

Our Party waged intense battles in accordance with the resolution of the Second Plenary Session of the Seventh Central Committee and the Party's general line for the transition period formulated by Chairman Mao. In 1956, the socialist transformation of the ownership of the means of production in agriculture, handicrafts, and capitalist industry and commerce was in the main completed. That was the crucial moment for the question of whether the socialist revolution could continue to advance. In view of the rampancy of revisionism in the international Communist movement and the new trends of class struggle in our country, Chairman Mao, in his great work *On the Correct Handling of Contradictions Among the People*, called the attention of the whole Party to the following fact: "In China, although in the main socialist transformation has been completed with respect to the system of ownership . . . there are still remnants of the overthrown landlord and comprador classes, there is still a bourgeoisie, and the remolding of the petty bourgeoisie has only just started." Countering the fallacy put forward by Liu Shao-chi * in 1956 that "in China, the question of which wins out, socialism or capitalism, is already solved," Chairman Mao specifically pointed out: "The question of which will win out, socialism or capitalism, is still not really settled. The class struggle between the proletariat and the bourgeoisie, the class struggle between the different political forces, and the class struggle in the ideological field between the proletariat and the bourgeoisie will continue to be long and tortuous and at times will even become very acute." Thus, for the first time in the theory and practice of the international Communist movement, it was pointed out explicitly that classes and class struggle still exist after the socialist transformation of the ownership of the means of production has been in the main completed, and that the proletariat must continue the revolution. . . .

The current Great Proletarian Cultural Revolution with the participation of hundreds of millions of revolutionary people has by no means occurred accidentally. It is the inevitable result of the protracted and sharp struggle between the two classes, the two roads, and the two lines in socialist society. The Great Proletarian Cultural Revolution is "a great political revolution carried out by the proletariat against the bourgeoisie and all other exploiting classes; it is a continuation of the prolonged struggle waged by the Chinese Communist Party and the masses of revolutionary people under its leadership against the Kuomintang reactionaries, a continuation of the class struggle between the proletariat and the bourgeoisie." The heroic Chinese proletariat, poor and lower-middle peasants, People's Liberation Army, revolutionary cadres, and revolutionary intellectuals, who were all determined to follow the great leader Chairman Mao closely in taking the socialist road, could no longer tolerate the restoration activities of Liu Shao-chi and his gang, and so a great class battle was unavoidable.

As Chairman Mao pointed out in his talk in February, 1967: "In the past we waged struggles in rural areas, in factories, in the cultural field, and we carried out the socialist education movement. But all this failed to solve the problem because we did not find a

---

* Until the Great Proletarian Cultural Revolution, Liu Shao-chi was President of the Chinese People's Republic, Vice-Chairman of the Communist Party, and, before Lin Piao's ascendancy, most probable successor to Mao Tse-tung. In October 1968 he was denounced as "a renegade, traitor, and scab . . . lackey of imperialism, modern revisionism, and the Kuomintang reactionaries," removed from all posts, and expelled from the party.—ED.

form, a method, to arouse the broad masses to expose our dark aspect openly, in an all-round way and from below." Now we have found this form—it is the Great Proletarian Cultural Revolution.

II. ON THE COURSE OF THE GREAT
PROLETARIAN CULTURAL REVOLUTION

The Great Proletarian Cultural Revolution is a great political revolution personally initiated and led by our great leader Chairman Mao under the conditions of the dictatorship of the proletariat, a great revolution in the realm of the superstructure. Our aim is to smash revisionism, seize back that portion of power usurped by the bourgeoisie, exercise all-round dictatorship of the proletariat in the superstructure, including all spheres of culture, and strengthen and consolidate the economic base of socialism so as to ensure that our country continues to advance in giant strides along the road of socialism. . . .

The *Circular* of May 16, 1966 worked out under Chairman Mao's personal guidance laid down the theory, line, principles, and policies for the Great Proletarian Cultural Revolution and constituted the great program for the whole movement. The *Circular* thoroughly criticized the "February Outline" turned out by Liu Shao-chi's bourgeois headquarters for the purpose of suppressing this great revolution. It called upon the whole Party and the whole nation to direct the spearhead of struggle against the representatives of the bourgeoisie who had sneaked into the Party and to pay special attention to unmasking "persons like Khrushchev . . . who are still nestling beside us." This was a great call mobilizing the people of the whole country to unfold a great political revolution. The Cultural Revolution Group under the Central Committee, which was set up by decision of the *Circular*, has firmly carried out Chairman Mao's proletarian revolutionary line.

Under the guidance of Chairman Mao's proletarian revolutionary line, the broad revolutionary masses plunged into the fight. In Peking University, a big-character poster was written in response to the call of the Central Committee.* And soon big-character posters

* On May 25, 1966, the Peking University Philosophy Department published a poster in large Chinese characters attacking the top officials of the University for sabotaging the Cultural Revolution. Mao subsequently endorsed the use of such posters and they were widely employed "to reveal the true face of sinister anti-Party and anti-socialist groups" (*People's Daily*, June 20, 1966).

criticizing reactionary bourgeois ideas mushroomed all over the country. Then Red Guards rose and came forward in large numbers and revolutionary young people became courageous and daring pathbreakers. Thrown into a panic, the Liu Shao-chi clique hastily hurled forth the bourgeois reactionary line, cruelly suppressing the revolutionary movement of the student youth. However, this did not win them much time in their death-bed struggle. Chairman Mao called and presided over the Eleventh Plenary Session of the Eighth Central Committee of the Party. The Plenary Session adopted the programmatic document, *Decision of the Central Committee of the Chinese Communist Party Concerning the Great Proletarian Cultural Revolution* (i.e., *the 16-Point Decision*). Chairman Mao put up his big-character poster *Bombard the Headquarters*, thus taking the lid off Liu Shao-chi's bourgeois headquarters. In his letter to the Red Guards, Chairman Mao said that the revolutionary actions of the Red Guards "express your wrath against and your denunciation of the landlord class, the bourgeoisie, the imperialists, the revisionists and their running dogs, all of whom exploit and oppress the workers, peasants, revolutionary intellectuals, and revolutionary parties and groups. They show that it is right to rebel against reactionaries. I warmly support you." Afterwards, Chairman Mao received 13 million Red Guards and other revolutionary masses from all parts of the country on eight occasions at Tien An Men in the capital, which heightened the revolutionary fighting will of the people of the whole country. The revolutionary movements of the workers, peasants, and revolutionary functionaries developed rapidly. Increasing numbers of big-character posters spread like raging prairie fire and roared like guns; the slogan "It is right to rebel against reactionaries" resounded throughout the land. And the battle of the hundreds of millions of the people to bombard Liu Shao-chi's bourgeois headquarters developed vigorously.

No reactionary class will ever step down from the stage of history of its own accord. When the revolution touched that portion of power usurped by the bourgeoisie, the class struggle became all the more acute. After Liu Shao-chi's downfall, his revisionist clique and his agents in various places changed their tactics time and again, putting forward slogans which were "Left" in form but Right in essence, such as "suspecting all" and "overthrowing all," in a futile attempt to go on hitting hard at the many and protecting their own handful. Moreover, they created splits among the revolutionary masses and manipulated and hoodwinked a section of the

masses so as to protect themselves. When these schemes were
shattered by the proletarian revolutionaries, they launched another
frenzied counterattack, and that is the adverse current lasting from
the winter of 1966 to the spring of 1967. . . .

III. On Carrying Out the Tasks of
Struggle-Criticism-Transformation Conscientiously

As in all other revolutions, the fundamental question in the current great revolution in the realm of the superstructure is the
question of political power, a question of which class holds leadership. The establishment of revolutionary committees in all provinces, municipalities, and autonomous regions throughout the
country (with the exception of Taiwan Province) marks the great,
decisive victory achieved by this revolution. However, the revolution is not yet over. The Proletariat must continue to advance,
"carry out the tasks of struggle-criticism-transformation conscientiously" and carry the socialist revolution in the realm of the superstructure through to the end.

Chairman Mao says: "Struggle-criticism-transformation in a
factory, on the whole, goes through the following stages: Establishing a three-in-one revolutionary committee; carrying out mass
criticism and repudiation; purifying the class ranks; consolidating
the Party organization; and simplifying the administrative structure, changing irrational rules and regulations and sending office
workers to the workshops." We must act on Chairman Mao's
instruction and fulfill these tasks in every single factory, every
single school, every single commune, and every single unit in a
deep-going, meticulous, down-to-earth, and appropriate way.

Confronted with a thousand and one tasks, a revolutionary committee must grasp the fundamental: It must put the living study
and application of Mao Tsetung Thought * above all work and
place Mao Tsetung Thought in command of everything. For
decades, Mao Tsetung Thought has been showing the orientation
of the revolution to the whole Party and the whole nation. However, as Liu Shao-chi and his gang of counterrevolutionary revisionists blocked Chairman Mao's instructions, the broad revolutionary masses could hardly hear Chairman Mao's voice directly.

---

* "Mao Tsetung Thought"—the elimination of the hyphen is part of a
conscious effort to rank Mao's thought with that of Marx and Lenin.—Ed.

The storm of the present great revolution has destroyed the "palaces of hell-rulers," big and small, and has made it possible for Mao Tsetung Thought to reach the broad revolutionary masses directly. This is a great victory. This wide dissemination of Mao Tsetung Thought in a big country with a population of 700 million is the most significant achievement of the Great Proletarian Cultural Revolution. In this revolution, hundreds of millions of people always carry with them *Quotations From Chairman Mao Tsetung*, which they study and apply conscientiously. As soon as a new instruction of Chairman Mao's is issued, they propagate it and go into action. This most valuable practice must be maintained and persevered in. We should carry on in a deep-going way the mass movement for the living study and application of Mao Tsetung Thought, continue to run well the Mao Tsetung Thought study classes of all types and, in the light of Chairman Mao's *May 7 Directive* of 1966, truly turn the whole country into a great school of Mao Tsetung Thought.

All revolutionary comrades must be clearly aware that class struggle will by no means cease in the ideological and political spheres. The struggle between the proletariat and the bourgeoisie by no means dies out with our seizure of power. We must continue to hold high the banner of revolutionary mass criticism and use Mao Tsetung Thought to criticize the bourgeoisie, to criticize revisionism and all kinds of Right or extreme "Left" erroneous ideas which run counter to Chairman Mao's proletarian revolutionary line, and to criticize bourgeois individualism and the theory of "many centers," * that is, the theory of "no center. . . ."

The People's Liberation Army is the mighty pillar of the dictatorship of the proletariat. Chairman Mao has pointed out many times: From the Marxist point of view the main component of the state is the army. The Chinese People's Liberation Army personally founded and led by Chairman Mao is an army of the workers and peasants, an army of the proletariat. It has performed great historic feats in the struggle for overthrowing the three big mountains of imperialism, feudalism, and bureaucrat-capitalism, and in the struggles for defending the motherland, for resisting U.S. aggression and aiding Korea, and for smashing

---

* "Many centers"—possibly a reference to the theory of "poly-centrism" in world Communism, first put forward by the Italian Communist Party.—ED.

aggression by imperialism, revisionism, and the reactionaries. In the Great Proletarian Cultural Revolution, large numbers of commanders and fighters have taken part in the work of "three supports and two militaries" (i.e., support industry, support agriculture, support the broad masses of the Left, military control, political and military training) and representatives of the army have taken part in the three-in-one combination; they have tempered themselves in the class struggle, strengthened their ties with the masses, promoted the ideological revolutionization of the army, and made new contributions to the people. And this is also the best preparation against war. We must carry forward the glorious tradition of "supporting the government and cherishing the people," "supporting the army and cherishing the people," strengthen the unity between the army and the people, strengthen the building of the militia and of national defense, and do a still better job in all our work. For the past three years, it is precisely because the people have supported the army and the army has protected the people that renegades, enemy agents, absolutely unrepentant persons in power taking the capitalist road, and counterrevolutionaries have failed in their attempts to undermine this great people's army of ours. . . .

IV. On the Policies of the Great Proletarian Cultural Revolution

The majority or the vast majority of the intellectuals trained in the old type of schools and colleges are able or willing to integrate themselves with the workers, peasants, and soldiers. They should be "re-educated" by the workers, peasants, and soldiers under the guidance of Chairman Mao's correct line, and encouragement should be given to those who have done well in the integration and to the Red Guards and educated young people who are active in going to the countryside or mountainous areas.

Chairman Mao has taught us many times: "Help more people by educating them and narrow the target of attack" and "carry out Marx's teaching that only by emancipating all mankind can the proletariat achieve its own final emancipation." With regard to people who have made mistakes, stress must be laid on giving them education and re-education, doing patient and careful ideological and political work, and truly acting "on the principles of 'learning from past mistakes to avoid future ones' and 'curing the sickness to save the patient,' in order to achieve the twofold objective of clarity in ideology and unity among comrades." With regard to good people who committed the errors characteristic of the capitalist-roader in power but have now raised their political consciousness and gained the understanding of the masses, they should be promptly "liberated," assigned to suitable work and encouraged to go among the masses of the workers and peasants to remold their world outlook. As for those who have made a little progress and become to some extent awakened, we should continue to help them, proceeding from the viewpoint of unity. Chairman Mao has recently pointed out: "The proletariat is the greatest class in the history of mankind. It is the most powerful revolutionary class ideologically, politically, and in strength. It can and must unite the overwhelming majority of people around itself so as to isolate the handful of enemies to the maximum and attack them."

In the struggle against the enemy, we must carry out the policy "make use of contradictions, win over the many, oppose the few, and crush our enemies one by one" which Chairman Mao has always advocated. "Stress should be laid on the weight of evidence and on investigation and study, and it is strictly forbidden to obtain confessions by compulsion and to give them credence." We must implement Chairman Mao's policies of "leniency toward those who confess their crimes and severe punishment of those who refuse to do so" and of "giving a way out." We rely mainly on the broad masses of the people in exercising dictatorship over the enemy. As for bad people or suspects ferreted out through investigation in the movement for purifying the class ranks, the policy of "killing none and not arresting most" should be applied to all except the active counterrevolutionaries against whom there is conclusive evidence of crimes such as murder, arson, and poisoning, and who should be dealt with in accordance with law. . . .

U.S. imperialism and Soviet revisionism are always trying to "isolate" China; this is China's honor. Their rabid opposition to China cannot do us the slightest harm. On the contrary, it serves to further arouse our people's determination to maintain independence and keep the initiative in our own hands, rely on our own efforts, and work hard to make our country prosperous and powerful; it serves to prove to the whole world that China has drawn a clear line between herself on the one hand and U.S. imperialism and Soviet revisionism on the other. Today, it is not imperialism, revisionism, and reaction but the proletariat and the revolutionary people of all countries that determine the destiny of the world. The genuine Marxist-Leninist Parties and organizations of various countries, which are composed of the advanced elements of the proletariat, are a new rising force that has infinitely broad prospects. The Communist Party of China is determined to unite and fight together with them. We firmly support the Albanian people in their struggle against imperialism and revisionism; we firmly support the Vietnamese people in carrying their war of resistance against U.S. aggression and for national salvation through to the end; we firmly support the revolutionary struggles of the people of Laos, Thailand, Burma, Malaya, Indonesia, India, Palestine, and other countries and regions in Asia, Africa, and Latin America; we firmly support the proletariat, the students and youth, and the masses of the Black people of the United States in their just struggle against the U.S. ruling clique; we firmly support the proletariat and the laboring people of the Soviet Union in their just struggle to overthrow the Soviet revisionist renegade clique; we firmly support the people of Czechoslovakia and other countries in their just struggle against Soviet revisionist social-imperialism; we firmly support the revolutionary struggles of the people of Japan and the West European and Oceanian countries; we firmly support the revolutionary struggles of the people of all countries; and we firmly support all the just struggles of resistance against aggression and oppression by U.S. imperialism and Soviet revisionism. All countries and people subjected to aggression, control, intervention, or bullying by U.S. imperialism and Soviet revisionism, unite and form the broadest possible united front and overthrow our common enemies! . . .

Let the whole Party unite, let the whole nation unite, hold high the great red banner of Mao Tsetung Thought, be resolute, fear no sacrifice and surmount every difficulty to win victory!

Long live the great victory of the Great Proletarian Cultural Revolution!

Long live the dictatorship of the proletariat!

Long live the Ninth National Congress of the Party!

Long live the great, glorious, and correct Communist Party of China!

Long live great Marxism-Leninism-Mao Tsetung Thought!
Long live our great leader Chairman Mao! A long, long life to
Chairman Mao.

3. Sukarno

*Sukarno, the former President of Indonesia, was born in 1901 at
Surabaya. He is the son of a village teacher. He attended a Dutch
elementary school, and later was sent to secondary school by a
nationalist friend of his father. He joined a nationalist organization, and entered the Engineering School at Bandung, where he
received his degree in 1925. Subsequently, Sukarno helped form the
Indonesian National Party (PNI). He was imprisoned by the
Dutch in 1929, and again in 1933, when he was exiled to a remote part of Indonesia. He was freed by the Japanese in 1942.
On August 17, 1945, before the return of the Dutch, Sukarno declared his country's independence. In 1949, after several years of
fighting, sovereignty was finally transferred by the Dutch, and he
became Indonesia's first President, a position he held until 1967
In 1963, he was declared President for Life, but this action was re-
versed by the People's Consultative Congress in 1966.*

*In 1960, Sukarno dissolved parliament and outlawed several of
the political parties. He proceeded to rule according to the principles of "guided democracy"—through leadership by an elite, consultation with an advisory parliament that represents social and
economic groups, and decision-making by discussion and consensus
rather than by voting. An unsuccessful Communist coup on September 30, 1965 led to their virtual elimination from Indonesian
political life, a sharp reduction in the political power of Sukarno,
and a great increase in that of the army. On March 12, 1967, the
People's Consultative Congress "replaced" him as President with
General Suharto, and he died on June 21, 1969. Suharto's government has promised elections and a return to parliamentary government in the near future.*

LECTURE TO THE STUDENTS OF HASANUDDIN UNIVERSITY*

Jefferson and Marx

... The British philosopher Bertrand Russell divides mankind at present into two groups, following two different philosophies. One group has faith in the Declaration of Independence of Thomas Jefferson, while the other group believes in the Communist Manifesto of Karl Marx. . . .

Bertrand Russell is not partial to one or the other group. He only hopes that the competition between the followers of these two philosophies would not be determined on the battlefield. It should not be solved through the destruction of men by men, because of the signs we see now and which have also been observed by themselves, but at the end they want to prove their stand by fighting one another, destroying one another in war.

Bertrand Russell said: Compete with each other, but do not try to reach a solution on the battlefield. Compete in a field that brings prosperity to mankind. Please compete and try to achieve prosperity of mankind by applying your respective ideas. Followers of Thomas Jefferson, please try to establish the prosperity of men according to your world of thought, and followers of Karl Marx, please try to bring prosperity to mankind. Those who will bring the greatest prosperity to men will prove to be the victors in this competition. . . .

I do not agree with Bertrand Russell when he said that humanity only consists of these two groups. There is a third group, which numbers more than a billion, maybe even more than one and a half billion people—namely, the people who live under the flags of nationalism in Asia and Africa.

Those are the people whose hearts throb eagerly, who are very anxious to realize their national independence by establishing a just and prosperous society without getting involved in any way with the two ways of thought mentioned by Bertrand Russell. These three groupings I regard as a phenomenon of the twentieth

* Translated and published by the Ministry of Information, Djakarta, Indonesia, 1959.

century: the group of Thomas Jefferson, the group adhering to the
Communist Manifesto, and the group of Asian and African nationalism. . . . We not only advocate the coexistence of what is
known as the Western bloc and the Communist bloc—the bloc
of the United States and that of the Soviet Union, we not only
want coexistence between these two blocs, but we also suggest that
these two blocs should coexist with Asian-African nationalism. I
suggest this because I have seen that Asian-African nationalism,
the third group, is always disturbed and attacked by people from
outside. It is not respected by people from outside. People even
try to suppress and destroy it.

It is my sincere hope, and this hope I put on all the Indonesian
students, that we should not, as a nation that has just been established as a state, that is eager to establish a just and prosperous
society, a nation that is eager to build up, a nation that thus needs
to look at the experiences of the outside world, indulge in too
many theories and look for the small mistakes in other people's
ideas, so that at the end we only see these mistakes. This attitude
is useless. . . . We do not have to look deliberately for errors in
the Declaration of Independence, concentrate and pounce on it
when we have found one. Neither do we look only for the mistakes
of Karl Marx and Friedrich Engels and doggedly criticize and analyze them. It is of no use for the community we are building. We
are looking for the experience of other nations outside of Indonesia,
especially in these later periods; we use their good experiences to
build up our community and country, and cast away the bad experiences.

That is why it is so important to send our scientists, cadres,
and youth to other parts of the world. If our government had
enough money, I would ask Pak Prijono, the Minister of Education, to send as many students as possible to the United States,
to the Soviet Union, to Canada, to the People's Republic of
China—everywhere—to get experience.

Do not say first, I do not want to go to the United States, as it
follows the world of thought of Thomas Jefferson. Or do not say,
I do not want to go to the People's Republic of China, as it is
within the world of thought of Karl Marx. This kind of opinion is
wrong. I have mentioned earlier that the world of thought of
Thomas Jefferson has a great number of followers. It is impossible
for human beings not to be rational, not to see some good things
in the world of thought of Thomas Jefferson. Because of the ex-

istence of some good points in the world of thought of Thomas
Jefferson, that world of thought has tens of millions, hundreds of
millions of followers, because human beings have sound minds.
The same applies to Karl Marx. . . .

The problem our country faces now is in the first place to provide our people with a good living. Therefore, the present is no
time for us for too much theorizing. We had better be practical
and pick out whatever is good from the ideas of Thomas Jefferson
as well as those from Karl Marx—without, however, taking sides.
In politics, this attitude is known as our independent and active
policy. But I would like this attitude to be taken in the field of
science, too. . . .

Guided Democracy

For reconstruction, three basic requirements are needed:
Firstly, capital. It is clear that one cannot build up without
capital. Furthermore, capital, if possible, should be our own capital—national capital—owned and raised by the Indonesian people
themselves. If our own capital is not sufficient, we can contract
loans from abroad. If we cannot obtain enough loans, then only
can we invite foreign capital to invest here, but remember, my
friends, I mention capital investment as number three here.
Firstly, we have to get our own capital. Whenever it is not enough,
there is nothing we can do except to borrow, to borrow capital
which we will repay in terms. Only when it is necessary, foreign
capital has to be imported.

Secondly, managerial know-how. One cannot build without the
knowledge of how to organize. That is the reason why we make a
blueprint, that is the reason why we established this university, to
train and educate cadres—as many as possible. . . . We are grateful that at present we have 30,000 students in the whole of Indonesia. But that is not enough yet. I think that we need more
than 150,000 students whose spirits are alert and whose minds are
filled with practical, managerial, and applied sciences.

Thirdly, a political atmosphere which is conducive to reconstruction. Even though we possess capital (the first requirement),
although we possess managerial know-how (the second requirement), if the political atmosphere is not conducive to reconstruction, development cannot be carried out smoothly. How is our
political atmosphere at present? I have said over and over again,

our political atmosphere is an unhealthy one, a liberal political atmosphere, an atmosphere of "free-fight liberalism." An atmosphere in which we continuously fight and quarrel, each claiming to be right, looking for mistakes of one another. It is a situation where there is no order and no unity, no one yielding to the other. One is eager to destroy the other. We must abandon this free-fight liberalism completely, if we want to develop and build up in the right way.

Indeed, the delegations which I sent have come back with an answer from the people of the countries they visited. Indonesia is richer than those countries. The Indonesians do not lack intelligence or brains. We also know that the Indonesian people have enough spirit. But why do we not build up speedily, why are we lagging behind? That is why, on the 17th of August, 1957, I said that the political atmosphere in Indonesia had to be changed. That is why I suggested that the free-fight liberalism which gives us this unhealthy atmosphere has to be abandoned. In order to draw up a blueprint, I suggested what is called democracy with leadership.

The day before yesterday, in Bogor, I was visited by a large delegation of 260, representing cooperative bodies of the whole of Indonesia. Their spokesman said the following: "Mr. President, with our cooperatives we have been able to raise the standard of living of the people a little. And for your knowledge, we would like to inform you that in the world of cooperatives, democracy with leadership or guided democracy is applied. In the world of co-operatives . . . we have a clear aim, a clear-cut way of working and distribution of profit—everything is clearly under leadership."

Within the world of cooperatives, then, guided democracy is applied. If the blueprint of the National Planning Council is finished, the execution thereof could not be carried out smoothly without guided democracy, without leadership. The number-one leader is the blueprint itself. One cannot carry out a blueprint and at the same time debate about it, after it has been approved by parliament. This blueprint becomes the property of the Indonesian people, becomes national property. . . . This blueprint has to be carried out, and its principles cannot be debated again.

I am myself a qualified engineer. Very often, when I was in the construction business, I received blueprints of things to be built. I carried out those blueprints as they were. I did not argue why, for instance, certain lines went a certain way, why a certain thing should be made of concrete and not of wood, why its stories were that high when they were not lower. It was a blueprint entrusted to me, for me to carry out, and I would carry it out. The blueprint was my guide, and I myself guided and led the employees. As a qualified engineer, I had under me superintendents and foremen. I was their leader, and I had conferences with them. But my conferences with them were not of that type of free-fight liberalism. I conferred with them about the execution of the blueprint. I asked the superintendents: These things have to be made out of concrete; what would be the best way to get them done? One superintendent would suggest: Pak, I think this is the best way; get stones, gravel, sand, and cement, call a lot of people—twenty, a hundred—and have everything mixed by hand. I then asked another superintendent what his opinion was. He answered: No, do not work by hand, Bung, this building is too large for that; buy a concrete mixer at once; with that we can mix concrete for this building and others. I conferred with my foremen—I practiced democracy with them—I asked for their opinion. I also discussed the choice of the materials; I conferred with my men. On all aspects of the execution of the blueprint, I held discussions, but these discussions were under guidance—the guidance of the blueprint, my guidance, the constructor of the building.

That is why it is wrong when people say that guided democracy is a false democracy, that it is a form of dictatorship. I even said in my statement of October 28, 1958, that democracy with leadership is a true Indonesian democracy. This is the danger you are facing, the danger that many of you become copyists. You have heard of the word "democracy"; democracy is indeed good. What does America say about democracy? It is to be found in certain American books. What does England say, France, the Netherlands, Germany? They each have their own reference books. Well, one of them must be the genuine democracy. Thus, you then try to apply in Indonesia democracy as it is practiced in America, Germany, France, England, the Netherlands, the U.S.S.R., or in other countries? You are only trying to copy!

No, as I have said before, we have to return to our own personality; we want to return to our own identity. Do not let us become a carbon-copy nation. We have had a democracy since olden times. I do not imply that we should remain as we were then. But the things of former times are good material for us today to refer to, because we are going to establish democracy in our own country.

How was democracy of former times in Indonesia? It still is practiced today in the villages in Java, Minangkabau, Sulawesi, Lombok, Bali, and other places—namely, in their laws and their system of *musjawarah* and *mufakat* (discussion and agreement). Every village practices democracy. But do they in these village meetings apply the practice of voting? Of free-fight liberalism, where half plus one is always right? No, the *musjawarah* is held under the guidance of Lurah, the Chief of the Elders, of Nini Mamak, the guidance of whoever is leader. Everybody says something different until at one time a compromise is achieved out of all these different opinions, without voting. This is what is called *mufakat* (agreement)—that by *musjawarah* (discussion) without voting, a joint compromise is achieved. There is no dictatorship in *musjawarah* and *mufakat*. That is why democracy with leadership is a true, original Indonesian democracy. This is one of the most important sources for us from which we can draw material to find a new, clear democracy—not American democracy, Dutch, French, British, German, or Soviet, or anybody else's democracy. Let us find a democracy which is suitable for our own identity. And use sources and material which are to be found in our own country.

Regarding our own democracy, I initiated the idea, calling on the people to join to fight the diseases that were the results of free-fight liberalism. I called on the people to destroy free-fight liberalism completely, and to change it into Indonesian democracy, guided democracy, or democracy with leadership. If people asked me to explain in detail what it means, I would not be able to give a proper answer. No, I want this guided democracy to become the property of the Indonesian people again. That is why I suggest to the people, especially the experts, scientists, students, to think. Please think and rethink, make and remake. Think, carry it out so that as a joint result we can achieve a new democratic system which I call democracy with leadership, or guided democracy, which is suitable for conditions in Indonesia. . . .

4. Mohandas K. Gandhi

Mohandas K. Gandhi was born in 1869 in western India, a member of the merchant caste. He studied law in London, was admitted to the bar in 1891, and then returned to India to practice law. Two years later, he went to South Africa, where he organized his first passive-resistance campaign against racial discrimination. On his return to India in 1915, he became one of the most influential members of the Indian Congress Party. After World War I, he organized campaigns of passive resistance calling for an end to British rule over India. Between 1922 and 1942, Gandhi was repeatedly imprisoned, but gained a vast following both in India and abroad. In 1948, after Indian independence had been established, Gandhi was assassinated by a Hindu fanatic—thus becoming a martyr to his belief in tolerance for all religions.

The Indian Congress Party still accepts Gandhi's philosophy as the basis of its ideology, although it has taken a more favorable attitude toward industrialization. Kwame Nkrumah has also mentioned Gandhi as one of the important influences upon his thinking.

The following selections are from a pamphlet Gandhi wrote in 1909. They include his explanation of passive resistance, and his defense of village and home industries as a more appropriate economic system than the machine civilization of the West.

INDIAN HOME RULE*

True Civilization

Reader: You have denounced railways, lawyers, and doctors. I can see that you will discard all machinery. What, then, is civilization?

---

* Excerpts from *Indian Home Rule* (Ahmedabad: Navajivan Trust, 1946); reprinted by permission.

Editor: The answer to that question is not difficult. I believe that the civilization India has evolved is not to be beaten in the world. Nothing can equal the seeds sown by our ancestors. Rome went; Greece shared the same fate; the might of the Pharaohs was broken; Japan has become Westernized; of China, nothing can be said; but India is still, somehow or other, sound at the foundation. The people of Europe learn their lessons from the writings of the men of Greece or Rome, which exist no longer in their former glory. In trying to learn from them, the Europeans imagine that they will avoid the mistakes of Greece and Rome. Such is their pitiable condition. In the midst of all this, India remains immovable, and that is her glory. It is a charge against India that her people are so uncivilized, ignorant, and stolid that it is not possible to induce them to adopt any changes. It is a charge really against our merit. What we have tested and found true on the anvil of experience we dare not change. Many thrust their advice upon India, and she remains steady. This is her beauty; it is the sheet anchor of our hope.

Civilization is that mode of conduct which points out to man the path of duty. Performance of duty and observance of morality are convertible terms. To observe morality is to attain mastery over our mind and our passions. So doing, we know ourselves. The Gujarati equivalent for civilization means "good conduct."

If this definition be correct, then India, as so many writers have shown, has nothing to learn from anybody else, and this is as it should be. We notice that the mind is a restless bird; the more it gets the more it wants, and still remains unsatisfied. The more we indulge our passions, the more unbridled they become. Our ancestors, therefore, set a limit to our indulgences. They saw that happiness was largely a mental condition. A man is not necessarily happy because he is rich, or unhappy because he is poor. The rich are often seen to be unhappy, the poor to be happy. Millions will always remain poor. Observing all this, our ancestors dissuaded us from luxuries and pleasures. We have managed with the same kind of plough as it existed thousands of years ago. We have retained the same kind of cottages that we had in former times, and our indigenous education remains the same as before. We have had no system of life-corroding competition. Each followed his own occupation or trade, and charged a regulation wage. It was not that we did not know how to invent machinery; but our forefathers knew that, if we set our hearts after such things, we would become slaves and lose our moral fiber. They therefore, after due deliberation, decided that we should only do what we could with our hands and feet. They saw that our real happiness and health consisted in a proper use of our hands and feet. They further reasoned that large cities were a snare and a useless encumbrance and that people would not be happy in them, that there would be gangs of thieves and robbers, prostitution, and vice flourishing in them, and that poor men would be robbed by rich men. They were, therefore, satisfied with small villages. They saw that kings and their swords were inferior to the sword of ethics, and they, therefore, held the sovereigns of the earth to be inferior to the rishis and the fakirs.* A nation with a constitution like this is more fit to teach others than to learn from others. This nation had courts, lawyers, and doctors, but they were all within bounds. Everybody knew that these professions were not particularly superior; moreover, they did not rob people; they were considered people's dependants, not their masters. Justice was tolerably fair. The ordinary rule was to avoid courts. There were not touts to lure people into them. This evil, too, was noticeable only in and around capitals. The common people lived independently and followed their agricultural occupation. They enjoyed true home rule.

And where this cursed modern civilization has not reached, India remains as it was before. The inhabitants of that part of India will very properly laugh at your newfangled notions. The English do not rule over them, nor will you ever rule over them. Those whose name we speak we do not know, nor do they know us. I would certainly advise you and those like you who love the motherland to go into the interior that has not yet been polluted by the railways, and to live there for six months; you might then be patriotic and speak of home rule.

Now you see what I consider to be real civilization. Those who want to change conditions such as I have described are enemies of the country and are sinners.

Reader: It would be all right if India were exactly as you described it, but it is also India where there are hundreds of child widows, where two-year-old babies are married, where twelve-year-old girls are mothers and housewives, where women practice poly-

---

* A rishi is an ancient sage of the Hindu religion; a fakir is a religious ascetic.—ED.

andry, where the practice of *niyog** obtains, where, in the name
of religion, girls dedicate themselves to prostitution, and where,
in the name of religion, sheep and goats are killed. Do you consider these also symbols of the civilization that you have described?

Editor: You make a mistake. The defects that you have shown
are defects. Nobody mistakes them for ancient civilization. They
remain in spite of it. Attempts have always been made, and will
be made, to remove them. We may utilize the new spirit that is
born in us for purging ourselves of these evils. But what I have
described to you as emblems of modern civilization are accepted
as such by its votaries. The Indian civilization, as described by
me, has been so described by its votaries. In no part of the world,
and under no civilization, have all men attained perfection. The
tendency of Indian civilization is to elevate the moral being, that
of the Western civilization is to propagate immorality. The latter is godless, the former is based on a belief in God. So understanding and so believing, it behooves every lover of India to cling
to the old Indian civilization even as a child clings to its mother's
breast. . . .

Passive Resistance

Reader: Is there any historical evidence as to the success of what
you have called soul-force or truth-force? No instance seems to
have happened of any nation having risen through soul-force. I
still think that the evildoers will not cease doing evil without
physical punishment.

Editor: The poet Tulsidas has said: "Of religion, pity or love
is the root, as egotism of the body. Therefore, we should not abandon pity so long as we are alive." This appears to me to be a
scientific truth; I believe in it as much as I believe in two and
two being four. The force of love is the same as the force of the
soul or truth. We would disappear without the existence of that
force. But you ask for historical evidence. It is therefore necessary
to know what history means. The Gujarati equivalent means: "It
so happened." If that is the meaning of history, it is possible to
give copious evidence. But if it means the doings of kings and
emperors, there can be no evidence of soul-force or passive resistance in such history. You cannot expect silver ore in a tin mine.

---

* *Niyog* is a practice that permits the husband to have sexual intercourse
with other women when his wife is ill or pregnant.—Ed.

History, as we know it, is a record of the wars of the world, and so there is a proverb among Englishmen that a nation which has no history—that is, no wars—is a happy nation. How kings played, how they became enemies of one another, and how they murdered one another is found accurately recorded in history; and, if this were all that had happened in the world, it would have been ended long ago. If the story of the universe had commenced with wars, not a man would have been found alive today. Those people who have been warred against have disappeared—as, for instance, the natives of Australia, of whom hardly a man was left alive by the intruders. Mark, please, that these natives did not use soul-force in self-defense, and it does not require much foresight to know that the Australians will share the same fate as their victims. "Those who wield the sword shall perish by the sword." With us, the proverb is that professional swimmers will find a watery grave.

The fact that there are so many men still alive in the world shows that it is based not on the force of arms, but on the force of truth or love. Therefore, the greatest and most unimpeachable evidence of the success of this force is to be found in the fact that, in spite of the wars of the world, it still lives on.

Thousands—indeed, tens of thousands—depend for their existence on a very active working of this force. Little quarrels of millions of families in their daily lives disappear before the exercise of this force. Hundreds of nations live in peace. History does not, and cannot, take note of this fact. History is really a record of every interruption of the even working of the force of love or of the soul. Two brothers quarrel; one of them repents and reawakens the love that was lying dormant in him; the two again begin to live in peace; nobody takes note of this. But if the two brothers, through the intervention of solicitors or some other reason, take up arms or go to law—which is another form of the exhibition of brute force—their doings would be immediately noticed in the press; they would be the talk of their neighbors, and would probably go down in history. And what is true of families and communities is true of nations. There is no reason to believe that there is one law for families, and another for nations. History, then, is a record of an interruption of the course of nature. Soul-force, being natural, is not noted in history.

Reader: According to what you say, it is plain that instances of this kind of passive resistance are not to be found in history. It is necessary to understand this passive resistance more fully. It will be better, therefore, if you enlarge upon it.

Editor: Passive resistance is a method of securing rights by personal suffering; it is the reverse of resistance by arms. When I refuse to do a thing that is repugnant to my conscience, I use soul-force. For instance, the government of the day has passed a law which is applicable to me. I do not like it. If, by using violence, I force the government to repeal the law, I am employing what may be termed body-force. If I do not obey the law, and accept the penalty for its breach, I use soul-force. It involves sacrifice of self.

Everybody admits that sacrifice of self is infinitely superior to sacrifice of others. Moreover, if this kind of force is used in a cause that is unjust, only the person using it suffers. He does not make others suffer for his mistakes. Men have before now done many things which were subsequently found to have been wrong. No man can claim to be absolutely in the right, or that a particular thing is wrong, because he thinks so, but it is wrong for him so long as that is his deliberate judgment. It is, therefore, meet that he should not do that which he knows to be wrong, and suffer the consequence whatever it may be. This is the key to the use of soul-force.

Reader: You would then disregard laws; this is rank disloyalty. We have always been considered a law-abiding nation. You seem to be going even beyond the extremists. They say that we must obey the laws that have been passed, but that, if the laws be bad, we must drive out the lawgivers even by force.

Editor: Whether I go beyond them or whether I do not is a matter of no consequence to either of us. We simply want to find out what is right, and to act accordingly. The real meaning of the statement that we are a law-abiding nation is that we are passive resisters. When we do not like certain laws, we do not break the heads of lawgivers, but we suffer and do not submit to the laws. That we should obey laws, whether good or bad, is a newfangled notion. There was no such thing in former days. The people disregarded those laws they did not like, and suffered the penalties for their breach. It is contrary to our manhood if we obey laws repugnant to our conscience. Such teaching is opposed to religion and means slavery. If the government were to ask us to go about without any clothing, should we do so? If I were a passive resister, I would say to them that I would have nothing to do with their law. But we have so forgotten ourselves and become so compliant, that we do not mind any degrading law.

A man who has realized his manhood, who fears only God, will fear no one else. Man-made laws are not necessarily binding on him. Even the government do not expect any such things from us. They do not say: "You must do such and such a thing," but they say: "If you do not do it, we will punish you." We are sunk so low that we fancy that it is our duty and our religion to do what the law lays down. If man will only realize that it is unmanly to obey laws that are unjust, no man's tyranny will enslave him. This is the key to self-rule or home rule.

It is a superstition and an ungodly thing to believe that an act of a majority binds a minority. Many examples can be given in which acts of majorities will be found to have been wrong, and those of minorities to have been right. All reforms owe their origin to the initiation of minorities in opposition to majorities. If, among a band of robbers, a knowledge of robbing is obligatory, is a pious man to accept the obligation? So long as the superstition that men should obey unjust laws exists, so long will their slavery exist. And a passive resister alone can remove such a superstition.

To use brute force, to use gunpowder, is contrary to passive resistance, for it means that we want our opponent to do by force that which we desire but he does not. If such a use of force is justifiable, surely he is entitled to do likewise by us. And so we should never come to an agreement. We may simply fancy, like the blind horse moving in a circle around a mill, that we are making progress. Those who believe that they are not bound to obey laws which are repugnant to their conscience have only the remedy of passive resistance open to them. Any other must lead to disaster.

Reader: From what you say, I deduce that passive resistance is a splendid weapon of the weak, but that when they are strong, they may take up arms.

Editor: This is gross ignorance. Passive resistance—that is, soul-force—is matchless. It is superior to the force of arms. How, then, can it be considered only a weapon of the weak? Physical-force men are strangers to the courage that is requisite in a passive resister. Do you believe that a coward can ever disobey a law that he dislikes? Extremists are considered to be advocates of brute force. Why do they, then, talk about obeying laws? I do not blame them. They can say nothing else. When they succeed in driving out the English and they themselves become governors, they will want you and me to obey their laws. And that is a fitting thing for their constitutions. But a passive resister will say he will not obey a law that is against his conscience, even though he may be blown to pieces at the mouth of a cannon.

What do you think? Wherein is courage required—in blowing others to pieces from behind a cannon, or with a smiling face to approach a cannon and to be blown to pieces? Who is the true warrior—he who keeps death always as a bosom-friend, or he who controls the death of others? Believe me that a man devoid of courage and manhood can never be a passive resister.

This, however, I will admit: that even a man weak in body is capable of offering this resistance. One man can offer it just as well as millions. Both men and women can indulge in it. It does not require the training of an army; it needs no jujitsu. Control over the mind is alone necessary, and when that is attained, man is free like the king of the forest, and his very glance withers the enemy.

Passive resistance is an all-sided sword; it can be used any way; it blesses him who uses it and him against whom it is used. Without drawing a drop of blood, it produces far-reaching results. It never rusts and cannot be stolen. Competition between passive resisters does not exhaust. The sword of passive resistance does not require a scabbard. It is strange indeed that you should consider such a weapon to be a weapon merely of the weak.

Reader: You have said that passive resistance is a specialty of India. Have cannons never been used in India?

Editor: Evidently, in your opinion, India means its few princes. To me, it means its teeming millions, on whom depends the existence of the princes and our own.

Kings will always use their kingly weapons. To use force is bred in them. They want to command; but those who have to obey commands do not want guns, and these are in a majority throughout the world. They have to learn either body-force or soul-force. Where they learn the former, both the rulers and the ruled become like so many madmen, but where they learn soul-force, the commands of the rulers do not go beyond the point of their swords, for true men disregard unjust commands. Peasants have never been subdued by the sword, and never will be. They do not know the use of the sword, and they are not frightened by the

use of it by others. That nation is great which rests its head upon
death as its pillow. Those who defy death are free from all fear.
For those who are laboring under the delusive charms of brute
force, this picture is not overdrawn. The fact is that, in India,
the nation at large has generally used passive resistance in all de-
partments of life. We cease to cooperate with our rulers when
they displease us. This is passive resistance.

I remember an instance when, in a small principality, the villagers were offended by some command issued by the prince. The
former immediately began vacating the village. The prince became nervous, apologized to his subjects, and withdrew his command. Many such instances can be found in India. Real home
rule is possible only where passive resistance is the guiding force
of the people. Any other rule is foreign rule. . . .

Machinery

Reader: When you speak of driving out Western civilization, I
suppose you will also say that we want no machinery.

Editor: By raising this question, you have opened the wound I
had received. When I read Mr. Dutt's *Economic History of India,*
I wept; and, as I think of it again, my heart sickens. It is machinery that has impoverished India. It is difficult to measure the
harm that Manchester has done to us. It is due to Manchester that
Indian handicraft has all but disappeared. . . .

Machinery has begun to desolate Europe. Ruination is now
knocking at the English gates. Machinery is the chief symbol of
modern civilization; it represents a great sin. The workers in the
mills of Bombay have become slaves. The condition of the women
working in the mills is shocking. When there were no mills, these
women were not starving. If the machinery craze grows in our
country, it will become an unhappy land. It may be considered a
heresy, but I am bound to say that it were better for us to send
money to Manchester and to use flimsy Manchester cloth, than to
multiply mills in India. By using Manchester cloth, we would only
waste our money, but by reproducing Manchester in India, we
shall keep our money at the price of our blood, because our very
moral being will be sapped, and I call in support of my statement
the very mill hands as witnesses. And those who have amassed
wealth out of factories are not likely to be better than other rich
men. It would be folly to assume that an Indian Rockefeller would
be better than the American Rockefeller. Impoverished India can

become free, but it will be hard for any India made rich through immorality to regain its freedom. I fear we will have to admit that moneyed men support British rule; their interest is bound up with its stability. Money renders a man helpless. The other thing as harmful is sexual vice. Both are poison. A snake bite is a lesser poison than these two, because the former merely destroys the body, but the latter destroys body, mind, and soul. We need not, therefore, be pleased with the prospect of the growth of the mill industry.

Reader: Are the mills, then, to be closed down?

Editor: That is difficult. It is no easy task to do away with a thing that is established. We therefore say that the nonbeginning of a thing is supreme wisdom. We cannot condemn millowners; we can but pity them. It would be too much to expect them to give up their mills, but we may implore them not to increase them. If they would be good, they would gradually contract their business. They can establish in thousands of households the ancient and sacred hand looms, and they can buy out the cloth that may be thus woven. Whether the millowners do this or not, people can cease to use machine-made goods.

Reader: You have so far spoken about machine-made cloth, but there are innumerable machine-made things. We have either to import them or to introduce machinery into our country.

Editor: Indeed, our gods even are made in Germany. What need, then, to speak of matches, pins, and glassware? My answer can be only one. What did India do before these articles were introduced? Precisely the same should be done today. As long as we cannot make pins without machinery, so long we will do without them. The tinsel splendor of glassware we will have nothing to do with, and we will make wicks, as of old, with home-grown cotton, and use handmade earthen saucers for lamps. So doing, we shall have our eyes and money, and will support Swadeshi,* and so shall we attain home rule. It is not to be conceived that all men will do all these things at one time, or that some men will give up all machine-made things at once. But if the thought is sound, we will always find out what we can give up, and will gradually cease to use this. What a few may do, others will copy, and the movement will grow like the coconut of the mathematical problem. What the leaders do, the populace will gladly follow. The matter

* Swadeshi was a program of the Indian nationalists to boycott British goods and to buy only Indian-made products.—ED.

is neither complicated nor difficult. You and I shall not wait until we can carry others with us. Those will be the losers who will not do it, and those who will not do it—although they appreciate the truth—will deserve to be called cowards.

Reader: What, then, of the tramcars and electricity?

Editor: This question is now too late. It signifies nothing. If we are to do without the railways, we shall have to do without the tramcars. Machinery is like a snake hole which may contain from one to a hundred snakes. Where there is machinery, there are large cities; and where there are large cities, there are tramcars and railways; and there only does one see electric light. English villages do not boast of any of these things. Honest physicians will tell you that where means of artificial locomotion have increased, the health of the people has suffered. I remember that when, in a European town, there was a scarcity of money, the receipts of the tramway company, of the lawyers, and of the doctors went down, and the people were less unhealthy. I cannot recall a single good point in connection with machinery. Books can be written to demonstrate its evils.

Reader: Is it a good point or a bad one that all you are saying will be printed through machinery?

Editor: This is one of those instances which demonstrate that sometimes poison is used to kill poison. This, then, will not be a good point regarding machinery. As it expires, the machinery, as it were, says to us: "Beware and avoid me. You will derive no benefit from me, and the benefit that may accrue from printing will avail only those who are infected with the machinery craze." Do not, therefore, forget the main thing. It is necessary to realize that machinery is bad. We shall then be able gradually to do away with it. Nature has not provided any way whereby we may reach a desired goal all of a sudden. If, instead of welcoming machinery as a boon, we would look upon it as an evil, it would ultimately go.

5. *Jawaharlal Nehru*

Jawaharlal Nehru, the late Prime Minister of India, was born in Allahabad in 1889, the only son of a Kashmiri Brahmin. His father was a wealthy and successful lawyer, and he was sent to Britain for his schooling. He attended Harrow and then Cambridge, where he was graduated with honors in science in 1910. For the next two years, he studied law in London. When he returned to India, he met Gandhi at the annual conference of the Indian National Congress in 1916, and became his lifelong disciple. He became General Secretary of the Congress in 1923, and was elected President of the Congress several times. He was repeatedly imprisoned by the British for passive-resistance activities. During World War II, Nehru began the negotiations with Britain that culminated in Indian independence on August 15, 1947. From that time until his death in May, 1964, he was Indian Prime Minister and Minister of Foreign Affairs, supported by a large Congress majority in the Indian parliament. Although he asserted a major role for India in international relations, he was equally concerned with the problem of economic development. A socialist in his early days in England, as Prime Minister Nehru took a more pragmatic view, favoring a mixed economy as more effective in development.

The first group of selections below is taken from The Discovery of India, a book that was written by Nehru in 1944. The contrast between his approach to modernization and economic development and that of Gandhi is evident in his discussion of his personal philosophy and his attitude toward industrialization. This is followed by a short selection illustrating the modification of his views on socialism.

THE DISCOVERY OF INDIA*

Philosophy of Life

Often, as I look at this world, I have a sense of mysteries, of unknown depths. The urge to understand it, insofar as I can, comes to me; to be in tune with it and to experience it in its fullness. But the way to that understanding seems to me essentially in the way of science, the way of objective approach, though I realize

---

* Excerpts from Jawaharlal Nehru, *The Discovery of India* (New York: The John Day Company, 1946); copyright 1946 by The John Day Company; reprinted by permission of The John Day Company, Inc., publisher.

that there can be no such thing as true objectiveness. If the subjective element is unavoidable and inevitable, it should be conditioned as far as possible by the scientific method.

What the mysterious is I do not know. I do not call it God
because God has come to mean much that I do not believe in. I
find myself incapable of thinking of a deity or of any unknown
supreme power in anthropomorphic terms, and the fact that many
people think so is continually a source of surprise to me. Any idea
of a personal god seems very odd to me. Intellectually, I can appreciate to some extent the conception of monism, and I have
been attracted toward the Advaita (nondualist) philosophy of the
Vedanta, though I do not presume to understand it in all its
depth and intricacy, and I realize that merely an intellectual appreciation of such matters does not carry one far. At the same
time, the Vedanta and other similar approaches rather frighten
me with their vague formless incursions into infinity. The diversity
and fullness of nature stir me and produce a harmony of the
spirit, and I can imagine myself feeling at home in the old Indian
or Greek pagan and pantheistic atmosphere, but minus the conception of god or gods that was attached to it.

Some kind of ethical approach to life has a strong appeal for
me, though it would be difficult for me to justify it logically. I
have been attracted by Gandhi's stress on right means, and I think
one of his greatest contributions to our public life has been this
emphasis. The idea is by no means new, but this application of
an ethical doctrine to large-scale public activity was certainly novel.
It is full of difficulty, and perhaps ends and means are not really
separable and form together one organic whole. In a world which
thinks almost exclusively of ends and ignores means, this emphasis
on means seems odd and remarkable. How far it has succeeded in
India I cannot say. But there is no doubt that it has created a
deep and abiding impression on the minds of large numbers of
people.

A study of Marx and Lenin produced a powerful effect on my
mind and helped me to see history and current affairs in a new
light. The long chain of history and of social development appeared to have some meaning, some sequence, and the future lost
some of its obscurity. The practical achievements of the Soviet
Union were also tremendously impressive. Often, I disliked or did
not understand some development there, and it seemed to me to
be too closely concerned with the opportunism of the moment or

the power politics of the day. But despite all these developments and possible distortions of the original passion for human betterment, I had no doubt that the Soviet Revolution had advanced human society by a great leap and had lit a bright flame which could not be smothered, and that it had laid the foundations for that "new civilization" toward which the world would advance. I am too much of an individualist and believer in personal freedom to like overmuch regimentation. Yet it seemed to me obvious that in a complex social structure individual freedom had to be limited, and perhaps the only way to real personal freedom was through some such limitation in the social sphere. The lesser liberties may often need limitation in the interest of the larger freedom.

Much in the Marxist philosophical outlook I could accept without difficulty: its monism and nonduality of mind and matter, the dynamics of matter, and the dialectic of continuous change by evolution as well as leap—through action and interaction, cause and effect, thesis, antithesis, and synthesis. It did not satisfy me completely, nor did it answer all the questions in my mind, and almost unawares a vague idealist approach would creep into my mind, something rather akin to the Vedanta approach. It was not a difference between mind and matter, but rather of something that lay beyond the mind. Also, there was the background of ethics. I realized that the moral approach is a changing one and depends upon the growing mind and an advancing civilization; it is conditioned by the mental climate of the age. Yet there was something more to it than that, certain basic urges which had greater permanence. I did not like the frequent divorce—in Communist, as in other, practice—between action and these basic urges or principles. So there was an odd mixture in my mind which I could not rationally explain or resolve. There was a general tendency not to think too much of those fundamental questions which appear to be beyond reach, and rather to concentrate on the problems of life—to understand, in the narrower and more immediate sense, what should be done and how. Whatever ultimate reality may be, and whether we can ever grasp it in whole or in part, there certainly appear to be vast possibilities of increasing human knowledge, even though this may be partly or largely subjective, and of applying this to the advancement and betterment of human life and social organization.

There has been in the past, and there is to a lesser extent even today among some people, an absorption in finding an answer to the riddle of the universe. This leads them away from the individual and social problems of the day, and when they are unable to solve that riddle, they despair and turn to inaction and triviality, or find comfort in some dogmatic creed. Social evils, most of which are certainly capable of removal, are attributed to original sin, to the unalterableness of "human nature," or the social structure, or (in India) to the inevitable legacy of previous births. Thus one drifts away from even the attempt to think rationally and scientifically, and takes refuge in irrationalism, superstition, and unreasonable and inequitable social prejudices and practices. It is true that even rational and scientific thought does not always take us as far as we would like to go. There is an infinite number of factors and relations which influence and determine events in varying degrees, and it is impossible to grasp all of them. Still, we can try to pick out the dominating forces at work and, by observing external material reality and by experiment and practice, trial and error, grope our way to ever-widening knowledge and truth.

For this purpose, and within these limitations, the general Marxist approach, fitting in as it more or less did with the present state of scientific knowledge, seemed to me to offer considerable help. But even accepting that approach, the consequences that flow from it and the interpretation of past and present happenings were by no means always clear. Marx's general analysis of social development seems to have been remarkably correct, and yet many developments took place later which did not fit in with his outlook for the immediate future. Lenin successfully adapted the Marxian thesis to some of these subsequent developments, but again, since then, further remarkable changes have taken place—the rise of fascism and Nazism and all that lay behind them. The very rapid growth of technology and the practical application of vast developments in scientific knowledge are now changing the world picture with an amazing rapidity, leading to new problems. . . .

Industrialization and the Machine

The Congress, under Gandhi's leadership, had long championed the revival of village industries, especially hand spinning and hand weaving. At no time, however, had the Congress been opposed to the development of big industries, and whenever it had the chance

—in the legislatures or elsewhere—it had encouraged this development. Congress provincial governments were eager to do so. In the twenties, when the Tata Steel and Iron Works were in difficulties, it was largely due to the insistence of the Congress Party in the central legislature that government aid was given to help to tide over a critical period. The development of Indian shipbuilding and shipping services had long been a sore point of conflict between nationalist opinion and the government. The Congress, as all other sections of Indian opinion, was anxious that every assistance should be given to Indian shipping; the government was equally anxious to protect the vested interests of powerful British shipping companies. Indian shipping was thus prevented from growing by official discrimination against it, although it had both capital and technical and managerial ability at its disposal. This kind of discrimination worked all along the line, whenever any British industrial, commercial, or financial interests were concerned. . . .

The Congress Party has thus always been in favor of the industrialization of India, and at the same time has emphasized the development of cottage industries and worked for this. Is there a conflict between these two approaches? Possibly there is a difference in emphasis, a realization of certain human and economic factors which were overlooked previously in India. Indian industrialists and the politicians who supported them thought too much in terms of the nineteenth-century development of capitalist industry in Europe and ignored many of the evil consequences that were obvious in the twentieth century. In India, because normal progress had been arrested for a hundred years, those consequences were likely to be more far-reaching. The kind of medium-scale industries that were being started in India under the prevailing economic system resulted not in absorbing labor, but in creating more unemployment. While capital accumulated at one end, poverty and unemployment increased at the other. Under a different system and with a stress on large-scale industries absorbing labor, and with planned development, this might well have been avoided.

This fact of increasing mass poverty influenced Gandhi powerfully. It is true, I think, that there is a fundamental difference between his outlook on life generally and what might be called the modern outlook. He is not enamored of ever-increasing standards of living and the growth of luxury at the cost of spiritual and moral values. He does not favor the soft life; for him, the straight way is the hard way, and the love of luxury leads to crookedness and loss of virtue. Above all, he is shocked at the vast gulf that stretches between the rich and the poor—in their ways of living and their opportunities of growth. For his own personal and psychological satisfaction, he crossed that gulf and went over to the side of the poor, adopting, with only such improvements as the poor themselves could afford, their ways of living, their dress or lack of dress. This vast difference between the few rich and the poverty-stricken masses seemed to him to be due to two principal causes: foreign rule and the exploitation that accompanied it, and the capitalist industrial civilization of the West, as embodied in the big machine. He reacted against both. He looked back with yearning to the days of the old autonomous and more or less self-contained village community where there had been an automatic balance between production, distribution, and consumption; where political or economic power was spread out and not concentrated as it is today; where a kind of simple democracy prevailed; where the gulf between the rich and the poor was not so marked; where the evils of great cities were absent, and people lived in contact with the life-giving soil and breathed the pure air of the open spaces.

There was all this basic difference in outlook as to the meaning of life itself between him and many others, and this difference colored his language as well as his activities. His language—vivid and powerful as it often was—drew its inspiration from the religious and moral teachings of the ages, principally of India, but also of other countries. Moral values must prevail; the ends can never justify unworthy means, or else the individual and the race perish.

And yet he was no dreamer living in some fantasy of his own creation, cut off from life and its problems. He came from Gujrat, the home of hardheaded businessmen, and he had an unrivaled knowledge of the Indian villages and the conditions of life that prevailed there. It was out of that personal experience that he evolved his program of the spinning wheel and village industry. If immediate relief was to be given to the vast numbers of the unemployed and partially employed; if the rot that was spreading throughout India and paralyzing the masses was to be stopped; if the villagers' standards were to be raised, however little, en masse; if they were to be taught self-reliance instead of waiting helplessly like derelicts for relief from others; if all this was to be done without much capital—then there seemed no other way. Apart from the evils inherent in foreign rule and exploitation, and the lack of freedom to initiate and carry through big schemes of reform, the problem of India was one of scarcity of capital and abundance of labor—how to utilize that wasted labor, that manpower that was producing nothing. Foolish comparisons are made between manpower and machine power; of course, a big machine can do the work of a thousand or ten thousand persons. But if those ten thousand sit idly by or starve, the introduction of that machine is not a social gain—except in long perspective which envisages a change in social conditions. When the big machine is not there at all, then no question of comparison arises; it is a net gain both from the individual and the national point of view to utilize manpower for production. There is no necessary conflict between this and the introduction of machinery on the largest scale, provided that machinery is used primarily for absorbing labor and not for creating fresh unemployment.

Gandhi's attitude to the use of machinery seemed to undergo a gradual change. "What I object to," he said, "is the craze for machinery, not machinery as such. . . . If we could have electricity in every village home, I should not mind villages plying their implements and tools with electricity." The big machine seemed to him to lead inevitably, at least in the circumstances of today, to the concentration of power and riches: "I consider it a sin and injustice to use machinery for the purpose of concentration of power and riches in the hands of the few. Today the machine is used in this way." He even came to accept the necessity of many kinds of heavy industries and large-scale key industries and public utilities, provided they were state-owned and did not interfere with some kinds of cottage industries which he considered essential. Referring to his own proposals, he said: "The whole of this program will be a structure on sand if it is not built on the solid foundation of economic equality."

Thus, even the enthusiastic advocates for cottage and small-scale industries recognize that large-scale industry is, to a certain extent, necessary and inevitable; only they would like to limit it as far as possible. Superficially, then, the question becomes one of emphasis and adjustment of the two forms of production and economy. It can hardly be challenged that, in the context of the modern world, no country can be politically and economically independent, even within the framework of international interdependence, unless it is highly industrialized and has developed its power resources to the utmost. Nor can it achieve or maintain high standards of living and liquidate poverty without the aid of modern technology in almost every sphere of life. An industrially backward country will continually upset the world equilibrium and encourage the aggressive tendencies of more developed countries. Even if it retains its political independence, this will be nominal only, and economic control will tend to pass to others. This control will inevitably upset its own small-scale economy which it has sought to preserve in pursuit of its own view of life. Thus an attempt to build up a country's economy largely on the basis of cottage and small-scale industries is doomed to failure. It will not solve the basic problems of the country or maintain freedom, nor will it fit in with the world framework, except as a colonial appendage.

Is it possible to have two entirely different kinds of economy in a country—one based on the big machine and industrialization, and the other mainly on cottage industries? This is hardly conceivable, for one must overcome the other, and there can be little doubt that the big machine will triumph unless it is forcibly prevented from doing so. Thus, it is not a mere question of adjustment of the two forms of production and economy. One must be dominating and paramount, with the other complementary to it, fitting in where it can. The economy based on the latest technical achievements of the day must necessarily be the dominating one. If technology demands the big machine, as it does today in a large measure, then the big machine with all its implications and consequences must be accepted. Where it is possible in terms of that technology to decentralize production, this would be desirable. But in any event, the latest technique has to be followed. To adhere to outworn and out-of-date methods of production—except as a temporary and stopgap measure—is to arrest growth and development.

Any argument as to the relative merits of small-scale and large-scale industry seems strangely irrelevant today, when the world and the dominating facts of the situation that confront it have decided in favor of the latter. Even in India, that decision has been made by these facts themselves, and no one doubts that India will be rapidly industrialized in the near future. She has already gone a good way in that direction. The evils of unrestricted and unplanned industrialization are well recognized today. Whether these evils are necessary concomitants of big industry, or derive from the social and economic structure behind it, is another matter. If the economic structure is primarily responsible for them, then surely we should set about changing that structure, instead of blaming the inevitable and desirable developments in technique.

The real question is not one of quantitative adjustment and balancing of various incongruous elements and methods of production, but a qualitative changeover to something different and new, from which various social consequences flow. The economic and political aspects of this qualitative change are important, but equally important are the social and psychological aspects. In India especially, where we have been wedded far too long to past forms and modes of thought and action—new experiences, new processes, leading to new ideas and new horizons, are necessary. Thus, we will change the static character of our living and make it dynamic and vital, and our minds will become active and adventurous. New situations lead to new experiences, as the mind is compelled to deal with them and adapt itself to a changing environment.

It is well recognized now that a child's education should be intimately associated with some craft or manual activity. The mind is stimulated thereby, and there is a coordination between the activities of the mind and the hands. So also the mind of a growing boy or girl is stimulated by the machine. It grows under the machine's impact (under proper conditions, of course, and not as an exploited and unhappy worker in a factory) and opens out new horizons. Simple scientific experiments, peeps into the microscope, and an explanation of the ordinary phenomena of nature bring excitement in their train, an understanding of some of life's processes and a desire to experiment and find out instead of relying on set phrases and old formulas. Self-confidence and the cooperative spirit grow, and frustration—arising out of the miasma of the past—lessens. A civilization based on ever-changing and advancing mechanical techniques leads to this. Such a civilization is a marked change, a jump almost, from the older type, and is intimately connected with modern industrialization. Inevitably, it gives rise to new problems and difficulties, but it also shows the way to overcome them. . . .

India and the West

A nation, like an individual, has many personalities, many approaches to life. If there is a sufficiently strong organic bond between these different personalities, it is well; otherwise, those personalities split up and lead to disintegration and trouble. Normally, there is a continuous process of adjustment going on, and some kind of an equilibrium is established. If normal development is arrested, or sometimes if there is some rapid change which is not easily assimilated, then conflict arises between those different personalities. In the mind and spirit of India, below the surface of our superficial conflicts and divisions, there has been this fundamental conflict due to a long period of arrested growth. A society, if it is to be both stable and progressive, must have a certain more or less fixed foundation of principles, as well as a dynamic outlook. Both appear to be necessary. Without the dynamic outlook, there is a stagnation and decay; without some fixed basis of principle, there is likely to be disintegration and destruction.

In India, from the earliest days, there was a search for those basic principles—for the unchanging, the universal, the absolute. Yet the dynamic outlook was also present, and an appreciation of life and the changing world. On these two foundations, a stable and progressive society was built up, though the stress was always more on stability and security and the survival of the race. In later years, the dynamic aspect began to fade away, and in the name of eternal principles the social structure was made rigid and unchanging. It was, as a matter of fact, not wholly rigid, and it did change gradually and continuously. But the ideology behind it, and the general framework, continued unchanged. The group idea as represented by more or less autonomous castes, the joint family, and the communal self-governing life of the village were the main pillars of this system, and all these survived for so long because—in spite of their failings—they fulfilled some essential needs of human nature and society. They gave security and stability to each group, and a sense of group freedom. Caste survived because it continued to represent the general power relationships of society, and class privileges were maintained, not only because of the prevailing ideology, but also because they were supported by vigor, intelligence, and ability, as well as a capacity for self-sacrifice. That ideology was not based on a conflict of rights, but on the individual's obligations to others and a satisfactory performance of his duties, on cooperation within the group and between different groups, and essentially on the idea of promoting peace rather than war. While the social system was rigid, no limit was placed on the freedom of the mind.

Indian civilization achieved much that it was aiming at, but in that very achievement life began to fade away, for it is too dynamic to exist for long in a rigid, unchanging environment. Even those basic principles which are said to be unchanging lose their freshness and reality when they are taken for granted, and the search for them ceases. Ideas of truth, beauty, and freedom decay, and we become prisoners following a deadening routine.

The very thing India lacked, the modern West possessed—and possessed to excess. It had the dynamic outlook. It was engrossed in the changing world, caring little for ultimate principles, the unchanging, the universal. It paid little attention to duties and obligations, and emphasized rights. It was active, aggressive, acquisitive, seeking power and domination, living in the present and ignoring the future consequences of its actions. Because it was dynamic, it was progressive and full of life, but that life was a fevered one, and the temperature kept on rising progressively.

If Indian civilization went to seed because it became static, self-absorbed, and inclined to narcissism, the civilization of the modern West—with all its great and manifold achievements—does not appear to have been a conspicuous success or to have thus far solved the basic problems of life. Conflict is inherent in it, and periodically it indulges in self-destruction on a colossal scale. It seems to lack something to give it stability, some basic principles to give meaning to life, though what these are I cannot say. Yet, because it is dynamic and full of life and curiosity, there is hope for it.

India—as well as China—must learn from the West, for the modern West has much to teach, and the spirit of the ages is represented by the West. But the West is also obviously in need of learning much, and its advances in technology will bring it little comfort if it does not learn some of the deeper lessons of life which have absorbed the minds of thinkers in all ages and in all countries.

India had become static, and yet it would be utterly wrong to imagine that she was unchanging. No change at all means death. Her very survival as a highly evolved nation shows that there was some process of continuous adaptation going on. When the British came to India, though technologically somewhat backward, she

was still among the advanced commercial nations of the world.
Technical changes would undoubtedly have come and changed
India as they had changed some Western countries. But her normal development was arrested by the British power. Industrial
growth was checked, and, as a consequence, social growth was also
arrested. The normal power relationships of society could not adjust themselves and find an equilibrium, as all power was concentrated in the alien authority, which based itself on force and
encouraged groups and classes which had ceased to have any real
significance. Indian life thus progressively became more artificial,
for many of the individuals and groups who seemed to play an
important role in it had no vital functions left and were there
only because of the importance given to them by the alien power.
They had long ago finished their role in history and would have
been pushed aside by new forces if they had not been given foreign protection. They became straw-stuffed symbols or protégés of
foreign authority, thereby cutting themselves further away from
the living currents of the nation. Normally, they would have been
weeded out or diverted to some more appropriate function by
revolution or democratic process. But so long as foreign authoritarian rule continued, no such development could take place. And
so India was cluttered up with these emblems of the past, and the
real changes that were taking place were hidden behind an artificial façade. No true social balances or power relationships within
society could develop or become evident, and unreal problems assumed an undue importance.

India must break with much of her past and not allow it to
dominate the present. Our lives are encumbered with the dead-
wood of this past; all that is dead and has served its purpose has
to go. But that does not mean a break with or a forgetting of the
vital and life-giving in that past. We can never forget the ideals
that have moved our race: the dreams of the Indian people
through the ages; the wisdom of the ancients; the buoyant energy
and love of life and nature of our forefathers; their spirit of curiosity and mental adventure; the daring of their thought, their
splendid achievements in literature, art, and culture; their love of
truth, and beauty, and freedom; the basic values that they set up;
their understanding of life's mysterious ways; their toleration of
other ways than theirs; their capacity to absorb other peoples and
their cultural accomplishments, synthesize them, and develop a

varied and mixed culture. Nor can we forget the myriad experiences which have built up our ancient race and lie embedded in our subconscious minds. We will never forget them or cease to take pride in that noble heritage of ours. If India forgets them, she will no longer remain India, and much that has made her our joy and pride will cease to be.

It is not this that we have to break with, but all the dust and dirt of ages that have covered her up and hidden her inner beauty and significance, the excrescences and abortions that have twisted and petrified her spirit, set it in rigid frames, and stunted her growth. We have to cut away these excrescences, and remember afresh the core of that ancient wisdom, and adapt it to our present circumstances. We have to get out of traditional ways of thought and living which, for all the good they may have done in a past age—and there was much good in them—have ceased to have significance today. We have to make our own all the achievements of the human race and join up with others in the exciting adventure of man, more exciting today perhaps than in earlier ages—realizing that this has ceased to be governed by national boundaries of old divisions and is common to the race of man everywhere. We have to revive the passion for truth and beauty and freedom which gives meaning to life, and develop afresh that dynamic outlook and spirit of adventure which distinguished those of our race who, in ages past, built our house on these strong and enduring foundations. Old as we are, with memories stretching back to the early dawns of human history and endeavor, we have to grow young again, in tune with our present time, with the irrepressible spirit and joy of youth in the present and its faith in the future. . . .

The Caste System

Caste is the symbol and embodiment of exclusiveness among the Hindus. It is sometimes said that the basic idea of caste might remain, but its subsequent harmful development and ramifications should go; that it should not depend on birth but on merit. This approach is irrelevant and merely confuses the issue. In a historical context, a study of the growth of caste has some value, but obviously we cannot go back to the period when caste began; in the social organization of today, it has no place left. If merit is the only criterion and opportunity is thrown open to everybody, then caste loses all its present-day distinguishing features and, in fact, ends. Caste has in the past not only led to the suppression of certain groups but to a separation of theoretical and scholastic learning from craftsmanship and a divorce of philosophy from actual life and its problems. It was an aristocratic approach based on traditionalism. This outlook has to change completely, for it is wholly opposed to modern conditions and the democratic ideal. The functional organization of social groups in India may continue, but even that will undergo a vast change as the nature of modern industry creates new functions and puts an end to many old ones. The tendency today everywhere is toward a functional organization of society, and the concept of abstract rights is giving place to that of functions. This is in harmony with the old Indian ideal.

The spirit of the age is in favor of equality, though practice denies it almost everywhere. We have got rid of slavery in the narrow sense of the word—that a man can be the property of another. But a new slavery, in some ways worse than the old, has taken its place all over the world. In the name of individual freedom, political and economic systems exploit human beings and treat them as commodities. And again, though an individual cannot be the property of another, a country and a nation can still be the property of another nation, and thus group slavery is tolerated. Racialism also is a distinguishing feature of our times, and we have not only master nations but also master races.

Yet the spirit of the age will triumph. In India, at any rate, we must aim at equality. That does not and cannot mean that everybody is physically or intellectually or spiritually equal or can be made so. But it does mean equal opportunities for all and no political, economic, or social barrier in the way of any individual or group. It means a faith in humanity and a belief that there is no race or group that cannot advance and make good in its own way, given the chance to do so. It means a realization of the fact that the backwardness or degradation of any group is not due to inherent failings in it, but principally to lack of opportunities and long suppression by other groups. It should mean an understanding of the modern world, wherein real progress and advance, whether national or international, have become very much a joint affair and a backward group pulls back others. Therefore, not only must equal opportunities be given to all, but special opportunities for educational, economic, and cultural growth must be given to backward groups so as to enable them to catch up to those who are ahead of them. Any such attempt to open the doors of opportunity to all in India will release enormous energy and ability and transform the country with amazing speed.

Democratic Collectivism

If the spirit of the age demands equality, it must necessarily also demand an economic system which fits in with it and encourages it. The present colonial system in India is the very antithesis of it. Absolutism is not only based on inequality, but must perpetuate it in every sphere of life. It suppresses the creative and regenerative forces of a nation, bottles up talent and capacity, and discourages the spirit of responsibility. Those who have to suffer under it lose their sense of dignity and self-reliance. The problems of India, complicated as they seem, are essentially due to an attempt to advance while preserving the political and economic structure more or less intact. Political advance is made subject to the preservation of this structure and existing vested interests. The two are incompatible.

Political change there must be, but economic change is equally necessary. That change will have to be in the direction of a democratically planned collectivism. "The choice," says R. H. Tawney, "is not between competition and monopoly, but between monopoly which is irresponsible and private and a monopoly which is responsible and public." Public monopolies are growing even in capitalist states, and they will continue to grow. The conflict between the idea underlying them and private monopoly will continue till the latter is liquidated. A democratic collectivism need not mean an abolition of private property, but it will mean the public ownership of the basic and major industries. It will mean the cooperative or collective control of the land. In India especially, it will be necessary to have, in addition to the big industries, cooperatively controlled small and village industries. Such a system of democratic collectivism will need careful and continuous planning and adaptation to the changing needs of the people. The aim should be the expansion of the productive capacity of the nation in every possible way, at the same time absorbing all the labor power of the nation in some activity or other and preventing unemployment. As far as possible, there should be freedom to choose one's occupation. An equalization of income will not result from all this, but there will be far more equitable sharing, and a progressive tendency toward equalization. In any event, the vast differences that exist today will disappear completely, and class distinctions, which are essentially based on differences in income, will begin to fade out.

Such a change would mean an upsetting of the present-day acquisitive society, based primarily on the profit motive. The profit motive may still continue to some extent, but it will not be the dominating urge, nor will it have the same scope as it has today. It would be absurd to say that the profit motive does not appeal to the average Indian, but it is nevertheless true that there is no such admiration for it in India as there is in the West. The possessor of money may be envied, but he is not particularly respected or admired. Respect and admiration still go to the man or woman who is considered good and wise, and especially to those who sacrifice themselves or what they possess for the public good. The Indian outlook, even of the masses, has never approved of the spirit of acquisitiveness. . . .

Behind these problems in India, as in many other countries, lies the real issue—which is not merely the establishment of democracy of the nineteenth-century European type, but also far-reaching social revolution. Democracy has itself become involved in that seemingly inevitable change, and hence among those who disapprove of the latter, doubts and denials arise about the feasibility of democracy, and this leads to fascist tendencies and the continuation of an imperialist outlook. All our present-day problems in India—the communal or minority problem, the Indian princes, vested interest of religious groups and the big landowners, and the entrenched interests of British authority and industry in India—ultimately resolve themselves into opposition to social change. And because any real democracy is likely to lead to such change, therefore democracy itself is objected to and considered unsuited to the peculiar conditions of India. So the problems of India—for all their seeming variety and difference from others—are of the same essential nature as the problems of China, or Spain, or many other countries of Europe and elsewhere. . . . Many of the resistance movements of Europe reflect these conflicts. Everywhere the old equilibrium of social forces has been upset, and till a new equilibrium is established, there will be tension, trouble, and conflict. From these problems of the moment, we are led to one of the central problems of our time: how to combine democracy with socialism, how to maintain individual freedom and initiative and yet have centralized social control and planning of the economic life of the people, on the national as well as the international plane. . . .

INDIAN SOCIALISM*

In a country like India—an underdeveloped country—socialism, a real socialist basis of society, can only come gradually. There is no help for it. Take the instance of China: They are very keen on changing their economy, and there are no such difficulties as we have—that is, parliamentary institutions and all kinds of "three readings" and select committees, which take a long time. They can pass a law overnight, if they want to. Even then, they go on saying that it will take them twenty years to lay the socialist basis of their society—to have a socialist economy—in spite of all the speed with which they may work. . . .

If by adopting some method which in theory appeals to us we reduce our production, then we are in effect undermining the growth toward socialism—although that particular step may be called a socialist step. For instance, I am quite clear in my mind that if we start nationalizing the existing institutions, industries, etc., by giving compensation, we reduce our capacity to go ahead. Here you have to be clear about one thing in your minds. Are we going in for possible seizure, expropriation without compensation, or are we not? Generally speaking, if we go in for possible seizure, then we think out its consequences, the consequences of conflict, the consequences of suffering of large numbers. Now, so far as our Constitution is concerned, that is ruled out. Apart from the Constitution, our general policy has been opposed to it. . . .

People do not generally realize how many years it took the Soviet Union to get the machines running. We see Russia today, forty years after the Revolution. It took them years to get the machines moving. Take one simple instance. In their Constitution, they said, in a sense as we say, compulsory free primary education

* From a speech delivered by Nehru to the Congress Parliamentary Party on December 22, 1954; excerpted from *Towards a Socialistic State* (New Delhi: All-India Congress Committee, 1956).

for everybody. As far as I remember, it took them fifteen years to do that, in spite of all the power of the state. These things do take time; you cannot help it, because it involves not only the money factor, but numerous other factors.

I think it is advantageous for the public sector to have a competitive private sector to keep it up to the mark. The public sector will grow. But I feel that, if the private sector is not there, if it is abolished completely, there is a risk of the public sector becoming slow, not having that urge and push behind it. It depends on men, of course. On the whole, it is a good thing to have a private sector, something where the surplus energies of people who are not employed in the public sector may have some play, provided, of course, we control that private sector in the interest of the National Plan. You can control it in a hundred ways. Control it by all means. But where you do not control, give them room to exercise initiative and bring results. That is only a sort of broad approach to this problem. I can understand that a government may gradually take steps which might be said to be in a wrong direction. It may strengthen the existing structure of society rather than weaken it. But in the final analysis, we want to break through the existing structure—the economic as well as the social—because it restricts progress. A country cannot grow if it allows rigid structures. . . . Similarly, we have to break through what might be called a capitalist structure and have something else. But breaking through it has to be in a way so as to replace it for all time, and to begin with—even while it exists—to control it.

6. The Indian National Congress (Ruling)

The Indian National Congress was founded in 1885 and since that time has been the leading nationalist movement in India. During most of the independence struggle, the Congress was led by Gandhi and Nehru. After independence, it was the majority party in India until after the death of Nehru in 1964. In 1966, Indira Gandhi, Nehru's daughter, became Prime Minister and leader of the party. When the Congress lost considerable support in the 1967 elections (dropping to 41 per cent of the vote, although narrowly retaining control of the Indian parliament), she determined to lead the Congress back to the socialist principles on which it was based. This led to a split in the party, although most of the members of the parliamentary group remained loyal to Mrs. Gandhi. In order to secure the parliamentary working majority that had been lost because of the party split, she called an election in March, 1971; it was fought over her program of nationalization of banks and insurance, abolition of princely purses, enforcement of agrarian reform, and limitations on urban property holdings. The Congress (Ruling) won 350 out of 518 seats in the lower house of parliament, enough to amend the constitution and to carry out Mrs. Gandhi's reform program without difficulty.

ELECTION MANIFESTO—1971 *

5. After the General Election of 1967, important and far-reaching political developments took place because of the tremendous mass upsurge and awakening. Only a genuine radical program of economic and social development could meet the challenge of this new situation. It is in this context that the Congress formulated the Ten-Point Programme and pledged itself to implement it effectively and speedily.

6. But these moves by the Congress to accelerate the pace of social and economic reforms aroused the opposition of vested interests and their advocates. Conservative elements inside the Congress organization, who were averse to and afraid of change, reacted sharply. When they became aware of our determination to implement the basic policies and radical programs which had earlier been decided upon jointly, they left and combined with those who had most bitterly opposed all that the Indian National Congress had stood for and fought for under the leadership of Mahatma Gandhi.

* From a pamphlet published by the Indian National Congress, New Delhi, 1971.

7. The alliance of reaction, composed of the Syndicate,* the Jana Sangh, and the Swatantra Party backed by vested interests, has been brought into being solely to fight against the progressive programs of the Congress. It is also not surprising that a section of the leadership of the Samyukta Socialist Party should have joined this unprincipled alliance, thus revealing not only their negative and destructive role but also the hollowness of their professed socialism.

8. With the consolidation of the reactionary forces, we are confronted with the most crucial fight in our postindependence history. But we are determined to press forward with a program of social change which is being challenged by disruptive and backward-looking element who are clinging to ideas and methods which are obstructing growth and social advance.

9. At the other end of the political spectrum are the Left extremists, trying to undermine the democratic process through ararchic violence. Their lawless activities have cost innocent lives of citizens and public property. Their aim is to make orderly and peaceful progress impossible.

10. Thus the ideologies of both the extreme Left and Right are a serious threat to the country. . . .

17. The Congress wants to make it clear that it has no intention of abolishing the institution of private property. On the other hand, the policy of the Congress is to ensure that the right to property becomes real for the largest number of people. But the Congress is pledged to prevent individual holdings and ownership of property beyond reasonable limits and the concentration of economic power and wealth in a few hands, as this is inconsistent with the concept of Democracy and Social Justice. . . .

AGRICULTURE

20. The great bulk of India's poor consists of the landless and small farmers. Any program which aims at benefiting them and improving the country's economy must, therefore, have a rural focus. The first item in such a program must be the speedy development of agriculture. New scientific methods should be

* The Syndicate refers to the former leaders of the Congress who opposed Mrs. Gandhi's program and formed the Congress (Opposition) in 1969. Jana Sangh is a Hindu communalist party, while the Swatantra (Freedom) Party is committed to free enterprise.—ED.

increasingly, consistently, and vigorously applied to agriculture which alone will create a vast field for additional employment. We have to ensure that this development secures for the people an adequate and nutritious diet and also leads to agrarian prosperity covering the entire countryside. The fruits of such development should be equitably spread out, particularly to benefit the small and marginal farmers and the landless.

21. For the spread of new technology, a positive program of agrarian reform is necessary. Insecurity of tenancies stands in the way of the adoption of new technology. In a share-cropping system neither the cultivating tenant nor the noncultivating owner would make the necessary investments. Uncertain ownership which has arisen out of the nonimplementation of existing land laws is a disincentive to proper investments.

22. The Green Revolution is now confined to irrigated areas and even there many of the small farmers have not been able to adopt new technology. Facilities by way of credit etc. are being extended to small farmers to enable them to adopt scientific agriculture. . . .

26. After Bank Nationalization we have embarked upon a new credit program, by extending credit facilities to small farmers, self-employed persons, and economically neglected sectors and areas. To serve these needs, banking institutions will be suitably restructured.

INDUSTRY

Public Sector

27. As far back as in 1931, the Congress had accepted that in any program for industrial development the public sector must have a dominant role. . . .

31. It is against this background that the Congress puts forward its proposals for the expansion of the public sector by taking over General Insurance; increasing state participation in the import-export trade; greater role of the State in industries where substantial public funds have been invested; and expansion of the activities of the Food Corporation of India, coordinated with cooperatives, which can ensure the implementation of a national policy for the distribution of food and fair prices for the farmer.

Private Sector

32. In our economy the private sector occupies an important

position. It should function in a manner that is consistent with our social objectives. . . .

CEILING ON URBAN PROPERTY

37. Limitations must be imposed on urban property. Measures will be taken to curb anti-social racketeering in the purchase and sale of urban land. . . .

HOUSING

49. Growing urbanization is creating new problems causing serious shortages of housing. The Congress is committed to undertake a large-scale housing program with special reference to the needs of the lower- and the middle-income groups. Slum clearance and provision of proper housing for slum-dwellers will have a high priority.

50. The Congress is also pledged to provide house sites free of cost to the landless in the rural areas and undertake measures to improve rural housing.

MINORITIES

51. In keeping with its past traditions, the Congress is pledged to protect the rights and interests of all minorities.

52. The dark and evil forces of Right reaction which masquerade in a variety of forms are intent upon destroying the very base of our democratic and socialist objectives. They are attempting to consolidate their position. They exploit some of the genuine grievances of the people and arouse the emotions of various sections by preaching religious fanaticism, racial supremacy, and chauvinism. History records that fascist forces always emerge through such nefarious maneuvers. The Congress is determined that this shall not happen in our country. And for this purpose, it will take effective measures in all fields, including education at all its stages.

53. The Constitution lays down that the State and local authorities should provide adequate facilities for instruction in the mother-tongue at the primary stage of education to children belonging to linguistic minority groups. It shall be our endeavour to implement this.

54. Secularism is one of the basic tenets of our Constitution. In accordance with this Constitutional imperative, the Congress

will strive to ensure that all minorities have full freedom to establish, manage, and run educational and other institutions. . . .

FOREIGN POLICY

59. For the last twenty-four years, India has raised her voice in the councils of the world to promote peace and fight the remnants of colonialism and all concepts of racial inequality. The Congress pledges itself to remain faithful to the vision of Jawaharlal Nehru who gave inspiration and direction to our foreign policy which is in India's own national interest and has helped to safeguard its sovereignty, security, and independence. The Congress pledges to uphold the principles of nonalignment and freedom from military blocs. This has received ever widening acceptance in the world and more specially amongst the newly independent nations. . . .

STRONG AND STABLE GOVERNMENT

64. To carry out the entire program, a strong and stable Government committed to radical policies backed by a decisive majority in Parliament is absolutely essential. Our Congress alone can provide such a Government and ensure effective implementation of programs. In this election we must think only of the nation and its advance.

65. The Congress, therefore, appeals to the people to return its candidates to the Lok Sabha and thus give it a clear mandate to:

i. continue the advance to socialism through the democratic process and devise administrative systems capable of speeding implementations;

ii. put down the forces of violence and disorder so that all our citizens can live in peace and harmony;

iii. defend secularism and safeguard the interests of the minorities and the weaker sections of the community, particularly the Scheduled Castes,* Scheduled Tribes, and the other backward sections so that they may attain "equality of status and opportunity and fraternity assuring the dignity of the individual";

iv. end anachronistic privileges such as privy purses, etc. and reduce glaring disparities of income and opportunity;

v. accelerate efforts to provide basic requirements to our people

* The "untouchables."—ED.

by undertaking a dynamic program of agricultural development by the application of science and technology and thereby usher in a new phase of rural prosperity, which will improve the condition of small farmers, farmers in dry areas, the landless, artisans, and others who eke out their existence through diverse skills;

vi. provide fresh avenues of employment and thus widen the participation of our citizens in nation-building activities;

vii. enlarge the role of the public sector and improve its performance;

viii. give scope to the private sector to play its proper role in the economy, while curbing the concentration of economic power and wealth;

ix. control prices and ensure to the people the supplies of essential commodities at reasonable rates;

x. launch upon a program of child welfare to provide nutritious diet to preschool children;

xi. provide elementary education to all children and reshape secondary and higher education to suit the needs of the country; and

xii. for these purposes, to effect such amendments of the Constitution as may be necessary. . . .

PART II

THE ISLAMIC WORLD

The area of Islamic religion and culture extends from Morocco to Pakistan. There are also substantial Moslem elements in Malaya, Indonesia, and some African countries, but the common tie of the Arab language—which links areas as distant as Morocco and Iraq—is not present, and Islam does not have the political significance in these areas that it possesses in North Africa, the Middle East, and Pakistan.

In the Islamic world, as in Africa, nationalism has taken several forms. Where the nation-state was the product of artificial divisions imposed by the Europeans, loyalties have been directed to a Pan-Arab or even Pan-Islamic ideal as much as to the individual nation. In these areas, the binding force of culture, language, and religion gives a common universe of discourse to political leaders. These ties are the basis of efforts toward common consultation and action through such bodies as the Arab League or the projected Maghreb (North African) Federation. The appeal of the Pan-Arab ideal may also be used—as in the case of Nasser—to extend the influence of an individual national leader throughout the Middle East.

Yet divisions remain—whether caused by personal rivalries, ideological differences (e.g., between Nasser and Saudi Arabia), permanent competition for influence (as between Iraq and Egypt), or different geographical situations and contacts with outside influences. North Africa, while maintaining links with the Middle East, seems destined to pursue a separate course, and Pakistan looks to Asia as much as to the Arab world.

All these areas are currently facing a common political problem (which Catholic Europe had to face earlier, in the nineteenth century): the adjustment of a traditional religion having a deep hold

147

on the population to the needs of the modern world. * This, in turn, is part of the larger problem of how to combine traditional culture and the European influences, to which the area has been subjected intensively during the last fifty years. In most Islamic countries, democracy has not functioned effectively, and reformist military rule has been more successful. Moreover, as the history of the Middle East—particularly the success of Nasser's policy and the failure of the Baghdad Pact—has demonstrated in the last decade, the Islamic world prefers a neutral position in the East-West conflict.*

Nasser's nationalization of a substantial sector of the Egyptian economy set off new discussions concerning the relationship of his "Arab socialism" and Islam. Nasser himself defended socialization as being in accord with the principles of the Prophet. While he has been both defended and criticized by Islamic leaders, his action was in accord with the modernizing elite's desire to assert political control over the production and distribution of goods in the interest of economic development and social reform.

No other careed or leader in the Islamic world shares the charismatic influence or ideological appeal of Nasser. In North Africa, Habib Bourguiba has espoused a more moderate position while Nasser's former rivals for influence in the Middle East such as the Ba'th Party in Syria and Iraq and the Saudis in Arabia continue to contend for leadership of a divided Pan-Arab movement. Cairo has also been active in the politics of the nonaligned nations, playing host to the Second Conference of Nonaligned Nations in 1964, and supporting various African liberation movements. However, with Nasser's death, regional and national interests are likely to be more important than the wider relationships that Nasser established.

* See Bourguiba's speech on Ramadan.

7. Gamal Abdel Nasser

Gamal Abdel Nasser, was born in 1918, the son of a postal clerk in Alexandria. He went to secondary school in Cairo, studied law for a time, and then attended military school, receiving his commission in 1938. He served in the Sudan, and fought in the Israeli War. Nasser had been a nationalist since his secondary-school days, and the corruption and inefficiency of the Egyptian politicians at the time of the war against Israel led him to form a Free Officiers' Committee, out of which grew the Council of Revolutionary Command, which seized power on July 23, 1952. General Naguib, the nominal head of the revolutionary junta, was removed in November, 1954, and Nasser took power as Premier and Chairman of the Council of Revolutionary Command. In 1956 he was elected President, and he was re-elected twice without opposition. Following his sudden death in September, 1970, he was succeeded by his vice-president, Anwar el-Sadat.

After the seizure of power in 1952, Nasser wrote a series of articles for the Egyptian magazine Akhar Saa, later published as The Philosophy of the Revolution. Nasser outlawed all political parties except the government party, reorganized in 1962 as the Arab Socialist Union. In July, 1961, he nationalized most major business enterprises and placed limits on landholding. His program of "Arab socialism," which he described in a speech on May 21, 1962, rejected the Marxist view of the inevitability of the class struggle and called for a mixed economy and the establishment of elected councils in factories and in local and national government. In the last years of his life Nasser had been more concerned with internal questions, and with relations with Israel, than with efforts to establish himself as the leader of the Pan-Arab movement or of the nonaligned countries.

THE PHILOSOPHY OF THE
REVOLUTION*

The Two Revolutions

Every people on earth go through two revolutions: a political revolution that helps them recover their right to self-government from the hands of a despot who had imposed himself upon them, or free themselves from the domination of alien armed forces which had installed themselves in the land against their will; and a social revolution—a class conflict that ultimately ends in the realization of social justice for all the inhabitants of the country.

People who preceded us on the path of human progress have all passed through those two revolutions, but not simultaneously. In certain cases, centuries have separated the one from the other. In our case, we are passing through the grueling ordeal of experiencing the two revolutions together. This ordeal, this acid test lies in the fact that each of these two revolutions has peculiar circumstances which are strangely conflicting and highly contradictory.

Unity, solidarity, and cooperation of all elements of the nation and self-denial and self-sacrifice on the part of the individual to ensure the safety, prosperity, and integrity of the motherland are the fundamental factors for the success of a *political* revolution. The disintegration of values, disruption of principles, dissension and discord among both classes and individuals, and domination of corruption, suspicion, and perversion of egoism form the foundation of *social* upheaval. Between these two millstones we find ourselves today, destined to go through two revolutions—one calling for unity, solidarity, self-sacrifice, and devotion to sacred duty, while the other imposes upon us, against our will, disunity, dissension, and nothing else but envy, hatred, vindictiveness, and egoism.

Between these two millstones, to cite a case in point, the 1919 Revolution failed to reach the results it ought to have realized. Hardly had the ranks designed to meet oppression been formed before they dispersed to engage in nothing else but strife. . . .

* Reprinted from *The Philosophy of the Revolution* (Cairo: Information Department, 1954).

Ignominious failure was the result; the oppressors tightened the screw, whether through the occupation forces or through their tools and instruments, who were then led by Sultan Fuad, and later by Farouk, his son. All that the people reaped was distrust, doubt, dissension, hatred, rancor, and strife among themselves—both classes and individuals. Thus faded the hope that was expected to be realized by the 1919 Revolution.

I said the hope faded. I did not say the hope disappeared, because the natural forces of resistance driven by the people's great hopes were still active and getting ready for yet another trial. Such was the situation that prevailed after 1919—a situation which made it imperative for the army to be the only force capable of any action.

In fact, the situation demanded a force concentrated within a framework that separates its members to a certain extent from the continual conflict between individuals and classes, a force drawn from the very heart of the people, whose members can trust one another and have full confidence in themselves—a force so equipped as to be capable of a swift and decisive action, and these conditions only prevailed in the army.

Thus it was not the army that determined the role it was to play in the course of events. The reverse was nearer to the truth. It was the events and their development that determined the army's part in the supreme struggle for the liberation of the homeland.

I realized from the outset that our success depended on our complete understanding of the nature of the circumstances in which we live in the present phase of our country's history. We could not with a mere stroke of the pen change these circumstances. We could not put back or forward the hands of the clock, and be masters of time. We also could not act the part of a traffic officer on the road of history, holding up the passage of one revolution to allow another revolution to pass through, and thus avert a collision. All that we could do was to act as best we could to escape being crushed between two millstones. There was no alternative to carrying out the two revolutions together.

In fact, the day we proceeded on the road to the political revolution and dethroned Farouk, we took a similar step on the road to the social revolution and limited the ownership of land. I still believe that the July 23 Revolution should continue to retain the initiative and its ability of rapid movement, so that it would be able to accomplish the miracle of carrying out the two revolutions simultaneously, no matter how contradictory our action may seem at times. . . .

Egypt at the Crossroads

Fate has decreed that we should stand at the world's crossroads. We have oftentimes been the invader's passageway and the adventurer's target. So numerous have been the circumstances through which we have lived that it would indeed be impossible to explain the factors latent in our people's souls unless these circumstances were taken into account.

In my opinion, Egypt's history under the Pharaohs cannot be overlooked. Then comes the interaction between the Greek culture and ours. The Roman invasion and the Islamic conquest, with the waves of Arab migration which followed, should also not be left out of the picture.

I am also of the opinion that we should dwell long on the circumstances through which we lived in the Middle Ages. It was those circumstances which brought about the situation in which we now are. If the Crusades marked the first dawnings of the Renaissance in Europe, they heralded the beginning of the ages of darkness in our country. Our people had borne alone almost the whole brunt of those battles, which left them completely impoverished and utterly helpless. And at the very time when they were shaking and tottering after the shattering blows of battle, it was their lot to suffer further humiliation and misery under the heels of Circassian tyrants and Mogul despots. . . .

My soul is torn with grief when I come to think, as I oftentimes do, of that period in our history in which a despotic feudalism was formed; a feudalism the sole object of which was to bleed the people white and deprive them of the last vestige of power and dignity. We shall indeed have to fight hard and long before we are able to rid ourselves completely of the deleterious effects of that system.

In fact, what still remains latent in our souls has on many an occasion provided me with an explanation of some of the aspects of our political life. It would seem to me sometimes, for instance, that many adopt toward the revolution the attitude of mere onlookers who are interested in nothing else but the result of a fight between two sides with whom they are in no way connected. . . .

Then what happened to us after the Mamelukes? There came the French expedition, the iron curtain drawn around us was smashed, new ideas followed, and horizons as yet invisible to us opened. The Mohammed Ali Dynasty inherited all the evils of the Mameluke regime, although it attempted to garb them in nineteenth-century garments. Our contacts with Europe and the whole world began anew. So also began our modern awakening, but it began with a new crisis.

In my opinion, our case very much resembled that of a sick man who had spent a long time in a closed room. The heat in that closed room had become so intense that the man was in anguish. Suddenly a violent storm blew, smashing all windows and doors, and strong currents of cold air began to lash the body of the sick man, who was still perspiring. The sick man needed a breath of air. Instead, a raging hurricane assailed him, and fever began to devour his feeble body. This was exactly the case of our society. It was indeed a dangerous case.

Undoubtedly, this state of affairs is responsible for the non-existence of a strong united public opinion in our country. The difference between one individual and another is vast; that between one generation and another is greater still.

There was a time when I complained that the people did not know what they were about, that they never agreed to follow the same road. I later realized, however, that I was asking for the impossible, that I had not taken the society in which we live into account. Actually, we live in a society which has not yet crystallized. It is still in a state of ferment and agitation and has not yet stabilized to continue its gradual development, like the other peoples who have gone before on the same road. I believe, with no intention to flatter the people in expressing such a belief, that our people have wrought a veritable miracle. Any other society subjected to the same severe trials as ours might have succumbed. It would have been swept by the powerful currents that had overtaken us. We have, however, weathered the tempest. It is true we have almost lost our balance, but we have not fallen down.

I sometimes consider the state of an average Egyptian family— one of the thousands of families which live in the capital of the country. The father, for example, is a turbaned *fellah*—a thoroughbred country fellow. The mother is a lady of Turkish descent. The sons and daughters attend schools following, respectively, the English and French educational systems—all this in an atmosphere in which the thirteenth-century spirit and twentieth-century manifestations intermingle and interact.

I see all this and feel in my heart of hearts that I know the cause of this bewildering perplexity which is torturing our minds and this astounding confusion which is destroying our very existence. Then I say to myself, "Surely our society will crystallize; surely it will be solidified; surely it will be welded into a strong homogeneous whole. All that is required is to strain every nerve to hold our ground during this period of transition."

The Three Circles

When I come to analyze the elements of our strength, I cannot help being struck by three sources standing in bold relief, which should be taken into account before everything else.

The first of these sources lies in the fact that we are a group of neighboring nations welded into a homogeneous whole by every possible material and moral tie that would unite any such group of nations. Moreover, our peoples possess peculiarities, potentialities, and a civilization inspired by the spiritual principles of the three divine religions which can never be overlooked in any attempt to build a new stable and peaceful world.

The second source is our land itself and the position it occupies on the map of the world—that important strategic position which rightly makes of it the world's crossroads, the main route of its trade and the highway of its armies.

There remains the third source. This is oil—which is considered the backbone of material civilization, and without which all the world's largest factories, all means of land, sea, and air communication, all war weapons would become mere iron . . .

If I have succeeded in explaining the extent of the importance of this vital element of strength, as I sincerely hope I have, it would thus follow that we are strong—strong not through wailing, shouting, or appealing for help at the top of our voices, but strong through our composure or our correct estimation (supported by figures) of our capacity for work, and our true understanding of the strength of the ties that bind our peoples together, those ties which make of our homeland an integral and indivisible whole, which should be defended as such and not as an isolated unit. So much for the First Circle—the Arab Circle, within the framework of which we should endeavor to turn, move, and act with all our force.

As for the Second Circle—the African Continent Circle . . . we cannot, under any condition, even if we want to, stand aloof from the terrible and terrifying battle now raging in the heart of that continent between 5 million whites and 200 million Africans. We cannot stand aloof for one important and obvious reason—we ourselves are in Africa.

Surely the people of Africa will continue to look to us—we who are the guardians of the Continent's northern gate, we who constitute the connecting link between the Continent and the outer world. We certainly cannot, under any condition, relinquish our responsibility to help to our utmost in spreading the light of knowledge and civilization to the very depths of the virgin jungles of the continent.

There remains another equally important reason: The Nile, the life artery of our country, springs from the heart of the continent. And still one more reason: the beloved Sudan, whose boundaries extend to the heart of the continent and which is bound by neighborly relations with the sensitive spots in its center.

There is no denying the fact that Africa is now the scene of a strange and stirring commotion. The white man, who represents several European nations, is again trying to change the map of the continent. We surely cannot, under any condition, stand as mere onlookers, deluding ourselves into the belief that we are in no way concerned with these machinations.

Indeed, I shall continue to dream of the day on which I shall see in Cairo a great Africa institute, seeking to reveal to us the various aspects of the continent, to create in our minds an enlightened African consciousness, and to associate itself with all those working in all parts of the world for the progress, prosperity, and welfare of the peoples of Africa.

There remains the Third Circle—the circle encompassing continents and oceans—the Circle of our Brethren in Islam, who, wherever their place under the sun, turn with us toward the same *kiblah*,* their lips solemnly saying the same prayers.

My faith in the magnitude of the positive effectiveness that could result from strengthening the Islamic tie that binds all Mos-

* *Kiblah* means "direction"; the reference is to Mecca, which Moslems must face during prayer.—ED.

lems grew stronger when I accompanied the Egyptian mission to Saudi Arabia to offer condolences on the death of its great King. As I stood before the Kaaba,* with my thoughts wandering around every part of the world which Islam has reached, I fully realized the need for a radical change of our conception of the pilgrimage. I said to myself: The journey to the Kaaba should no longer be construed as an admission card to paradise or as a crude attempt to buy forgiveness of sins after leading a dissipated life.

The pilgrimage should have a potential political power. The world press should hasten to follow and feature its news not by drawing attractive pen pictures of its rites and rituals for the delectation of readers, but by its representation as a periodic political conference at which the heads of all the Islamic states—leaders of opinion, scientists, eminent industrialists, and prominent businessmen—assemble to draw up at this world Islamic parliament the broad lines of the policies to be adopted by their respective countries, and lay down the principles ensuring their close cooperation until they have again gathered together in the following session.

They assemble, devout, but mighty; unambitious of power, but active and full of energy; submissive to divine will, but immutable in difficulties and implacable with their enemies.

They assemble, confirmed believers in the life to come, but equally convinced that they have a place under the sun which they should occupy in this life. . . .

ARAB SOCIALISM †

Political democracy cannot be separated from social democracy. No citizen can be regarded as free to vote unless he is given the following three guarantees:

1. He should be free from exploitation in all its forms.

---

* The Kaaba is the square structure in the center of the Great Mosque at Mecca which houses the sacred Black Stone.—ED.

† Excerpts from Nasser's speech on the draft charter, delivered on May 21, 1962; English translation published by the U.A.R. Information Department, Cairo.

2. He should enjoy an equal opportunity to have a fair share of the national wealth.

3. His mind should be free from all anxiety likely to undermine the security of his life in the future.

Only when a citizen possesses these three guarantees can he be said to have political freedom and can he take part, by means of his vote, in shaping the authority of the state he aspires to have.

Political democracy cannot exist under the domination of any one class. Democracy means, literally, the domination and sovereignty of the people—the entire people. The experiment started with the beginning of the organized revolutionary action has proved that it is indispensable that the revolution undertake to liquidate the force of reaction, deprive it of all its weapons, and prevent it from making any attempt to come back to power and subject the state machinery to the service of its own interests.

The bitterness and sanguinary nature of class strife, as well as the grave dangers likely to ensue, are in fact the creation of the force of reaction, which does not wish to give up the monopolies or privileged positions from which it continues to exploit the people. The force of reaction possesses the means of resistance; it possesses the power of the state, and if this is taken away from it, it turns to the power of capital. If, however, this is taken away from it, then it turns to its natural ally, imperialism.

Because of their monopoly of wealth, reactionary interests are bound to clash with the interest of the whole people. Consequently, the peaceful resolution of class struggle cannot be achieved unless the power of reaction is first and foremost deprived of all its weapons.

The removal of such clashes will pave the way to peaceful solutions to class struggles. It does not remove the contradictions in the rest of the social classes, but it creates a chance for the possibility of resolving them peacefully—namely, by means of democratic action. If, on the other hand, this clash of interests is allowed to remain, then it will not be resolved except by a civil war that will cause great damage to the country at a time of great international conflict and bitter Cold War.

The collaboration between the force of reaction and exploiting capital must, therefore, collapse. The road must then be paved for democratic interaction among the various powers of the working people—namely, the farmers, workers, soldiers, intellectuals, and national capital.

Cooperation among the powers representing the working people is the legitimate substitute for the collaboration between feudalism and exploiting capital. It alone is capable of replacing reactionary democracy by true democracy.

The national unity created by the cooperation between those representative powers of the people will be able to set up the Arab Socialist Union.* This union will constitute the authority representing the people and the driving force behind the possibilities of the revolution and the guardian of the values of true democracy.

These enormous popular powers—forming the Arab Socialist Union, and responsible for the unleashing of its energy and effectiveness—make it necessary that, when dealing with the form of the political organization of the state, the new constitution of the United Arab Republic must refer to a set of necessary guarantees:

1. The popular and political organizations based on free and direct election must truly and fairly represent the powers forming the majority of the population—the powers that have for long been exploited and have a deep interest in the Revolution, through their experience of deprivation. These powers are also naturally the storehouse of revolutionary energy, which is both dynamic and forceful.

This is only just and fair, since it means that the majority will be represented. It also provides a sure guarantee of the strength of the revolutionary impetus because it will then be springing from its genuine and natural sources.

It follows, then, that the new constitution must ensure that farmers and workers will get half the seats in political and popular organizations at all levels—including the house of representatives—since they form the majority of the people.† Moreover, they are the majority who have been longest deprived of their inalienable right to shape and direct their future.

* The creation of the Arab Socialist Union in 1962 marked Nasser's third attempt to establish an official political party. The two predecessors were the Liberation Rally (1953–57) and the National Union (1957–61).—ED.

† In the March, 1964, legislative elections, two candidates were nominated and elected in each district, one of whom was a worker or peasant.—ED.

2. The authority of the elected popular councils must be consolidated and raised above the authority of the executive machinery of the state, for that is the natural order regulating the sovereignty of the people, and ensures that the people will always lead national action. . . . Local government should gradually but resolutely transfer the authority of the state to the people, for they are in a better position to feel their own problems and find the proper solutions.

3. There is a dire need to create a new political organization within the framework of the Arab Socialist Union—recruiting the elements fit for leadership, organizing their efforts, clarifying the revolutionary motives of the masses, sounding their needs, and endeavoring to satisfy them.

4. Collective leadership is imperative in the period of the revolutionary drive. Collective leadership not only guards against the individual running loose, but also confirms and ensures the reign of democracy in its most sublime form.

Popular organizations, especially cooperatives and trade unions, can play an effective and influential role in promoting sound democracy. These organizations should form a vanguard force in the various fields of national democratic action. The development of the cooperative and trade-union movements provides an endless source to the conscious leadership that directly feels the reactions and responses of the masses. The pressure that stifled these organizations and paralyzed their movements has vanished.

Besides their productive role, the farmers' cooperatives are democratic organizations, capable of spotting and solving the problems of the farmers. So it is high time for agricultural labor unions to be established.

Industrial, commercial, and service trade unions were able, thanks to the July laws, to reach a position of leadership in the national struggle. The workers are no longer commodities in production processes. The forces of labor have become masters of the production process. They also share in its administration and profits, under the best terms of wages and working hours.

Criticism and self-criticism are among the most important guarantees to freedom. The greatest danger in the way of free criticism and self-criticism in political organizations is the infiltration of reactionary elements.

As a result of their control of economic interests, the reactionary forces controlled the press. Freedom of opinion was thus deprived of its most valuable instrument. The elimination of reaction puts an end to the dictatorship of one class and paves the way for the democracy of all the national powers of the people. It provides the surest guarantees for the freedom of assembly and freedom of discussion. . . .

Nationalization and Private Ownership

It is of prime importance that our outlook toward nationalization should be freed from the stigmas that private interests have tried to attach to it. Nationalization is but the transfer of the means of production from the sphere of private ownership to that of public ownership.

This is not a blow to individual initiative, as alleged by the enemies of socialism, but a guarantee to and an expansion of the range of general interest in cases affected by the socialist change, carried out for the benefit of the people.

Nationalization does not lead to a decrease in production. Experience has proved the ability of the public sector to shoulder the greatest responsibilities with maximum efficiency, whether in the achievement of the production targets or in the raising of the standard of its quality. Although some mistakes may occur during this great evolution, we must recall the new hands that have assumed the responsibility. At any rate it was inevitable that the major national interests should be handed over to the people even at the cost of facing temporary difficulties.

The great importance attached to the role of the public sector, however, cannot do away with the existence of the private sector. The private sector has its effective role in the development plan. It must be protected to fulfill that part. The private sector is now required to renovate itself and strike a new path of creative effort not dependent, as in the past, on parasitic exploitation.

The crisis which befell private capital before the Revolution actually stemmed from the fact that it had inherited the era of the foreign adventurers, who, in the nineteenth century, helped transfer abroad the wealth of Egypt. Private capital was accustomed to live under a protective trade policy that gave it benefits at the expense of the people. It was also accustomed to dominate the government with the aim of pursuing a policy of exploitation. . . . The people could not forever remain indifferent to maneuvers to direct the government to favor the minority controlling wealth, and to guarantee the maintenance of their privileged position at the expense of the people's interests.

Progress through socialism is a consolidation of the bases of sound democracy, the democracy of all the people. . . .

Moreover, the maintenance of the role of the private sector beside that of the public sector renders control over public ownership more effective. By encouraging free competition within the framework of the general economic planning, the private sector is also an invigorating element to the public sector. The July, 1961, revolutionary laws did not aim at destroying the private sector, but had two basic aims: The creation of some form of economic equality among citizens that ensures legitimate rights and removes the effects of a minority's monopolizing all opportunities at the expense of the majority contributes to the dissolution of class distinctions in a way that enhances the possibilities of a peaceful struggle between them, and paves the way for democratic solutions to the major problems confronting the process of development. The second objective is to step up the efficiency of the public sector, owned by the people, to consolidate its capacity to shoulder the responsibility of planning, and to enable it to play its leading role in industrial development on a socialist basis. These two objectives have been crowned with sweeping success, confirming the power of the revolutionary drive and the depth of national unity.

The realization of these two objectives wipes out the residue of the complexes (created by exploitation) that cast a shadow of doubt on the role of the private sector. Consequently, the path open to this sector today, to promote the process of development, is only restricted by the socialist laws now in force or by the steps deemed necessary by the popular authorities elected in future. . . .

Foreign Capital

Foreign capital is regarded with dark doubts in underdeveloped countries—particularly those which were colonized. The sovereignty of the people over their land and their restoration to the helm allow them to set the conditions under which foreign capital may be invested in the country.

The matter calls for the setting up of a system of priority, drawn from the essence of the national experience. It also takes into account the nature of world capital—always striving after unexploited raw materials in areas not yet ready for any economic or social revival, where it can obtain the highest share of profit.

In the first place, in the process of national evolution, all foreign aid with no strings attached is accepted to help attain the national objectives. The aid is accepted with sincere gratitude for those who offer it regardless of the colors of their flags.

In the second place, all unconditional loans are accepted, provided they can be refunded without difficulty or strain. Experience shows that loans are a clear operation; their problem ends with their amortization and the reimbursement of their interest.

In the third place, the participation of foreign capital as investment is accepted in indispensable operations, especially those requiring experience difficult to find in the national domain. Acceptance of foreign investment implies that a foreigner would participate in the administration. It also implies that a share of the annual profits would be transferred to the investors indefinitely. This matter should not be left without limitation.

First priority goes to unconditional aid. The second place is reserved to unconditional loans. Then follows the acceptance of foreign investment (in unavoidable circumstances) in aspects of modern evolution requiring international experience.

In their conscious revolutionary outlook, our people consider it the duty of the advanced states to offer aid to those still struggling for development. In their conception of history, our people believe the states with a colonialist past are, more than others, compelled to offer to the nations aspiring to development part of the national wealth they sapped when that wealth was a booty for all looters. . . .

The Class Struggle

We must clearly realize that no individual can be free unless he is first liberated from the shackles of exploitation. It is this fact that makes social freedom a way—in fact, the only way—to achieve political freedom.

Our immediate aim is to do away with exploitation and to make possible the exercise of the natural right of equal opportunity; to dissolve class distinctions and to end the domination of one class, and hence remove the struggle between classes, which constitutes a threat to the freedom of the individual citizen and even to freedom of the whole of the country by violating the rights of the people, and which creates the chance of exposing the country to the lurking dangers of foreign forces, vigilantly on the lookout to drag it to the arena of the Cold War and make of it its battlefield and of its people fodder for their guns. The removal of the struggle between classes which arises out of interests that can never be reconciled, between those who exercise exploitation and those crushed by exploitation in the past society, cannot overnight lead to the dissolution of all class distinctions, or lead to social freedom and true democracy.

Yet, the removal of the struggle between classes makes it possible—by eliminating the exploiting class—to dissolve class distinctions peacefully and to open the gates for democratic exchange, which brings the whole society nearer the age of true freedom. That was one of the great social objectives of the July laws, which directed a deadly blow at the centers of exploitation and monopolies. That great revolutionary action made it possible to have democracy for the first time in Egypt.

Land Reform

The Arab application of socialism in the domain of agriculture does not call for nationalizing the land and transforming it into the domain of public ownership. From experience and study, it believes in individual ownership of land within limits that do not allow for feudalism.

This conclusion is not just a response to the longing of the farmers for ownership of land. It is derived from the real circumstances of the agricultural problem in Egypt. These circumstances have confirmed the ability of the Egyptian farmer to work creatively if he is given favorable conditions. The efficiency of the Egyptian farmer throughout history has been able to exploit the land, especially when the opportunity is provided to benefit from scientific agricultural advances. Moreover, Egyptian agriculture long ago arrived at sound socialist solutions to its most complicated problems. Foremost among these were irrigation and drainage, which in Egypt are now and have been for a long time within the framework of the public services.

Thus the correct solution to the agricultural problem does not lie in transferring land to public ownership but requires individual ownership of land and the expansion of ownership by providing this opportunity to the largest number of wage-earners—and supporting this ownership by means of agricultural cooperation in all the stages of agricultural production.

Agricultural cooperation is much more than the simple credit to which it was confined until recently. It starts with the process of pooling agricultural exploitation which has proved to be very successful. It also involves the financial process which protects the farmer and liberates him from usurers and middlemen who take the largest part of the fruit of his labor. Cooperation also enables the farmer to use the most modern machines and scientific means to raise production. It helps the farmer in marketing, enabling him to obtain the highest return for his lengthy labor and toil.

The revolutionary solution to the land problem in Egypt is to increase the number of landowners. This was the aim of the land reform laws of 1952 and 1961.

It was also—in addition to the aim of raising production—one of the reasons for the great irrigation projects, the powerful symbol of which is the High Aswan Dam, for which the people of Egypt have suffered all kinds of military, economic, and psychological hardships. The dam has become the symbol of the will and determination of the people to fashion their lives. It is also a symbol of their will to provide the right of land ownership to large numbers of farmers for whom this opportunity was never provided through centuries of continuous feudal rule.

The success of this revolutionary attempt to solve the agricultural problem by increasing the number of landowners cannot be consolidated except by agricultural cooperation and the expansion of its scope to provide a strong and vital economy for small landholdings. . . .

8. *Mohammed Hasanein Heykal*

Mohammed Hasanein Heykal is editor-in-chief of al-Ahram, *the most influential Egyptian newspaper. Widely regarded as the ghost writer of* The Philosophy of the Revolution, *he was a close associate of Nasser during his life, and both reflected and influenced his views. After the 1961 nationalization laws, he wrote an article in* al-Ahram *that attempted to delineate the differences between the Communist ideology and that of Arab Socialism.*

The article is one of the most succinct summaries of the principal points on which many of the more radical nationalists differ from Marxism-Leninism, however willing they may be to cooperate with the Soviet Union on programs of mutual interest.

COMMUNISM AND OURSELVES:
SEVEN DIFFERENCES BETWEEN COMMUNISM
AND ARAB SOCIALISM *

My aim is to analyze the contents of Arab socialism and of Communism, in order to compare these two doctrines and highlight their differences. As preamble, however, I wish to indicate that my intention is neither to disparage Communism nor to vilify Communists, for several reasons:

The first is that our experience in socialism rose from nothing, but from now on is open to debate and confrontation. . . .

The second is that we believe in the right of the people to choose their own system. If the American people choose capitalism, it is their right, and if the people of the Soviet Union choose Communism, that is also their right.

The third is that no one can deny that Communism as experienced in the Soviet Union has achieved great results for the people of that country, even though the price they paid under the terror of Stalinism was tremendous. In fact, the Soviet Union has taken a great leap forward in the course of the last forty-three years, and together with the U.S.A. it has become one of the two great world powers as regards scientific progress and production.

Finally, the fourth reason is that the existence of a Communist world opposite the capitalist world has created an extremely important international balance, which has allowed many colonized and conquered people to rise up against their masters.

1. The first difference between Arab socialism and Communism lies in the conception of class by each. The existence of classes and their conflicting interests and the class struggle from which

---

* From *al-Ahram*, Cairo, August 4, 1961, translated in Kemal H. Karpat (ed.), *Political and Social Thought in the Contemporary Middle East* (New York: Praeger Publishers, 1968). Used by permission of the publisher.

the movement for social progress stems are accepted facts. It is here that the first difference appears between Arab socialism and Communism; it lies in the solution proposed by each of the two systems to the problem of conflicting contradictory class interests.

The solution proposed by Communism is proletarian dictatorship represented by the Communist Party, whereas Arab socialism proposes the fusion of the differences that exist between the classes. Communism asks the disposed to revolt and transform all the possessors into dispossessed. It also asks them to get rid of all property owners, by any means, if necessary by massacre—all such owners being in its eyes exploiters.

The Communist solution is therefore the final elimination of all classes by a single class. Arab socialism asks the dispossessed to revolt so that they may have access to property and take their rightful share of the national wealth. For Arabs, it is a question of eliminating the contradictions between the classes within a framework of national unity and revolutionary plotting, while society evolves to form only one class in which each member occupies a place commensurate with his work, without the impediment of any class barrier.

Thus punishment and vengeance mark the first steps of Communism, the class struggle inevitably assuming, in the eyes of the Communists, a bloody character. As to Arab socialism, its origins are in justice and equality. Revolutionary intrigue is carried out in a peaceful manner, unsoiled by bloodshed, and without the specter of the gallows in the background.

2. The second difference, which derives from the first, concerns the ideas of the two systems regarding private property. As far as Communism is concerned, every property owner is also an exploiter; hence, it is necessary to eliminate him in order to eliminate exploitation itself.

For Arab socialism, with its different point of view, property is of two kinds—that which exploits and that which results from work. Communism affirms: Whoever possesses exploits; he must be eliminated. Arab socialism says: There are proprietors and proprietors. In fact, there is a kind of property that represents the result of work and that cannot be used by the owner to exploit or dominate others. This property is an essential right. It is a right that should be extended so that as many as possible can share in it and benefit equally from it. As for the exploiting proprietor, Arab socialism continues: Do not kill him. Take from him rather the means that make him an exploiter, then allow him to live in the new society. It does not matter if he enters with anger and bitterness the society that is capable of educating him, since it is capable of educating its children and initiating them into a new way of life.

3. The third difference emerges from this logical chain of thought. Communism says: It is necessary to expropriate. Arab socialism says: It is necessary to compensate. This difference is the inevitable consequence of the two former differences. Arab socialism has as its aims justice and equality, not punishment and vengeance. Private property is a right—even an aim, one may say —on condition that it does not end in exploitation. The system of nationalization with compensation, as was practiced by Arab socialism in its attempt to increase the people's share in the national wealth and its revenues, is not only a guillotine that operates automatically, rising and falling to cut up and destroy. On the contrary, nationalization is carried out in a responsible, patriotic manner. This explains the apparent difference in the procedure employed with regard to certain firms affected by these measures. Total nationalization has struck first at all the international monopolies, starting with the Suez Canal Company, which was dominated by Britain and France. Then came the Company of New Egypt, a simple façade behind which lay Belgian interests, followed by banks and insurance companies, so as to prevent money's becoming the weapon of exploitation. Nationalization was then extended to public services closely linked to the public interest, such as the Tramway Company, for example, and the Lebon Company, and took in the heavy industry that exercised a direct influence on the national economy.

In other cases—altogether ninety-one cases affected by the revolutionary measures—nationalization has not been total but partial (50 per cent). Such is the case, for example, with the works of Yasin the glass manufacturers. Muhammad Sayyid Yasin, their founder, has made a real effort in a new productive bid. He has succeeded, and in his success lies a whole history of struggle and experience. . . .

4. Let us turn now to the role of the individual in society. In the Communist society, the state possesses everything. The individual is a tool; he receives what is necessary for his essential needs. . . . In Arab socialism, the state is an instrument of the people for achieving justice and guaranteeing its application.

While the individual in the Communist society feels he is only a small cog in a huge machine, the individual in the Arab socialist society feels that his capacities for invention are not subject to limitation or hindrance, so long as he does not indulge in exploitation.

In Arab socialism, the individual is the very basis of the social structure. There is nothing in it that fetters ambition. . . . Arab socialism desires that workers in the factories shall be co-proprietors, concerned with profit not only from the viewpoint of production but also from a personal point of view. . . .

5. Thus another difference appears between Communism and Arab socialism. Communism was founded on the sacrifice of several generations of men in order to arrive at a growth of production. Especially during the Stalinist period, it put these ideas into practice by confiscating all national resources and mobilizing the total work force toward production. The extreme cruelty of the conditions in factories and on collective farms, the coercion and oppression, could only be justified to the generation of that time by looking toward the future.

Arab socialism has another view on this question. To achieve an increase in production and eventually the highest level of production necessitates a general national mobilization of all resources, but the present generations have the right to live. . . .

6. We come to a sixth difference between Communism and Arab socialism. It is the difference between abject servility and free initiative. Above all, it is the difference between immobility and dynamism, or rather between blind fanaticism and free thought. Even though it undertakes to conform to Marxist dialectic, Communism cannot depart from the well-defined paths without being accused of deviationism, as was the case with Tito, who was attacked when he tried to transform, modernize, and free himself, and to become independent.

The Arab socialist feels that all the richness of thought throughout the world is available to him. He can benefit from it and explore its possibilities. Above all, he feels that he is capable of adding something to it and sharing in its growth. He adds to it his own national experience, and he helps it grow by his historical heritage.

In his speech made on the eve of the celebration of the revolution, Gamal Abdel Nasser expressed this idea in these words: "We do not open books to find all the answers, but we open the book of our reality [time] and try to find the solution of its problems."

That is the difference between the Communist and the Arab socialist. The Communist is a pupil who remains faithful to the words of Marx, Lenin, Stalin, Khrushchev, and Mao Tse-tung crammed into his head. Even though these words are in many cases divergent and remote . . . different and contradictory . . . the Communist must listen and obey. The Arab socialist is a pupil who remains faithful to the history of his nation, to his national heritage, to the problems of his people, and to their hopes.

It is possible that this is the reason for the failure of Arab Communists to achieve the least following among the people, particularly in the United Arab Republic. The Arab masses have heard nothing from the Communists but stiff foreign slogans. They see in the Communists only puppets, worked by string from behind their frontiers.

7. Communism believes that political organizations should be confined to the Communist Party alone. For this reason, that supreme and unchallenged authority is exclusively in the hands of the Party. No revolution can be lawful unless the Communist Party is the instigator and the master. Arab socialism considers that the organization encompassing political activity must extend to the whole nation.

9. *The Palestine Liberation Organization*

The Palestine Liberation Organization was formed in 1964 to coordinate the activities of the various Palestinian groups, dedicated to opposition to Israel. Recognized and financially supported by the Middle Eastern Arab governments, the organization was restructured and taken over by younger more militant resistance groups after the Six-Day War in 1967. At a Congress held in 1968, which was dominated by the Al Fatah group, a National Charter was adopted which outlined the Palestinians' basic principles, including commitment to armed struggle, opposition to the

*partition of Palestine, recognition of the Palestinian "people"
within a broader framework of "the Arab nation," and denial of
Palestinian citizenship to Jews who had arrived in Palestine since
"the Zionist invasion" (subsequently modified by Al Fatah to
allow all who accept a secular democratic state to remain). The
Charter also attempts to link Israel with imperialism, racism, and
fascism—a part of a general strategy of securing support from anticolonial, anticapitalist, and black liberation movements in other
parts of the world.*

THE PALESTINIAN
NATIONAL CHARTER (JULY, 1968) *

Article 1: Palestine is the homeland of the Arab Palestinian
people; it is an indivisible part of the Arab homeland, and the
Palestinian people are an integral part of the Arab nation.

Article 2: Palestine, with the boundaries it had during the British mandate, is an indivisible territorial unit.

Article 3: The Palestinian Arab people possess the legal right to
their homeland and have the right to determine their destiny
after achieving the liberation of their country in accordance with
their wishes and entirely of their own accord and will.

Article 4: The Palestinian identity is a genuine, essential, and
inherent characteristic; it is transmitted from parents to children.
The Zionist occupation and the dispersal of the Palestinian Arab
people, through the disasters which befell them, do not make
them lose their Palestinian identity and their membership of the
Palestinian community, nor do they negate them.

Article 5: The Palestinians are those Arab nationals who, until
1947, normally resided in Palestine regardless of whether they
were evicted from it or have stayed there. Anyone born, after
that date, of a Palestinian father—whether inside Palestine or
outside it—is also a Palestinian.

Article 6: The Jews who had normally resided in Palestine until

* Translated in Leila Kadi (ed.), *Basic Political Documents of the Armed
Palestinian Resistance Movement*, PLO Research Center, Beirut, 1969.

the beginning of the Zionist invasion will be considered Palestinians.*

Article 7: That there is a Palestinian community and that it has material, spiritual, and historical connection with Palestine are indisputable facts. It is a national duty to bring up individual Palestinians in an Arab revolutionary manner. All means of information and education must be adopted in order to acquaint the Palestinian with his country in the most profound manner, both spiritual and material, that is possible. He must be prepared for the armed struggle and ready to sacrifice his wealth and his life in order to win back his homeland and bring about its liberation.

Article 8: The phase in their history through which the Palestinian people are now living, is that of national struggle for the liberation of Palestine. Thus the conflicts among the Palestinian national forces are secondary, and should be ended for the sake of the basic conflict that exists between the forces of Zionism and of imperialism on the one hand, and the Palestinian Arab people on the other. On this basis the Palestinian masses, regardless of whether they are residing in the national homeland or in diaspora, constitute—both their organizations and the individuals—one national front working for the retrieval of Palestine and its liberation through armed struggle.

Article 9: Armed struggle is the only way to liberate Palestine. Thus it is the over-all strategy, not merely a tactical phase. The Palestinian Arab people assert their absolute determination and firm resolution to continue their armed struggle and to work for an armed popular revolution for the liberation of their country and their return to it. They also assert their right to normal life in Palestine and to exercise their right to self-determination and sovereignty over it.

Article 10: Commando (*fedayeen*) action constitutes the nucleus of the Palestinian popular liberation war. This requires its escalation, comprehensiveness, and the mobilization of all the Palestinian popular and educational efforts and their organization and involvement in the armed Palestinian revolution. It also re-

---

* In 1969, Al Fatah, the principal Palestinian resistance movement adopted a declaration proposing that "the new Palestine of tomorrow" should be "a progressive, democratic, and nonsectarian Palestine in which Christian, Moslem, and Jew will worship, work, live peacefully, and enjoy equal rights." It has proposed that Article 6 be reworded in this sense.—ED.

quires the achieving of unity for the national struggle among the different groupings of the Palestinian people, and between the Palestinian people and the Arab masses so as to secure the continuation of the revolution, its escalation, and victory.

Article 11: The Palestinians will have three mottoes: national unity, national mobilization, and liberation.

Article 12: The Palestinian people believe in Arab unity. In order to contribute their share toward the attainment of that objective, however, they must, at the present stage of their struggle, safeguard their Palestinian identity and develop their consciousness of that identity, and oppose any plan that may dissolve or impair it.

Article 13: Arab unity and the liberation of Palestine are two complementary objectives, the attainment of either of which facilitates the attainment of the other. Thus, Arab unity leads to the liberation of Palestine; the liberation of Palestine leads to Arab unity; and work toward the realization of the one objective proceeds side by side with work toward the realization of the other.

Article 18: The liberation of Palestine, from an international point of view, is a defensive action necessitated by the demands of self-defense. Accordingly, the Palestinian people, desirous as they are of the friendship of all people, look to freedom-loving, justice-loving, and peace-loving states for support in order to restore their legitimate rights in Palestine, to re-establish peace and security in the country, and to enable its people to exercise national sovereignty and freedom.

Article 19: The partition of Palestine in 1947 and the establishment of the state of Israel are entirely illegal, regardless of the passage of time, because they were contrary to the will of the Palestinian people and to their natural right in their homeland, and inconsistent with the principles embodied in the Charter of the United Nations, particularly the right to self-determination.

Article 20: The Balfour Declaration, the mandate for Palestine, and everything that has been based upon them, are deemed null and void. Claims of historical or religious ties of Jews with Palestine are incompatible with the facts of history and the true conception of what constitutes statehood. Judaism, being a religion, is not an independent nationality. Nor do Jews constitute a single nation with an identity of its own; they are citizens of the states to which they belong.

Article 21: The Arab Palestinian people, expressing themselves by the armed Palestinian revolution, reject all solutions which are substitutes for the total liberation of Palestine and reject all proposals aiming at the liquidation of the Palestinian problem or its internationalization.

Article 22: Zionism is a political movement organically associated with international imperialism and antagonistic to all action for liberation and to progressive movements in the world. It is racist and fanatic in its nature, aggressive, expansionist, and colonial in its aims, and fascist in its methods. Israel is the instrument of the Zionist movement, and a geographical base for world imperialism placed strategically in the midst of the Arab homeland to combat the hopes of the Arab nation for liberation, unity, and progress. Israel is a constant source of threat *vis-à-vis* peace in the Middle East and the whole world. Since the liberation of Palestine will destroy the Zionist and imperialistic presence and will contribute to the establishment of peace in the Middle East, the Palestinian people look for the support of all the progressive and peaceful forces and urge them all, irrespective of their affiliations and beliefs, to offer the Palestinian people all aid and support in their just struggle for the liberation of their homeland.

Article 23: The demands of security and peace, as well as the demands of right and justice, require all states to consider Zionism an illegitimate movement, to outlaw its existence, and to ban its operations, in order that friendly relations among peoples may be preserved and the loyalty of citizens to their respective homelands safeguarded.

Article 24: The Palestinian people believe in the principles of justice, freedom, sovereignty, self-determination, human dignity, and in the right of all peoples to exercise them.

10. The Baʻth Party

The Baʻth (Resurrection) Party was founded in Syria by Michel Aflaq and Salah Bitar in 1943; in 1953 it merged with the Arab Socialist Party in Syria. It is committed to Arab unity, neutralism, and socialism. The Ba'th thinks of itself as representing the Arab nation as a whole and it is organized under a National (i.e., Pan-Arab) Command and several Regional (i.e., Syrian, Iraqi, Jordanian) Commands. Originally suspicious of Nasser, the party supported the union of Egypt and Syria in the United Arab Republic in 1958. When it became evident that Nasser was interested in Arab unity only under his own auspices, the Ba'thists withdrew their support and favored the Syrian secession in 1961. The references in the Party Constitution to freedom of speech, organization, and expression and the need for an independent judiciary differentiate the party's view from those of Nasser, although when in power Ba'thists in Syria and Iraq have often disregarded those principles. The Ba'thist variety of socialism resembles that of Nasser in favoring nationalization of large and foreign-owned industries and the association of workers in the administration and profits of the factory. When a leftist-military faction in the party (the neo-Ba'th) came to power in Syria in 1966 it nationalized foreign trade and 80 per cent of industry, implemented a drastic agrarian reform, and adopted an attitude of intransigence toward Israel. The Syrian military continues to exert a decisive influence on the party in that country.

THE CONSTITUTION OF THE ARAB RESURRECTION SOCIALIST PARTY*

FUNDAMENTAL PRINCIPLES

The first principle: The unity and freedom of the Arab nation.

The Arabs are a single nation, having a natural right to exist within a single state and to be free to realize all its potentialities.

To these ends, the Arab Resurrection Socialist Party declares:

1. The Arab homeland is an indivisible politico-economic unit. It is impossible for any of the Arab regions to perfect the conditions of its life in isolation from the rest.

2. The Arab nation is a cultural unit. All of the differences

* Reprinted by permission from the *Middle East Journal*, XIII (Spring, 1959), 195–200; translated by Leonard Binder.

among its members are artificial accidents which will cease to exist as a consequence of the awakening of Arab consciousness.

3. The Arab homeland belongs to the Arabs. They alone have the right to utilize its resources and its wealth, and to control its potentialities.

The second principle: The special character of the Arab nation.

The Arab nation is distinguished by its special merit, revealed in its repeated awakenings; it is marked by the abundance of its vitality and inventiveness, and its tendency toward reform and resurgence. Its resurgence is ever related to the growth of individual freedom and the (extension of the) scope of harmony between individual freedom and the national interest.

Therefore, the Arab Resurrection Socialist Party declares that:

1. Freedom of speech, of association, of belief, and of science are sacred, and may not be limited by any government whatsoever.

2. The value of members of the nation is to be assessed—after they have been granted an adequate opportunity—exclusively on the basis of their efforts on behalf of the Arab nation and its efflorescence.

The third principle: The mission of the Arab nation.

The Arab nation is characterized by an eternal mission which manifests itself in the form of a complete regeneration through the stage of history, leading to the reformation of human existence, the advancement of human progress, and the enhancement of harmony and cooperation among nations.

Therefore, the Arab Resurrection Socialist Party declares that:

1. Colonialism and everything connected therewith is an evil which will be opposed by the Arabs by every possible means. They will make continuous and substantial efforts, within their capacity, to aid all people who are striving for freedom.

2. All humanity is mutually responsible for its common welfare, and collectively responsible for its protection and civilization. The Arabs benefit from world civilization, and they contribute to it in turn. The Arabs will extend a brotherly hand to the other nations and will cooperate with them in bringing about the rule of justice, guaranteeing to all peoples peace, well-being, and moral and spiritual elevation.

* For the verbatim text of a discussion between Nasser and leading Ba'thists in 1963 on their attitude toward "bourgeois democracy" see Kemal Karpat (ed.), *Political and Social Thought in the Middle East* (New York: Praeger Publishers, 1968, pp. 261–64).

GENERAL PROVISIONS

Article 1. The party is a universal Arab party, branches of which will be established in all the rest of the Arab regions. It will not pursue a regional policy, except out of regard for the higher Arab interest.

Article 2. The general headquarters of the party is in the district of Damascus, but it may be transferred to any other Arab country if the national interest so determines.

Article 3. The Arab Resurrection Socialist Party is nationalist, holding that nationalism has a truly permanent existence, and that the precious feeling of nationalism which firmly ties the individual to his nation is a sacred sentiment, full of creative power, encouraging sacrifice, reawakening the sense of responsibility, and striving to channel the individual personality purposefully, efficiently, and gloriously.

The nationalist idea which the party preaches is the will of the Arab people to be free and united; that the Arab people be given an opportunity to realize the Arab character in history; and that it cooperate with the rest of the nations on whatever will assure humanity's unswerving progress toward goodness and well-being.

Article 4. The Arab Resurrection Socialist Party is socialist, believing that socialism is necessarily derived from genuine Arab nationalism because it is the exemplary system which will permit the Arab people to realize its own potentialities. Socialism will cause the Arab genius to unfold in the most complete manner. Socialism will guarantee the continuous growth of the nation in its spiritual and material development; and it will guarantee close fraternization among its individual members.

Article 5. The Arab Resurrection Socialist Party is populist, believing that dominion belongs to the people, that they alone are the origin of all government and leadership, and that the value of the state derives from the will of the masses, even as its sanctity is in proportion to the extent of their freedom in choosing the government. Therefore the party depends upon the people for the accomplishment of its mission, and endeavors to tie itself closely to the people, and to raise their intellectual, moral, economic, and hygienic levels in order to increase their sense of individuality and to increase the exercise of their rights in the individualistic (sphere) of national life.

Article 6. The Arab Resurrection Socialist Party is revolutionary, believing that its principal goals of reawakening Arab nationalism and building socialism cannot be achieved except by revolution and strife. The party believes that dependence upon gradual change and contentment with superficial (because) partial amelioration will defeat these ends (through faintheartedness and loss of opportunities). Therefore the party decides to: (a) struggle against foreign colonialism in order to achieve absolute freedom for the Arab homeland; (b) struggle to achieve a union of Arabs in a single independent state; (c) rebel against existing evils affecting all intellectual, economic, social, and political aspects of life.

Article 7. The Arab national homeland is that part of the earth inhabited by the Arab people and which lies between the Taurus Mountains, the Zagros mountains, the Persian Gulf, the Arabian Sea, the mountains of Ethiopia, the Sahara Desert, the Atlas range, and the Mediterranean Sea.

Article 8. The official language of the state and the language of its people, authorized for publication and instruction, is the Arabic language.

Article 9. The subjects of the Arab state are the subjects of the Arab revolt which was begun in the year 1916 for the purpose of freeing and uniting the Arab people.

Article 10. An Arab is anyone whose language is Arabic, who lives in the Arab homeland or aspires to live therein, and who believes in his connection with the Arab people.

Article 11. Whoever agitates on behalf of or is connected with a racial group opposed to the Arabs, or whoever immigrates into the Arab homeland for the purpose of colonization, will be expelled from the Arab homeland.

Article 12. Arab women will enjoy all the rights of citizenship. The party will strive to raise the status of women so that they become worthy of these rights.

Article 13. In order that the citizens demonstrate their abilities in their true light and to their fullest extent in all fields of human activity, a true beginning is to be made with the equalization of educational and economic opportunity.

PROGRAM

The Domestic Policy of the Party

Article 14. The system of government in the Arab state will be representative and constitutional. The executive authority will be

responsible to the legislative authority, which is to be directly
elected by the people.

Article 15. The national tie will be the sole (social) bond existing in the Arab state. It will guarantee harmony among the citizens and it will guarantee their fusion in the crucible of a single
nationality. It will combat all other denominational, factional,
tribal, parochial, or regional loyalties.

Article 16. The system of administration in the Arab state will
be decentralized.

Article 17. The party will strive to make the populist spirit prevail, and to make it a living reality in the life of the individual.
The party will strive to enact a constitution for the state which
will guarantee absolute equality before the law to Arab citizens;
which will guarantee the complete freedom of the expression of
their will and the choice of their representatives in honest elections; thus organizing for them a life of freedom within the limits
of the laws.

Article 18. A single legislative code, in harmony with the spirit
of the contemporary period and based upon the experience of the
Arab nation in the past, will be enacted for the Arab state in
complete freedom.

Article 19. The judicial authority will be protected from and
independent of every other authority and it will enjoy complete
immunity.

Article 20. Full rights of citizenship will be bestowed upon every
citizen living in the Arab homeland who identifies himself solely
with the Arab homeland and disassociates himself from every racial
group.

Article 21. Military service will be compulsory in the Arab
homeland.

The Foreign Policy of the Party

Article 22. The foreign policy of the Arab state will be inspired
by the Arab national interest and the eternal Arab mission, and it
will be aimed at cooperation with other nations in improving the
harmony, freedom, faith, and righteousness of the world and its
continuous progress.

Article 23. The Arabs will struggle with all their power to undermine the supports of colonialism and foreign occupation and all
foreign political or economic influence in their country.

Article 24. When the Arab people alone become the source of all authority, all trade agreements and conventions made by the present governments which infringe upon the absolute sovereignty of the Arabs will be abrogated.

Article 25. The Arab foreign policy will be revealed to have received its correct form from the will of the Arabs to live in freedom, and from their desire to see all other nations similarly enjoying freedom.

The Economic Policy of the Party

Article 26. The Arab Resurrection Socialist Party is socialist, believing that the economic wealth of the homeland is the property of the nation.

Article 27. The distribution of immovable (landed) property in the Arab homeland is unjust, and therefore this distribution will be re-examined and (such property) will be redistributed among the citizens on a just basis.

Article 28. All citizens are to be recognized as equal in their capacity as human beings; therefore the party will prevent the exploitation of the labor of others.

Article 29. Public utilities, enterprises based on great natural resources, large-scale industries, and means of transport are the property of the nation to be administered directly by the state. All (relevant) foreign companies and concessions are to be abolished.

Article 30. Agricultural ownership will be limited in accordance with the capacity of the owner for proper exploitation and within the framework of the general economic plan, rather than (as presently regulated by) the exploitation of the labor of others by the dignitaries of the state.

Article 31. The ownership of small industries will be regulated in accordance with the economic level enjoyed by the rest of the citizens of the state.

Article 32. The workers will be associated with the administration of (their) factory, and the sum of their wages will be determined by the state in a proportion, also to be determined by the state, to the value of their work.

Article 33. The ownership of real property or buildings will be permitted to all citizens, provided that they will not have the right to rent it out nor to exploit it at the expense of others: moreover the government will guarantee a minimum of real property to all citizens.

Article 34. Ownership and inheritance are national and protected rights within the limits of the national interest.

Article 35. Lending at interest among the citizens will be abolished, and a single bank will be established which will issue bank-
notes guaranteed by national production, and which will apply
(credit) to essential agricultural and industrial enterprises.

Article 36. The state will supervise domestic and foreign commerce directly in order to eliminate exploitation between producer
and consumer to protect them both, to protect national production from the competition of foreign production, and to maintain
a balance between exports and imports.

Article 37. A comprehensive plan will be drawn up in the light
of experience and on the basis of economic theory for the purpose
of industrializing the Arab homeland, increasing national production, opening new (economic) horizons to it, and in order to
direct the economy in all spheres in accordance with its capacity
and in order to fulfill desired priorities.

The Social Policy of the Party

Article 38. The family, children, and marriage:

a) The family is the basic unit of the nation; its protection,
development, and welfare are responsibilities devolving upon the
state.

b) Children are first the responsibility of the family and secondly of the state. It is incumbent upon both to strive to increase
their number and to care for their health and education.

c) Marriage is essential to the nation; its encouragement, facili-
tation, and regulation is the duty of the state.

Article 39. Public health: The state will establish, at its own
expense, institutions of preventive medicine, clinics, and dispen-
saries which will supply the needs of all the citizens in accordance
with the highest standards, and which will guarantee scrupulous
medical treatment to them.

Article 40. Labor:

a) Work is to be required of all who are capable of it, and the
state will guarantee either intellectual or physical employment to
all citizens.

b) The product of labor must guarantee its producer at least a
proper standard of living.

c) The state will provide for the subsistence of invalids out of the total national product.

d) Just labor legislation will be enacted, limiting the daily hours of the worker, granting him weekly and annual paid vacations, safeguarding his rights, guaranteeing him old age insurance, and compensating partial or complete unemployment (occurring) during the course of work.

e) Free syndicates will be organized for workers and peasants. These syndicates will be encouraged to become beneficial instruments for defending their rights, raising their standards (of living), looking after their needs, increasing their opportunities, creating a spirit of mutual responsibility among them, and representing them in the high labor tribunal.

f) A tribunal specifically concerned with labor will be organized, in which the state and the worker and peasant syndicates will be represented, and which will decide in cases of disputes occurring among the latter (the syndicates), management, and the representatives of the state.

Article 41. The culture of the public:

a) The party will strive to create a general culture for the Arab homeland which will be nationalist, Arab, free, progressive, comprehensive, profound, and humane in its goals, and the party will cause it to prevail among all sections of the people.

b) The state will be responsible for protecting the freedoms of speech, publishing, association, protest, and of the press within the limits of the higher interest of the Arab nation; and the state will be responsible for promoting all instrumentalities which may assure these freedoms.

c) Intellectual work is of the most sacred kind of labor, and it will be incumbent upon the state to protect intellectuals and ulema and to encourage them.

d) There will be freedom—within the limits of Arab nationalist ideology—in the establishment of clubs, the formation of associations, parties, popular organizations, and institutions for travel, and in utilizing the benefits of the cinema, of broadcasting and television, and all the means of modern civilization for diffusing the national culture and improving the lot of the people.

Article 42. Manifestations and distinctions of class resulting in corrupted social conditions will be abolished. To that end the party will struggle in the ranks of the oppressed toiling classes of the public until such manifestation and distinction cease, until their full human dignity is restored to them, and until they will be enabled to live under a just social order without discrimination between one citizen and another except in the adequacy of the intellect and the skill of the hand.

Article 43. Nomadism: Nomadism is a primitive social state which weakens national productivity and renders a large part of the nation a paralyzed limb, hindering its growth and progress.

The party will strive to settle the Bedouin and to grant them lands; and the party will strive to abolish the tribal system and the adaptation of the laws of the state thereto.

The Educational and Instructional Policy of the Party

The educational policy of the party will be aimed at the creation of a new generation of Arabs which will believe in the unity of its nation and the permanence of its mission, which will seize hold of scientific thought free of the fetters of superstition and retrograde authority, which will be filled with the spirit of optimism and mutual responsibility with their fellow citizens in striving for a true, universal, Arab revolution and for human progress.

To this end the party decides that:

Article 44. Every manifestation of intellectual, economic, political, cultural, and artistic life will be stamped with the impress of Arab nationalism to remind the nation of its connection with its glorious history, and to direct it to advance toward a more glorious and exemplary future.

Article 45. Education is the function of the government alone; therefore all private or foreign institutions of learning will be abolished.

Article 46. Education, at all levels, will be free for all citizens, and compulsory in the primary and secondary levels.

Article 47. Higher professional schools will be established along the most modern lines, and instruction therein will be free.

Article 48. The teaching profession and all functions related thereto, except higher education, will be restricted to Arab nationals. . . .

11. Munif al-Razzaz

Munif al-Razzaz was born in Jordan in 1919. He studied at Amman Secondary School and did his university work in Beirut and Cairo. In 1949 he joined the Ba'th Party. During the last ten years he has held various positions of leadership in the party, most recently that of Secretary General. In February, 1966, he was imprisoned in Syria following a military coup by a splinter group within the party. He has written three books: Features of Arab Life *(1953), which won the Arab League prize as the best book on the Arab world;* The Evolution of the Meaning of Nationalism *(1960), which was published in English in 1963; and* Freedom and Its Problems in Underdeveloped Countries *(1965), from which the following selection is taken.*

The argument contained in this selection is an important criticism of the apologists for the one-party and the no-party state. Its defense of the rights of opposition parties has added significance because it was written at the time when the Ba'th Party was in power in Syria. Unlike some critics of the single party, al-Razzaz is a socialist and strongly anti-Western, but he is also deeply committed to freedom of expression and meaningful democracy. His work is typical of the reassessment of the claims of the strong man and the single party which has taken place in recent years in many parts of Asia, the Middle East, and Africa.

PARTIES—A PRECONDITION OF FREEDOM*

There is no doubt that freedom in these [underdeveloped] countries is passing through a severe crisis. . . . The gap between hope

* Excerpts from *al-Hurriyah wa-mushkilatuhā fī al-buldān al-mutakhallifah* (*Freedom and Its Problems in Underdeveloped Countries*) (Beirut, 1965); translated by John Mikhail.

and actual fulfillment is enormous. . . . Hence the masses' general feeling of disappointment and loss wherever you turn. . . . It is in order to disguise this stifling crisis, to deceive the masses, and to counter feelings of loss and disappointment that ruling authorities in these countries, and opposition movements as well, have resorted to employing the word "freedom" in a way which it was not intended to mean and cannot possibly signify. Freedom has been used to refer to systems that have the forms of parliamentarism but lack all other expressions of freedom; reactionary systems in which economic exploitation and political tyranny have been carried to the extreme; systems that have realized a measure of economic emancipation but have repressed all aspects of political freedom; and Communist systems that are no more than one-party dictatorships. In short, the word "freedom" has been used to describe both reactionary rightist and dictatorial leftist regimes. Most of the time the word "freedom" has come to be no more than a slogan disguising one or another form of dictatorship.

Has "freedom" lost its meaning? Has it become merely a propaganda symbol?

Because of the genuine crisis that the underdeveloped countries, including our Arab homeland, are going through, because of this continuous distortion in the use of the word "freedom" by both right and left, I have been induced to attempt to write this book. My aim is twofold: first, to restore to the word its [true] meaning lest it be lost in the labyrinth of assertion and counterassertion; second, to discuss the crisis of freedom in our country and countries with similar problems, out of a belief that discussion of these causes can indicate the way to overcome this crisis. . . .

Perhaps the understanding of freedom was initially dim and superficial, but it began to crystallize as a result of experience during the various phases that these countries passed through, especially after independence. There was first the realization that the democratic freedoms which nationalist governments had established in all these countries did not bring the masses closer to the fulfillment of their hopes for economic and social progress, despite the fact that imperialism, which they had imagined to be the sole obstacle to such progress, had been defeated. Then came the realization that in the absence of democracy and political freedom, economic progress, if achieved, is only achieved at the expense of the citizen's dignity and feeling of individuality, identity, freedom, and worth; his participation in bearing public responsibility; and his right to express his opinion and to determine his destiny.

The very crisis of freedom that these countries are passing through is, therefore, the way to educate the public as to the true meaning of freedom, and to bring it to the mature realization that freedom is indivisible, that it is impossible to realize economic freedom in the shadow of political tyranny, or political freedom in the shadow of economic enslavement. . . .

Disagreement as to the prerequisites of freedom has been greatest on the subject of parties. . . . Western democratic states have considered the existence of several parties as a guarantee of the expression of public opinion and an indispensable basis for political freedom. Communist thought, on the other hand, has considered the multiparty system in capitalist societies as an expression of the multiplicity of classes, and has thus championed the philosophy of the single party representing the single class.

As for the underdeveloped countries, most of them adopted the Western multiparty system at the time of independence. However, political life was dominated by one principal party—the party that personified the struggle for independence. After the collapse of democratic government, these countries went in one of two ways: either one-party rule, or the abolition of party activity and a call for government by the people without parties.

Parties are instruments for the organized expression of political opinion by the citizens. No political life can exist in any country without expressing itself in functioning parties. If party life is absent, then the participation of the people in charting their political destiny is absent.

The claim that parties are class expressions is a result of the rigid class theory of Marx, in which a class replaces man. Starting from the unity of interest, Marx arrives at the unity of opinion. Within any class, however, there is neither a single interest nor a unanimity of opinion. Otherwise, we would not have seen the intense differences among Communist parties themselves in Russia, Yugoslavia, and China. The mere existence of these differences is proof that disagreement is possible not only within a single class but also within a single-class party.

The claim that the people as a whole take the place of parties is further from the truth than the claim that parties are merely expressions of class interests. The people necessarily have greater contradictions and differences among themselves than has a given class. If a given class or its ideological representatives cannot agree, how can the whole people do so? The overwhelming majority of a people or class may come to an agreement about ultimate ends, but beyond that, disagreement is inevitable. Such disagreements cannot find expression except through party life.

Most underdeveloped countries in which democratic systems have collapsed have suffered greatly from anarchy, corruption, and internal conflict among the parties. There is no doubt that most of the parties that prevailed in Asia and Africa soon after independence were capitalist or feudalist parties that represented the interests of the exploiters. Having assumed power they used their positions for exploitation and destruction, thus discrediting party life in general and forcing the people to put an end to these parties when they revolted, as they often did.

However, granting that they can be instruments of anarchy and corruption, still parties are the only way to express a people's vitality, enthusiasm, and energy. We must remember that the struggle which the people undertook before and after independence was carried out by militant parties that have proved party organization to be the only means of organization capable of mobilizing the people, especially its militant elements.

Putting an end to all party life is quite a different matter from putting an end to corrupt parties. To end parties is to end the direct participation of the people in the determination of its destiny; it is to destroy the people's spirit of struggle which finds its expression in party organization, replacing it with a feeling of weariness, indifference, and irresponsibility among the citizenry. If in the West parties are an instrument for the expression of opinion, in the struggling underdeveloped countries they are something else. They are the way in which the people participate in the struggle.

The party has a function in awakening the people, associating them with responsibility, involving them in their future and in the politics of their country—a function that cannot be carried out by the state regardless of the means and organizations at its disposal. Moreover, a party cannot be imposed on a people from above. For a party is a conscious, voluntary, popular organization, and joining the party is an act that demands that the citizen be prepared to bear the responsibility of struggle, participation, and awakening.

A one-party system by its nature cannot be democratic, especially if the party itself is not democratic in its organization. A one-party state means domination by an organization in the name of the people. As for government without parties, it means the abolition of popular political life for the citizens and the replacement of the people by the state.

Many revolutions in the countries of Asia and Africa have found themselves faced with a choice between going back to the corrupt party life that prevailed during the period of reactionary rule, and abolishing political parties. They were forced to make the second choice.

However, there is a great difference between being forced to abolish political parties because they are corrupt, conspiratorial, and exploitative and considering the abolition of parties as an ideological starting point and a new basis for government.

Understanding the true meaning of party life and its fundamental importance is one of the conditions for passing from this crisis of freedom to true freedom. When a government is forced to abolish party activity or to be satisfied with one party, one must begin by introducing democratic procedures in the party itself where it exists and then permit the establishment of liberal democratic parties provided that their goals are not incompatible with the ultimate aims of the backward countries.

The claim that the party is the people, or that the government is the people, is a feeble attempt to disguise the dictatorial nature of the government. If over a short period of time such a claim is true, the longer run inevitably exposes this claim [as false]. . . .

The realization of freedom is a human as well as a national problem. Freedom cannot be fully realized in one country while it breaks down in another, for the threat to freedom in any country is a threat to freedom throughout the world. Similarly, the realization of freedom in any country is an example and a guide for the realization of freedom in other countries. For this reason the promotion of freedom is a service to the world. The promotion of freedom anywhere is a part of the promotion of freedom in one's own country. It is not enough that one country rid itself of imperialism and tyranny, but it must help to fight imperialism and tyranny wherever they may be. . . .

The realization of freedom is not an easy task. It will not be realized by issuing laws. It will not be realized over a short period of time. It will be realized only through continuous work and a permanent struggle. The underdeveloped countries themselves are faced with a reality that is full of contradictions. But they are also faced with a goal that is inextricably linked to their destiny. Setting out to realize freedom may call for lowering the ideal goal to the level of stubborn reality at which point improvement can commence. But it must also call for raising the level of reality to approach the ideal goal. Continuous interaction between the present reality and its demands, and the ideal goal and its requirements, given faith and will, is the guarantee for moving toward progress and freedom.

12. Habib Bourguiba

Habib Bourguiba was born in 1903, in a small fishing village in Tunisia. His father had been an officer in the army of the Bey of Tunis, but had resigned in protest against the establishment of the French protectorate. Bourguiba was educated at French schools in Tunis and at the Faculty of Law in Paris. On his return to Tunis, in 1928, he became active in the nationalist movement. In 1934, Bourguiba organized the Neo-Destour Party, which stood for complete independence of Tunisia. From 1934 until 1952, he was repeatedly imprisoned by the French for nationalist activities, but when Tunisia received internal autonomy in 1956, he became Prime Minister. When full independence was accorded a year later, he became President.

A modernizing Moslem, Bourguiba has campaigned—with only limited success—to persuade the Tunisians to abandon the traditional fast of Ramadan as not suited to a country trying to develop as rapidly as possible. Sometimes regarded as pro-Western, Bourguiba describes his policy as one of nonalignment and gradualism (Bourguibism). These policies are defended in the following selections from his speeches.

THE FAST OF RAMADAN*

. . .The cause of these obstacles to our progress and of the paralysis of our minds is not the Moslem religion. As I know it, as I have studied it and learned it—as it was lived and practiced by the

---

* From a speech delivered by Bourguiba on February 6, 1961; translated and published by the Tunisian Secretariat of State for Information.

earliest members and by the Prophet himself, his companions, contemporaries, and successors—the Moslem religion is not a doctrine of intellectual asphyxia.

The first leaders of Islam were infinitely bolder and infinitely freer in the application of the principles of their religion, in their creativeness and adaptation to circumstances than our Ulema of the period of decadence. The Prophet's life and history are witness of this. They did not hesitate to suspend the effects of a Koranic edict. The caliph Omar suspended the application of certain penalties because of special circumstances. The Prophet himself had done likewise before him.

Why should such boldness be forbidden today? Why should we always be bound by what so and so said or someone else forbade?

I do not want you to agree with me blindly. I shall be satisfied if the question is studied, thought about, and freely discussed. What surprises and pains me at the same time is to hear that problems of this sort are outside the field of reason. Here we see the poverty of the chained mind. "How can we discuss this problem, since it has never been discussed before?" This is the supreme argument. I cannot accept it. We must discuss it, with complete freedom. Allah has given us brains. Let us use them to discuss and understand his commands. After all, we allow ourselves to discuss his existence.

Let us see what all the talk is about. It is said that I want to abolish Ramadan and want to force civil servants, among others, not to fast. There has never been any question of this. Need I say that the Ramadan fast is perfectly valid. The institution of fasting is to be found in other religions. Its beneficial effects are well known: self-mastery, improvement perhaps of physical condition, treatment of certain illness. All this is reasonable, and we subscribe to it.

But, as we said, we are living today in special circumstances. Neither the Prophet nor the first Moslems would ever have imagined that this nation, which Allah said was the best ever to have existed among men, should be far behind the other nations and reduced to its present fate. You need only look around you. . . .

Thus, as soon as we took power, we considered it of the utmost importance to set resolutely to work. Work and still more work: productive, rational, and methodically organized work, undertaken to create new wealth and cause an upheaval comparable to what the Arabs achieved in passing from the pre-Islamic to the Islamic era.

I am convinced that the greatest contribution made by Islam is in the liberation of the human mind. The first Moslem Arabs owe their extraordinary advance to this liberation. In reading the *Koran* and the *Life of the Prophet,* we are struck by the boldness and the exceptional power of the thought expressed.

It is only natural that, in talking to the mass of believers, Islam should have made attractive promises and terrible threats. Paradise and hell were both described in minute detail. Of course, for the Arabs of that time, paradise represented every imaginable form of beauty: gently murmuring springs, trees, and gardens watered by rivers. The inhabitants of a harsh, bare country could imagine no greater delight than water and a green landscape. To this picture, a few houris were added, as well as rivers flowing with honey and melted butter—in fact, all that was needed for perfect happiness.

On the other side, however, there were the flames and burning coals of hell. One might imagine that, once the sinner was burned to ashes, his tortures would be ended. Far from it! His flesh would be reconstituted and his sufferings start all over again an infinite number of times.

In this way, primitive people were induced to behave well, so as to avoid hell and make themselves worthy of paradise.

However, when a higher outlook came into being—as during the golden age of Moslem civilization—the great doctrinal masters, such as Ghazali and others, taught that this belief is at a lower level than that of the faith which expects neither heavenly nor earthly reward for good works, but seeks only peace of conscience. The accomplishment of duty, the practice of charity, the forgiveness of injuries, all these Moslem virtues are gifts of self designed to bring the believer close to Allah.

At the same time, we should note that by working solely to deserve paradise and avoid hell, scrupulously carrying out divine teachings, man works for his happiness here on earth. This is of the utmost importance. After all, religion is made for men and to keep man from being a "wolf to man." There was no state organization at that time, but religion held out the prospect of reward or punishment so that men would do good and refrain from evil. By observing the commandments, abstaining from theft, drink, etc., by practicing charity and doing good around them, men were contributing to social harmony. When the Last Judgment sounded, they would have won happiness in heaven as well as here on earth.

As for those who are skeptical about the afterlife, they would have accomplished their duty; they would have produced and triumphed; their consciences would be at peace.

Then, spiritual decay set in. There was a tendency to disregard essential truths and abandon the substance while clinging to the form. And the Moslem world entered on a period of decadence.

As head of the state, responsible for the progress of the nation in the world, in the same way the Prophet was responsible for the Moslems of his day, I must think of every possible way of strengthening and building up the nation, making it creative and energetic. I must impress on you the need for a new approach to the problem of achieving national renewal. The means we use must be treated as sacred and as categorical obligations, like religious commands. Thus, work and behavior will no longer be dictated by the fear of the police or of the law, but will be ordered with the conviction that they come under the authority of religion, society, and individual conscience. Any disharmony between conscience, reason, and religious teaching would lead to complete disorganization.

I have developed these ideas as an introduction to the remarks I want to make today about Ramadan. This question has led to heated discussion and is being exploited in bad faith by a certain group. The seeds of doubt and hesitation are being sown in the minds of the unlearned, so that they will become agents of destruction and civil war.

Today, I shall repeat what I have already said about the fast of Ramadan. This practice was imposed by Islam. It is still so imposed today, as it will be till the end of time. However, Allah has allowed certain dispensations, which are laid down in the *Koran*. In certain circumstances, a man is not obliged to observe the fast. These dispensations are well known and have been thoroughly studied. In the Tunisian schools, they are not mentioned in certain teachings, but they are nonetheless authentic and valid. Originally, dispensations were only allowed in cases of sickness or when traveling. Then the Jihad (or holy war) was included. Later on, with the agreement of the Ulema, the risk of illness was added, by extension of principle.

If we study the question thoroughly and analyze the reasons given for the dispensations, we see that they have a common purpose—that of relieving Moslems of the obligation to fast if the effort involved is excessively arduous. For example, traveling was included in the dispensations because it was originally very tiring.

Under these circumstances, a traveler was not bound to observe the fast. He was excused because Allah did not want him to suffer excessively. If there were no dispensation, there would be a serious risk that Moslems would abstain from traveling during the month of Ramadan. This would reduce their means, and force idleness and unemployment upon them. But, far from encouraging laziness, religion gives dispensation from fasting in cases where it would stand in the way of traveling, that is to say, of work and effort.

Another case for dispensation is sickness. Why? Because fasting is likely to aggravate an illness, since the physical condition of a sick person is such that it is dangerous to deprive him of food. In fact, instead of fasting, he needs to eat properly.

If we meditate over these Koranic provisions and examine them closely, we realize how much trouble Islam has taken to spare men unnecessary causes of fatigue and impediments to their activity. You all know the origin of the dispensation allowed for the Jihad. The day before the capture of Mecca, Mohammed ordered the faithful to break their fast, so that they would be in the best physical condition to meet the enemy.

From a careful study of the purposes of the fast, the circumstances which surround this practice, the dispensations allowed, and the reasons for them, we find there is no room for hesitation. There are good grounds today for not observing the fast of Ramadan.

The *Koran* prescribes fasting, so as to accustom men to controlling their senses and appetites. But if fasting involves a risk, is harmful or impairs a man's physical condition, health, or working capacity, or lowers his potentialities or those of the Moslem community, he is dispensed from fasting.

We must keep a sense of proportion. Thus, traveling is one of the reasons for dispensation. But traveling is no longer as tiring today as it used to be. Today, we travel by air, ensconced in a comfortable seat. Modern travel bears no comparison with journeys across the desert by camel. All the same, some people argue that the dispensation allowed to travelers still holds good. Personally, I think that traveling today no longer gives dispensation from fasting. These same people maintain that no dispensation can be allowed to workers even when they toil to the point of fainting. Why should an allowance be made for a traveler surrounded by the most up-to-date comfort, and refused to an underfed worker with a weak constitution? The latter, it is argued, may only break his fast after fainting for the second time. Is this logical?

I invite the Tunisian people, its Ulema, and sheiks to study the whole problem from the point of view of the purpose of the fast and the reasons for dispensation. Everyone must acquaint himself with the problem of how to interpret divine law properly. Allah gave man his reasoning faculty so that he would be able to distinguish good from evil.

At a time when we are fighting against poverty and drawing up programs and plans to remedy our underdevelopment, when we contemplate calling to account those who do not produce enough, and restricting individual freedom, when the recovery of the Moslem nation depends on strenuous work—I urge you to make use of a dispensation which is based on a sound conception of religious law.

BOURGUIBISM*

The policy which has been described as Bourguibism is not a matter of accepting charity from the colonizing country and then begging for more. It is more like a war for positions, which consists of directing the weight of the attack against strategic points. This is the meaning of our policy of stages, each of which should facilitate accession to the next, until we achieve our final goal of independence, without which there can be no dignity.

This has been our concern from the very beginning. Since 1930, I have accepted many things: cosovereignty; participation in a ministry—most of whose members were tools of the colonialists—which we eventually left in order to take up armed resistance; internal autonomy, from which we achieved incomplete independence, which, in turn, enabled us to obtain partial evacuation. We have achieved all this after only seven years, starting with a regime of direct French administration, the like of which neither Syria, Lebanon, nor any other Middle East country has known. For although these countries have experienced French colonization, it had nothing in common with the regime installed in Tunisia. The form they knew did indeed make use of ruse, perfidy, and division in order to maintain its position, but the regime knew it was provisional because it was authorized by mandate. Here things were

* From a speech delivered by Bourguiba on October 12, 1961; translated and published by the Tunisian Secretariat of State for Information.

quite different. We experienced colonization by settlement. This came to an end barely seven years ago. All of you here and most of those listening to me remember this period. The protectorate which Tunisia underwent was harsher than was imposed on any other Arab country. In Egypt, for instance, the English protectorate came to an end in 1922, yet total evacuation was not obtained until 1957—over thirty years, in stages. Our stages barely lasted seven years, while our situation was much worse to start with.

We do not say this in order to boast of our successes, but only to give a comparable example, illustrating Bourguibism—which has sometimes been badly understood, to the extent of likening it to a policy of collusion or complicity with colonialism. It is nevertheless the policy of our means, the one which follows from our geographical position, our history, and the form of colonization imposed on us. . . .

My method is to advance by steps, thinking out every step as I go. Speed does not mean hasty, unthought-out actions. In the past, when I was a school child and had quarrels with my school-fellows, I did not rush to fight the enemy, but on the contrary I needed a certain amount of time to ponder and watch the situation evolve. It is too serious a matter for me to allow myself to throw the whole nation in with one bloc or another, with the excuse of French aggression.* In spite of the aggression we have suffered, we must not brutally change our policies. Naturally we must foresee matters, temper our policies, and allow them to evolve according to both circumstances and the means at our disposal.

We ourselves were fed on and formed by French culture. Through it, we found the principles of humanity, liberty, and dignity. We have always harbored feelings of affection for French culture and the French people and nation. We were even searching for explanations for the French attitude by saying that it is not possible for the French people to commit acts of aggression such as this. We distinguished between the French people and the supporters of colonialism. In spite of all this, the French used cultural relations as an object for low bargaining. We must refuse all bargaining. This refusal could lead to the reshaping of our programs. We may even have to envisage the use of a language other than French, and thus look toward other civilizations, countries, and

* Bourguiba is referring here to the Bizerte crisis.—ED.

friends. The problem is still of great importance and must be seriously examined and thought out.

Our decisions will be taken calmly by stages, in the light of our interests and the interests of the Tunisian state, and according to what suits our best interests. . . .

THE AGRICULTURAL ASPECT OF THE ECONOMIC BATTLE *

We are not inspired by any considerations of demagogy in the field of agrarian reform, a tempting formula covering a very simple operation: parceling out lands and distributing them. A regime which carries out such measures aims at gaining the support of the masses by satisfying those who are worst off. It is not greatly concerned with the effect of the reform on the curve of production. In fact, no thought is given to this. Agrarian reforms of this sort are generally accompanied by a vast propaganda campaign in which there is talk of social justice, of poor people to whom rights are restored, and of rich men despoiled—to the delirious applause of the populace.

What is important to me is the level of production. Admittedly, in some special cases, individual estates may be as much as 15,000 to 25,000 acres—which one man cannot farm properly. The state may intervene to help him and improve working conditions. If it decides to confiscate part of the estate, this is not done out of a desire for revenge. To create a hate psychosis like this would be contrary to the general interest. Poor and rich, we are one family. The state's role is to maintain the nation's unity. However, when a landowner has an agricultural estate which is too large for him to manage properly—or in conditions corresponding to the community's interest—it is the state's duty to dispossess him in whole or in part. The state performs its duty in the interest of all, whether poor or rich. It is concerned solely with the community's interest. An owner who has part of his lands confiscated must not feel he is being despoiled. In any case, the increase in production which would result from confiscation would help to raise the general level of the community. As a member of this community, a

* From a speech delivered by Bourguiba on October 27, 1961; translated and published by the Tunisian Secretariat of State for Information.

dispossessed owner will have his share of the general income. The sense of fraternity and association uniting the nation will be strengthened thereby. Sacrifices are accepted all the more readily if they are seen to be in the general interest. We do nothing with the intention of restricting the freedom of individuals. We do not apply any pressure. We do not impair individual freedom or the right of ownership, except in the general interest.

This is the path we have chosen in order to achieve socialism. Our method is based on respect for the individual, not on class hatred or the dictatorship of the poor over the rich. Our sole guide is the interest of the country, in which we are united for better or worse.

How can we compare the sacrifice of a few interests, a few minor rights, a few relatively unimportant freedoms, to the deportation, imprisonment, and death to which Tunisians were exposed in the past, and to which they are still prepared to expose themselves anew should the country be threatened once again?

If the state, which is in a position to weigh the situation, decides on measures implying a restriction of a given freedom, the reconversion of a given crop, the redivision of certain agricultural lands, it is because it has been led to do so for imperative reasons of general interest.

In carrying out this gigantic task, using the method of Neo-Destourian socialism,* we are at the same time respecting the dignity of the individual. The latter must be convinced that the sacrifice he accepts, by agreeing to the restriction of some of his freedoms, is in his country's interest. He is not so different from a conscript who relinquishes his individual freedom when he is called up. He makes this sacrifice willingly.

Freely accepted discipline is the motive power of progress. We must realize this and fully familiarize ourselves with the idea that the individual's interest lies in the progress and well-being of the community.

---

* Bourguiba only began to speak favorably of socialism in 1961. In October, 1964, his commitment to the doctrine became formalized when he changed the name of his party from the Neo-Destour to the Destourian Socialist Party.—ED.

THE NEED FOR BIRTH CONTROL*

. . . . The disequilibrium between births and available resources is still considerable and we must look for a solution to the problem of the birthrate in our country.

I should like you to realize how serious this problem is. In twenty years' time we shall number 6 million, perhaps more. Think of the new wealth we shall have to create in order to feed all these mouths. Think of the number of classes that will be needed in order to provide education for all children of school age. This is the underlying reason for planning, which many people still do not understand. However, every Tunisian must come to realize how necessary and urgent it is. We cannot help but feel some apprehension at the human tide rising implacably at a speed much greater than the rate of increase of subsistence.

Here arises the problem of birth control which preoccupies many countries in Latin America, Asia, and Africa. This is an endless task. The babies grow more rapidly than our food resources. What is the use of increasing our agricultural production and our mineral wealth, what is the use of raising our national income in order to bring about a fair distribution of wealth, if the population is to go on rising in a frenzied, uncontrolled manner? We should have achieved nothing, for we run the risk of dropping, in spite of all our efforts, to a general level lower than our point of departure.

We must find a solution to this vital problem. First of all, on the psychological level we must free ourselves from the archaic ideas that men and women in Tunisia hold on the subject of procreation. It is readily believed that the question is beyond us and is a matter solely of the divine will. We must stop abdicating our own will. By the use of reason, humanity has managed to master nature and progressively conquer disease, has created tools and changed the face of the world, and is able to govern itself and control the rate of procreation.

We must also discard the popular belief that Allah has endowed each newborn baby with its share of wealth, its subsistence. This is a false and dangerous opinion, and can only unduly aggravate the state's burdens.

* From a speech delivered by Bourguiba on December 26, 1962; translated and published by the Tunisian Secretariat of State for Information.

But I should like to clarify my thought further. What we want is not to do away with or hinder procreation, but only to discipline it, so that men and women should be able to procreate by an act of their will, in the light of reason. If a household can support seven, eight, or ten children, so much the better. But if it does not have the means to support more than two, we should help it to understand that it is not in its interest to exceed this limit and that it can effectively keep within it. . . .

We therefore do not aim to limit procreation systematically, but rather to improve the quality of our human potential. In any given society, what is important is not so much the number as the quality of the men. And quality is determined both by physical and moral health and by the standard of living. . . .

13. Bechir Ben Yahmed

Bechir Ben Yahmed is the general manager of Jeune Afrique, a journal of news and opinion published in Tunis and Paris and distributed in many parts of French-speaking Africa. Ben Yahmed was born in Djerba, Tunisia. The Minister of Information in the first Bourguiba government, he resigned after a year and has subsequently devoted himself to business and journalism. Jeune Afrique, like its predecessor, Afrique Action, has been increasingly critical of the concentration of power in the hands of Bourguiba. In 1963 and 1964, it devoted several issues to a general debate on the advantages and disadvantages of the African single-party system. The debate was concluded with the article translated below giving Ben Yahmed's own views in favor of a two-party system— a position not widely shared by African ideologists today.

FOR OR AGAINST
THE SINGLE PARTY?*

One of the merits of the debate begun in these columns under the above title has been to reveal or confirm several truths.

1. If the African countries live under governments which are dominated by a single party with all power, it is because this corresponds to a social and economic situation which demanded this solution at the time of independence. The colonizer constantly tried to break down the unity of our national movements. When we achieved independence, we thirsted for unity. We were haunted by the nightmare of our old divisions and also, I should note, by the spectacle of impotence and ridicule provided by the multiparty system of the French Fourth Republic between 1950 and 1958. When we became masters of our destinies, we also regarded independence as only a means to allow us to build a modern state and undertake the real battle for development. For this a strong, stable government, endowed with special powers, was necessary. We had confidence in those governments; we accepted the sacrifice of the liberties we had just acquired all the more readily because we were entrusting our fate to those who had liberated us from colonialism.

2. There is the single party which is an instrument of progress (at least in its early years) and the single party which, from the time of its creation, is a mask for immobilism and sterile dictatorship, an instrument of the domination of a single social group over the rest of the nation.

The single party means an unusual concentration of power in the hands of one man, aided and influenced by a group. What that man and group who monopolize power and the means of expression will do depends almost entirely upon their ideology, their force of character, and their capacity to resist the easy solution. Since they have force at their disposal, they have little need for persuasion. What they think is good for the country, they do. What in the long run is fatal is that even in their own consciences

* From "Pour ou contre le parti unique," *Jeune Afrique* (Tunis and Paris), No. 166 (January 13–19, 1964), p. 5. Translated by the editor, by permission.

they identify what is good for them with what is good for the country. In the party and in the nation they become an interest group instead of a government.

The result is that *in the optimal situation* the single party and personal power can only be helpful to a country during a transition period—that of the construction of the state, the consolidation of national unity, and the establishment of new economic structures. After that phase, the single party becomes unbearable, a factor making for sterility of thought, social immobility, and even political disorder.

3. Once the single party is established in power, it is the last to perceive the need for a change or for its own disappearance. It is practically incapable of democratizing itself or the country. It is accustomed to silencing the opposition and is persuaded that it represents the general interest; it therefore does not understand the need for concessions and is afraid to initiate them.

In these conditions what was the motor becomes the brake. The state just created is corrupted. The traditions which have hardly been established begin to decay. Confidence among companions in the struggle breaks down. The prisons fill up; the youth are alienated and revolt. The future becomes uncertain.

The single party and the leader who incarnates the state and the nation thus seem to be a sort of historical necessity for underdeveloped countries as they become independent. Directed by men who have sprung from the people and have been formed in battle, the party, when it establishes national goals, can be an incomparable instrument of progress for several years. After that, unable to see that its mission is ended, it becomes an obstacle to progress.

To go from the phase of the single party to that of democracy is in a way to go from underdevelopment to development, from the tribal phase to that of the nation, from the agricultural state to the industrial state. Just as one cannot modernize and industrialize a country without social dislocation, so one cannot democratize it without disagreement and adjustment.

Democracy is the result of education, and fortunately education is spreading through Africa like wildfire. Education produces citizenship and national horizons. Rather than plotting to overthrow a man or a group so as to replace them—fatally—with another man and another group, let us strive, we the youth, for a better and more widespread education of those below us. Just as our elders have struggled and suffered for independence, let us struggle and suffer, if necessary, for democracy.

When we say the word democracy, some of our elders . . . throw in our faces the formalism of Western democracy, the multi-party system of the French Fourth Republic, and stories about old man Queuille.*

Let us give a reasonable reply to that facile response—a form of government in which democracy does not prevent stability and efficiency in the state. We do not need to invent this form. It exists and has been tested by experience. It is the only one which has succeeded historically—that of a majority party in government and an opposition *united in a single organization* which checks the government and is prepared to take its place.

They will say that we are not sufficiently developed to adopt such a form of government. But when will we be?

14. Frantz Fanon

Frantz Fanon was born in Martinique in 1925. He studied medicine and psychiatry in France and practiced in Blida, Algeria, where he treated both colonizers and natives. He joined the National Liberation Front at the time of its founding, and later served as Ambassador to Ghana for the Algerian Provisional Government. He died of leukemia in 1961, at the age of thirty-six.

Fanon was known among leaders and intellectuals of the French-speaking world for his moving books on the Algerian Revolution and the anticolonial movement. His best-known work, translated into English as The Wretched of the Earth *(a reference to the second line of the "International"), endows the violence of the revolution with a mystical liberating quality. Writing from a radical nationalist point of view, Fanon was critical of the economic arrangements which many African governments have made with the former colonial powers, interpreting them as a "sell-out" to*

*Henri Queuille, twice Premier under the Fourth Republic. He was known for his ability to maintain himself in power by inaction.—ED.

capitalism and neocolonialism by the national bourgeoisie. His criticisms of the regime of the single party and the demagogy of the nationalist leader are similar in content to the more Western-oriented comments of Bechir Ben Yahmed.

This selection, showing the influence of the Algerian War but in no way Islamic in content, may be seen as an introduction to the African selections which follow, underscoring Algeria's dual orientation toward the Arab world and Africa. (Fanon's discussion of the revolutionary role of the Lumpenproletariat *of unemployed slum dwellers has also been quoted by the more radical black leaders in the United States, such as Eldridge Cleaver of the Black Panthers.)*

THE WRETCHED OF THE EARTH*

. . . The originality of the colonial context is that economic reality, inequality, and the immense difference of ways of life never come to mask the human realities. When you examine at close quarters the colonial context, it is evident that what parcels out the world is to begin with the fact of belonging to or not belonging to a given race, a given species. In the colonies the economic substructure is also a superstructure. The cause is the consequence; you are rich because you are white, you are white because you are rich. This is why Marxist analysis should always be slightly stretched every time we have to do with the colonial problem.

Everything up to and including the very nature of precapitalist society, so well explained by Marx, must here be thought out again. The serf is in essence different from the knight, but a reference to divine right is necessary to legitimize this statutory difference. In the colonies, the foreigner coming from another country imposed his rule by means of guns and machines. In defiance of his successful transplantation, in spite of his appropriation, the settler still remains a foreigner. It is neither the act of owning factories, nor estates, nor a bank balance which distinguishes the gov-

* Excerpts from *The Wretched of the Earth* (New York: Grove Press; London: McGibbon and Kee, 1965). Translated by Constance Farrington from *Les Damnés de la Terre*. Reprinted by permission of Grove Press, Inc. and McGibbon and Kee Ltd. Copyright 1963 by Présence Africaine.

erning classes. The governing race is first and foremost those who
come from elsewhere, those who are unlike the original inhabitants, "the others."

The violence which has ruled over the ordering of the colonial
world, which has ceaselessly drummed the rhythm for the destruction of native social forms and broken up without reserve the systems of reference of the economy, the customs of dress and external
life, that same violence will be claimed and taken over by the
native at the moment when, deciding to embody history in his
own person, he surges into the forbidden quarters. To wreck the
colonial world is henceforward a mental picture of action which is
very clear, very easy to understand, and which may be assumed by
each one of the individuals which constitute the colonized people.
To break up the colonial world does not mean that after the frontiers have been abolished lines of communication will be set up
between the two zones. The destruction of the colonial world is
no more and no less than the abolition of one zone, its burial in
the depths of the earth, or its expulsion from the country. . . .

The Revolutionary Role of the Peasants

What are the forces which in the colonial period open up new
outlets and engender new aims for the violence of colonized
peoples? In the first place there are the political parties and the
intellectual or commercial elites. Now, the characteristic feature
of certain political structures is that they proclaim abstract principles but refrain from issuing definite commands. The entire action of these nationalist political parties during the colonial period
is action of the electoral type: a string of philosophico-political
dissertations on the themes of the rights of peoples to self-determination, the rights of man to freedom from hunger and human
dignity, and the unceasing affirmation of the principle: "One man,
one vote." The national political parties never lay stress upon the
necessity of a trial of armed strength, for the good reason that their
objective is not the radical overthrowing of the system. Pacifists
and legalists, they are in fact partisans of order, the new order—
but to the colonialist bourgeoisie they put bluntly enough the demand which to them is the main one: "Give us more power." On
the specific question of violence, the elite are ambiguous. They
are violent in their words and reformist in their attitudes. When
the nationalist political leaders *say* something, they make quite
clear that they do not really *think* it.

This characteristic on the part of the nationalist political parties should be interpreted in the light both of the make-up of their leaders and the nature of their followings. The rank-and-file of a nationalist party is urban. The workers, primary schoolteachers, artisans and small shopkeepers who have begun to profit—at a discount, to be sure—from the colonial setup, have special interests at heart. What this sort of following demands is the betterment of their particular lot: increased salaries, for example. The dialogue between these political parties and colonialism is never broken off. Improvements are discussed, such as full electoral representation, the liberty of the press, and liberty of association. Reforms are debated. Thus it need not astonish anyone to notice that a large number of natives are militant members of the branches of political parties which stem from the mother country. These natives fight under an abstract watchword, "Government by the workers," and they forget that in their country it should be *nationalist* watchwords which are first in the field. The native intellectual has clothed his aggressiveness in his barely veiled desire to assimilate himself to the colonial world. He has used his aggressiveness to serve his own individual interests.

Thus there is very easily brought into being a kind of class of enfranchised slaves, or slaves who are individually free. What the intellectual demands is the right to multiply the emancipated, and the opportunity to organize a genuine class of emancipated citizens. On the other hand, the mass of the people have no intention of standing by and watching individuals increase their chances of success. What they demand is not the settler's position of status, but the settler's place. The immense majority of natives want the settler's farm. For them, there is no question of entering into competition with the settler. They want to take his place.

The peasantry is systematically disregarded for the most part by the propaganda put out by the nationalist parties. And it is clear that in the colonial countries the peasants alone are revolutionary, for they have nothing to lose and everything to gain. The starving peasant, outside of the class system, is the first among the exploited to discover that only violence pays. For him there is no compromise, no possible coming to terms; colonization and decolonization are simply a question of relative strength. The exploited man sees that his liberation implies the use of all means, and that of force first and foremost. When in 1956, after the capitulation of M. Guy Mollet to the settlers in Algeria, the National Liberation Front, in a famous leaflet, stated that colonialism only loosens its hold when the knife is at its throat, no Algerian really found these terms too violent. The leaflet only expressed what every Algerian felt at heart: colonialism is not a thinking machine, nor a body endowed with reasoning faculties. It is violence in its natural state, and it will only yield when confronted with greater violence.

At the decisive moment, the colonialist bourgeoisie, which up till then has remained inactive, comes into the field. It introduces that new idea which is in proper parlance a creation of the colonial situation: nonviolence. In its simplest form this nonviolence signifies to the intellectual and economic elite of the colonized country that the bourgeoisie has the same interests as they and that it is therefore urgent and indispensable to come to terms for the public good. Nonviolence is an attempt to settle the colonial problem around a green baize table, before any regrettable act has been performed or irreparable gesture made, before any blood has been shed. But if the masses, without waiting for the chairs to be arranged around the baize table, listen to their own voice and begin committing outrages and setting fire to buildings, the elites and the nationalist bourgeois parties will be seen rushing to the colonialists to exclaim "This is very serious! We do not know how it will end; we must find a solution—some sort of compromise."

This idea of compromise is very important in the phenomenon of decolonization, for it is very far from being a simple one. Compromise involves the colonial system and the young nationalist bourgeoisie at one and the same time. The partisans of the colonial system discover that the masses may destroy everything. Blown-up bridges, ravaged farms, repressions, and fighting harshly disrupt the economy. Compromise is equally attractive to the nationalist bourgeoisie, who, since they are not clearly aware of the possible consequences of the rising storm, are genuinely afraid of being swept away by this huge hurricane and never stop saying to the settlers: "We are still capable of stopping the slaughter; the masses still have confidence in us; act quickly if you do not want to put everything in jeopardy." One step more, and the leader of the nationalist party keeps his distance with regard to that violence. He loudly proclaims that he has nothing to do with these Mau Mau, these terrorists, these throat-slitters. At best, he shuts himself off in a no man's land between the terrorists and the settlers and willingly offers his services as go-between; that is to say, that as the settlers cannot discuss terms with these Mau Mau, he himself will be quite willing to begin negotiations. Thus it is that the rear guard of the national struggle, that very party of people who have never ceased to be on the other side in the fight, find themselves somersaulted into the van of negotiations and compromise—precisely because that party has taken very good care never to break contact with colonialism. . . .

. . . The militant nationalist who decides to throw in his lot with the country people instead of playing at hide-and-seek with the police in urban centers will lose nothing. The peasant's cloak will wrap him around with a gentleness and firmness that he never suspected. These men, who are in fact exiled to the backwoods, who are cut off from the urban background against which they had defined their ideas of the nation and of the political fight, these men have in fact become "Maquisards." Since they are obliged to move about the whole time in order to escape from the police, often at night so as not to attract attention, they will have good reason to wander through their country and to get to know it. The cafés are forgotten; so are the arguments about the next elections or the spitefulness of some policeman or other. Their ears hear the true voice of the country, and their eyes take in the great and infinite poverty of their people. They realize the precious time that has been wasted in useless commentaries upon the colonial regime. They finally come to understand that the changeover will not be a reform, nor a bettering of things. They come to understand, with a sort of bewilderment that will from henceforth never quite leave them, that political action in the towns will always be powerless to modify or overthrow the colonial regime.

These men get used to talking to the peasants. They discover that the mass of the country people have never ceased to think of the problem of their liberation except in terms of violence, in terms of taking back the land from the foreigners, in terms of national struggle and of armed insurrection. It is all very simple. These men discover a coherent people who go on living, as it were, statically, but who keep their moral values and their devotion to the nation intact. They discover a people that is generous, ready to sacrifice themselves completely, an impatient people with a stony pride. It is understandable that the meeting between these militants with the police on their track and these mettlesome masses of people, who are rebels by instinct, can produce an explosive mixture of unusual potentiality. The men coming from the towns learn their lessons in the hard school of the people; and at the same time these men open classes for the people in military and political education. The people furbish up their weapons; but in fact the classes do not last long, for the masses come to know once again the strength of their own muscles, and push the leaders on to prompt action. The armed struggle has begun. . . .

Moreover, the first overtures which the men of the Maquis make toward their former friends—precisely those whom they consider to be the most toward the left—will confirm their fears and will take away even the wish to see their old companions again. In fact the rebellion, which began in the country districts, will filter into the towns through that fraction of the peasant population which is blocked on the outer fringe of the urban centers, that fraction which has not yet succeeded in finding a bone to gnaw in the colonial system. The men whom the growing population of the country districts and colonial expropriation have brought to desert their family holdings circle tirelessly around the different towns, hoping that one day or another they will be allowed inside. It is within this mass of humanity, this people of the shanty towns, at the core of the *lumpenproletariat* that the rebellion will find its urban spearhead. For the *lumpenproletariat*, that horde of starving men, uprooted from their tribe and from their clan, constitutes one of the most spontaneous and the most radically revolutionary forces of a colonized people. . . .

So long as the uncertainty of colonialism continues, the national cause goes on progressing, and becomes the cause of each and all. The plans for liberation are sketched out; already they include the whole country. During this period spontaneity is king, and initiative is localized. On every hill a government in miniature is formed and takes over power. Everywhere—in the valleys and in the forests, in the jungle and in the villages—we find a national authority. Each man or woman brings the nation to life by his or her action, and is pledged to ensure its triumph in their locality. We are dealing with a strategy of immediacy which is both radical and totalitarian: the aim and the program of each locally constituted group is local liberation. If the nation is everywhere, then she is here. One step further, and only here is she to be found. Tactics are mistaken for strategy. The art of politics is simply transformed into the art of war; the political militant is the rebel. To fight the war and to take part in politics: the two things become one and the same. . . .

The National Bourgeoisie

The national middle class which takes over power at the end of the colonial regime is an underdeveloped middle class. It has practically no economic power, and in any case it is in no way commensurate with the bourgeoisie of the mother country which it hopes to replace. In its willful narcissism, the national middle class is easily convinced that it can advantageously replace the middle class of the mother country. But that same independence which literally drives it into a corner will give rise within its ranks to catastrophic reactions, and will oblige it to send out frenzied appeals for help to the former mother country. The university and merchant classes, which make up the most enlightened section of the new state, are in fact characterized by the smallness of their number and their being concentrated in the capital, and the type of activities in which they are engaged: business, agriculture, and the liberal professions. Neither financiers nor industrial magnates are to be found within this national middle class. The national bourgeoisie of underdeveloped countries is not engaged in production, nor in invention, nor building, nor labor; it is completely canalized into activities of the intermediary type. Its innermost vocation seems to be to keep in the running and to be part of the racket. The psychology of the national bourgeoisie is that of the businessman, not that of a captain of industry; and it is only too true that the greed of the settlers and the system of embargoes set up by colonialism has hardly left them any other choice.

Under the colonial system, a middle class which accumulates capital is an impossible phenomenon. Now, precisely, it would seem that the historical vocation of an authentic national middle class in an underdeveloped country is to repudiate its own nature insofar as it is bourgeois, that is to say, insofar as it is the tool of capitalism, and to make itself the willing slave of that revolutionary capital which is the people.

In an underdeveloped country an authentic national middle class ought to consider it as its bounden duty to betray the calling fate has marked out for it, and to put itself to school with the people: in other words to put at the people's disposal the intellectual and technical capital that it has snatched when going through the colonial universities. But, unhappily, we shall see that very often the national middle class does not follow this heroic, positive, fruitful, and just path; rather, it disappears with its soul set at peace into the shocking ways—shocking because antinational —of a traditional bourgeoisie, of a bourgeoisie which is stupidly, contemptibly, cynically bourgeois.

The objective of nationalist parties as from a certain given period is, we have seen, strictly national. They mobilize the people with slogans of independence, and for the rest leave it to future events. When such parties are questioned on the economic program of the state that they are clamoring for, or on the nature of the regime which they propose to install, they are incapable of replying, because, precisely, they are completely ignorant of the economy of their own country.

This economy has always developed outside the limits of their knowledge. They have nothing more than an approximate, bookish acquaintance with the actual and potential resources of their country's soil and mineral deposits; and therefore they can only speak of these resources on a general and abstract plane. After independence this underdeveloped middle class, reduced in numbers and without capital, which refuses to follow the path of revolution, will fall into deplorable stagnation. It is unable to give free rein to its genius, which, as it was formerly wont to lament, though rather too glibly, was held in check by colonial domination. The precariousness of its resources and the paucity of its managerial class forces it back for years into an artisanal economy. From its point of view, which is inevitably a very limited one, a national economy is an economy based on what may be called local products. Long speeches will be made about the artisan class. Since the middle classes find it impossible to set up factories that would be more profit-earning both for themselves and for the country as a whole, they will surround the artisan class with a chauvinistic tenderness in keeping with the new awareness of national dignity, and which moreover will bring them in quite a lot of money. This cult of local products and this incapability to seek out new systems of management will be equally manifested by the bogging down of the national middle class in the methods of agricultural production which were characteristic of the colonial period.

The national economy of the period of independence is not set on a new footing. It is still concerned with the peanut harvest, with the cocoa crop, and the olive yield. In the same way there is no change in the marketing of basic products, and not a single industry is set up in the country. We go on sending out raw materials; we go on being Europe's small farmers, who specialize in unfinished products.

Yet the national middle class constantly demands the nationalization of the economy and of the trading sectors. This is because, from their point of view, nationalization does not mean placing the whole economy at the service of the nation and deciding to satisfy the needs of the nation. For them, nationalization does not mean governing the state with regard to the new social relations whose growth it has been decided to encourage. To them, nationalization quite simply means the transfer into native hands of those unfair advantages which are a legacy of the colonial period.

Since the middle class has neither sufficient material nor intellectual resources (by intellectual resources we mean engineers and technicians), it limits its claims to the taking over of business offices and commercial houses formerly occupied by the settlers. The national bourgeoisie steps into the shoes of the former European settlement: doctors, barristers, traders, commercial travelers, general agents, and transport agents. It considers that the dignity of the country and its own welfare require that it should occupy all these posts. From now on it will insist that all the big foreign companies should pass through its hands, whether these companies wish to keep on their connections with the country, or to open it up. The national middle class discovers its historic mission: that of intermediary. . . .

As regards internal affairs and in the sphere of institutions, the national bourgeoisie will give equal proof of its incapacity. In a certain number of underdeveloped countries the parliamentary game is faked from the beginning. Powerless economically, unable to bring about the existence of coherent social relations, and standing on the principle of its domination as a class, the bourgeoisie chooses the solution that seems to it the easiest, that of the single party. It does not yet have the quiet conscience and the calm that economic power and the control of the state machine alone can give. It does not create a state that reassures the ordinary citizen, but rather one that rouses his anxiety.

The state, which by its strength and discretion ought to inspire confidence and disarm and lull everybody to sleep, on the contrary seeks to impose itself in spectacular fashion. It makes a display, it jostles people and bullies them, thus intimating to the citizen that he is in continual danger. The single party is the modern form of the dictatorship of the bourgeoisie, unmasked, unpainted, unscrupulous, and cynical.

It is true that such a dictatorship does not go very far. It cannot halt the processes of its own contradictions. Since the bourgeoisie has not the economic means to ensure its domination and to throw a few crumbs to the rest of the country, since, moreover, it is preoccupied with filling its pockets as rapidly as possible but also as prosaically as possible, the country sinks all the more deeply into stagnation. And in order to hide this stagnation and to mask this regression, to reassure itself and to give itself something to boast about, the bourgeoisie can find nothing better to do than to erect grandiose buildings in the capital and to lay out money on what are called prestige expenses.

The national bourgeoisie turns its back more and more on the interior and on the real facts of its undeveloped country, and tends to look toward the former mother country and the foreign capitalists who count on its obliging compliance. As it does not share its profits with the people, and in no way allows them to enjoy any of the dues that are paid to it by the big foreign companies, it will discover the need for a popular leader to whom will fall the dual role of stabilizing the regime and of perpetuating the domination of the bourgeoisie. The bourgeois dictatorship of underdeveloped countries draws its strength from the existence of a leader. We know that in the well-developed countries the bourgeois dictatorship is the result of the economic power of the bourgeoisie. In the underdeveloped countries, on the contrary, the leader stands for moral power, in whose shelter the thin and poverty-stricken bourgeoisie of the young nation decides to get rich.

The people who for years on end have seen this leader and heard him speak, who from a distance in a kind of dream have followed his contests with the colonial power, spontaneously put their trust in this patriot. Before independence, the leader generally embodies the aspirations of the people for independence, political liberty, and national dignity. But as soon as independence is declared, far from embodying in concrete form the needs of the people in what touches bread, land, and the restoration of the country to the sacred hands of the people, the leader will reveal his inner purpose: to become the general president of that company of profiteers impatient for their returns which is known as the national bourgeoisie. . . .

The economic channels of the young state sink back inevitably

into neocolonialist lines. The national economy, formerly protected, is today literally controlled. The budget is balanced through
loans and gifts, while every three or four months the chief ministers themselves or else their governmental delegations come to the
erstwhile mother countries or elsewhere, fishing for capital. . . .

From time to time the leader makes an effort; he speaks on the
radio or makes a tour of the country to pacify the people, to calm
them and bemuse them. The leader is all the more necessary in
that there is no party. During the period of the struggle for independence there was a party led by the present leader. But since
then this party has sadly disintegrated; nothing is left but the shell
of a party, the name, the emblem, and the motto. The living party,
which ought to make possible the free exchange of ideas which
have been elaborated according to the real needs of the mass of
the people, has been transformed into a trade union of individual
interests. Since the proclamation of independence, the party no
longer helps the people to set out its demands, to become more
aware of its needs and better able to establish its power. Today,
the party's mission is to deliver to the people the instructions
which issue from the summit. There no longer exists the fruitful
give-and-take from the bottom to the top and from the top to the
bottom which creates and guarantees democracy in a party. Quite
the contrary, the party has made itself into a screen between the
masses and the leaders. There is no longer any party life, for the
branches which were set up during the colonial period are today
completely demobilized. . . .

Europe and the Third World

The Third World today faces Europe like a colossal mass whose
aim should be to try to resolve the problems to which Europe has
not been able to find the answers.

But let us be clear: what matters is to stop talking about output,
and intensification, and the rhythm of work.

No, there is no question of a return to Nature. It is simply a
very concrete question of not dragging men toward mutilation,
of not imposing upon the brain rhythms which very quickly oblit-
erate it and wreck it. The pretext of catching up must not be used
to push man around, to tear him away from himself or from his
privacy, to break and kill him.

No, we do not want to catch up with anyone. What we want

to do is to go forward all the time, night and day, in the company of man, in the company of all men. The caravan should not be stretched out, for in that case each line will hardly see those who precede it; and men who no longer recognize each other meet less and less together, and talk to each other less and less.

It is a question of the Third World starting a new history of man, a history which will have regard to the sometimes prodigious theses which Europe has put forward, but which will also not forget Europe's crimes, of which the most horrible was committed in the heart of man, and consisted of the pathological tearing apart of his functions and the crumbling away of his unity. And in the framework of the collectivity there were the differentiations, the stratification, and the bloodthirsty tensions fed by classes; and finally, on the immense scale of humanity, there were racial hatreds, slavery, exploitation, and above all the bloodless genocide which consisted in the setting aside of fifteen billion men.

So, comrades, let us not pay tribute to Europe by creating states, institutions, and societies which draw their inspiration from her.

Humanity is waiting for something other from us than such an imitation, which would be almost an obscene caricature.

If we want to turn Africa into a new Europe, and America into a new Europe, then let us leave the destiny of our countries to Europeans. They will know how to do it better than the most gifted among us.

But if we want humanity to advance a step further, if we want to bring it up to a different level than that which Europe has shown it, then we must invent and we must make discoveries.

If we wish to live up to our people's expectations, we must seek the response elsewhere than in Europe.

Moreover, if we wish to reply to the expectations of the people of Europe, it is no good sending them back a reflection, even an ideal reflection, of their society and their thought with which from time to time they feel immeasurably sickened.

For Europe, for ourselves, and for humanity, comrades, we must turn over a new leaf, we must work out new concepts, and try to set afoot a new man.

PART III

AFRICA

African political and social thought, like African nationalism, has developed only in recent years. Yet, it has already made some important contributions to the common ideological stock of modernizing nationalism. In London and in Paris and in the African capitals, African students, intellectuals, and political leaders have drawn on Western democratic thought, on Marxism, on Gandhism, and (in the case of those studying in America) on Black Nationalism and combined them with a romanticized version of the African cultural heritage and history to produce a common Pan-African ideology shared by most African nationalist leaders—however much they may differ on its practical implementation.

The African nationalists face many of the same problems of underdevelopment as their counterparts in the Middle East, Asia, and Latin America, but there are also important differences. Since much of Africa has only recently achieved independence, no entrenched military class or feudal oligarchy impedes national development. In some areas, tribalism has broken down, either because cooperation with the colonizing power has discredited the traditional tribal leadership or because urbanization has loosened traditional loyalties. The nationalist leaders have thus been presented with a ready-made following, responsive to nationalistic and anti-colonial appeals.

Yet, the vast majority of Africans remain enmeshed in tribal and traditional structures of authority. The modernizing elite finds itself caught between the goals of democracy and development. The objective of modernization is by no means certain to win a majority.

The theory of the democratic single party—perhaps the distinctive African contribution to the ideology of modernizing national-

ism—offers a way out of this dilemma. Utilizing the slogans of development and national unity, the party educates a largely illiterate population to desire the goals that the modernizing elite considers desirable, at the same time making it possible for at least minimal controls to be exercised over the leadership by party members. Although it has not been universally accepted by African leaders, the theory of the single party has received its best formulation in the writings and speeches of African nationalists such as Sékou Touré, Julius Nyerere, and Madeira Keita, and its influence is wide.

In economic thought, the attempt to find a middle way between the individualism of the West and the collectivism of the Soviet bloc has received eloquent expression in Senghor's "African Socialism." A similar conception also underlies Julius Nyerere's emphasis on the harmony of the individual and the group in African social life.

The revival of African culture under the labels of Negritude and "the African personality" has a political as well as a cultural significance in the support it gives to the ideal of African unity. Already, however, there is among the Pan-Africanists a division, derived partly from varying conceptions of the method to reach African unity, partly from differing views regarding internal development and external ties, and partly from power rivalries.

There is no disagreement on the desirability of national independence, of the liberation of the remaining colonial territories, or of a nonaligned position in international relations. Above all, modernization and development are the objectives agreed upon by all educated Africans as the goals of African national and regional policy. This process has been termed "Westernization," but African leaders specifically reject some aspects of Western life—for example, its racialism, its individualism, and, in many instances, its political forms. Yet, the categories of their thought—the nation, the party, and the concept of modernization itself—are derived from Western sources and modified to fit African political and social realities.

The relations of Africa with the other developing areas are especially important in the United Nations. Voting records indicate that there is no clearly defined Afro-Asian bloc, but consultation does go on among Africans, Asians, and Middle Easterners. At the Bandung Conference of 1955, which was the first attempt to bring together the leaders of African and Asian governments, Ghana and

Liberia were the only African nations represented. Many more attended the Belgrade Conference in 1961, and thirty-two African governments were represented at the Third Conference of Non-Aligned Countries in Zambia in 1970. There is also a bridge to the Islamic world, through the North African countries and the United Arab Republic. The Algerians cultivated African support throughout the lengthy history of their revolt, and Nasser harbored anticolonial African leaders in Cairo for many years. Gandhi's system of thought has exercised influence upon a number of African leaders, but Indian-African relations may be strained in the future by the position of the Indian traders in East Africa.

The rise of African to self-assertion and independence has brought with it new contributions to the political theory of modernizing nationalism. While there has been a decline in the importance of ideology in some African states, as practical problems consume the energies of the leadership, or nontheoretical military men seize power, in others ideology remains a guiding force and a principal determinant of action.

15. The Organization of African Unity (OAU)

One of the most powerful currents in African thinking has been that favoring African unity. All African leaders have endorsed the concept but there has been some disagreement on how to achieve it. Kwame Nkrumah took the lead in the early days of African independence, calling a Conference of Independent African States in April, 1958, and later in the same year forging a rather vague union with Guinea (Guinea later provided him with refuge when he was overthrown). In 1959, Senegal and the French-speaking Sudan (now the Republic of Mali) formed the Federation of Mali, which split apart a year later. In the same year the Ivory Coast and its French-speaking neighbors formed the Entente, a loose organization for economic cooperation. In December, 1960, all the French-speaking states (except Guinea and Mali) met at Brazzaville; the following year they established the African and Malagasy Union. The 1961 Conferences at Casablanca and at Monrovia seemed to make more permanent the rapidly emerging split between radicals and moderates.* Yet in May, 1963, all the African states, meeting at Addis Ababa, agreed upon a Charter of African Unity which established the Organization of African Unity (OAU). The voting power of the moderates is evident in the Charter's emphasis on noninterference and its condemnation of subversion. In addition to setting up a Mediation Commission, which has already done important work in settling disputes involving Morocco, Algeria, and Mauritania and Somalia, Ethiopia, and

* The government of Morocco, the organizer of the Casablanca Conference, cannot properly be described as radical in orientation.

Kenya, the Addis Ababa Conference also established a Liberation Committee to supervise and coordinate Pan-African support for independence movements in the remaining colonial territories in Africa.

CHARTER OF THE ORGANIZATION OF AFRICAN UNITY*

We, the Heads of African and Malagasy States and Governments assembled in the city of Addis Ababa, Ethiopia;

Convinced that it is the inalienable right of all people to control their own destiny;

Conscious of the fact that freedom, equality, justice, and dignity are essential objectives for the achievement of the legitimate aspirations of the African peoples;

Conscious of our responsibility to harness the natural and human resources of our continent for the total advancement of our peoples in spheres of human endeavor;

Inspired by a common determination to promote understanding and collaboration among our States in response to the aspirations of our peoples for brotherhood and solidarity, in a larger unity transcending ethnic and national differences;

Convinced that, in order to translate this determination into a dynamic force in the cause of human progress, conditions for peace and security must be established and maintained;

Determined to safeguard and consolidate the hard-won independence as well as the sovereignty and territorial integrity of our States, and to resist neocolonialism in all its forms;

Dedicated to the general progress of Africa;

Persuaded that the Charter of the United Nations and the Universal Declaration of Human Rights, to the principles of which we reaffirm our adherence, provide a solid foundation for peaceful and positive cooperation among States;

Desirous that all African and Malagasy States should henceforth unite so that the welfare and well-being of their peoples can be assured;

* From OAU Provisional Secretariat, *Organization of African Unity, Basic Documents and Resolutions* (Addis Ababa, 1963).

Resolved to reinforce the links between our States by establishing and strengthening common institutions;

Have agreed to the present Charter.

ESTABLISHMENT

Article I

The High Contracting Parties do by the present Charter establish an Organization to be known as the Organization of African and Malagasy States.

PURPOSES

Article II

1. The Organization shall have the following purposes: (a) to promote the unity and solidarity of the African and Malagasy States; (b) to coordinate and intensify their collaboration and efforts to achieve a better life for the peoples of Africa; (c) to defend their sovereignty, their territorial integrity, and independence; (d) to eradicate all forms of colonialism from the continent of Africa; and (e) to promote international cooperation, having due regard to the Charter of the United Nations and the Universal Declaration of Human Rights.

2. To these ends, the Member States shall coordinate and harmonize their general policies, especially in the following fields: (a) political and diplomatic cooperation; (b) economic cooperation, including transport and communications; (c) educational and cultural cooperation; (d) health, sanitation, and nutritional cooperation; (e) scientific and technical cooperation; (f) cooperation for defense and security.

PRINCIPLES

Article III

The Member States, in pursuit of the purposes stated in Article II, solemnly affirm and declare their adherence to the following principles: (1) the sovereign equality of all African and Malagasy States; (2) noninterference in the internal affairs of States; (3) respect for the sovereignty and territorial integrity of each State and for its inalienable right to independent existence; (4) peaceful settlement of disputes by negotiation, mediation, conciliation, or arbitration; (5) unreserved condemnation, in all its forms, of political assassination as well as of subversive activities on the part of neighboring states or any other states; (6) absolute dedication to the total emancipation of the African territories which are still dependent; (7) affirmation of a policy of nonalignment with regard to all blocs.

MEMBERSHIP
Article IV

Each independent sovereign African and Malagasy State shall be entitled to become a Member of the Organization.

RIGHTS AND DUTIES OF MEMBER STATES
Article V

All Member States shall enjoy equal rights and have equal duties.

Article VI

The Member States pledge themselves to observe scrupulously the principles enumerated in Article III of the present Charter.

INSTITUTIONS
Article VII

The Organization shall accomplish its purposes through the following principal institutions: (1) the Assembly of Heads of State and Government; (2) the Council of Ministers; (3) the General Secretariat; (4) the Commission of Mediation, Conciliation, and Arbitration. . . .

COMMISSION OF MEDIATION, CONCILIATION, AND ARBITRATION
Article XIX

Member States pledge to settle all disputes among themselves by peaceful means and, to this end, agree to conclude a separate treaty establishing a Commission of Mediation, Conciliation, and Arbitration. Said treaty shall be regarded as forming an integral part of the present Charter.

SPECIALIZED COMMISSIONS

Article XX

The Assembly shall establish such Specialized Commissions as it may deem necessary, including the following: (1) Economic and Social Commission; (2) Educational and Cultural Commission; (3) Health, Sanitation, and Nutrition Commission; (4) Defense Commission; (5) Scientific, Technical, and Research Commission.

DECOLONIZATION RESOLUTION*

The summit conference of Independent African and Malagasy States meeting in Addis Ababa, Ethiopia, from 22 May to 25 May 1963; having considered all aspects of the questions of decolonization; unanimously convinced of the imperious and urgent necessity of coordinating and intensifying their efforts to accelerate the unconditional attainment of national independence by all African territories still under foreign domination; reaffirming that it is the duty of all African Independent States to support dependent people in Africa in their struggle for freedom and independence; noting with deep concern that most of the remaining dependent territories in Africa are dominated by foreign settlers; convinced that the colonial powers by their forcible imposition of the settlers to control the governments and administration of those territories are thus establishing colonial bases in the heart of Africa; have agreed unanimously to concert and coordinate their efforts and action in this field, and to this end have decided on the following measures:

Declares that the forcible imposition by the colonial powers of the settlers to control the governments and administration of the dependent territories is a flagrant violation of the inalienable rights of the legitimate inhabitants of the territories concerned;

Invites the colonial powers to take the necessary measures for the immediate application of the declaration on the granting of independence to colonial countries and peoples by insisting on

* From OAU Provisional Secretariat, *Organization of African Unity, Basic Documents and Resolutions* (Addis Ababa, 1963).

the fact that their determination to maintain colonies or semi-colonies in Africa constitutes a menace to the peace of the continent. . . .

Asks for an effective boycott of the foreign trade of Portugal and South Africa by : (a) prohibiting the import of goods from those two countries, (b) closing African ports and airports to their ships and planes, and (c) forbidding the planes of those two countries to overfly the territories of all African States;

Earnestly invites all national liberation movements to coordinate their efforts by establishing common action fronts wherever necessary so as to strengthen the effectiveness of their struggle and the rational use of the concerted assistance given them;

Establishes a coordinating committee consisting of Ethiopia, Algeria, Uganda, U.A.R., Tanganyika, Congo (Léopoldville), Guinea, Senegal, and Nigeria with headquarters in Dar-es-Salaam responsible for harmonizing assistance from African States and for managing the special fund to be set up for that purpose;

Establishes a special fund to be contributed by Member States to supply the necessary practical and financial aid to the various African national liberation movements. . . .

Receives, on the territories of Independent African States nationalists from liberation movements in order to give them training in all sectors, and afford young people all the assistance they need for their education and vocational training;

Promotes, in each state, the establishment of a body of volunteers in various fields, with a view to providing the various African national liberation movements with the assistance they need. . . .

16. The African and Malagasy Common Organization (OCAM)

At the 1963 meeting in Addis Ababa, it was understood that the various political groups already in existence would be dissolved or would fuse with the OAU. The French-speaking moderates, however, were reluctant to abandon the organization they had set up among themselves—the African and Malagasy Union. In 1964, they replaced it with an organization for economic cooperation (UAMCE). A recurrence of difficulties over the Congo exacerbated the differences between the moderates and radicals within the OAU, and in February, 1965, a new organization—the African and Malagasy Common Organization (OCAM)—was formed. Although the OCAM acts within the framework of the OAU, it has taken political action on its own—notably the recognition of the Tshombe government in the Congo (an action particularly abhorrent to the radicals) and an attack on Ghana for harboring and encouraging subversives working for the overthrow of neighboring states. The formation of OCAM marked a re-emergence of the earlier division between those who favored a Pan-African movement largely confined to technical and functional cooperation (the former Monrovia group) and those who saw it as an instrument for the encouragement and ultimate union of "progressive" forces throughout the continent (the former Casablanca group).

STATEMENT OF THE FIRST OCAM CONFERENCE*

The conference of chiefs of state convened by His Excellency Mokhtar Ould Daddah, President of the Islamic Republic of Mauritania, was held in Nouakchott from February 10 to 12, 1965. Its purpose was to examine the condition of the organization formed by the fourteen states involved in the light of the African and international situations, as had been done previously at the Cotonou and Dakar conferences.

The conference discussions took place in an atmosphere of complete frankness and cordiality. The participants were able, after careful examination of the African and international situation, to arrive at positive conclusions which will give a new impetus to their organization. The new organization, the OCAM (Organisation Commune Africaine et Malgache [African and Malagasy Common Organization]), is a regrouping of African states within the framework of the OAU. Its objective is to strengthen cooperation and solidarity among the African and Malagasy states in order to speed up their political, economic, social, technical, and cultural development. The new organization, with headquarters in Yaoundé, will concentrate its activities under the authority of one administrative secretary general. The conference took note of the decision of the states of the Entente to establish "multinationality."

With regard to the African situation:

Considering that the malaise from which the OAU is suffering derives essentially from the lack of respect given to its Charter;

Considering that respect for the sovereignty of the states and noninterference in their internal affairs constitute the sine qua non conditions for peace and development in Africa;

Considering that the situation in Congo-Léopoldville and the intensification of the Cold War between the two blocs in Africa constitute a permanent threat to the existence of the OAU and the independence of the African countries;

Considering that covetous designs from abroad are increasing in Africa,

* Translated in *Africa Report*, X, No. 3 (March, 1965), 10.

The chiefs of state of the Organization recommend prudence and vigilance to all.

They solemnly affirm the urgent necessity of bringing peace back to Congo-Léopoldville through aid to the legal government to hasten national reconciliation in order and liberty, in accordance with the resolutions of the Addis Ababa conference and the [United Nations] Security Council. They advocate at the same time the reconciliation of Congo-Léopoldville with its neighbors. They energetically condemn the action of certain states, notably Ghana, which harbor agents of subversion and organize training camps on their national territory.

They have decided, in consequence, to inform the OAU [of the problem] and make an appeal to the African feeling of all the chiefs of state of the continent in order that a climate of cooperation among equals can be substituted as soon as possible for the present climate of mistrust and false leadership through intervention in the internal affairs of the other states. . . .

17. Sékou Touré

Sékou Touré was born in 1922 in Kan-Kan, Guinea, of peasant parents. He received a primary education, but was expelled from a trade school for leading a food strike at the age of fifteen. He then secured a civil-service job and became active in Guinean trade unionism, becoming leader of the Guinean branch of the Confédération Générale du Travail (CGT), the Communist-influenced French trade-union federation. Touré organized the Parti Démocratique de Guinée (PDG), as the Guinean branch of the Rassemblement Démocratique Africain; his party lost the apparently rigged elections of 1954, but won complete control of the Guinea Assembly in 1957. He then broke ties with the CGT and formed an African trade-union federation. Using the French grant of internal autonomy to consolidate his political control and break the power of tribal chieftains, he was able to secure a 95 per cent en-

*dorsement of his position for immediate independence in the refer-
endum of September, 1958—at a time when all other French-speaking African territories were voting by equally lopsided margins for
continued association with France. An avowed Marxist, Sékou
Touré has pursued a leftist but independent policy in both internal and international politics. He demonstrated his nonalignment in 1961 when he expelled the Soviet Ambassador on charges
of plotting, and in 1962 when he refused the Soviet Union refuel-
ing rights during the Cuban missile crisis.*

*The selection below is taken from his speech to the congress of
the Parti Démocratique de Guinée, delivered on September 14,
1959, a year after independence. It explains how the PDG operates
as the single party in Guinea, and defends Touré's version of
"democratic centralism."*

AFRICAN EMANCIPATION*

The Contradictions of Colonialism

If the problem of the individual is a central concern in other continents—in countries that are free and independent—the first and
the only true problem for the colonial peoples is that of the attainment of independence. It is consequently a collective problem, a
political reality engendered by nationalist sentiments.

But if our party has been more successful than the other fraternal parties of Senegal, of the (French) Sudan, of Niger, etc.,
in guiding our country to its independence, it is because it has
found itself in favorable objective conditions. Political struggle involves laws, power relationships, a given level of maturity,
problems of unity, etc.—a number of objective conditions which,
combined, produce the rise of the dependent countries and govern
the rhythm of their political development.

The expansion of our political movement was achieved because

*Excerpts from *La Lutte du Parti Démocratique de Guinée pour l'Emanci-
pation Africaine* (Conakry: Imprimerie Nationale, 1959); translated by the
editor.

of the many contradictions between the interests of the people and the interests of the colonial regime. The principal contradiction was between the African interest and the interests of French imperialism, which had repercussions in all areas of social life. In addition to the moral domain (that of the dignity of our people) and the juridical domain, by which the illegitimate occupation of our country established by the colonial power was firmly entrenched, there were practices on the economic level and on the level of public activity, on the military level, and on the social level which constantly revealed these conflicts of interest. It was on the basis of these oppositions and in terms of these dichotomies that the struggle was organized and conducted, against both the colonial regime and those who by their actions, consciously or unconsciously, favored the programs of that regime.

Internal contradictions also existed. In the first place, the peasants—who constitute 80 per cent of the population of Guinea —turned against feudalism, which, perverted by the colonial regime, had ceased to be the true expression of the thought of our national social units. Created, supported, and used by the colonial regime, this feudalism, in opposition to the interests of the people, was better known under the name of "cantonal chiefdom." The chiefs lived on the exploitation of the peasant masses, and they justified the colonialist practices with which their own interests were intimately linked. There were still other internal contradictions, which were less apparent, but which had to be eliminated rapidly in order to reinforce the unity of the people. There was, notably, the nascent opposition between what we can call the intellectual elite on the one side and the peasant masses on the other. The education that was given to us was designed to assimilate us, to depersonalize us, to Westernize us—to present our civilization, our culture, our own sociological and philosophical conceptions, even our humanism as the expression of a savage and almost unconscious primitivism—in order to create a number of complexes in us which would drive us to become more French than the French themselves. In addition to this, there were the advantages and security of the material surroundings of the intellectual elite, which were absolutely foreign to the life of the immense majority of the people and constituted a privileged situation in comparison with general conditions. The satisfaction of the requirements of one group appeared immediately as a new obligation, a new burden on the others, who constituted not only the majority of the population, but also the most disinherited strata.

Contradictions existed in the economic domain, as they exist elsewhere in all colonial and imperialist regimes. Appropriate structures were used to facilitate the exploitation by the colonialists of the two aspects of the market: import and export. The shameful system of trading functioned through practices that none could deny because they were too simple and too apparent. There was speculation, with produce handled at three stages: purchase, storage, and resale to the producer in time of need. The difference between the cost of imported merchandise and the price to the consumer was exorbitant.

The feudal regime (despite the fact that the land is the first and natural property of the people) annexed the land and, under the name "national property," made it the property of the French state. The military regime contained the same contradictions because the African soldier had neither the material nor the moral advantages of his French colleague—just as the African veteran was treated in an inferior fashion in relation to his French counterpart. Finally, the administrative structure could be summed up by this simple formula: The French administration, the sole origin of all decisions involving the destiny of the country, was in fact the guarantor and manager of the interests of the colonialists. . . .

In its military organization, as in its administrative, economic, and political structure, assimilationist colonialism decreed laws that were to be applied unilaterally throughout the whole empire, without taking account of the particular characteristics of each part, or of its economic and social conditions or political evolution. This unification policy, the corollary of the aim of assimilation, created a feeling of equality in misery, and was bound to result in the emergence of an identity of interests of all those under colonial rule—whether in the north, south, or west of Africa. Thus the military and administrative organizations, with their broader and more general structures involving the whole of the former French empire, created new institutions favoring the unity of action of those under colonial rule against a common oppressor. . . .

Our party is a committed party which does not look for the golden mean between truth and falsehood. It is aware of the backwardness of the African peoples and does not want to lose time in useless evasions. From the moment that it has decided on a goal, it wants to attain that goal with the support and action of the people. Hence the anticolonial struggle did not end on the 28th

of September;* it has only started again with more power as a
double struggle against the consequences of the colonial regime
(by the adaptation of methods, structures, spirit and population to
the new requirements of a free national life) and against the
colonial domination that still weighs upon a good part of Africa.

We are aware that as long as all Africa is not free, Guinea will
feel threatened. Consider the man who has injured a finger. The
finger alone does not feel pain; if there is pain, it is the whole body
of the man that feels it. Guinea feels the pain of the colonized
people of Africa. In order to attempt to eliminate the pain of
soul and body of the inhabitants of Africa, whose welfare constitutes the object and the reason for our combat, we must first examine the state of the instruments—the Democratic Party of
Guinea, and its institutions, the people and their political, social,
economic, and cultural practices—that serve to lead us to victory
in the combat.

Principles of the PDG and Their Application

The Democratic Party of Guinea is a national movement grouping together (without distinction of race or sex) all those of good
will who are determined to work against colonialism and for the
building up of a solid democratic state in Guinea. There should
be no astonishment that in Guinea there is only one single national
party, the PDG. I want to emphasize that political unity is not an
end. It is only a means to develop a progressive movement that
serves the general interest. This unity can be maintained and developed to serve the national interest only if it involves unity of
action on the part of the whole population, mobilized for positive
ends and constantly confirming the democratic character of the
development of our country. We can also say that the life of a
society, of a social unit, or of a nation is not essentially governed
by laws, decrees, or regulations. The life of a society is governed
by habits, customs, historic traditions, and the necessity for its
maintenance and development. Thus, the value of a government
is determined by the balanced development it assures on the
national level. The various changes in living conditions that result

* September 28, 1958 was the date of the referendum on the Constitution
of the Fifth Republic of France. By voting "no" on the constitution and
thus refusing to join the new French Community, Guinea became the first
of the French colonies in sub-Sahara Africa to achieve independence.—ED.

from our progress clash with the conservative forces of the present
and the reactionary forces of the past, the former representing
vested interests and privileges and the latter the interests and
privileges that have been lost. These forces are not working for
the general interest because their demands only involve particular
and special cases which are, by their nature, opposed to social
justice and the national interest.

The most progressive and revolutionary law will remain without
application if it is not understood by the people and if the attitudes
and habits of the people are contrary to that law. Similarly, if the
principles of the party are not well understood by the party membership, and especially by all the leaders, the party will only list
its principles at its congresses without ever translating them into
reality in the living conditions of the nation. We must constantly
recall that the Democratic Party of Guinea is a popular movement,
uniting the entire mass of the population who wish to work together for the realization of its program in the general interest.
The party should not change its political line if this line remains
in conformity with the national interest. The essential principle
that we should never forget is that the Democratic Party of Guinea
is different from the ethnic movements we formerly knew in
Guinea. Our party operates scientifically—by analyzing concrete
situations to determine the objectives and forms of its action.

We constantly reiterate that the PDG is a party of men who
place their intelligence at the service of the masses. When we say
they are "intellectuals," it is in the true sense of the word. It is not
a question of those who know how to read and write, but of those
who determine their action on the basis of reason, starting out with
concrete study; of those who, guided by intelligence, can know
at any moment what has already been accomplished and what has
not yet been carried out; of those who can appreciate the real
value of the action of our party, so as to make it more efficient;
in short, of those men and women who look for the truth—starting
out with historic and present facts, determining their action by
the objectives that have been assigned to them. This intelligence
is found among peasants, workers, civil servants, laborers, women,
and children.

In the world today, there are three types of organizations and
movements. There is the party that speaks of the past and lives
on the basis of the past. The members of this party continually

say, "We have done such and such a thing in 1900, we have done such and such in 1910"; they are not capable of saying, "This is what we have done today, and this is what we should do tomorrow." The second category lives only in the present, and its workers are concerned exclusively with day-to-day problems and make no effort to analyze these problems or carry out the changes that would resolve them in the future. The Democratic Party of Guinea belongs neither to the first nor to the second category. Not forgetting what has taken place in the past, and keeping in mind what is taking place today, it is also concerned with what should take place tomorrow. Indeed, it is insofar as one is concerned with what will take place tomorrow that one can take the appropriate measures to make the future of the country more happy and prosperous. Party workers who only think of what is taking place today are those who are often surprised, have no general view, and are very quickly discouraged, for, at the least unhappy and unexpected event, they are disoriented and suffer panic, thus distorting the real significance of the party. When something happens that they cannot work out, they are immediately discouraged and lose all desire to continue their activity. It is the opposite with the worker who thinks of the program of the future while keeping in mind the present. Mistakes—far from discouraging him or limiting his action—are sources of profit, because once he has discovered them, thanks to criticism and self-criticism, he can henceforth avoid them in carrying out his future actions.

Indeed, it is when we discover a mistake committed by the whole party or by a worker or leader, that we seek to know its nature, its causes, and its consequences. There is no action without mistakes. Only a party that carries on no activity can avoid mistakes. Just as one cannot develop knowledge without study and apprenticeship, one cannot learn anything without the possibility of mistakes. That is why the party should stimulate action every day on the part of its workers. The officeholders and party workers ought to know that action feeds the intelligence and gives practical effect to the thinking of the party. We have often said that practice is superior to thought and theory. Suppose that the members of the party establish a program which everyone approves. Even when there is agreement on the program, it is action that will determine what part of the program is possible for the country and in the interest of the party, and what should be corrected, modified, or abandoned. The superiority of practice over theory is attainable only in action and results. Hence, the party should be organized at all levels—in the local districts, in the villages, in the administrative divisions, and at a national level—a perfect organization of militant activity, so that each one can contribute effectively to the realization of the party program.

When we say that the party works for democracy and the unity of the country, and against colonialism, this is only the general framework and spirit in which all daily actions should be taken, and a statement of future activities. On the level of local and village committees, as well as those of the sections and districts, there should be general assemblies and conferences to study and establish a concrete program, to work for the permanent mobilization of the energies of the PDG. Without a concrete and definite program according to the respective possibilities of the different branches of the party, action can be carried out in the abstract and come to an end before any positive result is attained. . . .

The workers ought to give an account of what they have done and an evaluation of the progress that has been realized every day. Action is necessary, but it is only possible within the framework of a program, and how is this program established? It is not the Political Bureau that establishes it. The Political Bureau only prepares a project, and the General Assembly discusses and determines it. Thus each one can understand its value and its implications.

It is necessary also to popularize the program among the masses, but it is not just a question of discussion of the program or of adopting it and understanding it. It is also a matter of distributing assignments; and the party must exercise some check over the carrying out of the tasks undertaken by each one.

For example, a delegation of the Political Bureau recently went into the regions of the interior. Its accounting, observation, and notes were discussed, after which a statement was made and circulars were sent out to the various sections, which drew lessons from this visit and determined new directives for action. The party should let no phenomenon or action take place without an appropriate analysis for the purpose of drawing from it a positive conclusion and determining the political line of its further activities. One can say that confidence does not exclude the review of action. When you benefit from the unlimited confidence of the masses, you have to act in such a way that the masses are aware that they have made a good decision, that they were not mistaken in granting you their confidence. . . .

In following the principles of the party, the officers of a local committee ought to have a meeting every evening and bring together all their information, review the execution of assignments, establish a program, distribute new assignments to be fulfilled, and, finally, organize a general assembly. At the assembly, everyone who is absent should be noted. If review is made in a rigorous manner, methodically and democratically, only real workers will continue in the party, for the bad elements will be eliminated of themselves.

When you cease to have criticism and self-criticism in the party, the party will die little by little. Everyone, as a matter of principle, must serve the party, and no one must serve himself. If there is no criticism and self-criticism, one cannot determine what is good and what is evil; one cannot locate mistakes that have been committed or evaluate the consequences; one cannot act against the enemies of the party, who are making use of it to operate against its objectives. . . .

Political Supremacy and Democratic Dictatorship

For the argument from force which the old colonialist state used, our new democratic state intends to substitute another basis of authority and draw its strength from arguments and from its guiding principles. Thus, the supremacy of political action is the consequence, the reality, of the political democracy that we have chosen for ourselves and have wished to be as real as possible and as vivid as the popular desire for a general revival in our country.

Democracy has different natures indeed and is interpreted in different ways, according to whether it is inspired by one or another form of thought, objective, or social force. We do not have to carry our analysis very far to become aware of the different social conceptions that utilize the name "democracy." Christianity acts politically under the name "Christian democracy," the bourgeoisie operate under the name "bourgeois democracy," and some social sectors talk about a "social democracy." Thus, if democracy represents a conception of the organization of society and peoples, its real content can be perverted or interpreted in different fashions.

As for ourselves, we are in favor of a democracy as real and as complete as possible and based solely on the interests of the people. This is the only form of democracy we recognize, the only interpretation we give to the word "democracy." . . .

Whether we are concerned with the democratic or nondemocratic state, both are governed by a man or a group of men who exercise power over the whole population. Both are dictatorships. Dictatorship is the concentration of powers exercised by a man or group of men over the whole. We can say, following that definition, that the driver of a vehicle imposes a dictatorship on the passengers of the vehicle. In a trade union, in a youth organization, in a women's organization, in an athletic team, there is this type of dictatorship. We can say, therefore, that states are democratic or nondemocratic—but whatever their nature, their direction toward specific objectives set out in advance necessarily implies a dictatorship.

To define the nature of this dictatorship, which is exercised differently in democratic states and nondemocratic states, we must consider the objective conditions surrounding the exercise of dictatorship to determine whether a state is democratic. . . . If the dictatorship exercised by the governmental apparatus emanates directly from the whole of the people, this dictatorship is popular in nature and the state is a democratic state—democracy being the exercise of national sovereignty by the people. It is power exercised of the people, by the people, and for the people.

A democratic state comes from the will of the people. Its program is therefore necessarily in conformance with the interests of the people. Likewise, its force, its authority, the powers it exercises, the discipline it imposes—in short, the dictatorship it exercises—arise exclusively from the interests, the requirements, and the principles of popular sovereignty. For every human society, democracy always corresponds in its form to given conditions and requirements, which are the result of the economic and social level at which the society has arrived. Hence, democracy can be more or less developed, more or less advanced. Democratic dictatorship—that is, the concentration of powers of the sovereignty of the people at the level of the people—can be more or less great and more or less developed. Thus, a state whose program of work and whose political power are determined, not in the interests of one level or part of the population, but exclusively in the interests of the whole people is a democratic state.

This means that on the level of the governing apparatus, there is an obligation to assure direct and free representation of the whole population, without discrimination of any sort. In a democratic state, the sovereign power is exercised directly by representatives whom the people have chosen freely.

But if the dictatorship is exercised by a king, a part of the population, a coalition of interests, or a feudal economic power, and if there is an interest other than the general interest operating in the exercise of the sovereignty, the dictatorship ceases to be exercised in the interests of the people. Economic dictatorship, financial dictatorship, personal dictatorship, military dictatorship are nothing else than the exercise of national sovereignty for the economic, financial, and personal benefit of one caste or social class. The state ceases to be democratic when the dictatorship it exercises arises solely out of the interests of the king, a social class, or any other group that does not represent the whole population. . . .

In a democratic state, sovereignty is the property of the nation as a whole. The responsibilities involved in running the state are, by the nature of its structure, shared collectively. Thus, all intelligence, all values, and all energies are mobilized for the benefit of the whole, so as to assure the best possible ways of achieving progress, creating the best conditions for the development of the country, and bringing about the maximum guarantee of the expansion of the society and the security of each of its members. . . .

On the other hand, there are states that are democratic in form, ruled by ministers, parliamentarians, and responsible people in power, elected according to sometimes quite complicated procedures; but the dictatorship practiced by these states is not democratic in fact, since it is exercised by one feudal group or coalition of private interests, or even by a clan or social caste. This is a dictatorship one can call ethnic or factional.

A first requirement for democracy is liberty. If men are to be considered as equals and are to participate with equal concern and involvement in the life of the nation, they must first be free. Without effective liberty, there is no possibility for men or societies to determine themselves freely. . . .

The Exercise of Democracy

We can say that our state is democratic, unitary, and progressive. We want Guinea to be a viable national entity. In three or four years, no one will think any longer of the tribal, ethnic, and religious rivalries that have in the past caused so much evil for our country and population. A considerable decentralization of administration and policy has been permitted on the level of electoral districts, and the district council has all authority to decide what needs to be done. But there is also a perfect concentration of powers in the national institutions: the assembly and the government. Our constitution has authorized this concentration of powers by stipulating that the chief of the state is also the chief of the army—as he is the one who names the ministers and can at any point remove them. Obviously, if we did not understand that behind the state there is a higher entity, the party, we could not comprehend the political value of the provisions of the Guinean constitution. That is why the party assumes a directing role in the life of the nation and exercises all the powers of the nation. Political, judiciary, administrative, economic, and technical powers are in the hands of the Democratic Party of Guinea. It is the party that designates the chief of state, by direct universal suffrage. The deputies to the National Assembly are elected for five years, directly by the population, under the same conditions as the chief of the state. Every seven years . . . popular elections take place for the selection of the President of the republic. . . .

There are contradictions in all societies. We refuse to regard them passively, for we want to direct our evolution in a harmonious and just fashion. But to govern is to choose, and to choose is to use authority for the realization of previously determined objectives. To govern is to apply a dictatorship. When an aroused people has chosen its future, it must follow the line that leads it efficiently and rapidly to that future. But to impose a discipline in the framework of principles set up in advance is to agree to subordinate oneself to the authority of principles and to accept the dictatorship that flows from them. Our fundamental principles are simple. We recognize as valuable only what serves the cause of the people and develops the history of the nation. This is the discipline to which we submit ourselves freely, and this orientation constitutes the principal task of a forward-looking party and a democratic state. This is the nature of the dictatorship. It can have a different content if it is applied by one man who considers himself superior to all others, or if it is the people themselves who have conceived its program of development and chosen the methods by which it will accomplish its daily tasks. Depending on how it is applied, dictatorship can be antidemocratic or democratic. As for ourselves, we say that in giving supremacy to the people and making them participate directly in all important decisions involving the nation, we want a popular democratic dictatorship.

For our decision to be more than a theoretical one—for it to be applied in every aspect of the life of every citizen and every branch of the state—we must immediately struggle against ourselves, against whatever in us is in contradiction to the decision we have taken. Thus, more than ever, there is a task of education on all levels and stages of thought, conception, and action. That is why, in the political field, the party has decided that our state, as a democratic state, will be at the same time a unitary and communitarian state.

Many nations in the world have 100–200 million inhabitants and are centuries ahead of us, disposing of enormous riches, which we do not have, and utilizing modern methods, which we lack today. We are just beginning, and our first chance to raise ourselves to the level of modern states in the world consists in our unity. Our desire for progress will be fruitless if individual wills are not identical and do not aim at attaining the same objectives, for internal contradiction will become more and more violent and hold us back, endangering our very independence. That is why we have said that at all levels the party must be extremely vigilant, intransigent, and severe, in order to force the unitary and dynamic character of its policy into the awareness and action of every citizen. . . .

The Unification of the Youth of Guinea

The constant concern of the Democratic Party of Guinea has been to . . . place all the institutions of the country at the service of the population. Thanks to its integral and solid structure, it has brought all organizations under its control. . . . It was the only party to choose independence in the name of the people of Guinea and of all of colonial Africa, by rejecting the French Community in a massive and historic vote.

Youth will play a primary role in the immense task of construction that we have begun since our accession to full sovereignty. It is important for each worker of the party, and particularly for the youth, that the specific problems of young people be approached with a clear conception of the general objectives of the nation. More than ever, the actions of young people must necessarily reflect the essential concerns of the country. We are guided by the central principle that the party has always considered of great importance—the absolute necessity of carrying out the program of youth on a national level, in the framework of the general program of the party. Youth ought to have an active part in the nation, be aware of its responsibilities, and be ready to play the dynamic role we assign to it.

The unification of youth movements was a response to the necessity of putting an end to the dispersion of energies that paralyzed the youth and prevented it from playing a worthy role as a front-ranking part of the Guinean people in the struggle for the emancipation of Africa. When the officers of the PDG, at the Congress of the JRDA* in March, 1959, emphasized the weakness of youth organizations in the fields of sport and art, they were right in thinking that it was urgent to abolish the individualism and mediocrity inherited from the colonial system and to place sport and art on the level of the most noble institutions of our nation. Henceforth, the spirit of competition should be developed among young people on the basis of an aroused sentiment of national pride. The PDG has therefore acted perfectly well in unifying the youth movements and in concretely realizing, within the JRDA, the unity of action of all the young people of the country. . . .

The Principles of Democratic Centralism

Democratic centralism consists of the following principles:

1. All the leaders of the party are directly elected, democratically, by the party workers, who have complete freedom of conscience and expression within the party.

2. The concerns of the state of Guinea are the concerns of all the citizens of Guinea. The program of the party is discussed democratically. As long as a decision has not been taken, each one is free to say what he thinks or wishes. But when—after a long discussion in the Congress or Assembly—the decisions have been taken by a unanimous vote or by a majority, the workers and the leaders are required to apply them faithfully.

3. There is no sharing of the responsibility of the leaders— only of the responsibility for a decision. Thus, discipline will not be undermined.

Democracy and the freedom of all party workers are expressed

---

* Jeunesse du Rassemblement Démocratique Africain, the youth section of the PDG.—Ed.

in the framing of problems, in their discussion, and in the choice of solutions for them. On the other hand, the leadership of the party has complete liberty in the execution of assigned responsibilities and in the evaluation of the forms of action appropriate for the objective conditions of their execution. Thus, at certain points, the leadership of the PDG has said to the masses: "Do not create any incidents. Even in the case of flagrant provocation, do not respond." Then, at other moments, when the power relationships and the development of the struggle required a strong attitude, the same leaders invited the militant masses to respond with force to the blows of the adversaries. Each movement of retreat or offense was linked to the political context of the moment. In other words, once the decisions had been democratically arrived at, it was up to the leadership to study the situation, the conditions, and the means, and to adopt the tactic to be employed to carry out effectively and efficiently the tasks assigned to the party. The choice of tactics to be employed was up to the leadership of the party. This required that the authority of the leadership be complete. If the leaders of the party abdicated their authority, if they were neither heard nor respected, what would the authority of the party be? If the party were without authority, what would be the character of the authority of the government or of the state of Guinea? Without the authority of the party, where would the government derive its own authority? The country would soon fall into disorder and anarchy, and rapidly lose its independence. As far as authority is concerned, there is no isolated problem. Everything holds together and makes one body. In the subdivisions of the party, if the leaders are without authority, there is no reason to be surprised if inefficient and mediocre administration results. There is no reason to be surprised if taxes are collected with difficulty, if human investment* is not fully carried out, and if discord arises. All that is normal. When supremacy is given to the party, nothing can go well in the places where the party is insufficient or lacks authority. The party ought to be continually mobilized if it wants the country to develop rapidly at an extraordinary rate of social, economic, and cultural progress.

---

* *Investissement Humain* is the title of the program organized by the PDG in Guinea in which the inhabitants of villages, towns, and other social units donate their free time to collective-work projects organized by the party.—ED.

In order to maintain this indispensable supremacy of the party, we have decided that the general secretaries of the local committees of Conakry are henceforth the official representatives of the mayor. No public act can take place in the future without the authorization of the party. In the local subdivisions (*quartiers*), the general secretary is the representative of the mayor. He represents him at the administrative and political level, at the level of authority and of public order. . . .

Conclusion

The foreign policy of our state is based on positive neutralism with regard to the antagonistic blocs that at present dominate the world with their influence. This is in order to safeguard the chance of the Republic of Guinea to lead the struggle for African independence to success. Indeed, Africa cannot accept the organic extension of any political or ideological system that does not respect its personality, its civilization, and its proper structure. And, as we have said recently at the Indian Congress of Transvaal, "Africa, land of the oppressed, cannot become, against its ardent will for liberation, a place for oppression." In its struggle for reconquest, there is no demand other than that its people have the right to life and to possession of their land, their sun, their sky, and to free utilization and free disposal of their goods. If Africa is a place of asylum for all those who have a sacred respect for man and wish to develop human society, it cannot allow brute force, exaction, and discrimination to be the laws governing the relations of men, people, and races. Against the old divisive practices utilized by the colonial dominators, against the continual diversionary maneuvers that attempt to reduce all coordinated action by arousing internal oppositions among the exploited and oppressed masses, we will respond with firmer cohesion and a renewed determination to assure the triumph of justice, dignity, and liberty.

18. Léopold Sédar Senghor

Léopold Sédar Senghor, President of Senegal, was born in 1907. He was educated at Catholic schools in Senegal, and at the Lycée Louis-le-Grand and the Sorbonne in Paris. Senghor was the first African to receive the prized agrégation *degree. In World War II, he served with the French infantry and was imprisoned for four years by the Germans. After the war, he became active in French African politics, was elected four times as a Senegalese representative in the French National Assembly, and held cabinet posts in French governments. In 1951, he organized the Bloc Démocratique Sénégalais, which received a majority of the seats in the 1957 internal elections for a representative assembly in Senegal. In 1958, his party joined with the Senegalese Socialists under Lamine Gueyé to form the Union Progressiste Sénégalaise (UPS). The following year, Senegal joined French-speaking Sudan in the short-lived Federation of Mali, which broke apart in 1960. In 1960, Senghor was elected President of Senegal, a position he has held since that time. Although Senghor has been critical of the one-party state, the UPS is the only party in Senegal, following its fusion with the single opposition party in 1966.*

The first selection below—detailing Senghor's program for a humanistic, democratic "African socialism"—is taken from an abridged English translation of Senghor's report to a party congress in Dakar (then the capital of the Mali Federation) on July 1, 1959. (The full French text is available under the title Nation et Voie Africaine du Socialisme *[Paris: Présence Africaine, 1961].)*

Senghor has also published four volumes of poetry, as well as an anthology of African poets. He is one of the leading spokesmen for the cultural revival associated with the concept of Negritude, and writes for the publication of the Society for African Culture, Présence Africaine. *The selection on this subject is taken from a speech Senghor delivered at Oxford University in October, 1961.*

AFRICAN SOCIALISM*

In the respective programs of our former parties, all of us used to proclaim our attachment to socialism. This was a good thing, but it was not enough. Most of the time, we were satisfied with stereotyped formulas and vague aspirations, which we called scientific socialism—as if socialism did not mean a return to original sources. Above all, we need to make an effort to rethink the basic texts in the light of Negro African realities.

The antifederalists† have accused us of being atheists, Marxists, and of outlawing religion. Though this smacks of propaganda, it poses a fundamental question. Can we integrate Negro African cultural values, especially religious values, into socialism? We must answer that question once and for all with an unequivocal "Yes."

We are not "Marxists" in the sense given the word today, in so far as Marxism is presented as atheistic metaphysics, a total and totalitarian view of the world, a *Weltanschauung*. In this sense, Marx himself once said: "As for me, I am not a Marxist." We are socialists. In other words, we shall exclude neither Marx nor Engels from our sources; we shall start from their works as from those of the "utopian socialists," and we shall add to these sources the works of their successors and commentators. But we shall retain only the method and the ideas: the method, which can help us to analyze our situation; the ideas, which can help us to solve our problems.

We shall start from Marx and Engels. Whatever their limitations, their inadequacies, or their errors, they, more than all others, revolutionized political and economic thought of the nineteenth century. . . .

We may wonder, first of all, whether the socialism, the economics of Marx, is really "scientific." Yes and no. *No*, if one means by science the exact knowledge and formulation of economic facts in laws which permit one to foresee and to organize a balanced economy. *Yes*, if science is defined as comprehension of the real, if it

---

* Excerpts from Léopold Sédar Senghor, *African Socialism*, translated by Mercer Cook (New York: American Society of African Culture, 1959); reprinted by permission.

† Those opposed to the Federation of Mali (now defunct).—Ed.

consists of deciphering the complexities basic to economic facts, especially man's reactions to these facts, and if its aim is to unveil "the economic law of motion of modern society."

So we must not seek in Marx—not even in *Capital*—an exposé of economic laws. Considering them more or less as contingent "appearances," Marx was not interested in them. Moreover, he went so far as to predict changes that have not occurred.

In *Conflit du Siècle*, Fritz Sternberg has analyzed almost all the changes that have taken place in economic, social, and political reality since the publication of *Capital*. They are impressive and have been listed by other writers. In our résumé of Marx's theories, we have skipped over most of them, and we shall now mention only a few, while noting the recent studies made in France by the Autonomous Socialist Party:

1. The class struggle is much more complex than Marx thought. In fact, the working class is not a simple reality. Moreover, it is diminishing while the several categories of salaried workers with dissimilar interests are increasing.

2. The peasants, whom Marx considered more or less impervious to revolutionary ferment and dedicated "to the stupidity of rural life," have belied his judgment in underdeveloped countries.

3. The theory of capitalist concentration has not been verified by the facts. On the contrary, the number of small and medium-sized businesses continues to grow in Western European countries.

4. Though periodic economic crises have not ceased, they are becoming rarer, and we cannot reasonably foresee a general cataclysm ending the capitalist system, which is adjusting to economic and social evolution.

5. "Socialism" has not triumphed, as Marx predicted, in the industrial nations of Western Europe, but in the underdeveloped nations of Eastern Europe and Asia.

By excessive simplification of the theory of class struggle—a more precise translation of *Klassenkampf* would be a "class war"— Marx overestimated the role of the determinism of things and underestimated man's freedom and the organizing power of the capitalist state. In fact, thanks to trade-union activity and a more enlightened middle class, the capitalistic state, by a policy of intervention and rational organization, has been able progressively to reduce the surplus value. This surplus value, reduced by more equitable taxation, has permitted the productive investments of the postwar era and the institution of social security. Marx advocated social legislation; in his opinion, it would lead to increased unemployment, bitter class antagonism, and, finally, to the revolution. However, social reforms have produced quite the opposite effects.

We may also observe, in passing, that he did not pay enough attention to the role of cooperatives, as preached by the utopian socialists. We know that these have proved their worth in the Scandinavian socialist democracies. Thus, a will to reform has replaced—in Western labor unions—the will to revolt. In the Communist countries, the "dictatorship of the proletariat," contrary to the teachings of Marx, has made the state an omnipotent, soulless monster, has stifled the natural freedoms of the human being, and has dried up the sources of art, without which life is not worth living.

One final word on this point. In Marx's day, colonialism was just beginning. He could not foresee its universal development during the second half of the nineteenth century. He spoke, of course, about "the modern theory of colonization,"* but merely in the etymological sense of the word. He had in mind only European colonization of the United States. Moreover, his macroeconomic theory, his almost blind confidence in proletarian generosity and conscience prevented him from anticipating the opposition that would develop between colonizing and colonized countries, between the well fed and the famished. It is a fact, now commonplace, that the standard of living of the European masses has been able to rise only at the expense of the standard of living of the masses in Asia and Africa. The economy of European nations consists fundamentally of selling manufactured products to underdeveloped countries at high prices and buying raw materials from them at the lowest possible cost. And I am not talking about the United States. The problem is different in France, but if the prices paid for raw materials in African countries are supported, it is no less true that French prices are generally the highest in Western Europe. This compensates for that. In a word, the European prole-

* Capital, IV, 314–28.

tariat has profited from the colonial system; therefore, it has never really—I mean effectively—opposed it.

There we have a series of facts that we must think about, we men from underdeveloped countries, we men inspired by socialism. We must not consider Marx as an economist like Keynes, but as a sociologist, a philosopher. This is something that would have astonished the founder of "scientific socialism," since he refrained from "philosophizing." And yet his thought remains that of a philosopher. Beyond the economic "appearances," it dives into the human reality that causes them. For the *factual* view of things, Marx substitutes a profound insight into human needs. His is a new humanism, new because it is *incarnate*.

Humanism, *philosophy of humanism*, rather than economics— this is the basic character, the positive contribution of Marxian thought. As we said earlier, Marx does not formulate economic facts; he defines "the economic law of motion of modern society," which is a social "tendency" rather than a law. In his analysis, he advances by *postulates* and theories which explain the facts. . . .

For an African Type of Socialism

Let us recapitulate Marx's positive contributions. They are: the philosophy of humanism, economic theory, dialectical method. To these we may add trade unionism, planning, and also federalism and cooperation, which come to us from the French idealistic socialists: Saint Simon, Proudhon, and Fourier—to name only the outstanding ones.

Thus, we are not Communists. Does this mean that we shall practice anti-Communism? Certainly not. Anti-Communism, the "witch hunt," can have but one result: increased tension between East and West and a continuation of the Cold War at the obvious risk of unleashing a third global conflict, from which humanity would not recover. We are not Communists for a theoretical reason. Lenin's definition of matter proceeds from a one-sided concept, from a purely materialistic and deterministic postulate. At the beginning of *Anarchy and Socialism*, Stalin goes even further: "Marxism is not only a theory of socialism, it is a definitive view of the world, a philosophical system."

We are not Communists for a practical reason. The anxiety for human dignity, the need for freedom—man's freedom, the freedoms of collectivities—which animate Marx's thought and provide its revolutionary ferment—this anxiety and this need are unknown to Communism, whose major deviation is Stalinism. The "dictatorship of the proletariat," which was to be only temporary, becomes the dictatorship of the party and state by perpetuating itself. "The Soviet Union," said Mamadou Dia on his return from Moscow, "has succeeded in building socialism, but at the sacrifice of religion, of the soul."

The paradox of socialistic construction in Communist countries —in the Soviet Union at least—is that it increasingly resembles capitalistic construction in the United States, the American way of life, with high salaries, refrigerators, washing machines, and television sets. And it has less art and freedom of thought. Nevertheless, we shall not be won over by a regime of liberal capitalism and free enterprise. We cannot close our eyes to segregation, although the government combats it; nor can we accept the elevation of material success to a way of life.

We stand for a middle course, for a *democratic socialism* which goes so far as to integrate spiritual values, a socialism which ties in with the old ethical current of the French socialists. Historically and culturally, we belong to the current. Besides, the French socialists—from Saint Simon to the Léon Blum of *A l'Echelle humaine*—are not so utopian as they are reputed to be. In so far as they are idealists, they fulfill the requirements of the Negro African soul, the requirements of men of all races and countries. *Not by Bread Alone*—this is the title of a novel by Dudintsev, a citizen of the Soviet Union, and the Russians read this book avidly. Khrushchev was not mistaken: "De-Stalinization was imposed by the people by the thirst for freedom, the hunger for spiritual nourishment."

Concluding his report on the German Democratic Republic [East Germany], Michel Bosquet writes: "But when I ask him [the head of a labor union] what the workers demand, he replies: 'Today they want TV sets and motorcycles. When they get them, they will demand a shorter work week. And then? . . . I can only answer for myself. What I would like, what I miss, is more good literature.' "* This fact is not unrelated to a phenomenon observed in America: the appeal of the contemplative life, as a reaction against the surrounding machinism. Among American Cath-

* *L'Express*, June 4, 1959, p. 24.

olics, the proportion of priests to laity is one of the highest in the world.

This thirst for freedom, this hunger for spiritual nourishment, strengthened by the moral tradition of French socialism, explains why numerous French Marxists in recent years have shunned Stalinism and even Communism: Henri Lefebvre, Pierre Fougeyrollas, and Edgar Morin, among others, who have stated their reasons lately in sorrowful but lucid volumes. * The major reason, common to all of them, is that the Party has come to submerge the individual under the collectivity, the person under the class, to hide reality behind the screen of ideology. If we reflect about these cases, we shall discover that not only Marxism but Marx himself is "called to question"—except perhaps by Lefebvre. For, if the person is submerged, it is because Marx did not pay sufficient attention to the "natural determination"—namely, the *nation*—that is not effaced by class.

Marx underestimated political and national idealism, which, born in France upon the ruins of provincial fatherlands with the Revolution of 1789, won over the world. "Justice," Marx writes, "humanity, liberty, equality, fraternity, independence . . . these relatively moral categories which sound so nice, but which, in historical and political questions, prove absolutely nothing." I repeat: independence. If the creator of scientific sociology returned to this earth, he would perceive with amazement that these "chimeras," as he called them, and above all the concept of *nation*, are living realities in the twentieth century.

What is left of the 1789 Revolution? A political doctrine and technique, accepted nowadays even by the devout. . . . From Marxism there will surely remain an economic doctrine and technique, inasmuch as they do not contradict the teachings of Christianity and Islam—far from it.

But a third revolution is taking place, as a reaction against capitalistic and Communistic materialism—one that will integrate moral, if not religious, values with the political and economic contributions of the two great revolutions. In this revolution, the colored peoples, including the African Negro, must play their part; they must bring their contribution to the construction of the new planetary civilization. As Aimé Césaire says: "They will not

* Cf. Lefebvre, *La Somme et le reste* (La Nef de Paris); Fougeyrollas, *Le Marxisme en question* (Editions du Seuil); Morin, *Autocritique* (Julliard).

come empty-handed to the rendezvous of give-and-take." Between
the two world wars, Paul Morand observed: "The Negroes have
rendered an enormous service to America. But for them, one
might have thought that men could not live without a bank
account and a bathtub."

For a Strong Federal Democracy

Our democracy will be *federal*. . . . We do not need to remind
you that local diversities, with their complementary qualities, will
enrich the federation. Conversely, the federation will preserve those
diversities. The decentralized federal structure will be extended,
within the framework of the federal state, to regional and communal collectivities, even into economic and social areas. The
Yugoslavian structures, adapted to our realities, will, in this instance, serve as a model.

Thus we shall fill the dangerous void now existing between the
federal state and the village. Our leaders are bored with their
freedom from responsibility. Even when they fill this void by the
political formation of militants, they tend to devote their activity
to contention over slogans. Regional and communal assemblies,
among others, would give them a practical opportunity to exercise
their responsibilities. A revolution remains ideological, therefore
ineffective, so long as it is not translated into concrete action
which, by transforming the structure, raises the standard of living
and culture of the citizens. . . .

A federal democracy, yes . . . but a strong democracy. As the
Secretary General suggests in his report, it is a question of avoiding two dangers: on the one hand, fascist dictatorship, which one
observes in the antifederalist states; on the other hand, governmental instability, which was common in France during the Third
and Fourth Republics. Both deviations are signs of weakness; in
the long run, they provoke the revolt of the people and the disintegration of the state.

The Federation of Mali, like the federated states, will be a democracy.* The electoral law will continue to be impartial . . . not
a law of circumstance, cut to the measure of the government or
the majority party. Freedom of opinion, speech, press, assembly,

* In August, 1960, after this report was made, the Federation of Mali
separated into its component parts, Senegal and the Sudan (which took the
name of the Republic of Mali).—ED.

and association is guaranteed by the constitutions of Mali and the federated states—in the antifederalist states also. But, with us, these freedoms do not exist only on paper; they are effectively enjoyed and will continue to be so. Above all, the right of *free settlement* of the citizens will be assured, whether or not they were born in Mali. A democratic policy pays dividends; in addition, it conforms to our humanitarian ideal. Already, public opinion in black Africa and France is grateful to us. This is excellent propaganda for Mali.

The rights of the minority, of the opposition, will therefore be respected in Mali. They will find their natural and legal limits in the rights of the majority, the popular will, which is sovereign; in other words, in the rights of the nation-state. For we are a quasi nation, as François Perroux says.

The stability of the executive is guaranteed by our constitutions. We need to assure it in actual political practice. It is necessary that governments govern, that they, along with the legislative assemblies, take the initiative of making laws within the framework of the doctrine and program of the majority party. Governments must apply the law firmly, and legislative assemblies must check on the action of the government. It is necessary that the party (congress, executive committee, and officers) have the final word in matters of control. Yet, to be effective, the various controls will be general and *a posteriori*. Meddling and harassing controls would not work. Here again, we shall avoid two dangers: granting government action a blank check, and taking away the executive power. The controls must be political, not technical.

Let us return to the rights of the opposition. Their role, certainly, is to criticize. But "criticism" means critical spirit, not spirit of criticism, systematic carping. In a democracy, criticism must be constructive and serve the general, not factional, interest. At any rate, one cannot grant the opposition more rights than the majority enjoys. The law also applies to the opposition, which is likewise required to observe it. Under the control of the majority party, the governments will take all necessary steps to curb demagogic opposition. They will not tolerate violations of the law, appeals to illegality or to violence, whether the pretexts be religious or racial. This is the democratic sense that we attach to the "dictatorship of the proletariat."

WHAT IS "NEGRITUDE"?*

Paradoxically, it was the French who first forced us to seek its essence, and who then showed us where it lay . . . when they enforced their policy of assimilation and thus deepened our despair. . . . Earlier, we had become aware within ourselves that assimilation was a failure; we could assimilate mathematics or the French language, but we could never strip off our black skins or root out black souls. And so we set out on a fervent quest for the "holy grail": our collective soul. And we came upon it.

It was not revealed to us by the "official France" of the politicians who, out of self-interest and political conviction, defended the policy of assimilation. Its whereabouts was pointed out to us by that handful of free-lance thinkers—writers, artists, ethnologists, and prehistorians—who bring about cultural revolutions in France. It was, to be quite precise, our teachers of ethnology who introduced us to the considerable body of work already achieved in the understanding of Africa, by the University of Oxford.

What did we learn from all those writers, artists, and teachers? That the early years of colonization and especially, even before colonization, the slave trade had ravaged black Africa like a bush fire, wiping out images and values in one vast carnage. That Negroid civilization had flourished in the Upper Paleolithic Age, and that the Neolithic revolution could not be explained without them. That their roots retained their vigor and would one day produce new grass and green branches . . .

Negritude is the *whole complex of civilized values—cultural, economic, social, and political—which characterize the black peoples*, or, more precisely, the Negro-African world. All these values are essentially informed by intuitive reason, because this sentient reason, the reason which comes to grips, expresses itself emotionally, through that self-surrender, that coalescence of subject and object; through myths, by which I mean the archetypal images of the collective soul; and, above all, through primordial rhythms, synchronized with those of the cosmos. In other words, the sense of communion, the gift of mythmaking, the gift of rhythm, such are the essential elements of Negritude, which you will find in-

* Excerpts from a speech delivered by Senghor at Oxford University in October, 1961; reprinted, by permission, from *West Africa*, November 4, 1961.

delibly stamped on all the works and activities of the black man. . . .

In opposition to European racialism, of which the Nazis were the symbol, we set up an "antiracial racialism." The very excesses of Nazism, and the catastrophes it engendered, were soon to bring us to our senses. Such hatred, such violence, above all, such weeping and such shedding of blood produced a feeling of revulsion. It was so foreign to our continent's genius: our *need to love*. And then the anthropologists taught us that there is no such thing as a pure race: Scientifically speaking—races do not exist. They went one better and forecast that, with a mere 200 million people, we would in the end disappear as a "black race," through miscegenation. At the same time, they did offer us some consolation. "The focal points of human development," wrote Teilhard de Chardin in 1939, "always seem to coincide with the points of contact and anastomosis of several nerve paths"—that is, in the ordinary man's language, of several races.* If, then, we were justified in fostering the values of Negritude and arousing the energy slumbering within us, it must be in order to pour them into the mainstream of cultural miscegenation (the biological process taking place spontaneously). They must flow toward the meeting point of all humanity; they must be our contribution to the civilization of the universal.

Biological miscegenation, then, takes place spontaneously, provoked by the very laws which govern life, and in the face of all policies of apartheid. It is a different matter in the realm of culture. Here, we remain wholly free to cooperate or not, to provoke or prevent the synthesis of cultures. This is an important point. For, as certain biologists point out, the psychological mutations brought about by education are incorporated in our genes and are then transmitted by heredity. Hence the major role played by culture.

Seen within this prospect of the civilization of the universal, the colonial policies of Great Britain and France have proved successful complements to each other, and black Africa has benefited. The policies of the former tended to reinforce the traditional native civilization. As for France's policy, although we have often reviled it in the past, it too ended with a credit balance, through forcing us actively to assimilate European civilization. This fertilized our

* On the relation of Teilhard de Chardin and Negritude, see Senghor's *Pierre Teilhard de Chardin et la Politique Africaine* (Paris: Editions du Seuil, 1962).—ED.

sense of Negritude. Today, our Negritude no longer expresses itself as opposition to European values, but as a *complement* to them. Henceforth, its militants will be concerned, as I have often said, *not to be assimilated, but to assimilate*. They will use European values to arouse the slumbering values of Negritude, which they will bring as their contribution to the civilization of the universal.

Nevertheless, we still disagree with Europe: not with its values any longer (with the exception of capitalism), but with its theory of the civilization of the universal. . . . In the eyes of the Europeans, the "exotic civilizations" are static in character, being content to live by means of archetypal images, which they repeat indefinitely. The most serious criticism is that they have no idea of the *pre-eminent dignity of the human person*. My reply is this: Just as much as black Africa, Europe and its North American offspring live by means of archetypal images. For what are free enterprise, democracy, and Communism but *myths*, around which hundreds of millions of men and women organize their lives? Negritude itself is a myth (I am not using the word in any pejorative sense), but a living, dynamic one, which evolves with its circumstances into a form of humanism. Actually, our criticism of the [European] thesis is that it is monstrously antihumanist. For if European civilization were to be imposed, unmodified, on all peoples and continents, it could only be by force. That is its first disadvantage. A more serious one is that it would not be *humanistic*, for it would cut itself off from the complementary values of the greater part of humanity. As I have said elsewhere, it would be a universal civilization; it would not be the civilization of the universal.

Our revised Negritude is humanistic. I repeat, it welcomes the complementary values of Europe and the white man, and, indeed, of all other races and continents. But it welcomes them in order to fertilize and reinvigorate its own values, which it then offers for the construction of a civilization which shall embrace all mankind. The neohumanism of the twentieth century stands at the point where the paths of all nations, races, and continents cross, "where the four winds of the spirit blow."

19. Kwame Nkrumah

Kwame Nkrumah was born in the Gold Coast, near the Ivory Coast border, in 1909. He was baptized a Catholic and attended mission schools for eight years. A German priest sent him to Achimota College—a secondary school near Accra—where he first acquired nationalist sentiments. After several years of teaching in the Gold Coast, he borrowed enough money to get to the United States where, in 1935, he received a scholarship from Lincoln University in Pennsylvania. After graduation, he taught political science at Lincoln University, and at the same time did graduate work toward advanced degrees at the University of Pennsylvania. In 1945, he went to England, where he became active in the nationalist movement. Two years later, he returned to the Gold Coast as organizing secretary of the United Gold Coast Convention, under J. B. Danquah. In 1949, he organized his own party, the Convention People's Party, which won all subsequent elections (including one in which Nkrumah campaigned while in prison, in 1951). On March 6, 1957, the Gold Coast was granted independence under the name of Ghana, and Nkrumah became its Prime Minister. In 1960, Ghana became a republic, and Nkrumah was elected President. In 1964, Ghana was officially declared a one-party state. Nkrumah's increasingly dictatorial exercise of power and Ghana's worsening economic situation led to an army coup d'état on February 24, 1966, while Nkrumah was on a state visit to China.

The selection below from Nkrumah's autobiography describes the principal influences on his political outlook and the methods that led to the independence of Ghana. It is followed by an excerpt from Consciencism, a recent attempt to develop an ideology of African revolution. Its contents give an indication of the increasingly radical character of Nkrumah's thinking before his overthrow in 1966. His obsession with neocolonialism reflects a widespread belief by the African left that nothing has really been changed by the granting of political independence.

BACKGROUND TO INDEPENDENCE*

Independence for the Gold Coast was my aim. It was a colony, and I have always regarded colonialism as the policy by which a foreign power binds territories to herself by political ties, with the primary object of promoting her own economic advantage. No one need be surprised if this system has led to disturbances and political tension in many territories. There are few people who would not rid themselves of such domination if they could.

At this time, I devoted much energy to the study of revolutionaries and their methods. Those who interested me most were Hannibal, Cromwell, Napoleon, Lenin, Mazzini, Gandhi, Mussolini, and Hitler. I found much of value to be gleaned and many ideas that were useful to me later in my own campaign against imperialism.

At first I could not understand how Gandhi's philosophy of nonviolence could possibly be effective. It seemed to me to be utterly feeble and without hope of success. The solution of the colonial problem, as I saw it at that time, lay in armed rebellion. How is it possible, I asked myself, for a revolution to succeed without arms and ammunition? After months of studying Gandhi's policy and watching the effect it had, I began to see that, when backed by a strong political organization, it could be the solution to the colonial problem. In Jawaharlal Nehru's rise to power I recognized the success of one who, pledged to socialism, was able to interpret Gandhi's philosophy in practical terms.

The Gold Coast revolt against colonialism is not a new thing. Its roots are deep. There was the Confederation of 1868, when certain chiefs came together to defend themselves not only against their tribal kin, the Ashantis, but also against political encroachments from abroad. After the bond of 1844, which gave Britain trading rights, the Gold Coast had come increasingly under her control.

The next great move of political cohesion and conscience was the formation of the Aborigines Rights Protection Society by

* Excerpts from *Ghana: The Autobiography of Kwame Nkrumah* (New York: Thomas Nelson and Sons, 1957; copyright by Thomas Nelson and Sons, 1957); reprinted by permission.

chiefs and literate Africans with the object of defending Gold Coast land. When this collapsed—because of an ever-widening rift between the chiefs and the educated people—the latter, binding themselves together and supported by their educated brothers in other West African territories, established the National Congress of British West Africa. This was the first indication of West African nationalism. However, because it lacked the support of the masses, it disintegrated in 1930.

The vacuum that this left in Gold Coast politics was eventually filled by the formation of the United Gold Coast Convention by the merchant and lawyer class of the country. It was when I realized that this movement was doomed to failure because it ignored the interests of the masses that I broke away, in 1949, and formed the Convention People's Party.

I saw that the whole solution to this problem lay in political freedom for our people; for it is only when a people are politically free that other races can give them the respect that is due them. It is impossible to talk of equality of races in any other terms. No people without a government of their own can expect to be treated on the same level as peoples of independent sovereign states. It is far better to be free to govern or misgovern yourself than to be governed by anybody else.

The formation of the CPP coincided with a political reawakening among the workers and young people of the country. Ex-servicemen who had taken part in World War II returned to the Gold Coast dissatisfied with their position after having been given the chance of comparing their lot with that of other peoples, and they were prepared to take up any line which would better their conditions. There was a general dissatisfaction with the British colonial policy that had been adopted until that time, especially the policy of indirect rule which so encouraged tribal feudalism. Again, the Russian Revolution and its aftermath had left its mark by spreading ideas of workers' solidarity, trade-union movements, freedom and independence. Events in Asia also added a glow to the political awakening.

The CPP was not merely a mass movement. Mass movements are well and good, but they cannot act with purpose unless they are led and guided by a vanguard political party. And when the time comes for a ruling power to accord self-government, it will do so more willingly if it can hand over to a properly constituted political party with a majority backing, rather than to a revolutionary nationalist movement. Rallying around me all those who genuinely wished for progress, I resisted both the opportunist element and the reactionary forces, and sought to establish the CPP as the democratic instrument of the people's will and aspirations. We were freely elected to power in 1951. Three years later, and again in 1956, the same confidence was shown by the country.

The first objective then is political independence, for which I believe the organization itself must take two forms. First there is the period of "positive action"—a combination of nonviolent methods with effective and disciplined political action. At this stage, open conflict with the existing colonial regime is inevitable, and this is a test of strength for the organization. Since it is marked by nonviolence, and since the forces of might are on the side of the colonial power, there is little chance of complete success in this period.

The second stage is one of "tactical action"—a sort of contest of wits. From now on, the movement must make its ideology clear and convincing. The ideology of my party may be formulated as follows: No race, no people, no nation can exist freely and be respected at home and abroad without political freedom.

Once this freedom is gained, a greater task comes into view. All dependent territories are backward in education, in science, in agriculture, and in industry. The economic independence that should follow and maintain political independence demands every effort from the people, a total mobilization of brain and manpower resources. What other countries have taken three hundred years to achieve, a once dependent territory must try to accomplish in a generation if it is to survive. Unless it is, as it were, "jet-propelled," it will lag behind and thus risk everything for which it has fought.

Capitalism is too complicated a system for a newly independent nation. Hence the need for a socialistic society. But even a system based on social justice and a democratic constitution may need backing up, during the period following independence, by emergency measures of a totalitarian kind. Without discipline, true freedom cannot survive. In any event, the basis must be a loyal, honest, hard-working, and responsible civil service on which the party in power can rely. Armed forces must also be consolidated for defense. . . .

I concentrated on finding a formula by which the whole colonial question and the problem of imperialism could be solved. I read Hegel, Marx, Engels, Lenin, and Mazzini. The writings of these men did much to influence me in my revolutionary ideas and activities, and Marx and Lenin particularly impressed me as I felt sure that their philosophy was capable of solving these problems. But I think that of all the literature that I studied, the book that did more than any other to fire my enthusiasm was *The Philosophy and Opinions of Marcus Garvey* . . . with his philosophy of "Africa for the Africans" and his "Back to Africa" movement.

CONSCIENCISM*

. . . Whereas capitalism is a development by refinement from slavery and feudalism, socialism is obviously not a development from capitalism. In order that socialism should be a development from capitalism, it needs to share a fundamental principle, that of exploitation, with capitalism. Socialism most avowedly has no share in this principle. Hence socialism cannot develop from capitalism. Rather it stands for the negation of that very principle wherein capitalism has its being, lives, and thrives, that principle which unites capitalism with slavery and feudalism.

If one seeks the social-political ancestor of socialism, one must go to communalism. Socialism stands to communalism as capitalism stands to slavery. In socialism, the principles underlying communalism are given expression in modern circumstances. Thus, whereas communalism in an untechnical society can be *laissez faire*, in a technical society where sophisticated means of production are at hand, if the underlying principles of communalism are not given centralized and correlated expression, class cleavages will arise, which are connected with economic disparities, and thereby with political inequalities. Socialism, therefore, can be and is the defense of the principles of communalism in a modern setting. Socialism is a form of social organization which, guided by the principles underlying Communism, adopts procedures and meas-

---

* Excerpts from *Consciencism: Philosophy and Ideology for Decolonization and Development* (London: Heinemann Educational Books; New York: Monthly Review Press, 1964); reprinted by permission of Heinemann Educational Books Ltd. and the Monthly Review Press.

ures made necessary by demographic and technological developments.

These considerations throw great light on the bearing of revolution and reform on socialism. The passage from the ancestral line of slavery via feudalism and capitalism to socialism can only lie through revolution: it cannot lie through reform. For in reform, fundamental principles are held constant and the details of their expression modified. In the words of Marx, it leaves the pillars of the building intact. Indeed, sometimes reform itself may be initiated by the necessities of preserving identical fundamental principles. Reform is a tactic of self-preservation.

Revolution is thus an indispensable avenue to socialism, where the antecedent social-political structure is animated by principles which are a negation of those of socialism, as in a capitalist structure (and therefore also in a colonialist structure, for a colonialist structure is essentially ancillary to capitalism). Indeed, I distinguish between two colonialisms, between a domestic one and an external one. Capitalism at home is domestic colonialism.

But from the ancestral line of communalism, the passage to socialism lies in reform, because the underlying principles are the same. But when this passage carries one through colonialism the reform is revolutionary since the passage from colonialism to genuine independence is an act of revolution. But because of the continuity of communalism with socialism, in communalistic societies, socialism is not a revolutionary creed, but a restatement in contemporary idiom of the principles underlying communalism. The passage from a noncommunalistic society to socialism is a revolutionary one which is guided by the principles underlying Communism.

In my autobiography, I said that capitalism might prove too complicated a system for a newly independent country. I wish to add to this the fact that the presuppositions and purposes of capitalism are contrary to those of African society. Capitalism would be a betrayal of the personality and conscience of Africa.

I have explained how society's desire to transform nature reflects itself in different social-political theories. I wish now to suggest how the same desire reflects itself in philosophy. Just as social-political theories, to the extent that they deploy forces for the harnessing and development of nature, fall into two lots, so do philosophies. From this standpoint, the two real social-political alternatives facing society are either that one section should produce, and another section batten thereon, or that all sections should produce and all sections should be fulfilled by the value created by labor.

In the same way, there are two real philosophical alternatives. These alternatives coincide with idealism and materialism. In the preceding chapter, I explained how idealism was connected with a tiered society, how through its mode of explaining nature and social phenomena by reference to spirit, idealism favored a class structure of a horizontal sort, in which one class sat upon the neck of another.

I also explained there how materialism, on the other hand, was connected with a humanist organization, how through its being monistic, and its referring all natural processes to matter and its laws, it inspired an egalitarian organization of society. The unity and fundamental identity of nature suggests the unity and fundamental identity of man in society. Idealism favors an oligarchy, materialism favors an egalitarianism.

Individuals have both idealist and materialist tendencies in them. So have societies both idealist and materialist streaks. But these streaks do not exist in equipoise. They are connected by a conflict in which now one streak predominates, now the other.

By reason of the connection of idealism with an oligarchy and of materialism with an egalitarianism, the opposition of idealism and materialism in the same society is paralleled by the opposition of conservative and progressive forces on the social level. When in the dialectical opposition of capitalism to socialism, the former for a time becomes triumphant, social progress is not thereby altogether arrested, though it is seriously attenuated. But since it is not arrested, it is hardly cause for wonder that the workers of today in many respects enjoy better circumstances of life than even a good many feudal lords of the past. To confess to this degree of progress is not to say, however, that capitalism has been without its shanty-towns and slums, its captive workers languishing and finally dying in public squares, victims of hunger, cold, and disease.

The question is not whether there has been discernible progress under capitalism, but rather whether what progress is admitted can be said to be adequate. . . .

Practice without thought is blind; thought without practice is empty. The three segments of African society . . . the traditional, the Western, and the Islamic, coexist uneasily; the principles animating them are often in conflict with one another. I have in illustration tried to show how the principles which inform capitalism are in conflict with the socialist egalitarianism of the traditional African society.

What is to be done then? I have stressed that the two other segments, in order to be rightly seen, must be accommodated only as experiences of the traditional African society. If we fail to do this our society will be racked by the most malignant schizophrenia.

Our attitude to the Western and the Islamic experience must be purposeful. It must also be guided by thought, for practice without thought is blind. What is called for as a first step is a body of connected thought which will determine the general nature of our action in unifying the society which we have inherited, this unification to take account, at all times, of the elevated ideals underlying the traditional African society. Social revolution must therefore have, standing firmly behind it, an intellectual revolution, a revolution in which our thinking and philosophy are directed towards the redemption of our society. Our philosophy must find its weapons in the environment and living conditions of the African people. It is from those conditions that the intellectual content of our philosophy must be created. The emancipation of the African continent is the emancipation of man. This requires two aims: first, the restitution of the egalitarianism of human society, and, second, the logistic mobilization of all our resources towards the attainment of that restitution.

The philosophy that must stand behind this social revolution is that which I have once referred to as philosophical consciencism; consciencism is the map in intellectual terms of the disposition of forces which will enable African society to digest the Western and the Islamic and the Euro-Christian elements in Africa, and develop them in such a way that they fit into the African personality. The African personality is itself defined by the cluster of humanist principles which underlie the traditional African society. Philosophical consciencism is that philosophical standpoint which, taking its start from the present content of the African conscience, indicates the way in which progress is forged out of the conflict in that conscience. . . .

Just as the placid appearance of matter only disguises the tension of forces underlying that appearance, like the bow of Heraclitus, so in a colonial territory, an opposition of reactionary and revolutionary forces can nevertheless give an impression of final and acquiescent subjugation. But just as a quality can be changed by quantitative (measurable) changes of a critical nature in matter, so this acquiescent impression can be obliterated by a change in the relation of the social forces. These opposing sets of forces are dynamic, in the sense that they seek and tend to establish some social condition. One may therefore refer to them by the name of action in order to make their dynamic nature explicit. In that case, one may say that in a colonial situation positive action and negative action can be discerned. Positive action will represent the sum of those forces seeking social justice in terms of the destruction of oligarchic exploitation and oppression. Negative action will correspondingly represent the sum of those forces tending to prolong colonial subjugation and exploitation. Positive action is revolutionary and negative action is reactionary.

It ought to be recognized at the outset that the introduced terms of positive and negative action are abstractions. But the ground for them is in social reality. It is quite possible by means of statistical analysis to discover the ways in which positive action and negative action are related in any given society. The statistical analysis will be of such facts as production, distribution, income, etc. Any such analysis must reveal one of three possible situations. Positive action may exceed negative action, or negative action may exceed positive action, or they may form an unstable equilibrium.

In a colonial situation, negative action undoubtedly outweighs positive action. In order that true independence should be won, it is necessary that positive action should come to overwhelm negative action. Admittedly, a semblance of true independence is possible without this specific relation. When this happens, we say that neocolonialism has set in, for neocolonialism is a guise adopted by negative action in order to give the impression that it has been overcome by positive action. Neocolonialism is negative action playing possum.

In order to forestall this, it is necessary for positive action to be backed by a mass party, and qualitatively to improve this mass so that by education and an increase in its degree of consciousness, its aptitude for positive action becomes heightened. We can therefore say that in a colonial territory, positive action must be backed by a mass party, complete with its instruments of education. This was why the Convention People's Party of Ghana developed from an early stage its education wing, workers' wing, farmers' wing, youth wing, women's wing, etc. In this way, the people received constant political education, their self-awareness was increased and such a self-image was formed as ruthlessly excluded colonialism in all its guises. It is also in the backing of millions of members and supporters, united by a common radical purpose, that the revolutionary character of the Convention People's Party consists, and not merely in the piquancy of its programs. Its mass and national support made it possible to think in realistic terms of instituting changes of a fundamental nature in the social hotch-potch bequeathed by colonialism.

A people's parliamentary democracy with a one-party system is better able to express and satisfy the common aspirations of a nation as a whole, than a multiple-party parliamentary system, which is in fact only a ruse for perpetuating, and covers up, the inherent struggle between the "haves" and the "have-nots." . . .

Any oblique attempt of a foreign power to thwart, balk, corrupt, or otherwise pervert the true independence of a sovereign people is neocolonialist. It is neocolonialist because it seeks, notwithstanding the acknowledged sovereignty of a people, to subordinate their interests to those of a foreign power.

A colonialist country can in fact offer independence to a people, not with the intention which such an act might be thought to imply, but in the hope that the positive and progressive forces thus appeased and quietened, the people might be exploited with greater serenity and comfort.

Neocolonialism is a greater danger to independent countries than is colonialism. Colonialism is crude, essentially overt, and apt to be overcome by a purposeful concert of national effort. In neo-colonialism, however, the people are divided from their leaders and, instead of providing true leadership and guidance which is informed at every point by the ideal of the general welfare, leaders come to neglect the very people who put them in power and incautiously become instruments of suppression on behalf of the neocolonialists.

It is far easier for the proverbial camel to pass through the needle's eye, hump and all, than for an erstwhile colonial administration to give sound and honest counsel of a *political* nature to its liberated territory. To allow a foreign country, especially one which is loaded with economic interests in our continent, to tell us what *political* decisions to take, what *political* courses to follow, is indeed for us to hand back our independence to the oppressor on a silver platter.

Likewise, since the motivation of colonialism, whatever protean forms it may take, is well and truly economic, colonialism itself being but the institution of political bonds fastening colonies to a colonialist country, with the primary object of the metropolitan economic advantages, it is essential that a liberated territory should not bind her economy to that of the ousted rulers. The liberation of a people institutes principles which enjoin the recognition and destruction of imperialistic domination, whether it is political, economic, social, or cultural. To destroy imperialistic domination in these forms, political, economic, social, and cultural action must always have reference to the needs and nature of the liberated territory, and it is from these needs and nature that the action must derive authenticity. Unless this self-reference is religiously maintained, a liberated territory will welcome with open arms the very foe which it has sought to destroy at cost of terrible suffering. . . .

20. K. A. Busia

Kofi A. Busia was born of the Royal House of Wenchi in the Ashanti area of Ghana in 1914. He took an external degree from the University of London and received his doctorate from Oxford. He returned to the Gold Coast and taught at the University College before entering politics in opposition to Kwame Nkrumah. Busia was leader of the parliamentary opposition in Ghana after independence in 1957, but left the country in 1959 when it became apparent that Nkrumah intended to establish a one-party state. While in exile, he taught at Oxford and in Mexico and was Professor of Sociology at the University of Leiden in Holland. Just before Nkrumah's overthrow in 1966, he completed Africa in Search of Democracy, *which was directed against the apologists for the one-party state, such as Nkrumah and Julius Nyerere. Arguing that traditional systems in Africa included checks on the power of the rulers, he defended the freedoms of the press, the judiciary, and opposition parties. When Nkrumah was overthrown, he returned to Ghana and re-entered politics as leader of the Progress Party. After his party won an overwhelming electoral victory in 1969, he became Prime Minister of Ghana.*

AFRICA IN SEARCH OF DEMOCRACY *

The best kind of democracy is the one which enables as many people as possible to share in the making of decisions, and in the actual functions of government. In the Ashanti system, the fact that each lineage, village, or part of a chiefdom managed as much of its own affairs as was consistent with the unity of the whole chiefdom enabled many to share in decision-making in local affairs; for the head of each unit was, like the chief at the center, obliged to act only on the concurrence and with the advice of his own local council.

However autocratic a chief was permitted to appear, he really ruled by the consent of the people. There was a balance between authority on the one side, and obligation on the other. A chief or king had the power to raise taxes, or exact tribute, or ask his people to work on his farm, or even call them to take up arms to defend the chiefdom. But he had the corresponding obligation to dispense justice, or to protect the interests of his people, or ensure their welfare by certain ritual acts and observances. The ruler's subjects knew what duties he owed them, and they could exert pressure to make him discharge those duties.

There can be no true democracy where there is no free expression of opinion in public affairs or criticism of the ruling body. Any member of the community could take part in the public discussions of community affairs, or in the public hearings and "anyone—even the most ordinary youth—will offer his opinion, or make a suggestion with an equal chance of its being heard as if it proceeded from the most experienced sage." †

* Excerpts from K. A. Busia, *Africa in Search of Democracy*, (New York: Praeger Publishers, London: Routledge, Kegan Paul, 1967), by permission of the author and publishers.

† Brodie Cruickshank, *Eighteen Years on the Gold Coast of Africa* (London, 1854).

The members of a chief's council were, in one aspect, representatives of the people; in another sense, they and the crief constituted the government. As representatives of a section of the chiefdom, they were to protect the sectional interests of those whom they represented, and to see to it that the chief did not abuse his power; but as members of the council which had responsibility for the affairs of the whole community, they were to help to ensure the welfare of all, and to see that the people obeyed and supported the constituted authority. They shared responsibility with the chief. It is never easy to reconcile the two functions. Somebody has to keep the government or the constituted authority to the mark. None can do this better than those over whom the government rules. The Ashanti system provided opportunities for the "commoners," those who were ruled, to express criticism, either through their lineage heads, or through a chosen leader recognized as spokesman for the commoners; through him the body of free citizens could criticize the government and express their wishes when they thought that undesirable measures were being contemplated or enforced; in the last resort, they could depose their rulers. Democracy cannot survive, unless people are able to make the government express their will; unless they have the power to choose their rulers and to change them. . . .

Neither authoritarianism nor the one-party State can be traced to traditional political systems like these. Arguments to justify the one-party State or authoritarianism cannot be based on the grounds of tradition. There were tribes which had hardly any institutional checks on their rulers, or where these were so ineffective as to make the system autocratic; but it is stretching the point too far to argue from this that one-party rule is a uniquely African innovation, uniformly in accord with her tradition. One-party governments can, in this twentieth century, be found in all continents, and cannot be appropriated by Africa as her own unique attribute. . . .

When a council, each member of which was the representative of a lineage, met to discuss matters affecting the whole community, it had always to grapple with the problem of reconciling sectional and common interests. In order to do this, the members had to talk things over: they had to listen to all the different points of view. So strong was the value of solidarity that the chief aim of the councillors was to reach unanimity, and they talked till this was achieved. Some have singled out this feature of talking till unanimity was reached as the cardinal principle of African democracy.* They have even gone farther to maintain that it is the essential mark of a democratic form of government, and that any government which has this is therefore democratic. This is going too far, for there are other important elements of a democracy. The principle is, however, noteworthy. The members of a traditional council allowed discussion, and a free and frank expression of opinions, and if there was disagreement, they spent hours, even days if necessary, to argue and exchange ideas till they reached unanimity. Those who disagreed were not denied a hearing, or locked up in prison, or branded as enemies of the community. . . .

It has often been stated both by Africans and Europeans that Africa should not be expected to have a "Westminster type democracy." One interpretation given to this seems to imply that Africans are incapable of practicing democratic rule. If this refers to the values of democracy, such as the rule of law, respect for human dignity, or the freedoms of speech, association, conscience, and the other ingredients of democracy we have referred to in this chapter, it can be seen from the evidence that Africans cherish democratic values, and that there are leaders whose political policies are inspired by them. The values of democracy must be seen as ideals which have universal validity.

Another interpretation of the statement is that Africans cannot be expected to adopt the same institutions as those of Westminster. This is, in fact, not saying something that is new; it has historical and sociological support. Countries borrow ideas and institutions from one another. Africa has already borrowed many ideas and institutions from Europe, including political institutions like the party, and political offices like Prime Minister, Minister, or President, and other institutions like schools and trade unions. The sociological fact is that institutions borrowed from one country into another are never exactly the same, for the borrowing country fits them into its own social context, and something therefore changes. The historical and social conditions of Africa are different from those of Europe, and the political institutions which African countries will find most suitable to express democratic values may well be different. No one can dispute the right

---

* The reference is to Julius Nyerere.—ED.

of Africans to evolve institutions which fit them best in their own historical and social context. But others have a right to expect the values of democracy to which the institutions give expression to be recognizable. The democratic institutions of France, Britain, and America, for example, have notable differences reflecting the history and social conditions of each country, but underlying them are perceptible values of democracy which they all share. In the same way, India has institutions reflecting Indian history and social structures, but there are recognizable values which she shares with the other democratic countries, and by which they are all judged. Since democracy expresses both principles and ideals, every country will be found to fall short in some respect or other. There are glaringly undemocratic practices in Africa also; we have already had evidence of this. . . . Good reasons may be given to explain some of the shortcomings, and it helps to promote international harmony for different countries to try to understand one another's problems. But it does not help Africa not to see her shortcomings for what they are, measured against the standards we have seen her leaders to avow. One of the sources of hope for world peace lies in the fact that democracy has a moral language which peoples of different cultures and races can understand. The democratic principle of racial equality has a moral foundation in the shared ideals of democracy. In so far as any country, wherever it may be, professes democracy, there should be common standards by which it can be judged. The countries of Africa which avow democratic ideals justifiably claim the right to evolve their own institutions; but they may not claim with equal justification to have their own particular brands of democracy with values so different from those of other nations that there are no meeting points. . . .

[Ghana's] Preventive Detention Bill was introduced into Parliament on July 14th, 1958, and it received the Governor-General's assent on July 18th, 1958. Since then it has been the principal instrument for stifling opposition to the government.* It was required by the Act that the list of those detained under the law should be published in the Government Gazette, and this was done for a while. In November 1958, 43 persons, most of them members of the United Party, were arrested and detained under the Act; some of them are still in prison, eight years later, without

* This was written before Nkrumah's overthrow in February, 1966.—ED.

trial. On December 23rd, 1960, 118 persons were also taken into preventive detention; On October 3rd, 1961, among 50 persons who were arrested and detained were Mr. J. E. Appiah, Deputy Leader of the Opposition, and Dr. J. B. Danquah, one of the most prominent political leaders in the country, a leading member of the opposition, and a Presidential candidate who stood against Dr. Nkrumah for the Presidency. Dr. Danquah was released after ten months, then was re-arrested and detained until his death in prison after thirteen months, on February 4th, 1965, at the age of seventy. . . .

The one-party régime in Ghana has meant the concentration of power over all the organs of State in the hands of one man. The foundations of democracy have been undermined.

A part of this process has been government and party control of the press as well as broadcasting. There is no independent paper in Ghana, and both press and radio only tell the people what the government wants them to know. There is also a censorship of news sent abroad by foreign correspondents. A further curtailment of freedom has been foreshadowed. In November, 1964, the government set up a committee of nine persons to "work out a system to ensure the removal of all publications which do not reflect the ideology of the party or are antagonistic to its ideas." Free access to information and knowledge appear to be in danger. . . .

Every democratic community must have effective checks on its rulers. Democracy rejects the view that the leader and the group around him who lead the single party always infallibly seek the interests of the people, or embody the will of all. The leader and the group and all who constitute the party are fallible men and women, on whom there must be effective checks in the exercise of the powers they wield. This implies the right of the people to oppose, and their right to choose and to change their rulers and leaders. The political institutions must provide democratic outlets for the exercise of these rights.

There appear to be two crucial questions for Africa: the way in which to institutionalize opposition, and how to make it possible to change a single-party government that has failed to satisfy the people. Some single-party devices are in effect self-perpetuating organs for the leaders. . . .

The right to criticize a government of which one is a member was one of the built-in checks of the traditional Ashanti political system. The lineages or areas were expected to criticize, and even though the ultimate objective was to reach consensus, there was also the constitutional right of the chief to take steps to destool a member of the Council, and the constitutional right of the members of the Council to destool the chief. Both rights were governed by traditional checks to prevent arbitrary action. It is as though there were arrangements not only for a Prime Minister or President to dismiss a Cabinet Minister, but also for the Cabinet to be able to initiate the deposition of the President or the Prime Minister. In either case, the ultimate power lay with the electors. The right to criticize did not abrogate the right to change the leader. Democratic restraints and discipline were obviously needed for the proper functioning of the system. Further, although there was no permanent opposition as such, the people had rights not only in the election and deposition of their rulers but also to criticize. This right was institutionalized. There were traditional ceremonies at which the people, particularly the women, could lampoon in song and dance against their rulers with impunity. So there were recognized occasions when the chief, in spite of the sacral nature of his office, was reminded that he was just as fallible as other mortals, and he had to listen to his wrongs as they were brought home to him.

It is right that Africa should seek her own institutions, and not pattern her institutions on those of Britain or France or America or Russia or any other country. But the single-party system is not an original or unique African institution. It exists in other parts of the world where its history and achievements can be studied. It is open to question whether it is the best way to ensure the democratic values of freedom, justice, human rights, and the Rule of Law which African States avow. Judged by these accepted standards and values, the records are not reassuring. Even the best examples of the one-party régimes smother some essential democratic rights, and the freedom of associations like trade unions, farmers', women's, youth, traders', and other associations; others are flagrant dictatorships which afford no democratic avenues for change, and, as the records abundantly testify, offer only the alternative of military coups. . . .

Social order does not rest on the imposition of restraints; but democracy demands that these should be as few as possible; it demands toleration and freedom of action; it seeks to prevent certain evils, the principal among them being dictatorship. Consequently, appropriate institutions are developed and fostered for the taming of power; for subjecting those who rule to constant criticism and checks. Among these institutions . . . are the party system, the organized opposition, the press, the Rule of Law, and the independent Judiciary.

In our review, we have presented evidence of the general desire for democracy. The new States of Africa are, however, in quest of appropriate institutions through which to express the democratic values they avow. In particular, many of them consider the institutions of opposition as established within Western political systems to be unsuitable for their communities. Democracy allows experimentation and innovation, for one of its demands is the readiness to compromise. We have, nevertheless, questioned whether the single-party experiments provide adequately for criticism and opposition. There is a need for new attitudes to the expression of criticism, and for the establishment and recognition of institutions through which opposition can function adequately. A basic tenet of democracy, as we have stated, is that all men, including party bosses and rulers, are fallible, and consequently that there should be effective institutions for the expression of criticism, and for a constitutional change of rulers. Intolerance of opposition often stems from the conviction that the party bosses are always right, and that only they understand and interpret the will of the people; so that whatever they say should be accepted without challenge. Such an attitude is very dangerous for the democratic life. We have questioned the adequacy of criticism when it is allowed only within the single party, since this presupposes that opposition must be confined within the limits set by the leadership, and the ideology and program of the one party. Challenge to its basic presuppositions cannot be tolerated, for that would spell rancorous dissensions, and instability. There are strict limits to the nonconformist ideas that a party which must govern can tolerate. There are some, as we have shown, who are prepared to accept that what they are practicing now falls short of the democratic principles they avow, but justify authoritarian practices as temporary and necessary expedients in their particular social context; the greater danger lies with those who seem prepared to defend their present experiments as the acme of democracy, despite its obvious shortcomings, and the sufferings they inflict on those who oppose or disagree with them. Hopefully, no human institutions can be static; there are already severe tensions which point compellingly to the need for continuing the quest for more appropriate forms.

21. The Cabinet of Kenya

While nearly all African leaders subscribe to the doctrine of African socialism, it is not always clear what they mean by the term. Senghor, Nkrumah, and Nyerere have made attempts to define it; in Kenya, the definition has been a joint effort of the entire cabinet under the leadership of President Jomo Kenyatta. Originally drafted in the Ministry of Economic Planning under Tom Mboya, the Sessional Paper on African Socialism was discussed, modified, and approved by the cabinet and subsequently endorsed by the Kenya Parliament.

The document attempts to spell out the implications of a commitment to African socialism for the future economic development of Kenya. As in the writings of other Africans, both Marxism and laissez-faire capitalism are criticized as antiquated and inapplicable to African problems. Socialism is seen as implying political democracy, social responsibility, and limits on the ownership of land. However, the paper indicates a wide range of choices available to the government as to the specific means to be utilized in developing the country. In terms perhaps stronger than those of any other socialist statement, the paper lists the reasons against a policy of nationalization, but recognizes that in some cases it may be necessary. There is also support for the creation of a single trade union but no mention of the establishment of a one-party state. After the paper was adopted, an opposition party, the Kenya People's Union (KPU), broke away from the governing Kenya African National Union (KANU) in 1966. In October, it was suppressed and its leaders imprisoned, but Kenya has still not officially declared itself a de jure one-party state.

AFRICAN SOCIALISM AND ITS
APPLICATION TO PLANNING
IN KENYA*

. . . The system adopted in Kenya is African socialism, but the characteristics of the system and the economic mechanisms it implies have never been spelled out fully in an agreed form.

In the phrase "African socialism," the word "African" is not introduced to describe a continent to which a foreign ideology is to be transplanted. It is meant to convey the African roots of a system that is itself African in its characteristics. African socialism is a term describing an African political and economic system that is positively African, not being imported from any country or being a blueprint of any foreign ideology, but capable of incorporating useful and compatible techniques from whatever source. The principal conditions the system must satisfy are: (i) it must draw on the best of African traditions; (ii) it must be adaptable to new and rapidly changing circumstances; and (iii) it must not rest for its success on a satellite relationship with any other country or group of countries.

African Traditions

There are two African traditions which form an essential basis for African socialism—political democracy and mutual social responsibility. Political democracy implies that each member of society is equal in his political rights and that no individual or group will be permitted to exert undue influence on the policies of the state. The state, therefore, can never become the tool of special interests, catering to the desires of a minority at the expense of the needs of the majority. The state will represent all of the people and will do so impartially and without prejudice.

Political democracy in the African traditional sense provided a genuine hedge against the exercise of disproportionate political power by economic power groups. In African society a man was born politically free and equal and his voice and counsel were heard and respected regardless of the economic wealth he possessed. Even where traditional leaders appeared to have greater

* Published by the Government of Kenya, Nairobi, 1965.

wealth and hold disproportionate political influence over their tribal or clan community, there were traditional checks and balances including sanctions against any possible abuse of such power. In fact, traditional leaders were regarded as trustees whose influence was circumscribed both in customary law and religion. In the traditional African society, an individual needed only to be a mature member of it to participate fully and equally in political affairs. Political rights did not derive from or relate to economic wealth or status. When this is translated into our modern state it means that to participate in political matters and party activities as an equal, the individual must prove nothing beyond age and citizenship and need take no oath beyond allegiance to country.

Political democracy in the African tradition would not, therefore, countenance a party of the elite, stern tests or discriminatory criteria for party membership, degrees of party membership, or first and second class citizens. In African socialism every member of society is important and equal; every mature citizen can belong to the party without restriction or discrimination; and the party will entertain and accommodate different points of view. African socialism rests on full, equal, and unfettered democracy. Thus, African socialism differs politically from Communism because it ensures every mature citizen equal political rights and from capitalism because it prevents the exercise of disproportionate political influence by economic power groups. Another fundamental force in African traditional life was religion, which provided a strict moral code for the community. This will be a prominent feature of African socialism.

Mutual social responsibility is an extension of the African family spirit to the nation as a whole, with the hope that ultimately the same spirit can be extended to ever larger areas. It implies a mutual responsibility by society and its members to do their very best for each other with the full knowledge and understanding that if society prospers its members will share in that prosperity and that society cannot prosper without the full cooperation of its members. The state has an obligation to ensure equal opportunities to all its citizens, eliminate exploitation and discrimination, and provide needed social services such as education, medical care, and social security.

To ensure success in the endeavors of the government, all citizens must contribute, to the degree they are able, to the rapid development of the economy and society. Every member of African traditional society had a duty to work. This duty was acknowledged and willingly accepted by members because the mechanism for sharing society's benefits, the reciprocal response of society to the individual's contribution, was definite, automatic, and universally recognized. But the response of society was not simply a passive one. African society had the power and duty to impose sanctions on those who refused to contribute their fair share of hard work to the common endeavor.

Drawing on this background, African socialism expects the members of the modern state to contribute willingly and without stint to the development of the nation. Society, in turn, will reward these efforts and at the same time will take measures against those who refuse to participate in the nation's efforts to grow. Sending needed capital abroad, allowing land to lie idle and undeveloped, misusing the nation's limited resources, and conspicuous consumption when the nation needs savings are examples of antisocial behavior that African socialism will not countenance.

While the modern economy is more complex than traditional society, the principle remains that to be successful, society and its members must each acknowledge fully and willingly its responsibility to the other. But the movement toward a modern, monetary economy changes the nature of these responsibilities and the mechanisms by which a member contributes to society and society shares benefits among its members. The people must be continually and carefully informed of what society expects of them and how these efforts will promote the welfare of all. . . .

Economic Nonalignment

. . . Ideologies and the theoretical systems on which they are based are rigid and uncompromising while the development over time of all viable practical systems has been marked by adaptability to change, frequently of substantial proportions. Marxian socialism and laissez-faire capitalism are both theoretical economic organizations designed to ensure the use of resources for the benefit of society. Both settled on the ownership of property as the critical factor in economic organization and advocated rigid systems based in the one case on state ownership and in the other on private ownership. But ownership is not an absolute, indivisible right subject only to complete control or none. Practical systems have demonstrated that the resources of society are best guided into proper uses by a range of sensitive controls each specifically designed for the task to be performed. . . .

As predictive models of what would happen to factory-system societies, both Marxian socialism and laissez-faire capitalism have been failures. The economic systems in actual use throughout the world today bear little resemblance to either model. The Industrial Revolution quickly led to the social protest of which Marx was a part and this in turn resulted in sweeping political and economic changes as the systems of the world adapted to the new state of technological change. Political democracy was achieved; private property rights were diluted; the state accepted increasing responsibilities for social services, planning, guidance, and control; taxes were made progressive to distribute benefits more widely. Capitalism did not evolve into Marxian socialism, as Marx predicted, but was indeed modified in directions that Marx might well have approved.

The adaptability of these systems has a parallel in those countries that have attempted to follow Marx. To become effective, these systems, too, have had to demonstrate an ability to adapt to changing circumstances. They have adopted wage differentials and management incentives, permitted various forms of ownership, and utilized interest rates or the equivalent in their planning procedures. All practical economic systems, regardless of their origin, have demonstrated adaptability. The problems of today are not the problems of a century ago. African socialism is designed to be a working system in a modern setting, fully prepared to adapt itself to changing circumstances and new problems. . . .

Relationships with Other Countries

. . . Economic nonalignment does not mean a policy of isolation, any more than political nonalignment implies a refusal to participate in world affairs. On the contrary it means a willingness and a desire: (i) to borrow technological knowledge and proven economic methods from any country—without commitment; (ii) to seek and accept technical and financial assistance from any source—without strings; and (iii) to participate fully in world trade —without political domination.

The ability of Africa to borrow advanced technological knowledge, modern methods of industrial organization, and economic techniques of control and guidance from more advanced countries provides the opportunity to leap over many of the hurdles that have restrained development in these modern societies in the past. It means also that African socialism as a system can profit from the mistakes of others. Unlike many countries that have eliminated many successful economic mechanisms on narrow ideological grounds, Kenya is free to pick and choose those methods that have been proven in practice and are adaptable to Kenya conditions regardless of the ideologies that others may attach to them. Kenya, therefore, is free to choose, among other things: (i) a wages-and-incomes policy that recognizes the need for differential incentives as well as an equitable distribution of income; (ii) techniques of production that combine efficiencies of scale with diffused ownership; (iii) various forms of ownership—state, cooperative, corporate and individual—that are efficient for different sectors or that compete with each other provided only that the form promotes the objectives of government; and (iv) techniques of control that vary with the needs of society and its members. . . .

African Socialism and Land Ownership

There is some conflict of opinion with regard to the traditional attitude toward rights to land. Some allege that land was essentially communally or tribally owned; others claim that individual rights were the distinguishing feature; still others suggest that ownership did not really exist in any modern context in many African tribes. Undoubtedly these traditions differed substantially from one tribe to another. In every case, however, and in sharp contrast to the European tradition, ownership was not an absolute indivisible bundle of rights. The ultimate right of disposal outside the tribe was essentially tribal and in this land was tribally owned. It must be remembered, however, that the political arrangements within the tribe were such that every mature member of the tribe would have a say in such a decision. Short of this right, others were assigned or allocated to clans, families, and individuals, including the right to transfer and reclaim property within the clan. Rights to use land were, in effect, assigned in perpetuity to various groups within the tribe, subject always, however, and this is significant to an understanding of African socialism, to the condition that resources must be properly used and their benefits appropriately distributed, not merely held idle, abused or misused, or the benefits hoarded. The rights normally associated in Europe with ownership as such scarcely mattered.

What does emerge with clarity and force and as a single, unifying principle from these discussions of traditional property rights is that land and other productive assets, no matter who owned or managed them, were expected to be *used*, and used for the general welfare. No individual family or clan could treat productive assets as private property unless the uses to which those assets were put were regarded as consonant with the general welfare. Unlike the traditional European approach to ownership, no person could treat a piece of land as his own with the freedom to use it or not as he chose. It is worth noting that over the past century, the European tradition of absolute ownership has gradually been eroded so that today the right of the state to guide, plan, and even order the uses to which property will be put is universally recognized and unquestioned.

These African traditions cannot be carried over indiscriminately to a modern, monetary economy. The need to develop and invest requires credit and a credit economy rests heavily on a system of land titles and their registration. The ownership of land must, therefore, be made more definite and explicit if land consolidation and development are to be fully successful. It does not follow, however, that society will also give up its stake in how resources are used. Indeed, it is a fundamental characteristic of African socialism that society has a duty to plan, guide, and control the uses of all productive resources.

Control of Resource Use

Under African socialism the power to control resource use resides with the state. To imagine, however, that the use of resources can only be controlled through their ownership or that the appropriate ownership will guarantee the proper use of productive assets are errors of great magnitude. Ownership can be abused whether private or public and ways must be found to control resource use in either case. African socialism must rely on planning to determine the appropriate uses of productive resources on a range of controls to ensure that plans are carried out. . . .

Class Problem

The sharp class divisions that once existed in Europe have no place in African socialism and no parallel in African society. No class problem arose in the traditional African society and none

exists today among Africans. The class problem in Africa, therefore, is largely one of prevention, in particular: (i) to eliminate
the risk of foreign economic domination; and (ii) to plan development so as to prevent the emergence of antagonistic classes. In
addition, Kenya has the special problem of eliminating classes
that have arisen largely on the basis of race.

The class divisions that Marx deplored in Europe a century ago
were supported and strengthened by three factors: (i) a concentration of economic power; (ii) the treatment of private ownership
as an absolute, unrestricted right; and (iii) the close relationship
between economic power and political influence. The concept of
political equality in Africa rules out in principle the use of economic power as a political base. The vigorous implementation of
traditional political democracy in the modern setting will eliminate,
therefore, one of the critical factors promoting class divisions. The
policy of African socialism to control by various means how productive resources are used eliminates the second of the factors supporting a class system. Without its two supporting allies, the
concentration of economic power cannot be the threat it once was,
but African socialism proposes to restrict and guard against this
factor as well with regard to both foreign and domestic concentrations.

Foreign Investors

Foreigners have no vote and can only have a political voice, now
that independence has been achieved, by enlisting the support of
Kenya citizens. Nevertheless, the foreign ownership and management of productive assets could mean that economic decisions in
Kenya might be dominated by foreign rather than domestic considerations. Foreign investors should therefore be prepared to accept the spirit of mutual social responsibility, for example: (i) by
making shares in the company available to Africans who wish to
buy them; (ii) by employing Africans at managerial levels as soon
as qualified people can be found; and (iii) by providing training
facilities for Africans. . . .

Nationalization

Nationalization is a useful tool that has already been used in
Kenya and will be used again when circumstances require. The
pertinent questions are at what cost, for what purpose, and when.

The Constitution and the KANU Manifesto make it clear that African socialism in Kenya does not imply a commitment to indiscriminate nationalization. These documents do commit the government to prompt payment of full compensation whenever nationalization is used. Kenya's policy with respect to nationalization should be more clearly defined within these stipulations.

It should be recognized that if the nation's limited domestic capital is used to buy existing land, livestock, buildings, machinery, and equipment, the nation has no more productive assets than before—only their ownership has changed. What may be lost are the new resources that could have been purchased instead—the new schools, hospitals, roads, water supplies, irrigation schemes, rolling stock, land surveys, housing, lodges, airports, and harbor development—and the employment opportunities and added output that these new developments would create. Further, the money paid for nationalized resources and the people who managed them before nationalization would most likely leave the country, increasing our foreign-exchange and skilled-manpower problems. There is also the firm likelihood that nationalization would discourage additional private investment, thus reducing further the rate of growth of the economy. It is also the case that the use of domestic capital to nationalize would reduce our ability to match foreign-aid funds leading to an even greater reduction in development expenditure. Finally, some speak of nationalization as though it should be applicable only to non-African enterprises. If the policy were applied to an economic activity, such as bus transportation, it would affect everyone, African and otherwise, owning productive resources in the industry.

Though the cost is great, there may be circumstances when nationalization will be needed: (i) when the assets in private hands threaten the security or undermine the integrity of the nation; or (ii) when productive resources are being wasted; or (iii) when the operation of an industry by private concerns has a serious detrimental effect on the public interest; and (iv) when other less costly means of control are not available or are not effective.

It must also be clear that, in most cases, when an industry is nationalized it must be operated efficiently, cover its costs, and earn a profit at least equivalent to the taxes paid when operated privately. If taxes must be used year after year to subsidize its operation, the nation has gained little if anything by the act of nationalization. . . .

Trade Unions

The rights of industrial workers must be fully protected as development takes place and much of this work can be left to responsible unions. But the unions now represent only a small minority of Kenya's adult population and they cannot be permitted to benefit these few at the expense of large numbers of less fortunate brothers. Experience in all developing countries has shown that in the interests of stability and good industrial relations government cannot permit the existence of more than one central organization for trade unions in the country. It is also desirable to have one central organization for employers.

The first responsibility of the unions must be to develop a disciplined, skilled, and responsible labor force. The nation's welfare and that of the workers depend much more on hard, productive work than on strikes and walkouts. Unions must concern themselves with training programs, apprentice programs, and workers' discipline and productivity. In addition, trade unions assisted by government should take an active role in organizing consumer cooperatives, generating savings for development, promoting cooperative housing development, initiating producer cooperatives, and making workers aware of their contribution to the development of the nation.

Strikes cost the nation output, the workers wages, the companies profits, and the government taxes. Wages in excess of those warranted by productivity increase the unemployment, encourage the substitution of capital for labor, and lead to bankruptcies. In order to avoid these drags on development, legislation will be needed providing for the compulsory arbitration of major issues not resolved through the regular bargaining process. Special legislation may be needed in sensitive industries and the government to avoid the economic paralysis that could result from work stoppages in these areas.

The Government will assume the responsibility for holding down the prices of basic commodities so that workers, farmers, and unemployed are not confronted with a rising cost of living. . . .

22. Kenya People's Union (KPU)

The Kenya People's Union was established in April, 1966, as a result of a split in the governing Kenya African National Union (KANU), which was based both on ideological and tribal differences. After Oginga Odinga, a Luo and a frequent critic of what he considered to be the excessively pro-Western policies of the Kikuyu-dominated government of President Jomo Kenyata, was removed from his post of vice-president of the KANU, he and his followers, most of them also Luos, formed the KPU and were compelled to run in a special by-election for the parliamentary seats which they had occupied as KANU members. The Wananchi Declaration, the KPU program published for these elections, favored accelerated land distribution to Africans, nationalization of banks, insurance companies, and public utilities, limitations on foreign capital, and closer relations with the Soviet Union. In the June, 1966, elections, nine KPU candidates were victorious, but in October, 1969, Odinga and all the party representatives were imprisoned after an antigovernment riot at the dedication of a hospital in a Luo area by Kenyatta had resulted in the deaths of eleven people. The party was also banned as subversive. In the December, 1969, primary elections within KANU, 616 candidates ran for 158 seats, and 74 incumbent legislators, five cabinet ministers, and fourteen assistant ministers were defeated. The winners ran unopposed in general elections in January, 1970.

THE WANANCHI DECLARATION *

SOCIALISM: KPU's PLAN FOR NATIONAL DEVELOPMENT

African society has always had strong elements of communal tradition in everyday life. In no African community were people

.* Published by the Kenya People's Union, Nairobi, 1966. Wananchi is Swahili for "the citizenry."

ever divided into classes. They shared their resources according to their needs, and they shared social and family responsibilities.

Under the cloak of something called "African Socialism," Kenya is moving toward one of the more orthodox forms of capitalism to be found in the world today. Why does the KANU government call its policy socialism, and not dare admit that it follows the capitalist road? Because it knows well that capitalism is utterly wrong and unsuited to the needs and aspirations of the people of Kenya. Most capitalist governments have learned to make a few concessions or gestures toward social reform when they have to. But KANU's "concessions" to social change in the economy center round a larger African share in capitalism: it seeks the Africanization of trade, land holding, executive positions in private firms, and more African share holdings in Kenya-based companies.

In Kenya today economic growth serves to strengthen the hand of the private interests which already determine how the bulk of the nation's wealth is used and divided. Their first motive in this is to make a profit for themselves and their shareholders. The international brotherhood of profit-seekers finds a "healthy and stable" economic climate in Kenya.

There are people who will argue that a rich country can afford capitalism. But in a developing country like Kenya there is no argument about it. Where most people lack the essentials for a decent life and where wealth is so unevenly divided, we will slide into dictatorship and generations of misery for the majority of our citizens under capitalism. It is not the business of the private profit-seekers to provide the social essentials. So we cannot afford to let our society be run by them. And changing the skin color of the profit-seekers is not social reform. It will make capitalism more difficult than ever to root out.

The only answer lies in the system known as socialism. For the first essential for a fair distribution in a poor society is to put *economic power into the hands of the people*. This is not done merely by installing a few Africans as directors of big companies, and parcelling out large tracts of land to Ministers and their relations.

The country's resources must be administered by and through a democratically-elected government whose policy-makers share *the interests of the small farmer and the worker*.

The government must be able to ensure that a reasonable share of the profits of economic activity is ploughed directly back into expansion. And it must protect the consumers from the high prices caused by excessive profits.

The government can encourage a measure of profit incentive in the working of the economy to sustain the desire to work hard and build the nation. But no one must have so much capital that he and his descendants can live off its profits without working. Higher incomes must be possible only through skills and hard work.

The managerial skills of all minorities who are prepared to use their entrepreneurial ability in the service of the people, and within a socialist framework, will be welcomed and rewarded. Likewise we will welcome all foreign capital and skills which are made available to us for achieving and furthering the above objectives. But we will accept them only on our terms.

These, then, are the objectives of KPU. A KPU government will manage the economy according to socialist principles, some of which are outlined above.

Socialism can stimulate economic growth. A state-run industry can plough back its returns into development and sustain itself much more easily than a private company. For, a private company must use a large proportion of the profits it would otherwise plough back into expansion to keep its shareholders happy. By taking control of key companies that are profitable, a socialist government can channel all returns into the development of the country, instead of allowing a big share to increase the incomes and luxury-spending of the privileged few. Further, with state control, the government has much greater freedom to determine *priorities in planning.* When most of the capital is in the hands of foreigners who owe no loyalty to the long-term development of the country, national needs get neglected. The capitalists want quick, high returns. Knowing that capitalism in a developing country is a basically unstable system—that is, it is "too good to last"—it is quite logical for them to squeeze as much profit as they can out of the country "while the going is good." The industries in which such quick returns are possible are not always those the country really needs. . . .

It is only by getting control over substantial areas of economic activity that the government can *free* itself *from the grip of private capital* and promote the kind of development it wants, using the capital it owns and creates itself. This a KPU government will do. . . .

Land

Uhuru * has no meaning until the land problem is solved.

Land has always been at the very heart of our struggle. It is the traditional source of our livelihood. The KANU leaders have betrayed the masses in their deep-felt need for land, grabbing it for themselves and sharing it with foreigners, just when opportunities for change were greatest and the hopes of the people reached new heights. As a first priority, therefore, KPU will introduce a new land policy.

KPU will put the *land in the hands of the people*. Failure to return the land stolen in colonial times is, for millions of people, the most serious in the string of broken promises since the end of colonial rule. It is the bitterest fruit of KANU "socialism" for the tens of thousands of landless and jobless people.

The KANU government, after strong pressure from KPU, has recently restricted *new* land purchases by noncitizens. But this has very little impact because large areas of land had already been purchased or transferred to noncitizens before the prohibition was imposed. KPU will not allow noncitizens to own any agricultural land, whether that land was acquired before prohibition or not.

European settlers have had good cause to make enthusiastic declarations of loyalty to the Kenyatta government. It has played their game well so far. Noncitizens were free to buy as much land as they liked. In the first four years after independence, more than 50 per cent of all land bought was purchased by Europeans. Asians moved in quickly and freely, largely for short-term speculative farming. Vast agricultural projects were handed over to the complete control of large foreign firms.

The KANU government's most specific betrayal is to fail even to look into limiting the size of individual land holdings in former European areas. But the government and KANU are now totally unable to take drastic action on the land question. Their ideological commitment to capitalism is reinforced by their individual ownership of hundreds and even thousands of acres. Most Ministers and Assistant-Ministers and other KANU leaders own big estates, some of them more than one. *One Minister holds six farms.* KANU's leaders have ceased to be the representatives of

* Swahili for "freedom."—Ed.

the people. They are the allies of European settlers and other capitalists.

KPU will immediately put a *ceiling on the size of land holdings*. In redistributing the larger holdings, KPU will introduce medium-sized farms where the land is not particularly suitable for small-scale farming. KPU will not be limited to the present extremes where farms are either very large or very small. The land released as a result of restrictions on noncitizens' ownership and the conditions imposed for maximum-sized holdings will be distributed among the needy, including *squatters*, and those who lost their lands in the struggle for independence.

When the terms for independence were being negotiated with Britain, those now in power were ready, some almost eager, to accept arrangements which saddled the new Kenya with a huge debt to buy out, at high prices, settlers who had acquired land and lived well off it for decades. It is one thing to borrow and repay for productive assets, it is quite another to borrow huge sums to buy your own land back, and sums which promptly leave the country. . . .

The KPU government will tackle the land problem immediately.

Noncitizens will not be allowed to own farming land, except in limited cases where they will lease it in partnership with state or parastate organizations, on specific conditions and for specific purposes.

A ceiling will be placed on all individual land holdings in former European settled areas.

As the above measures pave the way, free land will be distributed to the landless, including squatters and those who lost their land in the struggle for independence. KPU will reduce the indebtedness of the settlers by curtailing their debts on land and providing relief against other excessive burdens.

Cooperatives, either under state supervision in partnership with the state, or with government help, will be formed wherever desirable or convenient, on land acquired from European settlers. Cooperative systems will be strongly encouraged on settlement schemes and in consolidated areas.

Land consolidation will be promoted but only in a democratic manner according to the wishes of the people, and particular care will be taken to censure that individuals do not grasp too much for themselves to the detriment of the rest of the population in these areas.

KPU will honor the rights of tribes and clans to their land, but the state will have the right to direct land use in such a way as to make such usage most advantageous to the country. . . .

Nationalization

Nationalization is the main immediate method of putting economic power in the hands of the people and bringing about a more equitable distribution of the fruits of their labor.

Those industries, like the public utilities, which are vital to national economic independence, will be nationalized as a first step, as well as those which are profitable and can provide the necessary capital for development.

Where nationalization may not be used, KPU will accept a joint venture between the government and private entrepreneurs on the understanding that the nation's interest in the enterprise is paramount.

The *nationalized industries* will serve as a basis for further industrialization and domestic capital accumulation so vital for economic development. Thus at last KPU will provide a breakthrough out of the "vicious circle of poverty." The KPU will see to it that the banks and insurance companies are nationalized.

Investment and Aid

Kenya's development budget depends heavily on foreign capital. Some think that because Kenya is favored among those poor countries that have to beg, cap in hand, for aid and investment from rich Western countries, she is fortunate, but this is to live in a fool's paradise. She will accumulate not economic strength but an ever growing dependence from this type of aid.

There is room for foreign investment in Africa. Indeed, KPU will welcome it. But we will consider each investment proposal in the light of the return which the Kenya nation is going to derive from it. The foreign investor will have to ensure that Kenya, and not only his profits, will benefit. This may mean less profit for the investor to take out but it will mean a securer investment, because it will genuinely benefit the mass of the people, and the deal will be the result of genuine negotiation between the parties, not of misconceptions about what is "beneficial to the economy" —or of an under-the-table deal. Fewer profits will be leaving the country as firms are nationalized too, and these can help to balance any such loss of investment.

Not all foreign investment is beneficial. It can be argued there is too much.

Today the climate for foreign investment is so lush that there is sometimes a wasteful duplication of types of industry. Foreign investors expect too high a rate of return to compete with that prevailing in their own fully developed countries—plus extra for the "risk," such as in tax incentives, in the high amount of profit they are allowed to take out of the country, and in keeping labor cost low. On top of this, dividends have to be paid every year to the overseas shareholders out of the country's foreign exchange reserves, with guarantees for unrestricted repatriation of original capital.

It is a shocking fact that investors generally come to East Africa only on the basis that they can take out, within five years, what they originally put in.

Relying on foreign capital has established local rates of interest which are as high as the rates which have to be paid to foreign investors. There is no reason why *local capital* should get these high returns, provided strong measures are taken to keep capital from leaving the country. KPU government will redress this situation. While inviting investment on our own terms, stress will be laid more on government-to-government or multilateral loans to establish industries ourselves. Skilled people will be invited, on attractive terms, to help run these industries, but special *training schemes* will be launched for Kenyans to take over their management. . . .

DEMOCRATIC RIGHTS

The KPU will revive democratic government in Kenya. This means that at every level of government there will be *full participation of the wananchi*. This will be expressed not only in the casting of votes at the time of elections but through direct involvement in the formulation of policies right from the village level. People will be free to criticize government policy and the way in which policy is carried out. New policies will be initiated by the *wananchi* as much as by their leaders at different levels. KPU believes that good government is only possible through constant criticism; KPU will do all it can to encourage criticism and discussion of all aspects of its policies.

88 AFRICA

The Constitution

The KPU stands for a government legislating through Parliament which is voted into power and stays in power only through regular democratic elections by all adult citizens. KPU will not tolerate any interference in the right of the *wananchi* to choose representatives for Parliament and other institutions of government.

KPU will guarantee all *basic human rights*: freedom of speech, freedom of association, and freedom of the individual. But no guarantee of the "freedom" of one individual to exploit others and to entrench the privileges which are denied to others under the guise of unrestricted "free enterprise."

Independence of the Judiciary

Lip service can be paid to this principle yet at the same time the independence of the courts can be undermined by a growing number of oppressive laws which avoid the courts, and by discreet pressure on the courts from government quarters. These pressures can cause law officers to follow political expediency rather than real justice.

It has been quite obvious for the last five years since KANU government took power that justice has not been seen to be done because of the political interference by the KANU government in the judiciary and also the judiciary has remained in the hands of the expatriates who fear to lose their jobs if they go against the KANU government.

KPU therefore pledges to guard the independence of the judiciary which the KANU government has failed to do. . . .

FOREIGN POLICY

The KANU government is in the front ranks of the regimes which are selling out on the principles and evading the challenge of *African unity*. African unity has taken bad blows in recent years from the failures of Governments like the KANU government to strengthen a united front.

Nonalignment has given way and Kenya's government has become a satellite state of Britain, West Germany, and the United States, unable to think out or to follow its own foreign policies.

To achieve nonalignment, Kenya under KPU will strike a balance in her relations between East and West—not because we must be "fair to both sides," but because we must stop ourselves being forced to take sides in a power struggle which does not have our national or African interests at stake. . . .

KPU is fully aware of the great challenges and problems involved in these programs. They must be realistic and soundly planned. But they must be based on our own national priorities as we see them. We have to learn to think for ourselves, to work out what is realistic for us. But how, with our shortage of resources and skills, will KPU be able to provide these things for the *wananchi?* That is the key question in our whole policy.

The answer lies in socialism, applied to the Kenyan and the African situation. . . .

23. Julius Nyerere

Julius Nyerere, the President of the Republic of Tanzania, was born in 1922, the son of a Tanganyikan tribal chief. He was educated in Catholic schools, received his B.A. from Makerere College in Uganda, and his M.A. from the University of Edinburgh. After his return to Tanganyika, he became President of the Tanganyika African Association, which he transformed in 1954 into the Tanganyika African National Union (TANU). As Tanganyika moved toward independence, TANU virtually monopolized political activity, and when independence was granted in October, 1961, Nyerere became Prime Minister. In November, 1962, after a change in the Constitution, he was elected President of the Tanganyika Republic; when Zanzibar joined Tanganyika in the Republic of Tanzania in 1964, he became President of the new state, a position to which he was re-elected without opposition in 1965 and 1970.

His writing and speeches on African subjects have been prolific and original. One of the leaders of the Pan-African movement, he has been critical of both East and West in what he sees as their attempts to dominate independent Africa. In his attempt to define

African socialism, Nyerere has related the concept to traditional notions of familyhood; he has advocated limits on ownership and an extension of the family sense of mutual responsibility to the nation and ultimately to the world. Nyerere also argues that socialism implies a reorientation of education and development planning toward the rural areas, where 90 per cent of the population lives, and a reliance on self-help rather than on outside assistance.

Nyerere's most distinctive contribution is his defense of the one-party state in Africa. Arguing that a multiplicity of parties is the result of class conflicts, which are absent in Africa, he advocates a single "National Movement" in which there is complete freedom of individual criticism and action but no organized factions. His thinking received concrete application in the recommendations of a 1965 Presidential Commission that the party give the voter a choice by nominating several candidates in each constituency (although only one for President). In the elections carried out under this system in 1965 and 1970 several cabinet ministers were defeated.

THE ROLE OF AFRICAN TRADE UNIONS*

I think the time has come to re-examine our ideas about the trade-union movement in Africa and its relationship with the nationalist movements. Here again, we are in danger of accepting, without thought, the Western pattern, regardless of the fact that it makes little or no sense in Africa.

In Great Britain and in America, the trade unionists have come to believe that the trade-union movement must be "independent of any political party." Superficially, this sounds attractive; any slogan that can bring in the word "independence" always does sound attractive, so that its very appeal to the emotions automatically tends to stifle further thought about what it means. Let us try to find out how this idea of independence from the political parties grew, and what it does mean.

A great deal of the confused thinking on the part of those who

* Reprinted from *Labour* (Accra), June, 1961.

pontificate about African trade unions stems from their having forgotten a very important fact—that the trade unions and the labor, or socialist, parties of Europe are two wings of the same labor movement. Trade unionism first came into being as a result of the industrial revolution and the division of the Western countries between "labor" and "capital."

At first, unorganized labor was completely at the mercy of the employers, by whom it was exploited in more than one sense of the word. The workers then decided that they must organize themselves for the purpose of collective bargaining with the employers; to put it bluntly, they realized that they must fight for their rights against their exploiters, and that to do so they must organize.

It was not long before the workers found that their trade unions alone were not enough. In industry, the unions could bargain with the employers; but the employers still had the last word, for they were also the rulers of the country.

If the new labor movement was to have any influence over the laws affecting industrial conditions, it must have a voice in parliament. The workers must organize themselves into political parties as well as into trade unions; when the political prong had been added to the industrial one, the labor movement was complete.

In those early days there was no confusion of thought. The Labour Party in England, for instance, was quite clearly part of the same movement as the trade unions, and if anybody then had talked of the need for trade unions to be "independent of any political party," he would have been told he was talking nonsense.

If, on the other hand, he had said the trade-union movement must be independent of the government, he would merely have been stating the obvious; because at that time the "government" was the same thing as the industrialists—the exploiters—against whom the whole movement had been organized. The need for the labor movement to be free from any control by the capitalists is not a doctrine; it is a self-evident definition.

This fact, however, has gradually been forgotten, and forgetting it has led to some ridiculous results. In Britain, for instance, one would have expected that when once the labor movement succeeded in forming a government of its own, the whole movement would rejoice. But no! When this did eventually happen, only one prong of the labor movement rejoiced—the political prong. The other, the industrial prong, from long force of habit remained sulky and suspicious! . . .

Habit, no less than emotion, has an unhappy tendency to stop people from thinking. The rule that you must not allow yourself to be controlled by the enemy springs from the very definition of "enemy." The labor movement applied this rule correctly in the days when Britain was controlled by the capitalists. But then, somehow, the rule slipped imperceptibly into some general doctrine of the independence of trade unions from *any* political control.

As a result, when the labor movement won its resounding victory after the end of World War II, the victory, instead of being seen in its true light as a victory of the whole movement, was looked at as only a Labour Party victory. . . . They [the unions] had for so long accepted the doctrine that trade unions must be independent and suspicious of the government that they had come to believe this meant *any* government—including, I suppose, a government 100 per cent trade unionist.

A socialist government either is socialist or it is not. A trade-union movement either is socialist or it is not. If a government *is* a socialist government, representing the working peoples of the country, then it must be acknowledged and treated as such, not only by the capitalists, but by the workers themselves. The workers can no more be independent of it than it can be independent of the workers.

Of course, if the particular individuals who happen at any given time to form the government do not carry out the policies for which the labor movement as a whole stands, they can be replaced, in the normal democratic way, by the labor movement itself. But there can be no logic in any *part* of the labor movement trying to have it both ways. . . .

I said the time had come to re-examine our ideas about the trade-union movement in Africa. So far, I have been dealing with European, and particularly British, trade unions. I have done this deliberately, in order to bring out one thing: that particular patterns or traditions grow up in different countries because of the historical circumstances peculiar to those countries during the period of growth, and that these habits of thought tend to become accepted as essential to trade unionism when, in fact, they are not.

I have tried to indicate why, in the case of Great Britain especially, the doctrine or habit of trade unions being independent of political control is the result of the original necessity for their independence from what was then a capitalist government, and

how this habit of thought has slipped into a meaningless formula
of independence from political control generally.

In Britain, the fact that the formula is meaningless saves it from
doing much harm, for the British are accustomed to taking their
political slogans with a pinch of salt, with a ruling class of industrialists or employers associated with political power, against
whom it has been necessary for the workers to organize first an
industrial and then a political movement. Our development has
been the other way around. When, six years ago, we established our
nationalist movement, its first aim was political—independence
from colonialism. Within this nationalist movement, and very
much a part of it, one of our objectives was to help the growth of
a trade-union movement.

We have an officer in the organization whose special duty it
was to stimulate and help the growth of trade unionism. Once
firmly established, the trade-union movement was, and is, part
and parcel of the whole nationalist movement. In the early days,
when a trade union went on strike, for instance, and its members
were in direct need of funds to keep them going, we saw no doctrine that would be abrogated by our giving financial support from
the political wing to the industrial wing of the same nationalist
movement.

It was simply a case of the right hand helping the left hand, or
vice versa. It would clearly have been ridiculous to preach an imported doctrine of independence of the Tanganyika Federation of
Labour from political control, and so to deny them the assistance
they needed from the Tanganyika African Nationalist Union.*

NATIONALISM AND PAN-AFRICANISM†

You have asked me to speak on African unity. I am an advocate
of African unity. I believe firmly that, just as unity was necessary
for the achievement of independence in Tanganyika or any other
nation, unity is equally necessary to consolidate and maintain the

independence which we are now achieving in different parts of Africa.

I believe that, left to ourselves, we can achieve unity on the African continent. But I don't believe that we are going to be left to ourselves! I believe that the phase through which we are emerging successfully is the phase of the first scramble for Africa—and Africa's reaction to it. We are now entering a new phase. It is the phase of the second scramble for Africa. And just as in the first one tribe was divided against another tribe to make the division of Africa easier, in the second the technique will be to try to divide one nation against another nation, to make it easier to control Africa by making her weak and divided against herself.

It is for this reason, therefore, that before we can talk complacently about "African unity," we should examine carefully the external ideas that are likely to be imposed upon us, imposed not for the purpose of uniting us, but for the purpose of dividing us!

Two Blocs

Today the world is divided into two blocs—what one might call the "capitalist bloc" and the "socialist bloc," but generally referred to as the "Western bloc" and the "Eastern bloc." I have said "capitalist" and "socialist" for a good reason—it makes it easier to understand the forces behind these divisions.

What is wrong with capitalism? To my mind, capitalism went wrong when it divorced wealth from its true purpose. The true purpose of wealth is to satisfy very simple needs: the need for food, the need for shelter, the need for education, and so on. In other words, the end of wealth is the banishment of poverty—and wealth is to poverty what light is to darkness.

There is enough wealth in every state for every individual to satisfy these simple needs. But the moment individuals in any single state begin to use wealth not for the satisfaction of those needs, not for the banishment of poverty, but for the purpose of acquiring power and prestige—then there is no longer enough. Then wealth tolerates poverty; then wealth is no longer to poverty what light is to darkness. For there is not enough wealth in any nation to satisfy the desire for power and the prestige of every individual.

So what happens? There is then ruthless competition between individuals—not to get wealth to feed themselves, or to clothe themselves, or to house themselves, but to seize enough wealth to give themselves more power, more prestige than their fellows, i.e., wealth that exceeds their real needs and will enable them to dominate other individuals. When that stage is reached, one millionaire is prepared to spend millions simply in order to destroy another millionaire.

I believe that the purpose of socialism was to remove this sin of capitalism and to return wealth to its original use—the satisfaction of simple human needs, the banishment of poverty. I think it would be hypocrisy on the part of the capitalist countries—not to recognize the fact that this is happening in the socialist countries; that, within those countries, personal wealth is not a symbol of power or prestige, and wealth is used to banish poverty.

But I believe that the socialist countries themselves, considered as individuals in the larger society of nations, are now committing the same crime that was committed by capitalists before. I believe that, on the international level, they are now beginning to use wealth for the purpose of acquiring power and prestige! It would be equally hypocritical on the part of the socialist countries to deny this. Internationally, they are now engaged in using wealth in exactly the same way as the capitalist countries—for power and prestige.

And socialist countries, no less than capitalist countries, are prepared to behave like the millionaire—to use millions to destroy another millionaire; and it need not necessarily be a capitalist millionaire—it is just as likely to be a socialist millionaire. In other words, socialist wealth now tolerates poverty—which is an even more unforgivable crime!

Lure of Slogans

I believe that no underdeveloped country can afford to be anything but socialist. I think, therefore, that we in Africa are bound to organize ourselves on a socialist pattern. But let us at least provide another corrective to socialism, and prevent the wealth we are beginning to build in our own countries from being used for the purpose of acquiring national power or prestige. Let us make sure that it is used solely for raising the standards of our people. Let us not allow the wealth that we are creating to live side by side with poverty, and tolerate that poverty.

. . . I have said already that socialism arose to remedy the mistakes capitalism had made. Karl Marx felt there was an inevitable clash between the rich of one society and the poor of that society. In that, I believe, Karl Marx was right. But today it is the international scene which is going to have a greater impact on the lives of individuals than what is happening within Tanganyika or within Uganda. And when you look at the international scene, you must admit that the world is still divided between the "haves" and the "have-nots." This division is not a division between capitalists and socialists, or between capitalists and Communists; this is a division between the poor countries of the world and the rich countries of the world.

The poor countries of the world should be very careful not to allow themselves to be used as the "tools" of any of the rich countries of the world, however much the rich countries may seek to fool them that they are on their side! And don't forget that the rich countries of the world today may be found on either side of the division between capitalist and socialist countries.

I have said all this as a rather long introduction to what I am going to say about African unity. I believe the danger to African unity is going to come from these external forces and slogans which bear no relation to the facts of the world today; from the fact that today the rich countries of the world—both capitalist and socialist—are using their wealth to dominate the poor countries. And they are ready to try to weaken and divide the poor countries for that purpose of domination. That is why I said at the beginning that if we in Africa were left on our own, we would achieve unity on our continent—but that I do not believe we are going to be left alone. And I have explained why I think we are not going to be left alone.

But there is no need for fear. All we need to do is to use our intellect, to know what is good for us. We need to listen to the outside world, to accept from them what we believe is in the best interests of Africa and of African unity, and to reject—and reject in no uncertain terms—what we believe is not in the best interests of Africa and of African unity. And that includes all those attractive but misleading slogans about "democracy" and "socialism" which are too often used to cloak the real designs of the power-hungry. These old slogans bear no relation at all to what Africa is doing, and they are generally used for the purpose of dividing Africa into camps.

Artificial Nations

At the beginning, I used the phrase "the second scramble for Africa." It may sound farfetched, in the context of the Africa of the 1960's. . . . But anybody who thinks this is farfetched has been completely blind to what is happening on the African continent. Take, for example, the Congo: There were obvious weaknesses in the Congo situation, but those weaknesses were deliberately used in a scramble for the control of the Congo.

There are obvious weaknesses on the African continent. We have artificial "nations" carved out at the Berlin Conference;* we are struggling to build these nations into stable units of human society. And these weaknesses, too, are being exploited. We are being reminded daily of these weaknesses. We are told that tribalism will not allow us to build nations. But when we try to take measures to deal with tribalism, we are accused of dictatorship.

Whenever we try to talk in terms of larger units on the African continent, we are told that it can't be done; we are told that the units we would so create would be "artificial." As if they could be any more artificial than the "national" units on which we are now building! Some of the people who say this are genuinely pointing to a difficulty; but I believe many of them are deliberately emphasizing the difficulties on our continent for the express purpose of maintaining them and sabotaging any move to unite Africa.

The technique is very simple. One power bloc labels a move for unity a "Communist plot"—not because it is Communist, but because they don't like it. Another power bloc labels another move for unity an "imperialist plot"—not because it is so, but because they don't like it. What annoys me is not the use of these slogans by power-hungry nations, for this is something we do expect; but what does infuriate me is that they should expect us to allow ourselves to be treated as if we were a bunch of idiots!

So I believe that the second scramble for Africa has begun in real earnest. And it is going to be a much more dangerous scramble than the first one. For what happened in the first scramble? One imperialist power fought another imperialist power for the booty. What do you think is going to happen in the second scramble? No imperialist power is going to fight another imperialist power for

* The Berlin Conference of 1884–85 agreed on the basic principles governing the partition of Africa among the European colonial powers.—ED.

the control of Africa; that would be too crude a method in the context of the 1960's. No. This time, one imperialist power is going to arm one African nation, and another imperialist power is going to arm another African nation, and African brother is going to slaughter African brother—not in the interests of Africa, but in the interests of the imperialists both old and new!

That is why I have often thought we must try and find a method which will enable us, in Africa, to avoid the weaknesses of the "national" state. We have the example of Europe before us, where one national state arms itself against another national state. In the world as it is today, nobody could seriously suggest that an African state can arm itself, or be armed, in order to defend itself against one of the great powers of the world. If an African state is armed realistically, it can only be armed against another African state. I think we should be very careful about this. We must not find ourselves committing the same mistakes committed by the nation-states of other continents; arming ourselves against ourselves, destroying our chances not only of raising the standards of living of our people—which is what we are here for—but also destroying forever the chances of African unity.

African Command

That is why, during the difficulties in the Congo, when the idea of an African Command was first proposed, I was very taken with it. I do think we in Africa should think very seriously of a method by which that idea could be put into practice. All that we need within our national boundaries are sufficient police forces for the purpose of maintaining law and order within those boundaries. As far as large military commitments are concerned, these should be on an African basis.

If such a thing could be done, it would achieve two objectives at least. First, it removes the danger I have already referred to—the danger of arming ourselves against ourselves, and thus depriving ourselves of the chance of achieving African unity, as well as of the materials for raising our people's standards of living. And secondly, it provides a real force for the defense of Africa against external aggression. Once again, I know, people have said that this is impossible, that it can't be done; but I believe it can be done.

What can be the role of the young people of Africa in all this? First, I would like to say that Africa is a young continent in two respects. Internationally, its nations are young nations. But Africa is also young in another sense—it is governed by young people. I think one of the troubles in the modern world is that nuclear power is being handled by people who were born in the nineteenth century and educated in the nineteenth century—people with a Victorian turn of mind who have been overtaken by the achievement of science and by modern ideas about human society.

They have not been able to adjust themselves; and while they repeat some of the slogans which sound very "modern" (and I have already said that many of the ones they shout are not modern at all), their actions are the actions of the past. They talk "unity" —and they divide. One advantage of youth is that it doesn't have this dichotomy. The young have had an education which is a present-day education; their ideas are present-day ideas. Youth, bred from the prejudices of the past, should be able to put into action the ideas which modern society demands—but to which the slogan-shouters do little more than pay lip service. Young leaders everywhere in the world find they are having to fight that Victorian attitude, and you can help them.

I believe that you, the youth of Africa, can understand that the role of African nationalism is different—or should be different— from the nationalism of the past; that the African national state is an instrument for the unification of Africa, and not for dividing Africa; that African nationalism is meaningless, is dangerous, is anachronistic, if it is not at the same time Pan-Africanism.

"UJAMAA": THE BASIS OF AFRICAN SOCIALISM*

. . . In the individual, as in the society, it is an attitude of mind which distinguishes the socialist from the nonsocialist. It has nothing to do with possession or nonpossession of wealth. Destitute people can be potential capitalists—exploiters of their fellow human beings. A millionaire can equally well be a socialist; he may value his wealth only because it can be used in the service of his

* Excerpts from a pamphlet published by the *Tanganyika Standard*, Dar-es-Salaam, 1962.

fellow men. But the man who uses wealth for the purpose of dominating any of his fellows is a capitalist. So is the man who would if
he could! . . .

Defenders of capitalism claim that the millionaire's wealth is the
just reward for his ability or enterprise. But this claim is not borne
out by the facts. The wealth of the millionaire depends as little on
the enterprise or abilities of the millionaire himself as the power
of a feudal monarch depended on his own efforts, enterprise, or
brain. Both are users, exploiters, of the abilities and enterprise of
other people. Even when you have an exceptionally intelligent and
hard-working millionaire, the difference between his intelligence,
his enterprise, his hard work, and those of other members of society, cannot possibly be proportionate to the difference between
their "rewards". . . .

Acquisitiveness for the purpose of gaining power and prestige is
unsocialist. In an acquisitive society wealth tends to corrupt those
who possess it. It tends to breed in them a desire to live more com-
fortably than their fellows, to dress better, and in every way to
outdo them. They begin to feel they must climb as far above their
neighbors as they can. The visible contrast between their own comfort and the comparative discomfort of the rest of society becomes
almost essential to the enjoyment of their wealth, and this sets off
the spiral of personal competition—which is then antisocial.

Apart from the antisocial effects of the accumulation of personal
wealth, the very desire to accumulate it must be interpreted as a
vote of "no confidence" in the social system. For when a society
is so organized that it cares about its individuals, then, provided
he is willing to work, no individual within that society should
worry about what will happen to him tomorrow if he does not
hoard wealth today. Society itself should look after him, or his
widow, or his orphans. This is exactly what traditional African society succeeded in doing. Both the "rich" and the "poor" individual were completely secure in African society. Natural catastrophe
brought famine, but it brought famine to everybody—"poor" or
"rich." Nobody starved, either of food or of human dignity, because he lacked personal wealth; he could depend on the weal
possessed by the community of which he was a member. That was
socialism. That *is* socialism. There can be no such thing as acquisitive socialism, for that would be another contradiction in terms.
Socialism is essentially distributive. Its concern is to see that those
who sow reap a fair share of what they sow. . . .

In traditional African society *everybody* was a worker. There was no other way of earning a living for the community. Even the Elder, who appeared to be enjoying himself without doing any work and for whom everybody else appeared to be working, had, in fact, worked hard all his younger days. The wealth he now appeared to possess was not *his*, personally; it was only "his" as the Elder of the group which had produced it. He was its guardian. The wealth itself gave him neither power nor prestige. The respect paid to him by the young was his because he was older than they, and had served his community longer; and the "poor" Elder enjoyed as much respect in our society as the "rich" Elder.

When I say that in traditional African society everybody was a worker, I do not use the word "worker" simply as opposed to "employer" but also as opposed to "loiterer" or "idler." One of the most socialistic achievements of our society was the sense of security it gave to its members, and the universal hospitality on which they could rely. But it is too often forgotten, nowadays, that the basis of this great socialistic achievement was this: that it was taken for granted that every member of society—barring only the children and the infirm—contributed his fair share of effort toward the production of its wealth. Not only was the capitalist, or the landed exploiter, unknown to traditional African society, but we did not have that other form of modern parasite—the loiterer, or idler, who accepts the hospitality of society as his right but gives nothing in return! Capitalistic exploitation was impossible. Loitering was an unthinkable disgrace. . . .

. . . In the old days, the African had never aspired to the possession of personal wealth for the purpose of dominating any of his fellows. He had never had laborers or factory hands to do his work for him. But then came the foreign capitalists. They were wealthy. They were powerful. And the African naturally started wanting to be wealthy too. There is nothing wrong in our wanting to be wealthy; nor is it a bad thing for us to want to acquire the power which wealth brings with it. But it most certainly is wrong if we want the wealth and the power so that we can dominate somebody else. Unfortunately there are some of us who have already learned to covet wealth for that purpose—and who would like to use the methods which the capitalist uses in acquiring it. That is to say, some of us would like to use, or exploit, our brothers for the purpose of building up our own personal power and prestige. This is completely foreign to us, and it is incompatible with the socialist society we want to build here.

Our first step, therefore, must be to re-educate ourselves; to regain our former attitude of mind. In our traditional African society we were individuals within a community. We took care of the community, and the community took care of us. We neither needed nor wished to exploit our fellow men.

And in rejecting the capitalist attitude of mind which colonization brought into Africa, we must reject also the capitalist methods which go with it. One of these is the individual ownership of land. To us in Africa, land was always recognized as belonging to the community. Each individual within our society had a right to the use of land, because otherwise he could not earn his living and one cannot have the right to life without also having the right to some means of maintaining life. But the African's right to land was simply the right to *use* it; he had no other right to it, nor did it occur to him to try and claim one.

The foreigner introduced a completely different concept—the concept of land as a marketable commodity. According to this system, a person could claim a piece of land as his own private property *whether he intended to use it or not*. I could take a few square miles of land, call them "mine," and then go off to the moon. All I had to do to gain a living from "my" land was to charge a rent to the people who wanted to use it. If this piece of land was in an urban area, I had no need to develop it at all; I could leave it to the fools who were prepared to develop all the other pieces of land surrounding "my" piece, and in doing so automatically to raise the market value of mine. Then I could come down from the moon and demand that these fools pay me through the nose for the high value of "my" land; a value which they themselves had created for me while I was enjoying myself on the moon! Such a system is not only foreign to us, it is completely wrong. Landlords, in a society which recognizes individual ownership of land, can be—and they usually are—in the same class as the loiterers I was talking about: the class of parasites.

We must not allow the growth of parasites here in Tanganyika. The TANU [Tanganyika African National Union] government must go back to the traditional African custom of landholding. That is to say, a member of society will be entitled to a piece of land *on condition that he uses it*. Unconditional, or freehold, ownership of land (which leads to speculation and parasitism) must be abolished. We must, as I have said, regain our former attitude of mind—our traditional African socialism—and apply it to the new societies we are building today. . . .

There are bound to be certain groups which, by virtue of the market value of their particular industry's products, *will* contribute more to the nation's income than others. But the others may actually be producing goods or services which are of equal, or greater, *intrinsic* value although they do not happen to command such a high *artificial* value. For example, the food produced by the peasant farmer is of greater social value than the diamonds mined at Mwadui. But the mineworkers of Mwadui could claim, quite correctly, that their labor was yielding greater financial profits to the community than that of the farmers. If, however, they went on to demand that they should therefore be given most of that extra profit for themselves, and that no share of it should be spent on helping the farmers, they would be potential capitalists!

This is exactly where the attitude of mind comes in. It is one of the purposes of trade unions to ensure for the workers a fair share of the profits of their labor. But a "fair" share must be fair in relation to the whole society. If it is greater than the country can afford without having to penalize some other section of society, then it is *not* a fair share. Trade-union leaders and their followers, as long as they are true socialists, will not need to be coerced by the government into keeping their demands within the limits imposed by the needs of society as a whole. Only if there are potential capitalists among them will the socialist government have to step in and prevent them from putting their capitalist ideas into practice!

As with groups, so with individuals. There are certain skills, certain qualifications, which, for good reasons, command a higher rate of salary for their possessors than others. But, here again, the true socialist will demand only that return for his skilled work which he knows to be a fair one in proportion to the wealth or poverty of the whole society to which he belongs. He will not, unless he is a would-be capitalist, attempt to blackmail the community by demanding a salary equal to that paid to his counterpart in some far wealthier society.

European socialism was born of the Agrarian Revolution and the Industrial Revolution which followed it. The former created the "landed" and the "landless" classes in society; the latter produced the modern capitalist and the industrial proletariat.

These two revolutions planted the seeds of conflict within society, and not only was European socialism born of that conflict, but its apostles sanctified the conflict itself into a philosophy. Civil war was no longer looked upon as something evil, or something unfortunate, but as something good and necessary. As prayer is to Christianity or to Islam, so civil war (which they call "class war") is to the European version of socialism—a means inseparable from the end. Each becomes the basis of a whole way of life. The European socialist cannot think of his socialism without its father —capitalism! . . .

African socialism, on the other hand, did not have the "benefit" of the Agrarian Revolution or the Industrial Revolution. It did not start from the existence of conflicting classes in society. Indeed, I doubt if the equivalent for the word "class" exists in any indigenous African language; for language describes the ideas of those who speak it, and the idea of "class" or "caste" was nonexistent in African society.

The foundation, and the objective, of African socialism is the extended family. The true African socialist does not look on one class of men as his brethren and another as his natural enemies. He does not form an alliance with the brethren for the extermination of the nonbrethren. He rather regards *all* men as his brethren— as members of his ever extending family. . . .

Ujamaa, then, or "familyhood," describes our socialism. It is opposed to capitalism, which seeks to build a happy society on the basis of the exploitation of man by man; and it is equally opposed to doctrinaire socialism which seeks to build its happy society on a philosophy of inevitable conflict between man and man.

We, in Africa, have no more need of being "converted" to socialism than we have of being "taught" democracy. Both are rooted in our own past—in the traditional society which produced us. Modern African socialism can draw from its traditional heritage the recognition of society as an extension of the basic family unit. But it can no longer confine the idea of the social family within the limits of the tribe, nor, indeed, of the nation. For no true African socialist can look at a line drawn on a map and say, "The people on this side of that line are my brothers, but those who happen to live on the other side of it can have no claim on me"; every individual on this continent is his brother.

It was in the struggle to break the grip of colonialism that we learned the need for unity. We came to recognize that the same socialist attitude of mind, which in the tribal days gave to every individual the security that comes of belonging to a widely extended family, must be preserved within the still wider society of the nation. But we should not stop there. Our recognition of the family to which we all belong must be extended yet further— beyond the tribe, the community, the nation, or even the continent—to embrace the whole society of mankind. This is the only logical conclusion for true socialism.

DEMOCRACY AND THE PARTY SYSTEM*

. . . Democracy, in Africa or anywhere else, is government by the people. Ideally, it is a form of government whereby the people—*all* the people—settle their affairs through free discussion. The appropriate setting for this basic, or pure, democracy is a small community. The city-states of ancient Greece, for example, practiced it. And in African society, the traditional method of conducting affairs is by free discussion. Mr. Guy Clutton-Brock, writing about a typical African village community, puts it neatly: . . . "The Elders sit under the big tree, and talk until they agree." In larger communities, however, government by the people is possible only in a modified form.

After pure democracy, the next best thing is government by the people's representatives. Where it is the affairs of several million people that are to be settled by discussion, it is obviously not possible for all the people to come together and take a direct part in the discussion. So instead, we have a Parliament in which a number of spokesmen, or representatives, conduct the discussion on their behalf. And if these representatives are truly to represent the people, they must be freely chosen by the people from among themselves. So free elections are the essential instruments of representative democracy.

The purpose of a general election, then, is to elect these people's representatives. But, because of the historical circumstances of the countries in which representative democracy has been most highly developed, such elections are usually organized on a party basis. The electorate is offered a choice between contending parties. It could be said that the object is not so much to elect representatives as to elect a representative party. The countries

* Excerpts from a pamphlet published by the *Tanganyika Standard*, Dar-es-Salaam, 1962.

where this system works most successfully are those which have two major political parties. Now the two-party system requires certain disciplines. I will mention two in particular which are relevant to the case I want to argue. These affect elections and debate—both vital aspects of any form of democracy.

First, where one party is fighting an election against another, it cannot afford to allow more than one of its members to contest the same seat. If it did, it would split the votes of its own supporters and risk handing an easy victory to the rival party. So the first thing such a party must do is select its official candidate, usually by means of some kind of preliminary balloting within its own organization. Once this has been done, *all* party members must support the official candidates only, and fight the public elections as a united group. On this point party discipline is very strict.

Secondly, party candidates who have won the elections and taken their seats in Parliament must remain bound by the rules of party discipline. Once their own leaders have decided on a particular line of policy (even though it may be the purely negative line of opposing the policies of another party), the backbenchers must follow that line, for fear that they might increase the strength or prestige of the rival party by appearing to agree with it.

These disciplines, however, do not apply when each party is conducting what is purely party business. When, for instance, party officials are elected, any member may freely oppose another member, or when the official party candidates for election to national bodies are being selected from within the party organization, fellow members may compete with one another for adoption. The American primary is a typical example of this democratic freedom within a party. Another freedom follows from this: when debate takes place within party circles, it is a free and very often heated debate—each member saying exactly what he feels. The British Labour Party goes as far as allowing this kind of debate to be conducted in public. The Conservatives are more reticent, but it may be presumed that their private debates are just as free and, no doubt, at times as heated.

Those whose political thinking has been molded by the Western parliamentary tradition have now become so used to the two-party system that they cannot imagine democracy without it. It is no good telling them that when a group of a hundred people have sat together as equals and talked until they agreed about where they should dig a well, for example, or whether they should build a new school (and "until they agreed" implies that they will have produced many conflicting arguments before they did eventually agree), they have practiced democracy. No, the Western parliamentarians will want to know whether the talking was properly organized. They will want to know whether there was an organized group whose duty was to talk *for* the motion, and another organized group whose duty was to talk *against* it. They will also want to know whether, at the next debate, the same two groups will remain opposed to each other. In other words, they will be asking whether the opposition is organized and therefore automatic, or whether it is free and therefore spontaneous. Only if it is automatic will they concede that here is democracy! The way they generally put it is: "How can you have democracy with a one-party system?" It may surprise them to know, therefore, that some "heretics" like myself—who also claim to be democrats—are now beginning to ask: "How can you have democracy with a two-party system?"

I must confess that, not so long ago, I would have been content to answer the first of those questions. If I had posed the second it would have been in jest rather than in earnest. Recently, however, I have found myself questioning the democracy of the two-party system very seriously indeed.

Here in Tanganyika, for instance, we have adopted the Westminster type of representative democracy. With it, we took over the whole pattern of parliamentary and local government elections designed for a multiparty system. But it soon became clear to us that however ready we leaders might have been to accept the theory that an official opposition was essential to democratic government, our own people thought otherwise, for the idea did not make sense to them. As a result of the people's choice freely expressed at the polls, we found ourselves with a one-party system.

Now nobody who knew anything about Tanganyika could deny that, in spite of our having only one party, we were very democratic. But we were more democratic within the party than we were outside it. When, for instance, we met to elect our party leaders, nothing could have been more democratic. And our members' freedom of expression during our debates at the party's national executive meetings left nothing to be desired! But since we had adopted the method of election to Parliament and local government bodies which was designed for a contest between parties, we had to apply the party-unity rule. Once we had selected an official TANU candidate, we required all party members to support him. And if any other member disobeyed this rule and stood in opposition to our official candidate, he had to be punished. Invariably his punishment was expulsion from the party. As there is only one party in Tanganyika, the inevitable result of enforcing this rule was to make a contested election a very rare thing indeed. Most TANU candidates for Parliament and for local government councils are returned unopposed, which means, in effect, that they are elected by a party committee. Again, when it came to debates in Parliament we "naturally" (according to the book of rules of the two-party system) had to apply the party-unity rule. . . .

Because of the absence of any rival party, the membership of the TANU Parliamentary Party [TPP] is almost identical with that of the Parliament itself. Yet it is at private meetings of the TPP, and not in the Parliament, that we expect members to speak their minds freely. Here it is that they learn from their leaders what the "party line" is to be, and just how far they may go in criticizing any particular piece of legislation when this comes up for "debate" in Parliament. Fortunately, and I use the word deliberately, this has not so far prevented our members of Parliament (particularly those who are accustomed to the freedom of speech which is characteristic of the national executive) from expressing their own opinions in Parliament from time to time with a most "un-parliamentary" independence of the party line! Nevertheless, whenever one of them does this, we leaders are rather disconcerted, and we generally feel obliged to rebuke him severely for his lapse from party discipline.

Now if we can encourage this freedom of expression at national executive meetings, and within the TPP, why do we discourage it in Parliament? There is, of course, a good theoretical reason. At the national-executive level we are deciding in broad terms what the party's policy shall be. This, naturally, requires a free discussion —to which anybody may contribute his suggestions, objections, countersuggestions, and so on. There obviously cannot be a "party line" to conform to at that stage, because the policy has not yet been agreed upon. And this is equally true under a one-party or a two-party system. But when we go into the Parliament we are no longer debating *what* the policy shall be, for by that time it has been settled—at least in outline. Theoretically, then, all that is still open to discussion in Parliament is detail—the question of exactly how, when, in what order of priority, and so on, the agreed policies shall be put into effect. And here we assume that the party leaders

know best, and therefore the rest of us must support their decisions. But *why* should we assume this? Why should the question
of timing and detail be left entirely to the leaders to decide? In a
two-party Parliament there would be, of course, the need to avoid
giving accidental support or encouragement to the rival party by
any lack of unity between the leaders and their backbench supporters. Where there is only one party, the sole reason—apart
from sheer habit—is that the leaders (i.e., the government) are
said to have based their decisions on advice made available to
them by experts. But this is really nonsense. For there is no valid
reason why the relevant information could not also be placed before the people's representatives in the Parliament, so that such
decisions were approved after a free and informed discussion had
taken place in public. It is not particularly democratic to say,
simply, that the details have been decided by the government "in
the light of certain knowledge which is available to us but not to
you people," and to leave it at that. Nor is it particularly democratic if the people's representatives are given this inside information
privately. An intelligent public must know that decisions are only
reached after argument. Why, then, should we try to fool them by
keeping these arguments out of Parliament? In fact, where there is
no opposition party, there is no reason why the debate in Parliament should not be as free as the debate in the national executive.

Given the two-party system, then, some limitation of freedom is
essential—both at election time and in debate—in order to en-
force party discipline and unity. And we have seen that these
restrictions are not necessary where you have only one party. It
seems at least open to doubt, therefore, that a system which forces
political parties to limit the freedom of their members is a democratic system, and that one which can permit a party to leave its
members their freedom is *un*democratic!

I realize that the political theorists are so attached to the pattern
of democracy which depends on the existence of opposing parties,
that they are likely to have been shocked by my expressing a doubt
as to its being so very democratic after all. I am afraid they may be
even more shocked by what I am now going to suggest: that where
there is *one* party, and that party is identified with the *nation as a
whole*, the foundations of democracy are firmer than they can
ever be where you have two or more parties, each representing only
a section of the community!

After all, we do have it on very reliable authority that a house

divided against itself cannot stand! So it is surely up to the advocates of the two-party system to defend their own case more con-
vincingly. It is not enough for them simply to insist that it *is* more
democratic than a one-party system, and then be horrified when we
presume to disagree with them!

Now my argument is that a two-party system can be justified
only when the parties are divided over some fundamental issue;
otherwise it merely encourages the growth of factionalism. Or, to
put it another way, the only time when a political group can represent the interests of a section of the community, *without* being
a faction, is when that group fights to remove a grievous wrong
from society. But then the differences between this group and
those responsible for the wrong it fights are fundamental; and
there can therefore be no question of national unity until the
differences have been removed by change. And "change" in that
context is a euphemism, because any change in fundamentals is
properly termed "revolution." What is more, the reason why the
word "revolution" is generally associated with armed insurrection
is that the existence of really fundamental differences within any
society poses a "civil war" situation, and has often led to bloody
revolution. Benjamin Disraeli, who was certainly no advocate of a
one-party system, once referred to this situation as tantamount to
"two nations" within a state. . . .

. . . In any country which is divided over fundamental issues
you have the "civil war" situation we have been talking about. If,
on the other hand, you have a two-party system where the differences between the parties are *not* fundamental, then you immediately reduce politics to the level of a football match. A football
match may, of course, attract some very able players; it may also be
entertaining; but it is still only a game, and only the most ardent
fans (who are not usually the most intelligent) take the game
very seriously. This, in fact, is not unlike what has happened in
many of the so-called democratic countries today, where some of
the most intelligent members of society have become disgusted by
the hypocrisy of the party games called politics, and take no interest in them. They can see no party whose "line" they could support without reservation and are therefore left with no way of
serving their country in the political field, even should they wish to,
except, perhaps, by writing a book! For the politics of a country
governed by the two-party system are not, and cannot be, *national*
politics; they are the politics of *groups*, whose differences, more

often than not, are of small concern to the majority of the people.

It is hard to avoid the conclusion that people who defend the two-party system are actually advocating "football politics"; that they really consider a spirit of purely artificial rivalry, like that which exists between a couple of soccer teams, is appropriate to the relationship between opposing political parties. . . .

Our critics should understand that, in Africa, we have to take our politics a little more seriously. And they should also remember the historical difference between parties in Africa and those in Europe or America. The European and American parties came into being as the result of existing social and economic divisions —the second party being formed to challenge the monopoly of political power by some aristocratic or capitalist group. Our own parties had a very different origin. They were not formed to challenge any ruling group of our own people; they were formed to challenge the *foreigners* who ruled over us. They were not, therefore, political "parties"—i.e., factions—but nationalist movements. And from the outset they represented the interests and aspirations of the whole nation. . . .

Now that the colonialists have gone, there is no remaining division between rulers and ruled; no monopoly of political power by any sectional group which could give rise to conflicting parties. There can, therefore, be only one reason for the formation of such parties in a country like ours—the desire to imitate the political structure of a totally dissimilar society. What is more, the desire to imitate where conditions are not suitable for imitation can easily lead us into trouble. To try and import the idea of a parliamentary opposition into Africa may very likely lead to violence— because the opposition parties will tend to be regarded as traitors by the majority of our people—or, at best, it will lead to the trivial maneuverings of opposing groups whose time is spent in the inflation of artificial differences into some semblance of reality "for the sake of preserving democracy"! The latter alternative, I repeat, is an oversophisticated pastime which we in Africa cannot afford to indulge in; our time is too short and there is too much serious work to be done. . . .

The parties of our friends in the older parliamentary democracies outside Africa are sectional groups. So, too, are those within Africa which seek to imitate them. Nowadays such parties do not restrict their membership to those who can claim noble birth, or to the wealthy; but there are some which restrict it, instead, to those who belong to an equally exclusive aristocracy of the intellect! And in certain such modern "aristocracies," instead of the blueness of blood which was once the qualification for membership of the ruling class, we now find that it is by the "redness" of his thought that a man is judged worthy of entry into the ranks of the elite. . . . And in all such parties—whether the factional parties of a two-party democracy, or the vanguard aristocracies of an ideological dictatorship—it is the leaders themselves who "elect" each other. The elections, if any, in which the people are permitted to take part, are not for the purpose of choosing their own representatives; they are merely for the purpose of deciding from which sectional group the "people's representatives" shall be selected for them! . . .

. . . Our friends, the Communists, have made their policies a creed, and are finding that dogmatism and freedom of discussion do not easily go together. They are as much afraid of the "other party" as any government in a two-party democracy. In their case the "other party" is only a phantom, but a phantom can be even more frightening than a living rival! And their fear of this phantom has blinded them to the truth that, in a one-party system, party membership must be open to everybody and freedom of expression allowed to every individual. No party which limits its membership to a clique can ever free itself from the fear of overthrow by those it has excluded. It must be constantly on the watch for signs of opposition, and must smother "dangerous" ideas before they have time to spread.

But a national movement which is open to all—which is identified with the whole nation—has nothing to fear from the discontent of any excluded section of society, for there is then no such section. Those forming the government will, of course, be replaced from time to time; but this is what elections are for. The leadership of our movement is constantly changing; there is no reason why the leadership of the nation should not also be constantly changing. This would have nothing to do with the overthrowing of a party government by a rival party. And, since such a national movement leaves no room for the growth of discontented elements excluded from its membership, it has nothing to fear from criticism and the free expression of ideas. On the contrary, both the movement itself and the nation have everything to gain from a constant injection of new ideas from within the nation and from outside. It would be both wrong, and certainly unnecessary, to feel we must wait until the leaders are dead before we begin to criticize them!

Any member of the Movement (which; in this context, means any patriotic citizen since it is a National Movement we are talking about) would be free to stand as a candidate if he so wished. * And in each constituency the voters themselves would be able to make their choice freely from among these candidates; they would no longer be obliged to consider the party label rather than the individual. Of such elections it could truly be said that they were for the purpose of letting the people choose their own representatives. If that is not democracy, I do not know the meaning of the word!

THE ARUSHA DECLARATION †

THE POLICY OF SOCIALISM

(A) *Absence of Exploitation:* A truly socialist state is one in which all people are workers and in which neither capitalism nor feudalism exists. It does not have two classes of people, a lower class composed of people who work for their living, and an upper class of people who live on the work of others. In a really socialist country no person exploits another; everyone who is physically able to work does so; every worker obtains a just return for the labor he performs; and the incomes derived from different types of work are not grossly divergent.

* Under the system adopted for the elections of September, 1965, the TANU District Conferences chose two candidates in each constituency from among those who had received twenty-five signatures on nominating papers. The entire list of nominees was then forwarded to the National Executive Committee, which could (and occasionally did) substitute other nominees for the candidates endorsed by the District Conference. In 6 out of 107 constituencies, a single candidate was unopposed. The same system was used in the elections of September 1970.—ED.

† TANU Document, reprinted in Julius K. Nyerere, *Ujamaa, Essays on Socialism* (Dar es Salaam, Oxford University Press, 1968).

In a socialist country, the only people who live on the work of others, and who have the right to be dependent upon their fellows, are small children, people who are too old to support themselves, the crippled, and those whom the state at any one time cannot provide with an opportunity to work for their living.

Tanzania is a nation of peasants and workers, but it is not yet a socialist society. It still contains elements of feudalism and capitalism—with their temptations. These feudalistic and capitalistic features of our society could spread and entrench themselves.

(B) *The Major Means of Production and Exchange are under the Control of the Peasants and Workers:* To build and maintain socialism it is essential that all the major means of production and exchange in the nation are controlled and owned by the peasants through the machinery of their government and their cooperatives. Further, it is essential that the ruling party should be a party of peasants and workers.

The major means of production and exchange are such things as: land; forests; minerals; water; oil and electricity; news media; communications; banks, insurance, import and export trade, wholesale trade; iron and steel, machine-tool, arms, motor-car, cement, fertilizer, and textile industries; and any big factory on which a large section of the people depend for their lives, or which provides essential components of other industries; large plantations, and especially those which provide raw materials essential to important industries.*

Some of the instruments of production and exchange which have been listed here are already owned or controlled by the people's Government of Tanzania.

(C) *The Existence of Democracy:* A state is not socialist simply because its means of production and exchange are controlled or owned by the government, either wholly or in large part. For a country to be socialist, it is essential that its government is chosen and led by the peasants and workers themselves. If the minority governments of Rhodesia or South Africa controlled or owned the entire economies of these respective countries, the result would

---

* Since the Arusha Declaration, Tanzania has nationalized the banks, insurance companies, trading, and food processing. It has also bought a majority interest in the breweries and the cement, sisal, and tobacco industries.—ED.

be a strengthening of oppression, not the building of socialism. True socialism cannot exist without democracy also existing in the society.

(D) *Socialism is a Belief:* Socialism is a way of life, and a socialist society cannot simply come into existence. A socialist society can only be built by those who believe in, and who themselves practise, the principles of socialism. A committed member of TANU will be a socialist, and his fellow socialists—that is, his fellow believers in this political and economic system—are all those in Africa or elsewhere in the world who fight for the rights of peasants and workers. The first duty of a TANU member, and especially of a TANU leader, is to accept these socialist principles, and to live his own life in accordance with them. In particular, a genuine TANU leader will not live off the sweat of another man, nor commit any feudalistic or capitalistic actions. . . .

THE POLICY OF SELF-RELIANCE

We Are at War

TANU is involved in a war against poverty and oppression in our country; the struggle is aimed at moving the people of Tanzania (and the people of Africa as a whole) from a state of poverty to a state of prosperity.

We have been oppressed a great deal, we have been exploited a great deal and we have been disregarded a great deal. It is our weakness that has led to our being oppressed, exploited, and disregarded. Now we want a revolution—a revolution which brings to an end our weakness, so that we are never again exploited, oppressed, or humiliated.

A Poor Man Does Not Use Money as a Weapon

But it is obvious that in the past we have chosen the wrong weapon for our struggle, because we chose money as our weapon. We are trying to overcome our economic weakness by using the weapons of the economically strong—weapons which in fact we do not possess. By our thoughts, words, and actions it appears as if we have come to the conclusion that without money we cannot bring about the revolution we are aiming at. It is as if we have said, "Money is the basis of development. Without money there can be no development." . . .

We made a mistake in choosing money—something we do not

have—to be the big instrument of our development. We are making a mistake to think that we shall get the money from other countries; first, because in fact we shall not be able to get sufficient money for our economic development; and secondly, because even if we could get all that we need, such dependence upon others would endanger our independence and our ability to choose our own political policies.

We Have Put Too Much Emphasis on Industries

Because of our emphasis on money, we have made another big mistake. We have put too much emphasis on industries. . . . It is a mistake bacause we do not have the means to establish many modern industries in our country. We do not have either the necessary finances or the technical know-how. It is not enough to say that we shall borrow the finances and the technicians from other countries to come and start the industries. The answer to this is the same one we gave earlier, that we cannot get enough money and borrow enough technicians to start all the industries we need. And even if we could get the necessary assistance, dependence on it could interfere with our policy on socialism. The policy of inviting a chain of capitalists to come and establish industries in our country might succeed in giving us all the industries we need, but it would also succeed in preventing the establishment of socialism unless we believe that without first building capitalism, we cannot build socialism.

Let Us Pay Heed to the Peasant

Our emphasis on money and industries has made us concentrate on urban development. We recognize that we do not have enough money to bring the kind of development to each village which would benefit everybody. We also know that we cannot establish an industry in each village and through this means effect a rise in the real incomes of the people. For these reasons we spend most of our money in the urban areas and our industries are established in the towns.

Yet the greater part of this money that we spend in the towns comes from loans. Whether it is used to build schools, hospitals, houses, or factories, etc., it still has to be repaid. But it is obvious that it cannot be repaid just out of money obtained from urban and industrial development. To repay the loans we have to use foreign currency which is obtained from the sale of our exports.

But we do not now sell our industrial products in foreign markets, and indeed it is likely to be a long time before our industries produce for export. The main aim of our new industries is "import substitution"—that is, to produce things which up to now we have had to import from foreign countries.

It is therefore obvious that the foreign currency we shall use to pay back the loans used in the development of the urban areas will not come from the towns or the industries. Where, then, shall we get it from? We shall get it from the villages and from agriculture. What does this mean? It means that the people who benefit directly from development which is brought about by borrowed money are not the ones who will repay the loans. The largest proportion of the loans will be spent in, or for, the urban areas, but the largest proportion of the repayment will be made through the efforts of the farmers. . . .

If we are not careful we might get to the position where the real exploitation in Tanzania is that of the town dwellers exploiting the peasants. . . .

The Roots of Development

We should not lessen our efforts to get the money we really need, but it would be more appropriate for us to spend time in the villages showing the people how to bring about development through their own efforts rather than going on so many long and expensive journeys abroad in search of development money. This is the real way to bring development to everybody in the country.

None of this means that from now on we will not need money or that we will not start industries or embark upon development projects which require money. Furthermore, we are not saying that we will not accept, or even that we shall not look for, money from other countries for our development. This is *not* what we are saying. We will continue to use money; and each year we will use more money for the various development projects than we used the previous year because his will be one of the signs of our development.

What we are saying, however, is that from now on we shall know what is the foundation and what is the fruit of development. Between *money* and *people* it is obvious that the people and their *hard work* are the foundation of development, and money is one of the fruits of that hard work. . . .

Because the economy of Tanzania depends and will continue

to depend on agriculture and animal husbandry, Tanzanians can live well without depending on help from outside if they use their land properly. Land is the basis of human life and all Tanzanians should use it as a valuable investment for future development. Because the land belongs to the nation, the government has to see to it that it is used for the benefit of the whole nation and not for the benefit of one individual or just a few people. . . .

THE ARUSHA RESOLUTION

Therefore, the National Executive Committee, meeting in the Community Centre at Arusha from January 26, 1967 to January 29, 1967 resolves:

1. Every TANU and Government leader must be either a peasant or a worker, and should in no way be associated with the practices of capitalism or feudalism.

2. No TANU or Government leader should hold shares in any company.

3. No TANU or Government leader should hold the directorships in any privately owned enterprise.

4. No TANU or Government leader should receive two or more salaries.

5. No TANU or Government leader should own houses which he rents to others. . . .

EDUCATION FOR SELF-RELIANCE *

The education provided by the colonial government in the two countries which now form Tanzania had a different purpose. It was not designed to prepare young people for the service of their own country; instead it was motivated by a desire to inculcate the values of the colonial society and to train individuals for the service of the colonial state. In these countries the state interest in education therefore stemmed from the need for local clerks and junior officials; on top of that, various religious groups were interested in spreading literacy and other education as part of their evangelical work.

* From *Ujamaa—Essays in Socialism* (Dar es Salaam: Oxford University Press, 1968), by permission of Julius K. Nyerere.

This statement of fact is not given as a criticism of the many individuals who worked hard, often under difficult conditions, in teaching and in organizing educational work. Nor does it imply that all the values these people transmitted in schools were wrong or inappropriate. What it does mean, however, is that the educational system introduced into Tanzania by the colonialists was modelled on the British system, but with even heavier emphasis on subservient attitudes and on white-collar skills. Inevitably, too, it was based on the assumptions of a colonialist and capitalist society. It emphasized and encouraged the individualistic instincts of mankind, instead of his cooperative instincts. It led to the possession of individual material wealth being the major criterion of social merit and worth. . . .

The third action we have taken is to make the education provided in all schools much more Tanzanian in content. No longer do our children simply learn British and European history. Faster than would have been thought possible our University College and other institutions are providing materials on the history of Africa and making these available to our teachers. Our national songs and dances are once again being learned by our children; and our national language has been given the importance in our curriculum which it needs and deserves. Also, civics classes taken by Tanzanians are beginning to give the secondary school pupils an understanding of the organization and aims of our young state. In these and other ways changes have been introduced to make our educational system more relevant to our needs.

Tanzania will continue to have a predominantly rural economy for a long time to come. And as it is in the rural areas that people live and work, so it is in the rural areas that life must be improved. This is not to say that we shall have no industries and factories in the near future. We have some now and they will continue to expand. But it would be grossly unrealistic to imagine that in the near future more than a small proportion of our people will live in towns and work in modern industrial enterprises. It is therefore the villages which must be made into places where people live a good life; it is in the rural areas that people must be able to find their material well-being and their satisfactions.

This improvement in village life will not, however, come automatically. It will come only if we pursue a deliberate policy of using the resources we have—our manpower and our land—to the best advantage. This means people working hard, intelligently,

and together; in other words, working in cooperation. Our people
in the rural areas, as well as their government, must organize
themselves cooperatively and work for themselves through working for the community of which they are members. Our village
life, as well as our state organization, must be based on the principles of socialism and that equality in work and return which is
part of it.

This is what our educational system has to encourage. It has
to foster the social goals of living together, and working together,
for the common good. It has to prepare our young people to play
a dynamic and constructive part in the development of a society
in which all members share fairly in the good or bad fortune of
the group, and in which progress is measured in terms of human
well-being, not prestige buildings, cars, or other such things,
whether privately or publicly owned. Our education must therefore inculcate a sense of commitment to the total community, and
help the pupils to accept the values appropriate to our kind of
future, not those appropriate to our colonial past.

This means that the educational system of Tanzania must
emphasize cooperative endeavor, not individual advancement; it
must stress concepts of equality and the responsibility to give
service which goes with any special ability, whether it be in
carpentry, in animal husbandry, or in academic pursuits. And, in
particular, our education must counteract the temptation to intellectual arrogance; for this leads to the well-educated despising
those whose abilities are nonacademic or who have no special
abilities but are just human beings. Shuch arrogance has no place
in a society of equal citizens.

It is, however, not only in relation to social values that our
educational system has a task to do. It must also prepare young
people for the work they will be called upon to do in the society
which exists in Tanzania—a rural society where improvement
will depend largely upon the efforts of the people in agriculture
and in village development. . . .

The education now provided is designed for the few who are
intellectually stronger than their fellows; it induces among those
who succeed a feeling of superiority, and leaves the majority of
the others hankering after something they will never obtain. It
induces a feeling of inferiority among the majority, and can thus
not produce either the egalitarian society we should build, nor

the attitudes of mind which are conducive to an egalitarian society. On the contrary, it induces the growth of a class structure in our country.

Equally important is the second point; the fact that Tanzania's education is such as to divorce its participants from the society it is supposed to be preparing them for. This is particularly true of secondary schools, which are inevitably almost entirely boarding schools; but to some extent, and despite recent modifications in the curriculum, it is true of primary schools too. We take children from their parents at the age of seven years, and for up to seven-and-a-half hours a day we teach them certain basic academic skills. In recent years we have tried to relate these skills, at least in theory, to the life which the children see around them. But the school is always separate; it is not part of the society. It is a place children go to and which they and their parents hope will make it unnecessary for them to become farmers and continue living in the villages.

Our present system encourages school pupils in the idea that all knowledge which is worthwhile is acquired from books or from "educated people"—meaning those who have been through a formal education. The knowledge and wisdom of other old people is despised, and they themselves regarded as being ignorant and of no account. Indeed it is not only the education system which at present has the effect. Government and party themselves tend to judge people according to whether they have "passed school certificate," "have a degree," etc. If a man has these qualifications we assume he can fill a post; we do not wait to find out about his attitudes, his character, or any other ability except the ability to pass examinations. If a man does not have these qualifications we assume he cannot do a job; we ignore his knowledge and experience.

The education given in our primary schools must be a complete education in itself. It must not continue to be simply a preparation for secondary school. Instead of the primary school activities being geared to the competitive examination which will select the few who go on to secondary school, they must be a preparation for the life which the majority of the children will lead. Similarly, secondary schools must not be simply a selection process for the university, teachers' colleges, and so on. They must prepare people for life and service in the villages and rural areas of this country. For in Tanzania the only true justification for secondary education is that it is needed by the few for service to the many.

We should not determine the type of things children are taught in primary schools by the things a doctor, engineer, teacher, economist, or administrator need to know. Most of our pupils will never be any of these things. We should determine the type of things taught in the primary schools by the things which the boy or girl ought to know—that is, the skills he ought to acquire and the values he ought to cherish if he, or she, is to live happily and well in a socialist and predominantly rural society, and contribute to the improvement of life there. Our sights must be on the majority; it is they we must be aiming at in determining the curriculum and syllabus. Those most suitable for further education will still become obvious, and they will not suffer. For the purpose is not to provide an inferior education to that given at present. The purpose is to provide a different education—one realistically designed to fulfill the common purposes of education in the particular society of Tanzania. The same thing must be true at post-primary schools. The object of the teaching must be the provision of knowledge, skills, and attitudes which will serve the student when he or she lives and works in a developing and changing socialist state; it must not be aimed at university entrance.

Alongside this change in the approach to the curriculum there must be a parallel and integrated change in the way our schools are run, so as to make them and their inhabitants a real part of our society and our economy. Schools must, in fact, become communities—and communities which practice the precept of self-reliance. The teachers, workers, and pupils together must be the members of a social unit in the same way as parents, relatives, and children are the family social unit. There must be the same kind of relationship between pupils and teachers within the school community as there is between children and parents in the village. And the former community must realize just as the latter do, that their life and well-being depend upon the production of wealth—by farming or other activities. This means that all schools, but especially secondary schools and other forms of higher education, must contribute to their own upkeep; they must be economic communities as well as social and educational communities. Each school should have, as an integral part of it, a farm or workshop which provides the food eaten by the community, and makes some contribution to the total national income. . . .

The education provided by Tanzania for the students of Tanzania must serve the purposes of Tanzania. It must encourage the growth of the socialist values we aspire to. It must encourage the development of a proud, independent, and free citizenry which relies upon itself for its own development, and which knows the advantages and the problems of cooperation. It must ensure that the educated know themselves to be an integral part of the nation and recognize the responsibility to give greater service the greater the opportunities they have had.

This is not only a matter of school organization and curriculum. Social values are formed by family, school, and society—by the total environment in which a child develops. But it is no use our educational system stressing values and knowledge appropriate to the past or to the citizens in other countries; it is wrong if it even contributes to the continuation of those inequalities and privileges which still exist in our society because of our inheritance. Let our students be educated to be members and servants of the kind of just and egalitarian future to which this country aspires.

24. *Nelson Mandela*

Nelson Mandela, born in 1918, the son of a chief in the Transkei, was one of the leaders of the African National Congress (ANC) in South Africa. He received a law degree from the University of South Africa in 1942 and led the African opposition to the increasingly repressive South African racial laws. Imprisoned for five years for inciting a strike in 1961 and leaving the country without a passport, he was taken from his cell in October, 1963 to face trial for sabotage and conspiracy to overthrow the government by revolution. In his statement to the court he explained why he and his associates decided on recourse to violent resistance to the South African government. Mandela was subsequently convicted and sentenced to life imprisonment.

THE QUESTION OF VIOLENCE *

I am the First Accused.

I hold a Bachelor's Degree in Arts and practiced as an attorney in Johannesburg for a number of years in partnership with Oliver Tambo. I am a convicted prisoner serving five years for leaving the country without a permit and for inciting people to go on strike at the end of May, 1961.

. . . I have done whatever I did, both as an individual and as a leader of my people, because of my experience in South Africa. . . .

In my youth in the Transkei, I listened to the elders of my tribe telling stories of the old days. Among the tales they related to me were those of wars fought by our ancestors in defense of the fatherland. . . . I hoped then that life might offer me the opportunity to serve my people and make my own humble contribution to their freedom struggle. This is what has motivated me in all that I have done in relation to the charges made against me in this case.

Having said this, I must deal immediately and at some length with the question of violence. Some of the things so far told to the court are true and some are untrue. I do not, however, deny that I planned sabotage. I did not plan it in a spirit of recklessness, nor because I have any love of violence. I planned it as a result of a calm and sober assessment of the political situation that had arisen after many years of tyranny, exploitation, and oppression of my people by the whites.

. . . We had no doubt that we had to continue the fight. Anything else would have been abject surrender. Our problem was not whether to fight, but was how to continue the fight. We of the African National Congress had always stood for a nonracial democracy, and we shrank from any action which might drive the races further apart than they already were. But the hard facts were that fifty years of nonviolence had brought the African people nothing but more and more repressive legislation, and fewer and fewer rights. It may not be easy for this Court to understand, but it is a fact that for a long time the people had been talking of violence—of the day when they would fight the white man and win back their country—and we, the leaders of the ANC, had

* From a pamphlet published by *Christian Action* (London, 1964).

nevertheless always prevailed upon them to avoid violence and to pursue peaceful methods. When some of us discussed this in May and June of 1961, it could not be denied that our policy to achieve a nonracial State by nonviolence had achieved nothing, and that our followers were beginning to lose confidence in this policy and were developing disturbing ideas of terrorism.

At the beginning of June, 1961, after a long and anxious assessment of the South African situation, I, and some colleagues, came to the conclusion that as violence in this country was inevitable, it would be unrealistic and wrong for African leaders to continue preaching peace and nonviolence at a time when the government met our peaceful demands with force.

. . . As far as the ANC was concerned, it formed a clear view which can be summarized as follows:

(1) It was a mass political organization with a political function to fulfill. Its members had joined on the express policy of nonviolence.

(2) Because of all this, it could, and would, not undertake violence. This must be stressed. One cannot turn such a body into the small, closely knit, organization required for sabotage. Nor would this be politically correct because it would result in members ceasing to carry out this essential activity: political propaganda and organization. Nor was it permissible to change the whole nature of the organization.

(3) On the other hand, in view of this situation I have described, the ANC was prepared to depart from its fifty-year-old policy of nonviolence to this extent: that it would no longer disapprove of properly controlled violence. Hence members who undertook such activity would not be subject to disciplinary action by the ANC.

I say "properly controlled violence" because I made it clear that if I formed the organization I would at all times subject it to the political guidance of the ANC and would not undertake any different form of activity from that contemplated without the consent of the ANC. And I shall now tell the Court how that form of violence came to be determined. . . .

The avoidance of civil war had dominated our thinking for many years, but when we decided to adopt violence as part of our policy, we realized that we might one day have to face the prospect of such a war. This had to be taken into account in formulating our plans. We required a plan which was flexible and which permitted us to act in accordance with the needs of the times; above all, the plan had to be one which recognized civil war as the last resort, and left the decision on this question to the future. We did not want to be committed to civil war, but we wanted to be ready if it became inevitable.

Four forms of violence were possible. There is sabotage, there is guerrilla warfare, there is terrorism, and there is open revolution. We chose to adopt the first method and to exhaust it before taking any other decision.

In the light of our political background, the choice was a logical one. Sabotage did not involve loss of life, and it offered the best hope for future race relations. Bitterness would be kept to a minimum and, if the policy bore fruit, democratic government could become a reality. . . .

The initial plan was based on a careful analysis of the political and economic situation of our country. We believed that South Africa depended to a large extent on foreign capital and foreign trade. We felt that planned destruction of power plants, and interference with rail and telephone communications, would tend to scare away capital from the country, make it more difficult for goods from the industrial areas to reach the seaports on schedule, and would in the long run be a heavy drain on the economic life of the country, thus compelling the voters of the country to reconsider their position.

Attacks on the economic life lines of the country were to be linked with sabotage on government buildings and other symbols of apartheid. These attacks would serve as a source of inspiration to our people. In addition, they would provide an outlet for those people who were urging the adoption of violent methods and would enable us to give concrete proof to our followers that we had adopted a stronger line and were fighting back against government violence.

In addition, if mass action were successfully organized, and mass reprisals taken, we felt that sympathy for our cause would be roused in other countries, and that greater pressure would be brought to bear on the South African government. . . .

I was completely objective. The Court will see that I attempted to examine all types of authority on the subject—from the East and from the West, going back to the classic work of Clausewitz, and covering such a variety as Mao Tse-tung and Che Guevara on the one hand, and the writings on the Anglo-Boer War on the other.

. . . I also made arrangements for our recruits to undergo military training. . . . I consequently obtained the permission of the ANC in South Africa to do this. To this extent then there was a departure from the original decision of the ANC, but it applied outside South Africa only. The first batch of recruits actually arrived in Tanganyika when I was passing through that country on my way back to South Africa.

I returned to South Africa and reported to my colleagues on the results of my trip. It was decided to go ahead with the plans for military training because of the fact that it would take many years to build up a sufficient nucleus of trained soldiers to start a guerrilla campaign, and whatever happened the training would be of value. . . .

Africans want to be paid a living wage. Africans want to perform work which they are capable of doing, and not work which the government declares them to be capable of. Africans want to be allowed to live where they obtain work, and not be endorsed out of an area because they were not born there. Africans want to be allowed to own land in places where they work, and not to be obliged to live in rented houses which they can never call their own. Africans want to be part of the general population, and not confined to living in their own ghettoes. African men want to have their wives and children to live with them where they work, and not forced into an unnatural existence in men's hostels. African women want to be with their menfolk and not be left permanently widowed in the Reserves. Africans want to be allowed out after eleven o'clock at night and not to be confined to their rooms like little children. Africans want to be allowed to travel in their own country and to seek work where they want to and not where the Labor Bureau tells them to. Africans want a just share in the whole of South Africa; they want security and a stake in society.

Above all, we want equal political rights, because without them our disabilities will be permanent. I know this sounds revolutionary to the whites in this country, because the majority of voters will be Africans. This makes the white man fear democracy.

But this fear cannot be allowed to stand in the way of the only solution which will guarantee racial harmony and freedom for all. It is not true that the enfranchisement of all will result in racial domination. Political division, based on color, is entirely artificial and, when it disappears, so will the domination of one color group by another. The ANC has spent half a century fighting against racialism. When it triumphs it will not change that policy.

This then is what the ANC is fighting. Their struggle is a truly national one. It is a struggle of the African people, inspired by their own suffering and their own experience. It is a struggle for the right to live.

During my lifetime, I have dedicated myself to this struggle of the African people. I have fought against white domination, and I have fought against black domination. I have cherished the ideal of a democratic and free society in which all persons live together in harmony and with equal opportunities. It is an ideal which I hope to live for and to achieve. But if needs be, it is an ideal for which I am prepared to die.

PART IV

LATIN AMERICA

The Latin American experience is different from that of Asia, Africa, or the Middle East, yet the area faces many of the same problems of modernization and development. Although Latin America has been politically independent since the early nineteenth century, government has until recently been the monopoly of a small, European-oriented upper class, which wielded economic, political, and often military and ecclesiastical power. Ideological conflicts among the Latin American elite reflected the ideologies of Europe—with the positivism and anticlericalism of the European radicals, as well as the conservatism of the European landowning feudal classes.

In this century, radical and reformist ideologies have begun to involve the masses in political life. In some cases, European doctrines have been altered to fit the Latin American scene. (Christian Democratic, socialist, and Communist theories are represented in the selections by Eduardo Frei, José Figueres, Salvador Allende, and Fidel Castro.) In others, new formulations or combinations have been developed to deal with the special situation in Latin America (e.g., the theories of Haya de la Torre and General Velasco in Peru). Even when the political leader has no systematic and integrated political theory, he is still aware of the necessity to respond to the pressing problems of Latin America— the concentration of economic power in the hands of a few wealthy landowners, the lack of industrial development, and the preponderance of foreign (particularly American) influences in Latin American economic life.*

* It should be noted that there are considerable variations among the Latin American countries in the extent of industrialization and the seriousness of

Latin American leaders share the reforming zeal and anti-imperialist sentiments of those of Asia, Africa, and the Middle East. Until recently, however, there has been little awareness of a community of interest with other underdeveloped nations—partly because of cultural and linguistic barriers, partly because of the absence of the political links that the French and British colonial empires provided to bring the African and Asian nationalists into contact with one another. The Cuban revolution has considerably altered this situation. Certainly at its outset, and even today, the politically conscious elements in Asia, Africa, and the Middle East consider it a nationalistic, anticolonial revolution similar to their own. Thus Cuba continues to be invited to the Conference of Nonaligned Countries.

In addition to a desire for social reform and opposition to imperialism, other goals of modernizing nationalism are present in Latin American political thought. Economic development through planning and government action, industrialization at a rapid rate, and the expansion of literacy and educational opportunity are all objectives of the Latin American leaders. Although a multiparty system flourishes in such countries as Chile and Uruguay, there is also a desire for strong government and an end to party strife. The single party has not been defended with the vigor with which the Africans defend it, but in the case of Mexico, an effective and democratic dominant party system has been in control for a number of years. Latin American nationalism has not led to a significant revival of interest in traditional culture, but Haya de la Torre of Peru has spoken of "Indo-America" as a distinctive cultural entity, and Eduardo Frei of Chile has called upon Latin America to make its distinctive contribution to world civilization. That a loosening of political and economic ties with the United States also appeals to many Latin Americans is evident in the support for programs of Latin American political and economic integration.

Counterbalancing the neutralist and anti-American tendencies are programs of political cooperation (through the Organization of American States), of military alliance (through the 1947 Treaty of Rio de Janeiro), and of economic assistance (through the Alliance for Progress, initiated in 1961). In addition, there is

the economic and social problems. Thus Walt W. Rostow, in *The Stages of Economic Growth*, classes Argentina and Mexico as already in the "take-off" stage of economic development.

the vigorously anti-Communist attitude of many groups in Latin America, although this has diminished recently. It may thus be possible to attain the social and economic objectives of modernization without destroying the inter-American system, but the task will be among the most difficult ones confronted by United States policymakers in the years to come.

25. Fidel Castro

Fidel Castro was born in 1926, on a sugar farm owned by his father. He received his primary and secondary education in Catholic schools. At the University of Havana, where he studied law and was active in student politics, he was elected president of the student government. Castro joined an unsuccessful expeditionary force against General Trujillo of the Dominican Republic in 1947. A year later, he attended a student meeting in Bogotá, Colombia, and participated in the riots marking the meeting of the Organization of American States there. He received his law degree in 1950, and two years later sued unsuccessfully in the Constitutional Court of Havana for a decision that Batista's seizure of power had been unconstitutional. On July 26, 1953, after an attack on the Moncada barracks in Santiago de Cuba, he was captured, tried (his defense was later published as History Will Absolve Me*), and sentenced to fifteen years in prison on the Isle of Pines. Released in 1955 under an amnesty law, he went to Mexico, where he formed the 26th of July Movement. In November, 1956, he returned to Cuba and began the resistance movement in the hills of Sierra Maestre that was finally to come to power on January 1, 1959.* History Will Absolve Me *promised a return to the 1940 constitution, an agrarian reform, and the nationalization of the telephone and electricity "trusts." After coming to power, Castro did not hold elections (although this was implied by his promise to restore the 1940 constitution and by his references to the "popularly elected" government that would follow). In May, 1959, however, at the Economic Council of the Organization of American States in Buenos Aires, he spoke of elections as a check against oppression, and asked the United States to set up a $30 billion aid program for Latin America in the next ten years. At this time, he also repeatedly denied that he or his revolution was Communist. A year later, he* *asserted that because of "the intimate union and identification of the government with the people," elections were not necessary (see Castro's speech on "A Real Democracy"). In late 1959 and 1960, with the defection of many of the original revolutionaries on the grounds of increasing Communist control of Cuba, it became apparent that the Popular Socialist Party (PSP)—as the Cuban Communist Party was known—was becoming dominant in the group around Castro. This development was reinforced by Castro's increasingly close military and economic ties with the Soviet bloc, links that were strengthened after the United States cut off the Cuban sugar quota in mid-1960. Finally, in December, 1961, Castro announced his allegiance to Marxism-Leninism (although he did not say, as press reports first had it, that he had always been a Marxist-Leninist), and described the newly established Revolutionary Integrated Organizations as a preparatory step to the creation of an elite party, the United Revolutionary Socialist Party, under collective leadership along Leninist lines (now known as the Communist Party of Cuba). Supported economically by the Soviet Union, he has differed with it on the appropriateness of guerrilla activity in Latin America. Since late 1968, Castro's attention has been devoted primarily to internal economic matters.*

HISTORY WILL ABSOLVE ME*

In the brief of this case there must be recorded the five revolutionary laws that would have been proclaimed immediately after the capture of the Moncada barracks and would have been broadcast to the nation by radio. It is possible that Colonel Chaviano may deliberately have destroyed these documents, but even if he has done so, I conserve them in my memory.

The First Revolutionary Law would have returned power to the people and proclaimed the Constitution of 1940 the supreme law of the land, until such time as the people should decide to modify or change it. And, in order to effect its implementation and punish those who had violated it—there being no organization for holding elections to accomplish this—the revolutionary movement,

* Excerpts from Fidel Castro's defense statement at his trial (see biographical sketch) in 1953, later published as *History Will Absolve Me* (New York: Lyle Stuart, 1961); reprinted by permission.

as the momentous incarnation of this sovereignty, the only source of legitimate power, would have assumed all the faculties inherent to it except that of modifying the Constitution itself. In other words, it would have assumed the legislative, executive, and judicial powers.

This approach could not be more crystal-clear or more free of vacillation and sterile charlatanry. A government acclaimed by the mass of rebel people would be vested with every power, everything necessary in order to proceed with the effective implementation of the popular will and true justice. From that moment, the judicial power, which since March 10 has placed itself *against* the Constitution and *outside* the Constitution, would cease to exist, and we would proceed to its immediate and total reform before it would again assume the power granted to it by the Supreme Law of the Republic. Without our first taking those measures, a return to legality—by putting the custody of the courts back into the hands that have crippled the system so dishonorably—would constitute a fraud, a deceit, and one more betrayal.

The Second Revolutionary Law would have granted property (not mortgageable and not transferable) to all planters, subplanters, lessees, partners, and squatters who hold parcels of five or less *caballerias** of land, and the state would indemnify the former owners on the basis of the rental they would have received for these parcels over a period of ten years.

The Third Revolutionary Law would have granted workers and employees the right to share 30 per cent of the profits of all the large industrial, mercantile, and mining enterprises, including the sugar mills. The strictly agricultural enterprises would be exempt, in consideration of other agrarian laws which would have been implemented.

The Fourth Revolutionary Law would have granted all planters the right to share 50 per cent of the sugar production and a minimum quota of 40,000 *arrobas†* for all small planters who had been established for three or more years.

The Fifth Revolutionary Law would have ordered the confiscation of all holdings and ill-gotten gains of those who had committed frauds during previous regimes, as well as the holdings and ill-gotten gains of all their legatees and heirs. To implement this,

---

* A *caballeria* is a tract of land equivalent to about 33.3 acres.—ED.
† An *arroba* is equivalent to 25 pounds.—ED.

special courts with full powers would gain access to all records of all corporations registered or operating in this country, in order to investigate concealed funds of illegal origin, and to request that foreign governments extradite persons and attach their holdings. Half of the property recovered would be used to subsidize retirement funds for workers, and the other half would be used for hospitals, asylums, and charitable organizations.

Furthermore, it was to be declared that the Cuban policy in the Americas would be one of close solidarity with the democratic people of this continent, and that those politically persecuted by bloody tyrants oppressing our sister nations would find generous asylum, brotherhood, and bread in the land of Martí—not the persecution, hunger, and treason that they find today. Cuba should be the bulwark of liberty and not a shameful link in the chain of despotism.

These laws would have been proclaimed immediately, as soon as the upheaval was ended and prior to a detailed and far-reaching study. They would have been followed by another series of laws and fundamental measures, such as agrarian reform, integral reform of education, nationalization of the utilities trust and the telephone trust, refunds to the people of the illegal excessive rates this company has charged, and payment to the treasury of all taxes brazenly evaded in the past.

All these laws and others would be inspired in the exact fulfillment of two essential articles of our Constitution. One of these orders the outlawing of feudal estates by indicating the maximum area of land any person or entity can possess for each type of agricultural enterprise, by adopting measures which would tend to return the land to the Cubans. The other categorically orders the state to use all means at its disposal to provide employment for all those who lack it and to ensure a decent livelihood for each manual laborer or intellectual.

None of these articles may be called unconstitutional. The first popularly elected government would have to respect these laws, not only because of moral obligation to the nation, but because when people achieve something they have yearned for throughout generations, no force in the world is capable of taking it away again.

The problems concerning land, industrialization, housing, unemployment, education, and the health of the people—these are the six problems we would take immediate steps to resolve, along with the restoration of public liberties and political democracy....

It is not by statesmen such as Carlos Saladrigas*—whose statesmanship consists of preserving the *status quo* and mouthing phrases like the "absolute freedom of enterprise," "guarantees to investment capital," and "the law of supply and demand"—that we will solve these problems. Those ministers can chat gaily in a mansion on Fifth Avenue† until there remains not even the dust of the bones of those whose problems required immediate solution. In this present-day world, social problems are not solved by spontaneous generation.

A revolutionary government with the backing of the people and the respect of the nation, after purging the various institutions of all venal and corrupt officials, would proceed immediately to industrialize the country, mobilizing all inactive capital (currently estimated at about $500 million) through the National Bank and the Agricultural, Industrial, and Development Bank and submitting this mammoth task to experts and men of absolute competence, completely removed from all political machinations, for study, direction, planning, and realization.

After establishing the 100,000 small farmers as owners on land they had previously rented, a revolutionary government would proceed immediately to settle the land problem. First, as the Constitution orders, we would establish the maximum amount of land to be held by each type of agricultural enterprise and would acquire the excess acres by expropriation: recovery of the lands stolen from the state, improvement of swampland, planting of large nurseries, and reserving of zones for reforestation. Secondly, we would distribute the remaining land among peasant families (with priority given to the larger ones) and would promote agricultural cooperatives *for the common use of expensive equipment,*‡ with a single technical, professional direction of farming and cattle raising. Finally, we would provide resources, equipment, protection, and useful guidance to the peasants.

---

* Batista's presidential candidate in 1944 elections, Saladrigas was defeated. He became an influential member of Batista's government after 1952.—ED.

† Located in the Miramar residential district in Havana.—ED.

‡ Italicized words omitted in the translation from which this excerpt is taken.—ED.

A revolutionary government would solve the housing problem by cutting all rents in half, by providing tax exemptions on homes inhabited by the owners, by tripling taxes on rented homes, by tearing down hovels and replacing them with modern multiple-dwelling buildings, and by financing housing all over the island on a scale heretofore unheard of, with the criterion that, just as each rural family should possess its own tract of land, each city family should own its home or apartment. There is plenty of building material and more than enough manpower to make a decent home for every Cuban. But if we continue to wait for the miracle of the golden calf, a thousand years will have gone by and the problem will still be the same. On the other hand, today there are greater possibilities than ever of bringing electricity to the remotest corner of the island. The use of nuclear energy in this field is now a reality and will greatly reduce the cost of producing electricity.

With these three projects and reforms, the problem of unemployment would automatically disappear, and the work to improve public health and to fight against disease would be made much less difficult.

Finally, a revolutionary government would undertake the integral reform of the educational system, bringing it in line with the foregoing projects, with the idea of educating those generations who will have the privilege of living in a happy land. Do not forget the words of the Apostle:* "A serious error is being made in Latin America: Where the inhabitants depend almost exclusively on the products of the soil for their livelihood, the educational stress is on urban rather than farm life." "The happiest people are the ones whose children are well educated and instructed in philosophy; whose sentiments are directed into noble channels." "A well-educated people will always be strong and free."

The spirit of education lies, however, in the teacher himself, and in Cuba the teaching profession is miserably underpaid. Despite this, no one is more dedicated than the Cuban teacher. Who among us has not learned his ABC's in the little public schoolhouse? It is time we stopped paying pittances to these young men and women who are entrusted with the sacred task of teaching the young. No teacher should earn less than $200, no secondary pro-

* "The Apostle" refers to Jose Martí.—Ed.

fessor should get less than $350, if they are to devote themselves exclusively to their high calling without suffering want. Moreover, all rural teachers should have free use of the various systems of transportation, and, at least every five years, all teachers should enjoy a sabbatical leave of six months with pay so they may attend special refresher courses at home and abroad to keep abreast of the latest developments in their field. In this way, the curriculum and the teaching system may be constantly improved.

Where will the money be found for all this? When there is an end to rife embezzlement of government funds, when public officials stop taking graft from the large companies that owe taxes to the state, when the enormous resources of the country are brought into full use, when we no longer buy tanks, bombers, and guns for this country (which has no frontiers to defend, and where these instruments of war, now being purchased, are used against the people), when there is more interest in educating the people than in killing them—then there will be more than enough money.

Cuba could easily provide for a population three times as great as it now has, so there is no excuse for the abject poverty of a single one of its present inhabitants. The markets should be overflowing with produce, pantries should be full, all hands should be working. This is not an inconceivable thought. What is inconceivable is that anyone should go to bed hungry, that children should die for lack of medical attention; what is inconceivable is that 30 per cent of our farm people cannot write their names and that 99 per cent of them know nothing of Cuba's history. What is inconceivable is that the majority of our rural people are now living in worse circumstances than the Indians Columbus discovered living in the fairest land that human eyes had ever seen.

To those who would call me a dreamer, I quote the words of Martí: "A true man does not seek the path where advantage lies, but rather, the path where duty lies, and this is the only practical man, whose dream of today will be the law of tomorrow, because he who has looked back on the upheavals of history and has seen civilizations going up in flames, crying out in bloody struggle, throughout the centuries, knows that the future well-being of man, without exception, lies on the side of duty."

THE ACCUSATION OF COMMUNISM*

I do not know whether the calumny against the Revolution—that it is Communist and infiltrated by Communism—is due solely to the fact that we do not persecute the Communists and do not shoot them. I do not know how the ideas of the Revolution can be defined in such a way that there will be no more intrigues or lies than there are at present, and that the infamous attacks against our Revolution will finally cease. Is it perhaps because we have a firm conviction of the freedom of mankind and the rights of man, and of equity and human equality, that we cannot conceive that anyone would desire to have rights that he keeps from others? Is it because we have pledged to discuss our ideas in conditions of equality with all others? Is it because we have pledged to carry out our ideals, not by force, but by reason and justice? On the contrary, if the theory is accepted that someone has a right to suppress others' rights, the easiest thing for the Revolution would be to suppress the right of everyone except those who are members of the revolutionary government to speak. But that would not be democratic, nor is it our philosophy, for clearly the right to think and speak belongs to all equally. Is it because we think this way, because this is our political philosophy, that the fear of Communists is being aroused, in order to incite division in the country and bring together the enemies in other countries against us? Can our Revolution be accused of being Communist? Can the ideals of our Revolution be confused? Have we not spoken with sufficient clarity on the doctrine of the 26th of July Movement? Are our purposes not clearly defined? Then why are these fears and fantasies pursued? Are they not trying to create obstacles for the path of our Revolution? If our ideas are very clear, if the majority of the people are behind those ideas, and we are all at the command of that movement and that Revolution, do the people not trust us? Can someone perhaps maintain that we have ever lied to the people? Can anyone think that we have lacked courage to

* Excerpts from a speech delivered by Castro in the Plaza Cívica, Havana, on May 8, 1959; translated by the editor from the text in *Guia del Pensamiento Político Económico de Fidel* (Havana: Diario Libre, 1959).

speak to the people? Can anyone think that we lack the necessary sincerity to speak what we think to the people? Can anyone perhaps think that we are hypocrites or cowards? Then why do we say that our Revolution is not Communist? Why, when we prove that our ideals are different from Communist doctrine, that the Revolution is not Communist or capitalist, that it is a revolution of its own . . . that it has its own ideology—entirely its own— which has a Cuban basis and is entirely Cuban, entirely Latin American, why then, do they start to accuse our Revolution of being something it is not? It is necessary to explain for once that if our ideas were Communist, we would say so here, and if our ideas were capitalist, we would say so here. We do not give anyone the right to decide for our conscience what we are and what we have a right to be. . . .

PLAN FOR THE ADVANCEMENT
OF LATIN AMERICA*

Democracy and Dictatorship

How is it possible for democracy to be preserved under these conditions? We have declared the democratic ideal to be the ideal of the peoples of this hemisphere. We have declared that the democratic ideal is the ideal that can best satisfy the dreams of the peoples of this continent. Nevertheless, the economic and social conditions of Latin America make it impossible for our countries to attain their ideal of democracy. Be it a dictatorship of the Left or a dictatorship of the Right, a dictatorship is a dictatorship, and those in power completely deny the principles toward which the peoples of Latin America aspire. . . . The Pan-American ideal is true democracy with absolute respect for the dignity of man, a true democracy in which all the liberties prevail, a true democracy in a regime of social justice. The peoples of Latin America want neither bread without liberty nor liberty without bread. . . .

* Excerpts from a speech delivered by Castro in Buenos Aires, on May 21, 1959, at the Sixth Plenary Economic Council of the Organization of American States, reprinted from *Plan for the Advancement of Latin America* (Havana, 1959).

We have said that underdevelopment is an insidious enemy of constitutional governments—governments that find themselves so strangled by conditions of poverty that they are pushed into the grip of armed minorities. We made this statement precisely because we have known two kinds of governments. We have been subjected to strong-arm governments that suppress all liberties—freedom of press, of assembly, of association, of election—and use fire and sword to maintain the so-called peace and order about which they brag so much. Under these strong-arm governments, resentment grows, poverty worsens, suffering increases.

Thus, as soon as the people can overcome the restrictions imposed upon them, they put constitutional governments into effect. Full of dreams, and with their hopes high, they begin to exercise the rights that the new regime guarantees them. They begin trying to satisfy all their needs as quickly as possible. Then, since the tremendous problem is precisely that there are not enough resources to satisfy their needs, since the resources available do not reach far enough, all kinds of conflicts arise. These conflicts are forthwith called disorder or anarchy by the enemies of democracy —by those who are waiting for the opportunity to seize power again by force.

Democratic governments cannot solve these problems which are becoming more and more acute—with theories, or arguments, or reasoning. The theory is advanced that if investments are to be attracted, there must be complete peace and order. The theory is advanced that in order to attract investments, there should be no strikes. In other words, these are the requisites often cited for the economic development of a country. But what is never explained is just how such conditions can be achieved by the use of democratic procedures and without placing further restrictions on the people, without further depriving the people. What democratic government can stay in office after placing restrictions on the people, after depriving the people further in order to comply with the conditions demanded as a requisite for capital investment—sacrificing thereby its popular support at the very time that armed minorities are waiting for the democratic government's vulnerable moment in order to seize power? . . .

No system of government is more corrupt than a dictatorship. It is true that some constitutional governments are also corrupt, but the constitutional governments must be careful because they have to submit to elections; and if there is true democracy, if the citizens really vote, the governments can lose these elections. Furthermore, in a democracy, public protest serves as a check on corruption. In a democracy, freedom of expression serves as a check. In a democracy, the electoral process serves as a check, and this electoral process is repeated every few years. . . .

Sources of Development Capital

There are three ways to obtain capital—by saving, by obtaining financing of our own, or by private investments. I understand that until now, the economists have discovered no other way. Saving would be a solution, if we could freely sell all we produce. If the United States and Canada should remove all the protective tariffs that affect our basic products, if they should remove the subsidies on those articles, then we could sell to them everything that we produce and thereby obtain the gold and dollar reserves necessary for our industrialization. If Cuba, for example, could sell 8 million tons of sugar, we would be able to obtain the capital needed for our industrial development. But such changes would imply a change in the economic structure of the United States, and I am not going to be utopian because our experience has taught us the difficulties that, as a result of certain well-established interests, are always to be encountered when an attempt is made to eliminate some of those restrictions. . . .

The second way to obtain capital is by private investment. This is the formula that has been proposed lately as a solution, but it is no solution. On other occasions, when the possibilities for our economic development have been studied, it has been insinuated and more or less implied that private investment could provide the capital for industrialization, but that certain previous conditions were required for private investments. To begin with a "climate": What is meant by a "climate"? In the midst of 700,000 unemployed, can there be a "climate"? . . . A "climate" cannot be achieved in the midst of conflicts that stem from hunger, poverty, and unsatisfied need. . . . Private capital would go to those countries with the best conditions, those countries which are in the best economic situation and in which for that very reason the social conflicts are less. Private capital would not go to the countries in which the greatest social conflicts appear. Then large areas of the continent would remain neglected and abandoned to their own fate. Private investment would not solve the problem in these areas.

Furthermore, there are investments that do not interest private capital—for example, hydroelectric plants, which require $200 million or $300 million as initial investment. Private capital prefers to exploit petroleum resources. That is a sure investment. Private capital is not interested in certain kinds of investment that do not produce big profits. These investments have to be financed by loans rather than by private investments.

We are not opposed to private investment. But in our industrialization program, the private investments we should encourage are those that can be made by private sources of capital within our respective countries. Funds should be made available to them by government credit institutions, mobilizing resources provided through international credit institutions. We believe in the usefulness, the experience, and the enthusiasm of private investors. But we should hope for the private investments to be made by firms within our respective countries. Does this mean that we will exclude international investors? No. Companies with international investments will have the same guarantees and the same rights as the national firms. . . .

The third type of investment, the one that is made through public finance, remains. Why not agree that under the present conditions the best way to cooperate in a program of economic development is through a program of public financing? . . . The financial consultants of the Cuban delegation estimate that a ten-year loan of $30 billion is needed to carry out the economic development of Latin America. . . . I declare that what we need we can obtain only from the United States and through public financing. We understand, furthermore, that this is the easiest way for the United States to help Latin America; experience in recent years shows us that any other procedure—such as that of eliminating trade tariffs —would be politically more difficult. Furthermore, the large-scale loan is the foreign-aid program that the United States has used in Europe and the Near East. Why ignore in Latin America the program that was considered best for other places and would benefit both Latin America and the United States? . . . The important thing is that we should be convinced that the solutions I have discussed are the true solutions and that the assistance that Latin America needs should be made available in the amount needed really to solve the problem of underdevelopment—not to solve it halfway, but to solve it completely, so that we can build a lasting foundation for a democratic family of nations in this hemisphere.

A REAL DEMOCRACY*

You who produce things, you who work, who sacrifice yourselves, who have been missing the pleasant things of life, you always were, are now, and will be tomorrow, members of the majority of the people.

And yet, you did not run things; you were the majority, and others used to run things for you. You were managed, you were governed by others who not only did what you were supposed to do, but as a rule did it to the detriment of your interests. They ruled in your place and against you.

They invented a democracy for you, a strange, peculiar democracy in which you, who represented the majority, had nothing whatever to say about anything; in which you, peasant, and you, workman, you fellows who produce most of what is worth anything and who, combining efforts with the white-collar workers, produce all our wealth, all our income—you, who produced everything, did not even have the chance to learn how to read or write, often not even to sign your name.

They invented a very peculiar democracy for you who were the majority and yet were practically nonexistent as a political element of our society. They spoke to you about rights and privileges of the citizen, and all those rights and privileges only meant that your child had to starve to death before the closed eyes of an indolent government, that your other child had to go through life without learning his ABC's, that you yourself had to sell your hard work for whatever they condescended to pay for it—if you were lucky enough to find someone who would buy it.

They spoke to you about rights that never existed as far as you were concerned. Your children were not sure of even the right to a country school, or the right to medical attention, or

* Excerpts from Castro's May Day, 1960, speech; reprinted, by permission, from *Monthly Review*, XII, No. 5 (September, 1960).

the right to a piece of bread; and you yourself were not sure of even the right to work!

They invented a democracy in which you, who represented the majority, did not mean anything. And thus, despite your tremendous strength, regardless of your colossal might, in spite of your sacrifice and your endless toil for others as a mere cog in our national life, you, who were the majority all the time, neither governed anything nor could even manage your own affairs!

A democracy is that form of government in which the majority runs things, where the majority means something, and the interests of that majority are protected; a democracy is that in which a man is assured of all his rights, not only the right to think freely, but also the right to know how to think, the right to know how to write what he thinks, the right to know how to read what others think and say. Also the right to eat, to work, to become educated, and to mean something within your society. That is why this is real democracy, the democracy brought to you by the Cuban Revolution, by our Revolution.

A real democracy is one in which you, peasant, get the land we have been recovering for you, after wresting it from foreign hands! A true democracy is one in which you, sugar-cane plantation worker, receive nearly 3 million acres of planted land so that you will no longer have to live as an outcast! A true democracy is one in which you, workman, are assured of your right to work, and know that nobody can kick you out into the gutter to starve to death! A real democracy is that in which you, poor student, have just the same opportunity to get a university degree, if you are talented enough, as the son of any rich man. A true democracy is one in which you who are the son of a laborer, or of a poor peasant, or of any poor family have a schoolteacher and a decent school to educate you. A real democracy is one in which you, old man, will not live in want when you no longer can earn enough for your own support! A true democracy is one in which Cuban Negroes have the right to work and do not have to be afraid of seeing anybody take it away from them because of stupid racial prejudices! A bona fide democracy is one in which you, woman, are recognized as an equal of all other citizens, and even have the right to take up arms to defend your country, next to your man! A pure democracy is one in which the government transforms fortresses into schools and is trying to build a house for every family, so that every Cuban father will have a roof for his children!

A real democracy is one in which whoever falls sick has a physician to treat him. A true democracy is one that does not go around recruiting peasants to convert them into soldiers (who, after being thoroughly corrupted, are converted into enemies of the workman and of their own peasant brothers), but changes that peasant soldier, not into a protector of the privileged, of the heartless landlords, but into a defender of his brothers, the peasants and the workers of his country. A real democracy is this, your democracy, which does not divide the people and does not play brothers against brothers; whose government discovers the strength of the people and combines its various elements, makes the people stronger by uniting them, hands a gun to the peasant, to the workman, to the student, and the women, and the Negroes —hands a gun to the poor man and to whoever is willing to fight for a just cause.

A real democracy is this, our and your democracy, in which not only the majority's rights prevail, but loaded weapons are handed to that majority! That, my friends, can be done only by a really democratic government, ruled and managed by the majority. This is the sort of thing that could never be done in any of those phony democracies.

I would like to know what would happen if a loaded rifle were delivered to each of those Negroes of the South in the United States, where so many of them have been lynched, abused, humiliated, and robbed for centuries!

What an oligarchy of despoilers or a military caste of plunderers and tyrants can never do, what no minority government will ever dare to do is to hand a gun to each worker and to each student, to each young man and each poor citizen—to each one of those who make up the majority of the people!

Of course, that does not mean that the rights of the others should not be considered. The rights of the other people are worth considering in the same measure as the interests of the majority, to the same extent that the rights of the majority are considered. However, the truth is that the rights and interests of the majority are the ones that should prevail over the rights and interests of the minority, and not vice versa.

And that real democracy, that pure, bona fide democracy, that true and honest democracy, is the kind of democracy we have in this country now, the kind of democracy we have had since January 1, 1959.

That democracy has asserted itself directly in the intimate union and identification of the government with the people, in this direct dealing, in this determination to do things and strive for the good of the great majority, in the interest of the great majority of the country. That direct type of democracy has been exercised here more purely, a thousand times more purely, than that false democracy, that phony democracy that resorts to sly methods, predicated on corruption and fraud, to distort and falsify the true will of the peoples.

And this democracy of ours has operated in that direct way because we are going through a revolutionary process. Tomorrow it will be as the people say, as the people decide, as may be demanded by the needs of the people, by the aspirations, hopes, and desires of the people. Today we have here a direct interdependence between the people and the government. Someday, when this revolutionary process will have advanced far enough, when the people freely decide (and the revolutionary government will immediately interpret and obey the will of the people) that we should adopt new policies and procedures; once the most important tasks have been completed and the most fundamental goals of the Revolution (among which is, in the first place today, the defense of our Revolution and of the country) have been reached, then the people and the government will adopt the procedure considered most fitting to the circumstances and characteristics of a revolution already consolidated and victorious in every way—a procedure chosen by you and us, the people and the government!

Nobody holds a public office for sport or personal gain; we are only fulfilling our duty, all of us; we are all willing and ready to sacrifice everything, to work until sheer exhaustion overcomes us; we are all intent on reaching a single goal, a single purpose, and that purpose is to serve our cause and to carry it to final victory! ...

I AM A MARXIST-LENINIST*

The Revolution and Socialism

This was the method the Revolution had to follow, the method of anti-imperialist struggle and of socialism—that is, the nationalization of all the large industries and businesses, the nationalization and social ownership of the basic means of production, and the planned development of our whole economy at the pace permitted by our resources and by the aid we have been receiving from outside. This is something else very favorable to our Revolution: the fact that we can count on aid and solidarity, which enable us to carry our Revolution forward without the enormous sacrifices that other countries are required to make.

We have had to carry out an anti-imperialist and socialist revolution. The anti-imperialist and socialist revolution had to be a single revolution because there is only one revolution. This is the great dialectic truth of humanity: imperialism, and, opposed to imperialism—socialism. The result of this opposition is the triumph of socialism, the supremacy of the epoch of socialism, the overcoming of the stage of capitalism and imperialism, the establishment of the era of socialism and, after that, the era of Communism.

If there are still any anti-Communists here, they need not be afraid. We will not have Communism in less than thirty years. This is the way it is with Marxism. One cannot simply leap over a historical stage. Perhaps the historical stage that some underdeveloped countries can omit today is the construction of capitalism —that is, they can begin the development of the economy of the country by way of planning and socialism. What cannot be skipped is socialism. The Soviet Union itself, after forty years, is beginning to construct Communism and hopes to have advanced considerably in this direction at the end of twenty years.

Thus we are in a stage of construction of socialism. What is this socialism we should apply? Is it utopian socialism? Clearly, we must apply scientific socialism. On this subject I had to begin by saying with complete frankness that we believe in Marxism,

* Excerpts from a speech delivered by Castro on December 1, 1961; translated by the editor from the text printed in *Revolución*, December 2, 1961.

that we believe it is the most correct, most scientific theory, the only true theory, the only true revolutionary theory. I say this here with complete satisfaction and confidence. I am a Marxist-Leninist, and I will be a Marxist-Leninist until the last day of my life.

Past Attitude toward Communists

And how am I a Marxist-Leninist? Am I one halfway? We revolutionaries do not know how to be anything halfway. We can only be something 100 per cent. And we will devote our energy entirely to this. Besides, it is a great satisfaction to have been an illiterate at eighteen years of age and to be a revolutionary, which I feel I am, at thirty and a "little." The "little" I believe is thirty and six. At eighteen, I had learned something, but there was much that I did not know. And we say this with all frankness to the people, with loyalty and clarity, as we have always spoken to the people—I have always spoken with complete frankness.

Did I have prejudices? I believe it is good to speak of this. Did I have prejudices with regard to Communists? Yes. Was I at times influenced by the propaganda of imperialism and by the reaction against the Communists? Yes. What did I believe regarding the Communists? Did I believe they were thieves? No, never. I always considered the Communists both in the university and elsewhere to be honorable people, honest and all that. But this has no special merit, because nearly everybody recognizes this. Did I have the idea that they were sectarian? Yes. Why did I have these opinions about the Communists? I am absolutely convinced that the ideas I had concerning the Communists (not with regard to Marxism, but with regard to the Communist Party) were like the ideas of many people, the product of propaganda and prejudices inculcated practically since childhood, almost since school days—in the universities, in the movies, and everywhere. Do I consider they could be wrong? Yes, I feel that they could be wrong. Marx, Engels, and Lenin are themselves the first to admit that they could be wrong, that they could make mistakes, because they did not consider themselves infallible.

What was my opinion of the militants of the Communist Party? Was it the opinion they really merited? If for a long time they were ignored, attacked, excluded, left out because they were considered a kind of plague, we should also recognize that it took great courage to be a Communist. Not today—no, we are going to see to it that it is rewarded from now on, of course!

It took courage to be a Communist at that time. Felix Torres has told me how they took him out of the prison of Santa Clara and made him go to Yaguajay on foot—on foot to Yaguajay! And this was the way it was, an infinity of sacrifices and efforts. The merit in being Communists when they were persecuted, when all doors were closed to them, when all presses, newspapers, and opportunities were shut off—we should recognize that merit. Much more, of course, than to be one today. Today, conditions are different. On that point, I have said that we must make efforts that the socialists and Marxists are real Marxists in the complete meaning of the word, that they are prepared for all contingencies.

But I wanted to say that I had prejudices against the [Popular] Socialist Party, prejudices that originated in the electoral campaigns. I confess it with the complete honesty with which I should confess all things. I am not going to ask anything from the Socialists. I say this when we are completely united and are all comrades, all socialists.

At certain moments at the beginning of the Revolution, we had some friction which arose out of differing conceptions on some points, but, fundamentally, because we were not talking to one another. I ought to say that there are people here who were victims of the intrigues of the first days, when, each time something happened, it was said that a group of Communists was creating a problem and instigating a riot. I must say myself that at one time I thought it was the Communists that were creating a riot in one place where a group of people had taken action with clubs against a citizen. . . . Afterward, I discovered that it was not Communists who had created the riot, but divisionist elements. . . .

This is the way it was at the first stage—the conflict between two things, in reality between prejudices, between a series of things. If a Communist was working on anything, his Communism had to be clandestine. But immediately there were the UPI, AP, and all the American newspapers crying out "ten, twelve, fifteen Communists." It was curious in those days that they called all the comrades Communists, and there were a number of comrades who were not members of the Communist Party but members of the 26th of July Movement. They called them that already, and published their Communist antecedents to all the world. They began a campaign that had, in many areas, a response influenced by the propaganda of anti-Communism and imperialism. Fortunately for all our efforts, these stages have passed.

I think that one of the bad aspects of those first days was the lack of greater interchange among the various organizations. Each of us was going somewhat on his own. It was the same revolutionary struggle which should have been more and more in contact, in discussion, and in interchange, to promote more and more unification.

I should mention one of the things in our terrible experience. Someday, when historians write about this stage and want to describe some characteristic of this revolution, they may say that we were establishing a socialist revolution without socialists. At that time, there was so much anti-Communist prejudice that when a Communist functionary was assigned to the smallest matter, a wave of protest arose, followed by numerous intrigues on the subject. At that time, our methods were socialist—a collective farm, a cooperative, a nationalized industry—those were all socialist institutions. We had good comrades for those jobs—wonderful comrades of the revolutionary movement of the 26th of July—but they did not succeed. If those men did not succeed, how were we going to succeed?

One of the most difficult things, then, was to carry out a socialist revolution without socialists. Later, when the process of unification of the revolutionary forces and the revolutionary organizations had begun, when anti-Communism was being defeated and destroyed, a stage came in which it was easier for a number of the members of the Socialist Party to carry out numerous functions without so much intrigue and divisionism.

The Integrated Revolutionary Organizations (ORI)

What was the meaning of this union? What was the significance of this moment in which the unification of all the revolutionary organizations took place? It meant—among other things—hundreds, thousands of cadres, of trained people, of people who had passed through sacrifices, through hard and difficult tests, and had a political education. On this point, I remember that some people came to me and said, "When are we going to carry out the program of the 26th?" And I said, "What program of the 26th are we going to carry out? Why not a Marxist-Leninist program?" And, "Why are we going to carry out two Marxist-Leninist programs?" This is reality. Anything else is a figment of the imagination.

352 LATIN AMERICA

Therefore, it meant the addition of thousands of trained leaders, who were indispensable, fundamental, and necessary for the creation of socialism. It signified the addition of all the cadres of the Revolutionary Directorate. They did not have the number of experienced leaders that the Socialist Party had, because there were people who said that no, they would rather do this or they would rather do that. You have to be a complete ignoramus with regard to the facts of revolution to think that a revolutionary can choose to do this or that. What we know about all revolutions is that work is divided today among all, and it is so great that it cannot be carried out; that many comrades, if they are in the army, would prefer to go to a military academy; if they are civil servants, they would prefer to go for something like a vacation to a school of revolutionary instruction. That is, the revolutionary considers it a rest—compared to the work which he must do—to be a pupil in the school.

The revolution today can count on all the cadres of all the revolutionary organizations. The important addition of the [Popular] Socialist Party has brought the cadres of the old militants educated in socialism by the Socialist Party. The addition of the Directorate has brought young people. The 26th of July Movement could not bring older, politically educated people, but has brought many young persons who were enthusiasts and revolutionists by vocation. It has also added all the experience acquired in the seizure of power. That is, we all have brought something, one way or another, and we represent the basic forces.

These forces were asked to unite in one single organization, and they have, therefore, joined together in the ORI. It was not easy. It took a long time, and at the end they joined together into the Integrated Revolutionary Organizations (ORI).

The manifestations of sectarianism have been disappearing in the same way that exclusiveness is going to disappear, in the same way that the practice of excluding people because they are Socialists is going to disappear, naturally, and so will sectarianism and these manifestations.* Certain manifestations of extremism are also going to disappear. Often extremism is a type of disease

* On March 26, 1962, Castro criticized a number of leaders of the Popular Socialist (Communist) Party for their "sectarianism" and attempt to dominate the ORI. Other groups in the ORI include the Union of Pioneers, the Cuban Women's Federation, the Young Rebels (later changed to Young Communists), and the Committees for the Defense of the Revolution.—ED.

that should not be confused, of course, with revolutionary firmness. Extremism is also a manifestation of a petty-bourgeois spirit
in the revolutionary movement, and we must struggle against
extremism just as much as against sectarianism.

There are many things that our people have had time to learn.
They have had time to get rid of widespread prejudices picturing
socialism as something terrible, inhuman, and hard—as a type of
slavery—which is precisely the description that imperialism tries
to impute to socialism. . . .

The Party of the Vanguard

We have all contributed to this unity, and we feel satisfied that
we have contributed to it. We are all of us struggling to organize
and create a strong, disciplined, and firm political organization of
the vanguard of the working class and of the Cuban Revolution.
How are we trying to do this? In the same way that the traditional
parties do it—by inviting everyone, by opening up one's gates
wide, so that all can come into the party? No.

What did the bourgeois parties, when in power, do? They
opened their gates wide and invited everyone. Whatever party
came to power immediately had a million members—all of a sudden. When we were naïve and did not know anything about
politics, we accepted what the newspapers said—"As proof of
what the Soviet Union is, the Communist Party does not have
more than 5 million members in a population of 200 million"—
as evidence, by capitalism and imperialism, that a minority ruled!
In this way, they tried to make us see a Marxist revolutionary
party from the standpoint of a bourgeois party. With a bourgeois
party, the more people, the more boasting. The bourgeois party
does not have ideology: It is a gang of politicians, a group of individuals who stick together and defend class interests. When more
people belong, then there are more jobs and more boasting. They
are not in the least concerned with the thinking of the members of
the party. Hence, they try to conceal very carefully the fact that a
Marxist revolutionary party is a party of the vanguard, a party
that gives direction, and an elite party—that if the Soviet Union
attempted to enlist Party members, there would be tens of millions of them. They conceal the fact that . . . a revolutionary party
is an elite party, which directs and works fundamentally through
mass organizations, through trade unions, through the youth,

through women's federations, through committees for defense (an invention of the Cuban Revolution and a phenomenal mass organization), the peasant associations, the cooperatives (the collective farms are already in the trade unions). That is, the party gives direction and orientation through all the mass organizations.

Thus, the standard which the political organization of the Cuban Revolution should have is, in the first place, that of selection and quality. It will not be a quantitative organization; it will be a qualitative organization. . . .

And since, besides, we are conscious of the great enthusiasm of the masses, and of their revolutionary spirit, a party that is developing and becoming articulate in these conditions has all favorable conditions to select the best elements and the most positive and valuable people from the masses, and, to make them members of this organization. It is fundamental that these be precisely the best people, the best of the mass organizations—those who attain the honorable function of being members of the United Party of the Socialist Revolution (PURS).

The more that this is the case, the more every worker, peasant, intellectual, and citizen will realize that it means that every citizen can be a member of the United Party of the Socialist Revolution apart from whether he is a worker or not. That is, the gates are open for every true revolutionary who builds the revolution and is disposed to carry out his assignments and accept the program of the United Party of the Socialist Revolution fully and with complete conviction. . . .

Thus, I think that the ideal system, the most perfect encountered by man for governing a country (a system that does not aspire to be eternal but simply transitory, as are the stages which the history of a country is destined to realize) is a system of government with a revolutionary, democratically organized party under collective leadership. This means that this party ought to exercise the functions of leadership.

This is the best system if democratic standards function, if the standards of collective leadership function. If democratic standards do not function, if the standards of collective leadership do not function, then the system can be very bad, like any other system. But if the fundamental principles of internal democracy maintain a collective leadership, this is without any doubt the most perfect method of government, especially for a country in a stage of revolutionary transition.

What does this mean? In the first place, if this party is not a party that amasses membership but a party that selects them, the best citizens of the country will enter this party, on the basis of their conditions and merits. They will enter into revolutionary cells. There will be a long-term process of learning, direct experience, and the fulfillment of duty.

Little by little, because of his merit, a citizen can go on assuming responsibilities that continually grow greater. This citizen can arrive at membership of the regional directorate, of the central directorate, of the national directorate. He can hold these positions according to his merit. This is not the case of the king who passes on his power to his idiot son. It is not the case of a military leader who happens to be successful, because there can be men who are excellent war-makers and, as war-makers, acquire fame and prestige and, as rulers, are perfectly stupid. This is not a question of demagogues, or of clowns, or of theatrical personalities. In a party where the standards of discipline, principle, selection, internal democracy, and collective leadership predominate, a stupid person cannot advance—an idiot cannot become head of state. The lucky adventurer cannot do so. This school will be a school in which men are proving themselves, where they are learning and where they are acquiring proficiency. . . .

So what can the party of this revolutionary people do? This party will be the great instrument of merit, the instrument of revolutionary calling and revolutionary intelligence. This party should be above individuals, because it is the party that is going to include not the value of one intelligence, but the value of tens of thousands, of hundreds of thousands of intelligences; not the value of one hero, but the value of the heroism of all; not the value of one spirit of sacrifice, but the value of the spirit of hundreds of thousands of citizens and the spirit of combat, of love of the revolution. This is what the United Party of the Cuban Socialist Revolution must be.

THE COMMUNIST PARTY OF CUBA*

Starting from the conception of the Party as the representative of
the laboring masses, organized and operated with the constant participation of the workers, we conclude that the Party, as the most
legitimate representative of the workers of the country, can and
has the right to elect local government officials. And at the same
time, the Party can and should, if necessary, remove from office
any officeholder, even the head of the local government, if he does
not carry out his responsibilities.

As to the title which we were going to give the officeholders, we
discussed some earlier titles and finally decided almost unanimously
that they should be called president—president of the local government, president of the regional government, and president of the
provincial government. We did not work out the manner in which
they should be elected. Later, when the comrades were preparing
the report, they decided that they should be elected at a meeting
of all the Party members. . . .

Since it is not possible for all the representatives of the [Party]
cells to participate in a provincial or national election, all the cells
will meet together up to the regional level, where they will elect
representatives to a provincial assembly, which will then elect representatives to a National Congress. What does this mean? That the
cell will be the base of the Party, the cell members will go to the
municipality and to the region and there in the region the representatives of all the cells will elect representatives of the Party for
the province and the nation. This is a very direct method, a more
efficient method, and a method that will certainly work better.
The other way, in an assembly of five or six thousand, it is difficult
to have any discussion of an election. In practice certain formulas
and proposals are simply presented without any possibility of analyzing and considering the reasons for a decision or in favor of
one person or another. . . .

I think we can go to any part of the world and convince anyone
that our system is a thousand times more revolutionary, a thousand
times more democratic, than all those systems by which the bour-

* Excerpts from speeches by Fidel Castro at the first meeting of the Central
Committee of the Communist Party of Cuba, September 30–October 2, 1965;
translated by the editor from *Granma*, October 10, 1965.

geoisie try to sell their worthless representative democracy, their bourgeois democracy in which they have elections every four years but the masses have no participation in [solving] social and economic problems. The so-called representatives of the masses who are the representatives of a specific class are a thousand miles from the masses. They do not represent anyone, certainly not those who elect them.

When the time comes to defend the institutions of our Revolution, we can discuss them in any university or intellectual center in the world and prove that we have a very superior governmental system, a much more democratic governmental system, a government henceforth by one class, that of the workers. When all the citizens are workers, then it is a government of the whole people. To achieve this we must keep this objective before us and struggle unceasingly to establish this society—the Communist society. . . .

When the forces of the revolution began to unite, the name we used was the Integrated Revolutionary Organizations (ORI). Because there were errors in the way in which this was done, problems of sectarianism arose and consequently it was necessary to make a thorough criticism of that vice which had developed. Instead of the name which had been used thus far, we conceived the idea of using a new and, we may say, more advanced name. First, there was the Integrated Revolutionary Organizations, then came the name, the United Party of the Cuban Socialist Revolution. There is no doubt that this name is a valued one, one which has been used throughout the process of formation of the Party. But still it is not a name which can be used for all time. . . .

We are fighting for a higher type of society, the Communist society. This name has been calumniated by the exploiters in the capitalist society, and even before capitalism—in the period of slavery, in the period of feudalism, and even in the period of the bourgeois revolutions—it has been a name which the exploiters, those who live by the sweat and labor of other men and other peoples, have tried to blot out.

When we say a Communist society, we are speaking of a higher type of society, a thousand times more just and perfect than that rotten bourgeois imperialist society which discriminates against men and sacrifices them, which condemns women to prostitution and children to misery, which shows no mercy and has no ideal but the worship of riches and money.

We are fighting for a new higher type of society which no nation today has achieved and I think that we can compete in this effort to try to be among the first to achieve these more advanced forms of human society. If we pursue this objective, we should raise up the ideals of the Revolution for men to see, expressed in the name of the Party so that the members of our Party may always keep in mind what those objectives are and how we must try to achieve them—objectives which I am sure our people will achieve among the first in the world.

And therefore to adopt a name which implies both the absolute unity of all the people and at the same time expresses the final goals of our Revolution, we have suggested the name of the Communist Party of Cuba. . . .

THE ERRORS OF THE VENEZUELAN
COMMUNIST PARTY (1967) *

There is no doubt that the Venezuelan revolutionaries, like all revolutionaries everywhere, committed mistakes in both strategy and tactics. The fact that the revolutionary movement was strongest in the capital while, as in the case of many other Latin American countries, it was very weak in the countryside, due to the inactivity of the Communist Party, contributed to those mistakes. Why? Because the [Latin American] Marxist parties preferred to concentrate their attention on the cities and in many cases (although there are exceptions to this generalization) greatly underestimtated the importance of the peasantry as a revolutionary force. . . .

The revolutionary leadership of the [Venezuelan Communist] Party tried to direct the guerrillas from the capital. It did not do what it should have done, what a bold and truly revolutionary leadership would have done, what the leaders of all successful contemporary historic movements have done—go to the mountains and join the guerrillas, direct the war from the field of battle, direct the war from the mountains.

It is absurd and almost criminal to try to lead the guerrillas

* Excerpts from a speech delivered by Fidel Castro, March 13, 1967; translated by the editor from *Punto Final* (Santiago, Chile), April 1–15, 1967.

from the city. The city and the countryside are two things so different and distinct, two scenes so completely dissimilar, that it is madness to wish to lead the guerrillas from the city. And the guerrillas were not really considered as a force that could develop and take revolutionary power in countries like ours but as a tool to exert pressure, an instrument for political maneuvering or negotiation. . . .

For us, the international Communist movement is first of all a movement of Communists, or fighters for the revolution. And whoever is not a fighter for the revolution cannot be called a Communist. We conceive of Marxism as revolutionary thought and action. Those who do not possess a true revolutionary spirit cannot call themselves Communists. . . .

The international Communist movement, as we understand it, is not a church or a religious or Masonic sect that obliges us to sanctify every weakness, to consecrate every error, to be associated with every kind of reformist and pseudorevolutionary. Our position with respect to the Communist parties is based on strictly revolutionary principles. Above all, we support those parties that hold a line without vacillation or weakness, the parties that in our judgment follow a consistently revolutionary line. But parties which think that because they have the name "Communist" or "Marxist" in their title they have a monopoly on revolution, when in reality they only represent reform, we do not consider as revolutionary parties. And if those who call themselves Communists in any country do not know how to fulfill the requirements of Marxism, we will support those who, although they do not call themselves Communists, act like true Communists in action and struggle.

Every true revolutionary who has within himself the spirit of revolution and a calling as a revolutionary will end up as a Marxist. It is impossible for a man with a revolutionary calling who is on the road to revolution not to end as a Marxist. Every consistent revolutionary on this continent will arrive at the Marxist conception of society. And they are the ones who matter, the revolutionaries who are able to make revolutions and to develop in the revolutionary struggle.

Often, practice comes first and theory afterward. Our [Cuban] people are an example of this, for the immense majority of those who today proudly proclaim themselves to be Marxist-Leninists came to Marxism by way of the revolutionary struggle. . . .

The revolution that arose out of nothing, the revolution that arose out of a small group of men who lived for years surrounded by forces through which nothing could pass, is a revolution with its own right to exist, and a revolution—hear this, you puppets, oligarchs, vacillators, and pseudorevolutionaries of all types—that nothing and nobody can destroy or delay. And this revolution will maintain its own absolutely independent position with that independence that belongs by right to people who know how to fight, who possess dignity. And we proclaim it to the world, this revolution will follow its course, this revolution will follow its own line, this revolution will never be a satellite of anybody, and it will never seek permission from anybody to maintain its own ideological position domestically and internationally. With head held high and a proud heart in its breast, this people will face the future, whatever it may be.

THE EVENTS IN CZECHOSLOVAKIA *

Throughout that entire process [of liberalization] a whole series of events of a political nature took place. A real liberal fury was unleashed; a whole series of political slogans in favor of the formation of opposition parties began to develop, in favor of openly anti-Marxist and anti-Leninist theses such as the thesis that the Party should cease to play the role which the Party plays within socialist society and begin to play the role there of a guide, supervising some things but, above all, exerting a sort of spiritual leadership—in short, that the reins of power should cease to be in the hands of the Communist Party; the revision of certain fundamental postulates to the effect that a socialist regime is a regime of transition from socialism to Communism, a governmental form known as the dictatorship of the proletariat. This means a government where power is wielded in behalf of one class and against the former exploiting classes, by virtue of which in a revolutionary process political rights, the right to carry on political activities, cannot be granted to the former exploiters, whose objective would be precisely to struggle against the essence and the *raison d'etre* of socialism. A series of slogans began to be put for-

* From *Granma* (English edition), August 25, 1968, Año 3, No. 34. (Speech delivered, August 23, 1968.)

ward, and in fact certain measures were taken, such as the establishment of a bourgeois form of "freedom" of the press. This
means that the counterrevolution and the exploiters, the very
enemies of socialism, were granted the right to speak and write
freely against socialism. As a matter of fact, a process of seizure
of the principal information media by the reactionary elements
began to develop. As regards foreign policy, a whole series of
slogans of open *rapprochement* toward capitalist concepts and
theses and of *rapprochement* toward the West appeared. Of
course, all of this was linked to a series of unquestionably correct
slogans. It was some of these slogans that won a certain amount
of sympathy for the liberalization of democratization movement.
Even some European Communist Parties, facing their own problems and contradictions, began to express their sympathy for the
liberalization movement. It was a situation which everyone was
trying to use to his advantage, to resolve related problems stem-
ming from incorrect methods of government, bureaucratic policy,
separation from the masses and, in short, a whole series of problems for which the former leadership was held responsible. There
was also talk about the need to create their own forms for the
development of the socialist revolution and the socialist system
in Czechoslovakia. . . .

And right here I wish to make the first important affirmation:
we considered that Czechoslovakia was moving toward a counterrevolutionary situation, toward capitalism and into the arms of
imperialism.

So this defines our first position in relation to the specific fact
of the action taken by a group of socialist countries. That is, we
consider that it was absolutely necessary, at all costs, in one way
or another, to prevent this eventuality from taking place.

Bear with me, because I plan to analyze this in the light of
our ideas.

Discussion of the form is not, in the final analysis, the most
fundamental factor. The essential point to be accepted, or not
accepted, is whether or not the socialist camp could allow a
political situation to develop which would lead to the breaking
away of a socialist country, to its falling into the arms of imperialism. And our point of view is that it is not permissible and
that the socialist camp has a right to prevent this in one way
or another. I would like to begin by making it clear that we look
upon this fact as an essential one.

Nevertheless, it is not enough simply to accept the fact—and nothing more—that Czechoslovakia was headed toward a counterrevolutionary situation and that it was necessary to prevent it. It is not enough simply to come to the conclusion that there was no alternative there but to prevent this, and nothing more.

We must analyze the causes and ask what factors made this possible and created the necessity for such a dramatic, drastic, and painful measure. What are the factors that created the necessity for a step which unquestionably entailed a violation of legal principles and international norms that, having often served as a shield for the peoples against injustice, are highly esteemed by the world?

Because what cannot be denied here is that the sovereignty of the Czechoslovak State was violated. This would be a fiction, an untruth. And the violation was, in fact, of a flagrant nature.

And I am going to refer to this point, to our concept of sovereignty, to legal principles and political principles. From a legal point of view, this cannot be justified. This is very clear. In our opinion, the decision made concerning Czechoslovakia can only be explained from a political point of view, not from a legal point of view. Not the slightest trace of legality exists. Frankly none whatever. . . .

Obviously, this is not the time to make or pretend to make profound analysis, but we can cite some facts and ideas: bureaucratic methods in the leadership of the country, lack of contact with the masses—contact which is essential in every true revolutionary movement—neglect of Communist ideals. And what do we mean by neglect of Communist ideals?

We mean forgetting that men in a class society, the exploited in a class society, the enslaved, struggle for a whole series of ideals, and when they speak of socialism and Communism they are not only speaking of a society where exploitation does actually disappear and the poverty resulting from that exploitation disappears, and the underdevelopment resulting from that exploitation disappears, but they are speaking also of all those beautiful aspirations that constitute the Communist ideal of a classless society, a society free from selfishness, a society in which man is no longer a miserable slave to money, in which society no longer works for personal gain, and all of society begins to work for the satisfaction of all needs and for the establishment among men of the rule of justice, fraternity, equality, and all those ideals of human society and of the people who have always aspired to achieve those objectives. And these objectives are possible, as we have explained on other occasions, as we explained amply last July 26.

In future stages it will be necessary for our revolutionary people to go deeply into the concepts of what they understand by a Communist society. The ideal of the Communist society cannot be the ideal of the industrialized bourgeois society; it cannot under any circumstances, be the ideal of a bourgeois-capitalist consumers' society.

The Communist ideal cannot, for a single moment, exist without internationalism. Those who struggle for Communism in any one country in the world can never forget the rest of the world. They can never forget the suffering, underdevelopment, poverty, ignorance, and exploitation that exist in a part of the world or how much poverty and destitution have accumulated there. They can never forget, for a single moment, the needs of that part of the world, and we believe that it is impossible to instill in the masses a truly internationalist outlook, a truly Communist outlook, if they are allowed to forget the realities of the world, the dangers of confrontation with imperialism that those realities entail and the dangers of growing soft when the people are made to forget those real problems and when the attempt is made to move the masses through material incentives and the promises of more consumer goods alone.

We can say—and today it is necessary to speak clearly and frankly—that we have seen to what extent those ideals and those internationalist sentiments, that state of alertness and that awareness of the world's problems have disappeared or are very weakly expressed in certain socialist countries of Europe. We would not say in all those countries, but in more than one socialist country of Europe. Those who have visited those countries, including the Cuban scholarship students, have often come back completely dissatisfied and displeased and have said to us: "Over there the youth are not being educated in the ideals of Communism and in the principles of internationalism; the youth there are highly influenced by all the ideas and tastes prevalent in the countries of Western Europe. In many places the main topic of conversation is money and incentives of this or that type, material incentives of all kinds, material gains and salaries." As a matter of fact, an internationalist and Communist conscience is not being developed in those places. . . .

We are against all those bourgeois liberal reforms within

Czechoslovakia. But we are also against the liberal economic reforms that were taking place in Czechoslovakia and that have been taking place in other countries of the socialist camp, as well.

Naturally, we maintain the position that we should not tell them how to carry out the construction of socialism, but we can analyze what they did—a series of reforms that increasingly tended to accentuate mercantile relations within a socialist society: personal gain, profit, all those things. . . .

It is understandable that the countries of the Warsaw Pact sent their armies to destroy the imperialist conspiracy and the progress of counterrevolution in Czechoslovakia. However, we have dsagreed with, been displeased at, and protested against the fact that these same countries have been drawing closer economically, culturally, and politically to the oligarchic governments of Latin America, which are not merely reactionary governments and exploiters of their peoples, but also shameless accomplices in the imperialist aggressions against Cuba and shameless accomplices in the economic blockade of Cuba. And these countries have been encouraged and emboldened by the fact that our friends, our natural allies, have ignored the vile and treacherous role enacted by those governments against a socialist country, the policy of blockade practiced by those countries against a socialist country.

And at the same time that we understand the need for the spirit of internationalism, and the need to go to the aid—even with troops—of a fraternal country to confront the schemes of the imperialists, we ask ourselves if their policy of economic, political and cultural *rapprochement* toward those oligarchic governments that are accomplices in the imperialist blockade against Cuba will come to an end. . . .

The imperialists have not given up for one instant their dream of destroying our country. Those dangers will naturally increase now. Therefore, now, precisely now—because things must be spoken of at the right time—we are once more going to explain what our position is, the position of our Revolutionary Government, regarding the United States. And we state it now, precisely when speaking out has very real significance and is not simply declamatory or theoretical, and we state it with all the more reason because of certain speculations that have been circulated concerning a possible bettering of relations between Cuba and the United States.

The Revolutionary Government has at no time shown the slightest interest in bettering its relations with the imperialist Government of the United States; it has not shown it and it will not show it, nor will it give it the slightest attention or express directly or indirectly, tacitly or openly, any kind of willingness to hold conversations with that government as long as that government remains the international *gendarme*, bulwark of world reaction, enemy of the revolutionary movements. This has been, is, and will unquestionably continue to be the position of the Revolutionary Government of Cuba.

Never, under any circumstance, and the comrades of our Central Committee know this, they know that this is the line adopted by our Committee, never, under any circumstance, even in the most difficult circumstances, will this country approach the imperialist Government of the United States—not even should it one day place us in the situation of having to choose between the continued existence of the Revolution or such a step. Because, gentlemen, that would be the moment at which the Revolution would have ceased to exist.

And if the day should ever come when this Revolution had to buy its security and its survival at the price of some concession to the Yankee imperialists, we would prefer—as our Central Committee unanimously would prefer and as our people would prefer —this people to disappear with the Revolution rather than survive at such a price!

THE ECONOMIC PROBLEMS OF CUBA *

We have just finished waging a heroic battle, a battle that can truly be called heroic. The heroes of that battle are represented here. The people were the heroes of that battle, the battle for the 10 million tons, both in the planting and in the harvesting. And enough cane was cut to produce practically 10 million tons, enough to have resulted in 10 million tons if the industrial side of the sugar-making process had held up its end.†

The people were heroes—not only in fulfilling that task, but

* From *Granma* (English edition), August 2, 1970, Año 5, No. 31. (Speech delivered, July 26, 1970).

† The actual figure for the 1970 sugar crop was 8 million tons.—ED.

even more so in deciding to cut every last stalk of cane, even when they knew that the 10 million tons would not be reached.

The heroic effort to increase production, to raise our purchasing power, resulted in imbalances in the economy, in diminished production in other sectors, and, in short, in an increase in our difficulties.

Of course the enemy insisted that the 10-million-ton sugar harvest would lead to some of these problems. It was our duty to do everything possible to avoid it. And actually we haven't been capable of doing so.

Our enemies say we have problems, and in this our enemies are right. Our enemies say we have problems, and in reality our enemies are right. They say there is discontent, and in reality our enemies are right. They say there is irritation, and in reality our enemies are right.

As you can see, we aren't afraid to admit it when our enemies are right. . . .

There are objective difficulties. Some of them have been pointed out. But we aren't here to discuss the objective difficulties. We must discuss the concrete problem, and man must contribute what nature or our means and resources have not been able to provide. It depends on man. Men are playing a key role here and especially the men in leadership positions.

We are going to begin, in the first place, by pointing out the responsibility which all of us, and I in particular, have for these problems. I am in no way trying to pin the blame on anyone not in the revolutionary leadership and myself. Unfortunately, this self-criticism cannot be accompanied by other logical solutions. It would be better to tell the people to look for somebody else. It would be better, but it would be hypocritical on our part.

I believe that we, the leaders of this Revolution, have cost the people too much in our process of learning. And, unfortunately, our problem—not when it is a case of the Revolution; the people can replace us whenever they wish—right now if you so desire! One of our most difficult problems—and we are paying for it dearly—is our heritage of ignorance. . . .

In the past, industries, schools, and hospitals were often run by private owners. Today this is not the case. In the past, all a citizen expected from the state was that it build post offices or telegraph stations. He didn't dream of the state's solving his housing problem or any of his other problems. Today the citizen feels that the state should solve the problems. And he is right. This is a really collective mentality, a socialist mentality. Today everything is expected from the administrative apparatus, and especially from the political apparatus that represents it. Today it is not possible to depend on individual effort and means, as was the case in the past.

The fact that today the people expect everything is in keeping with the socialist awareness the Revolution has created in the people. An inefficiency in a service—I am not referring to those problems which cannot be solved by man but those which are within his power to solve and are delayed and left unsolved—can affect thousands of people.

Today it is impossible to direct and coordinate this entire apparatus. We must create a political structure to coordinate the different sectors of social production.* . . .

The Revolution has survived through this day. But today we have to wage a more difficult battle. It is perhaps easier, a thousand times easier, to crush the Playa Girón [Bay of Pigs] mercenaries in a few hours than to really solve the problems of one of our industrial plants. It is easier to win a score of wars than to win the battle of underdevelopment. . . .

26. *Ernesto "Che" Guevara*

Ernesto "Che" Guevara was born in Rosario, Argentina, in 1928. His family moved to Buenos Aires, but when it became evident that the climate was bad for Ernesto's asthma, they moved again to a resort town in the province of Cordoba. He attended secondary school in Cordoba where he joined an anti-Peron nationalist youth group. In 1947, Guevara entered the University of Buenos Aires as a medical student. In 1952, he traveled to Chile, Peru, Colombia, Venezuela, and Miami. After returning to Buenos

---

* On the lack of a political structure in Cuba, see René Dumont, *Cuba: est-il socialiste?* (Paris: Editions du Seuil, 1970) and K. S. Karol, *Guerrillas in Power: The Course of the Cuban Revolution* (New York: Hill and Wang, 1970).—Ed.

Aires to take the examinations for his medical degree, he set out once again in 1953, intending to work at a leprosarium in Venezuela. Instead, passing through Bolivia shortly after it experienced a major revolution, Guevara secured passage on a United Fruit boat from Ecuador to Panama and from there hitchhiked through Central America, ending his trip in Guatemala. After a U.S.-sponsored invasion overthrew the left-wing government of Jacobo Arbenz, he left Guatemala and went to Mexico City where he joined the group of Cubans led by Fidel Castro who were organizing an invasion of that country to overthrow the dictator, Fulgencio Batista. One of the twenty or so who survived the fierce attacks of the Batista air force when the Castro group landed in Oriente province in December, 1956, Guevara achieved a brilliant military record during the guerrilla operations of the next two years. After Castro's victory, Guevara became chief of the Industrial Department of the National Institute of Agrarian Reform, and later head of the National Bank. During the years following the Revolution, he engaged in extensive international travel. In the policy debates within the Castro regime he was a proponent of moral rather than material incentives and argued for the creation of a new socialist man in Cuba (see "Socialism and Man in Cuba"). A perennial revolutionary, he left Cuba for the last time in 1965; his attempt to organize a guerrilla movement in Bolivia ended in his death after capture in October, 1967. Since his death, he has become an international symbol of revolution and his life and writings have exerted a wide influence. His argument for giving priority to the establishment of a guerrilla foco (focal point) in the countryside has been further developed in the writings of Regis Debray, and attacked as a Marxist heresy by the orthodox Communist parties of Latin America.*

* See Regis Debray, *Revolution within the Revolution?* (New York: Monthly Review Press, 1967), and "A 'Revolution within the Revolution' Is Impossible" by the Central Committee of the Argentine Communist Party, in Paul E. Sigmund (ed.), *Models of Political Change in Latin America* (New York: Praeger Publishers, 1970), pp. 111–15.

GUERRILLA WARFARE: A METHOD *

We consider that the Cuban revolution made three fundamental contributions to the laws of the revolutionary movement in the current situation in [Latin] America. They are: First, peoples' forces can win a war against the army. Second, we need not always wait for all the revolutionary conditions to be present; the insurrection itself can create them. Third, in the underdeveloped patrs of America, the battleground for armed struggle should in the main be the countryside. . . .

In all the countries in which oppression becomes unbearable, the banner of rebellion must be raised, and this banner of historical necessity will have a continental character. As Fidel said, the Andes will be the Sierra Maestra of America, and all the immense territories that make up this continent will become the scene of a life-and-death struggle against the power of imperialism.

We cannot tell when this struggle will acquire a continental character, or how long it will last; but we can predict its advent and its triumph, because it is the inevitable result of historical, economic, and political conditions and its direction cannot be changed. It is the task of the revolutionary force in each country to initiate [the struggle] when the conditions are present, regardless of the situation in other countries. The general strategy will emerge as the struggle develops. The prediction of the continental character of the struggle is borne out by analysis of the strength of each contender, but this does not in the least exclude independent outbreaks. Just as the beginning of the struggle in one part of a country is bound to develop it throughout its area, the beginning of a revolutionary war contributes to the development of new conditions in the neighboring countries.

The development of revolution has normally produced high and low tides in inverse proportion; to the revolutionary high tide corresponds the counterrevolutionary low tide, and conversely, at moments of revolutionary decline, there is a counterrevolutionary ascendency. At such moments, the situation of the people's forces becomes difficult, and they should resort to the best measures in order to suffer the least loss. The enemy is extremely powerful,

* Excerpts from an article published in *Cuba Socialista* No. 25, Havana, September, 1963; translated in a pamphlet published by the Foreign Languages Press, Peking, 1964.

continental in stature. Therefore, the relative weaknesses of the local bourgeoisie cannot be analyzed with a view to making decisions within restricted limits. Still less can one think of an eventual alliance of these oligarchies with an armed people. The Cuban revolution has sounded the alarm. The polarization of forces is becoming complete: exploiters on one side and exploited on the other. The mass of the petty bourgeoisie will lean to one side or the other according to their interests and the political skill with which it is handled; neutrality will be an exception. This is how revolutionary war will be.

Let us consider the way in which a guerrilla *foco* may start.

Nuclei of relatively few persons choose places favorable for guerrilla warfare, sometimes with the intention of launching a counterattack or to weather a storm, and there they begin to take action. But the following must be made clear: At the beginning, the relative weakness of the guerrilla fighters is such that they should endeavor to pay attention only to the terrain, in order to become acquainted with the surroundings, establish connections with the population, and fortify the places that eventually will be converted into bases.

The guerrilla unit can survive only if it starts by basing its development on the three following conditions: constant mobility, constant vigilance, constant wariness. Without the adequate use of these elements of military tactics, the unit will find it hard to survive. It must be remembered that the heroism of the guerrilla fighter at such times consists in the scope of the planned objective and the long series of sacrifices that must be made in order to attain it.

These sacrifices will not mean daily combat or face-to-face struggle with the enemy; they will assume forms more subtle and difficult for the individual guerrilla fighter to endure physically and mentally.

The guerrillas will perhaps suffer heavily from the attacks of enemy armies, at times be split up while those taken prisoner will be martyred. They will be pursued like hunted animals in the areas they have chosen to operate in, with the constant anxiety of having the enemy on their track, and on top of all this with the constant doubt that in some cases the terrorized peasants will give them away to the repressive troops in order to save their own skins. They have no alternative but death or victory at times when death is a concept a thousand times present and victory a myth that only a revolutionary can dream of.

That is the heroism of the guerrilla. That is why it is said that to be on the march is also a form of fighting and to avoid combat at a given moment is another form. Faced with the general superiority of the enemy, the way to act is to find a form of tactics with which to gain a relative superiority at a chosen point, either by being able to concentrate more troops than the enemy or by making the best use of the terrain to secure advantages that upset the correlation of forces. In these conditions tactical victory is assured; if relative superiority is not clear, it is preferable not to take action. As long as one is in a position to choose the "how" and the "when," no battle should be fought that will not end in victory.

Guerrilla forces will grow and be consolidated within the framework of the great politico-military action of which they are a part. And within this framework they will go on forming the bases that are essential for their success. These bases are points that the enemy can penetrate only at the cost of heavy losses; they are bastions of the revolution, both shelters and starting points for bolder and more distant raids.

Such a time will come if the difficulties of both tactical and political discipline have been overcome. The guerrillas must never forget their function as the vanguard of the people, the mandate entrusted to their care, and therefore they should create the necessary political conditions for the establishment of a revolutionary power based on the full support of the masses. The main demands of the peasantry should be met to the degree and in the form that circumstances permit, so as to bring about the unity and solidarity of the whole population.

If the military situation is difficult from the first moments, the political situation will be no less delicate; and if a single military error can wipe out the guerrillas, a political error can check their development for a long period.

The struggle is politico-military; so it must develop, and so it must be understood.

In the course of its growth, guerrilla fighting reaches a point at which its capacity for action covers a given region, for which there are too many men and too great a concentration. Then begins the beehive action, in which one of the commanding officers, a distinguished guerrilla, hops to another region and repeats the chain development of guerrilla warfare, but still subject to a central command.

Now, it is necessary to point out that one cannot hope for victory without the formation of a people's army. The guerrilla forces can be expanded to a certain size; the people's forces in the cities and in other enemy-occupied zones can inflict losses, but the military potential of the reactionaries would remain intact. It must always be remembered that the final outcome should be the annihilation of the enemy. Therefore, all these new zones that have been created, as well as the penetrated zones behind the enemy lines and the forces operating in the principal cities, should be under a unified command. It cannot be claimed that there exists among guerrilla forces the closely linked chain of command that characterizes an army, but there is a strategic command. Within certain conditions of freedom of action, the guerrillas should carry out all the strategic orders of the central command, which is set up in one of the safest and strongest areas, preparing conditions for the union of the forces at a given moment.

The guerrilla war, or war of liberation, will generally have three stages: First, the strategic defensive, when a small force nibbles at the enemy and makes off, not to shelter in passive defense within a small circumference but rather to defend itself by limited attacks that it can carry out successfully. After this comes a state of equilibrium, during which the possibilities of action on the part of both the enemy and the guerrillas are established; then comes the final stage of overrunning the repressive army, ending in the capture of the big cities, large-scale decisive encounters, and the total annihilation of the enemy.

After reaching a state of equilibrium, when both sides are on guard against each other, in the ensuing development guerrilla war acquires new characteristics. The concept of maneuver is introduced: Big columns attack strong points, and there is mobile warfare, with the shifting of forces and of considerable means of attack. But owing to the capacity for resistance and counterattack that the enemy still retains, this war of maneuver does not entirely replace guerrilla fighting; it is only one form of action taken by the larger guerrilla forces until finally they crystallize into a people's army with army corps. Even at this time, the guerrillas will play their "original" guerrilla role, moving ahead of the

actions of the main forces, destroying communications and sabotaging the whole defensive apparatus of the enemy.

We have predicted that the war will be continental. This means
it will be protracted; it will have many fronts, and will cost much
blood and countless lives over a long period. But besides this, the
polarization of forces that is occurring in America—the clear
division between exploiters and exploited that will exist in future
revolutionary war—means that when the armed vanguard of the
people seize power, the country or countries that attain it will
at one and the same time liquidate both their imperialist and
their national exploiting class oppressor. The first stage of the
socialist revolution will have crystallized; the people will be ready
to staunch their wounds and begin to build socialism.

SOCIALISM AND MAN IN CUBA *

Looking at things from a superficial standpoint, it might seem
that those who speak of the submission of the individual to the
state are right; with incomparable enthusiasm and discipline, the
masses carry out the tasks set by the government whether they
are economic, cultural, defense, sports, etc. The initiative generally comes from Fidel or the high command for the Revolution:
It is explained to the people, who make it their own. At times,
local experiences are taken up by the party and the government
and are thereby generalized, following the same procedure.

However, the state at times makes mistakes. When this happens the collective enthusiasm diminishes palpably as a result of
a quantitative diminishing that takes place in each of the elements that make up the collective, and work becomes paralyzed
until it finally shrinks to insignificant proportions; this is the time
to rectify.

This was what happened in March, 1962 as a result of the
sectarian policy imposed on the party by Anibal Escalante.

It is evident that this mechanism is not sufficient to ensure a
sequence of sensible measures; what is missing is a more structured relationship with the mass. We must improve this connec-

---

* Translated by the editor from *El Socialismo y el Hombre en Cuba*
(Havana: Ediciones Politicas, 1967).

tion in the years to come, but in the case of the initiatives arising at the top levels of government, we are using the almost intuitive method of keeping our ears open to the general reactions in the face of the problems that are posed.

Fidel is a past-master at this; his particular mode of integration with the people can only be appreciated by seeing him in action. In the big public meetings one can observe something like the dialogue of two tuning forks whose vibrations summon forth new vibrations each in the other. Fidel and the mass begin to vibrate in a dialogue of growing intensity which reaches its culminating point in an abrupt ending crowned by our victorious battle cry.

What is hard to understand for anyone who has not lived the revolutionary experience is this close dialectical unity which exists between the individual and the mass, in which both are interrelated and the mass, as a whole made up of individuals, is in turn related to the leaders. . . .

Pursuing the chimera of achieving socialism with the aid of the blunted weapons left to us by capitalism (the commodity as the economic unit, profitability and individual material interest as levers, etc.), it is possible to come to a blind alley. And the arrival there comes about after covering a long distance in which there are many crossroads where it is difficult to realize just when the wrong turn was taken. Meanwhile, the adapted economic base has undermined the development of consciousness. To build Communism, a new man must be created simultaneously with the material base.

That is why it is so important to choose correctly the instrument of mass mobilization. The instrument must be fundamentally of a moral character, without forgetting the correct use of material incentives, especially those of a social nature.

As I already said, in moments of extreme danger it is easy to activate moral incentives: To maintain their effectiveness, it is necessary to develop a consciousness in which values acquire new categories. Society as a whole must become a huge school.

The broad characteristics of the phenomenon are similar to the process of formation of capitalist consciousness in the system's first stage. Capitalism resorts to force, but it also educates people in the system. Direct propaganda is carried out by those who are entrusted with the task of explaining the inevitability of a class regime, whether due to its divine origin or due to the imposition of nature as a mechanical entity. This placates the masses, who see themselves oppressed by an evil against which it is not possible to struggle.

This is followed by hope, which differentiates capitalism from the previous caste regimes that offered no way out. For some, the caste formula continues in force: The obedient are rewarded by arrival after death in other wonderful worlds where the good are rewarded and thus the old tradition is continued. For others, there is innovation: The division in classes is a matter of fate, but individuals can leave the class to which they belong through work, initiative, etc. This process, and that of self-education for success, must be deeply hypocritical: It is the interested demonstration that a lie is true.

In our case, direct education acquires much greater importance. Explanation is convincing because it is true; subterfuges are not needed. It is carried out through the state's educational apparatus in the form of general, technical, and ideological culture, by means of bodies such as the Ministry of Education and the party's information apparatus. Education takes hold among the masses, and the new attitude that is praised tends to become habit; the mass gradually takes it over and exerts pressure on those who have still not become educated. This is the indirect way of educating the masses, as powerful as the other one.

But the process is a conscious one: The individual receives the impact of the new social power and perceives that he is not completely adequate to it. Under the influence of the pressure implied in indirect education, he tries to adjust to a situation that he feels to be just and whose lack of development has kept him from doing so thus far. He is educating himself.

We can see the new man who begins to emerge in this period of the building of socialism. His image is as yet unfinished. In fact it will never be finished, since the process advances parallel to the development of new economic forms. Discounting those whose lack of education makes them tend toward the solitary road, toward the satisfaction of their ambitions, there are others who, even within this new picture of over-all advances, tend to march in isolation from the accompanying mass. What is important is that people become more aware every day of the need to incorporate themselves into society and of their own importance as motors of that society.

They no longer march in complete solitude along wandering bypaths toward distant goals. They follow their vanguard, composed of the party, of the most advanced workers, of the advanced men who move along bound to the masses and in close communion with them. The vanguard have their eyes on the future and its rewards, but the latter are not envisioned as something individual; the reward is the new society, where human beings will have different characteristics: the society of Communist man.

The road is long and full of difficulties. At times, the route strays off course, and it is necessary to retreat; at times, a too rapid pace separates us from the masses, and on occasions the pace is slow, and we feel upon our necks the breath of those who follow upon our heels. Our ambition as revolutionaries makes us try to move forward as far as possible, opening up the way before us, but we know that we must be reinforced by the mass, while the mass will only be able to advance more rapidly if we encourage it by our example.

In spite of the importance given to moral incentives, the existence of two principal groups (excluding, of course, the minority fraction of those who do not participate for one reason or another in the building of socialism) is an indication of the relative lack of development of social consciousness. The vanguard group is ideologically more advanced than the mass; the latter is acquainted with the new values, but insufficiently. While in the former a qualitative change takes place that permits them to make sacrifices as a function of their vanguard character, the latter see only by halves and must be subjected to incentives and pressures of some intensity; it is the dictatorship of the proletariat being exercised not only upon the defeated class but also individually upon the victorious class.

To achieve total success, all of this involves the necessity of a series of mechanisms, the revolutionary institutions. The concept of institutionalization fits in with the images of the multitudes marching toward the future as that of a harmonic unit of canals, steps, well-oiled apparatuses that make the march possible, that permit the natural selection of those who are destined to march in the vanguard and who dispense rewards and punishments to those who fulfill their duty or act against the society under construction.

The Revolution has still not been institutionalized. We are seeking something new that will allow a perfect identification between the government and the community as a whole, adapted to the special conditions of the building of socialism and avoiding to the utmost the commonplaces of bourgeois democracy transplanted to the society in formation (such as legislative houses, for example). Some experiments have been carried out with the aim of gradually producing the institutionalization of the Revolution, but without too much hurry. We have been greatly restrained by the fear that any formal aspect might separate us from the masses and make us lose sight of the ultimate and most important revolutionary aspiration: to see man freed from alienation.

Notwithstanding the lack of institutions, which must be overcome gradually, the masses now make history as a conscious aggregate of individuals who struggle for the same cause. In spite of the apparent standardization of man in socialism, he is more complete; his possibilities for expressing himself and making himself heard in the social apparatus are infinitely greater, in spite of the lack of a perfect mechanism to do so.

It is still necessary to accentuate his conscious, individual and collective, his participation in all the mechanisms of direction and production and to associate it with the idea of the need for technical and ideological education, so that the individual will realize that these processes are closely interdependent and their advances are parallel. He will thus achieve total awareness of his social being, which is equivalent to his full realization as a human being, having broken the chains of alienation.

This will be translated concretely into the reappropriation of his nature through liberated work and the expression of his own human condition in culture and art.

In order for it to develop, work must acquire a new condition; man as commodity ceases to exist, and a system is established that allows the fulfillment of social duty. The means of production belong to society, and the machine is only the front line where duty is performed. Man begins to free his thought from the bothersome fact that presupposed the need to satisfy his animal needs by working. He begins to see himself portrayed in his work and to understand its human magnitude through the created object, through the work carried out. This no longer involves leaving a part of his being in the form of labor power sold, which no longer belongs to him; rather it signifies an emanation from himself, a contribution to the life of society in which he is reflected, the fulfillment of this social duty.

We are doing everything possible to give work this new cate-

gory of social duty and to join it to the development of technology, on the one hand, which will provide the conditions for
greater freedom, and to voluntary work on the other, based on
the Marxist concept that man truly achieves his full human condition when he produces without being compelled by the physical
necessity of selling himself as a commodity.

It is clear that work still has coercive aspects, even when it is
voluntary: Man has still not transformed all the coercion surrounding him into conditioned reflexes of a social nature and in
many cases he still produces under the pressure of the environment (Fidel calls this moral compulsion). He has still to achieve
complete spiritual recreation in the presence of his own work,
without the direct pressure of the social environment but bound
to it by new habits. That will be Communism. . . .

It is not a question of how many kilograms of meat are eaten
or how many times a year someone may go to the beach or how
many pretty imported things can be bought with present wages.
It is rather that the individual feels greater fulfillment, that he
has greater inner wealth and many more responsibilities. In our
country the individual knows that the glorious period in which
it has fallen to him to live is one of sacrifice; he is familiar with
sacrifice.

The first came to know it in the Sierra Maestra and wherever
there was fighting; later we have known it in all Cuba. Cuba is
the vanguard of America and must make sacrifices because it
occupies the advance position, because it points out to the Latin
American masses the road to full freedom.

Within the country, the leaders have to fulfill their vanguard
role; and it must be said with complete sincerity that in a true
revolution, to which you give yourself completely without any
thought for material retribution, the task of the vanguard revolutionary is both magnificent and anguishing.

Let me say, at the risk of appearing ridiculous, that the true
revolutionary is guided by strong feelings of love. It is impossible
to think of an authentic revolutionary without this quality. This
is perhaps one of the great dramas of a leader; he must combine
an impassioned spirit with a cold mind and make painful decisions without flinching. Our vanguard revolutionaries must idealize
their love for the people, for the most hallowed causes, and make
it one and indivisible. They cannot descend, with small doses of
daily affection, to the terrain where ordinary men put their love
into practice.

The leaders of the Revolution have children who do not learn to call their father with their first faltering words; they have wives who must be part of the general sacrifice of their lives to carry the Revolution to its destination; their friends are strictly limited to their comrades in revolution. There is no life outside the Revolution.

In these conditions, the revolutionary leaders must have a large dose of humanity, a large dose of a sense of justice and truth, to avoid falling into dogmatic extremes, into cold scholasticism, into isolation from the masses. They must struggle every day so that their love of living humanity is transformed into concrete deeds, into acts that will serve as an example, as a mobilizing factor.

The revolutionary, the ideological motor of the Revolution within his party, is consumed by this uninterrupted activity that ends only with death, unless its construction is achieved on a worldwide scale.

TWO, THREE . . . MANY VIETNAMS *

What role shall we, the exploited people of the world, play? The peoples of the three continents focus their attention on Vietnam and learn their lesson. Since imperialists blackmail humanity by threatening it with war, the wise reaction is not to fear war. The general tactics of the people should be to launch a constant and a firm attack on all fronts where the confrontation is taking place.

In those places where this meager peace we have has been violated, what is our duty? To liberate ourselves at any price.

The world panorama is of great complexity. The struggle for liberation has not yet been undertaken by some countries of old Europe, sufficiently developed to realize the contradictions of capitalism, but weak to such a degree that they are unable either to follow imperialism or even to start on its own road. Their contradictions will reach an explosive stage during the forthcoming years—but their problems and, consequently, their own solutions are different from those of our dependent and economically underdeveloped countries.

* From *Tricontinental* (English edition), no. 14 (Sept.-Oct., 1969). The message was first published by the Organization for Solidarity among the Peoples of Africa, Asia, and Latin America—OSPAAAL—in April, 1967.

The fundamental field of imperialist exploitation comprises the three underdeveloped continents: [Latin] America, Asia, and Africa. Every country also has its own characteristics, but each continent, as a whole, also presents a certain unity. . . .

We must bear in mind that imperialism is a world system, the last stage of capitalism—and it must be defeated in a world confrontation. The strategic end of this struggle should be the destruction of imperialism. Our share, the responsibility of the exploited and underdeveloped of the world, is to eliminate the foundations of imperialism: our oppressed nations, from which they extract capital, raw materials, technicians, and cheap labor, and to which they export new capital—instruments of domination —arms, and all kinds of articles, thus submerging us in an absolute dependence.

The fundamental element of this strategic goal will be the real liberation of all people, a liberation that will be brought about through armed struggle in most cases and which will be, in Our America, almost certainly a Socialist Revolution.

While envisaging the destruction of imperialism, it is necessary to identify its leader, which is none other than the United States of America.

We must carry out a general task with the tactical purpose of getting the enemy out of his natural environment, forcing him to fight in regions where his own life and habits will clash with the existing reality. We must not underrate our adversary; the U.S. soldier has technical capacity and is backed by weapons and resources of such magnitude that render him frightful. He lacks the essential ideological motivation, which his bitterest enemies of today—the North Vietnamese soldiers—have in the highest degree. We will only be able to overcome that army by undermining its morale—and this is accomplished by defeating it and causing it repeated sufferings.

But this brief outline of victories carries within itself the immense sacrifices of the people, sacrifices that should be demanded beginning today, in plain daylight, and that perhaps may be less painful than those we would have to endure if we constantly avoided battle in an attempt to have others pull our chestnuts out of the fire. . . .

[What are] the real possibilities that dependent America may have of liberating itself through peaceful means? For us, the solution to this question is quite clear: The present moment may or may not be the proper one for starting the struggle, but we cannot harbor any illusions, and we have no right to do so, that freedom can be obtained without fighting. And these battles will not be mere street fights with stones against tear-gas bombs, or peaceful general strikes; neither will they be the battles of a furious people destroying in two or three days the repressive scaffolds of the ruling oligarchies; the struggle will be long, harsh, and its front will be in the guerrilla's refuge, in the cities, in the homes of the fighters—where the repressive forces will go seeking easy victims among their families—in the massacred rural population, in the villages or cities destroyed by the bombardments of the enemy.

They are pushing us into this struggle; there is no alternative: We must prepare for it and we must decide to undertake it. . . .

We must carry the war into every corner the enemy happens to carry it—to his home, to his centers of entertainment: a total war. It is necessary to prevent him from having a moment of peace, a quiet moment outside his barracks or even inside; we must attack him wherever he may be; make him feel like a cornered beast wherever he may move. Then his moral fiber will begin to decline. He will even become more beastly, but we will notice how the signs of decadence begin to appear. . . .

How close we could look into a bright future should two, three, or many Vietnams flourish throughout the world with their share of deaths and their immense tragedies, their everyday heroism and their repeated blows against imperialism—impelled to disperse its forces under the sudden attack and the increasing hatred of all peoples of the world! . . .

Our every action is a battle cry against imperialism, and a battle hymn to the people's unity against the great enemy of mankind: the United States of America. Wherever death may surprise us, let it be welcome, provided that this, our battle cry, may have reached some receptive ear and another hand may be extended to wield our weapons and other men be ready to intone the funeral dirge with the staccato singing of the machine guns and new battle cries of war and victory.

27. *Victor Raúl Haya de la Torre*

*Victor Raúl Haya de la Torre was born in Trujillo, Peru, in 1895,
and educated both in that country and in England. He began political activity as a student and, after leading a protest movement
against the government, was jailed and expelled from the country.
While in exile in Mexico, in 1924, he formed the Alianza Popular
Revolucionaria Americana (usually referred to as the APRA, or
Aprista Party). Its program called for the involvement of the Indian
in political life, Latin American unity, and opposition to foreign
imperialism. In 1931, he returned to Peru from exile to run for
the Presidency. He probably won the election, but the government
imprisoned him and killed many of his followers. He was released
in 1933, but went underground to avoid being arrested again. In
1945, he came out of hiding, and his party, supporting the election
of a Conservative President, won a considerable electoral victory.
In 1948, however, dictatorship returned to Peru, and Haya de la
Torre took refuge in the Colombian Embassy, where he remained
until 1954, when he was given a guarantee of safe conduct to leave
the country. After the overthrow of the dictatorship in 1957, he
returned to Peru.*

*Now once again active in national politics, Haya de la Torre was
a Presidential candidate in June, 1962. The military annulled this
election, and he ran again unsuccessfully a year later.*

*His political writings are characterized by an effort to develop
a distinctively Latin American (he would say Indo-American)
political formula which does not imitate European or American models. He is anti-Communist and anti-imperialist, but believes that an alliance of the workers, the peasants, and the middle
classes can control and utilize foreign investment (for "imperialism
is the first stage of capitalism in underdeveloped countries"), establish rural cooperatives, and develop the countries of Latin
America under a "directed" economy which also allows private enterprise and initiative. The works from which the following selections are taken were published two decades apart. In his more*

recent writing, as is evident here, Haya de la Torre has somewhat softened the dogmatism of his original theory, particularly with regard to nationalization and relations with the United States.

INDO-AMERICA*

In my opinion, the term "Spanish America" corresponds to the colonial epoch, the term "Latin America" corresponds to the republican period, and the term "Pan-America" is an expression of Yankee imperialism. "Indo-America" is the expression of the new revolutionary conception of America which, having passed through the period of Spanish and Anglo-Saxon conquests, will create a definite political, economic, and social organization on the national base of its workers, who represent the tradition, and the race of the exploited indigenous masses who, throughout the economy of [Central and South] America (the unity of which is indestructible) have formed the basis of our productivity and the core of our collective life from the time of the period before Columbus.

It is true that the terms are used at the same time. Some say Pan-America, others Spanish America, some Latin America, and others Indo-America. But this coexistence has a social and economic significance. Up to the present day in [Latin] America, there has also been both a coexistence and an opposition between the various periods of historic evolution that followed after one another in other continents. In [Central and South] America, we have, living together and at the same time in opposition, within the frontiers of our continent or even within the frontiers of each country, all forms of social organization and every level of economic development—savagery, barbarism, and civilization, communal primitive agriculture, feudalism, manufacturing, industrialism, and imperialism. Indians who have never known the use of a wheel as a means of locomotion see swift airplanes in the skies above their mountains. The young gentleman of Buenos Aires who plays golf and visits London has as compatriot and fellow citizen the half-naked Indian in the Chaco. The same thing is true in Peru and Mexico and Colombia and Central America.

* Excerpts from Victor Raúl Haya de la Torre, *¿A Dónde Vá Indoamérica?* (Santiago de Chile: Biblioteca América, 1936); translated by the editor, by permission.

This lack of definition, this contradiction, this historic juxta-position, if the terms are appropriate, describes in great part the dialectic of our educational development. [Latin] America has been and is a land that has experienced invasions—as Europe once did. From the immigrations and transmigrations of the period before Columbus . . . from Asia, from Indo-America, from Oceania, from the North to the South and back, America has been the site of invasions and countless conquests. Three centuries of Spanish domination represent a long period in our history. It seems to us almost an eternity because it was so recent, but it is less in time than the eight centuries of Arab domination over Spain, for example. The Arabs gave Spain a great civilization and formed a southern racial mixture. They left behind 10 per cent of the word-roots in the language, according to the philologists. The Arabs would have the right to demand, as thanks from the Spaniards, that they call Spain Ibero-Arabia or something similar. But the Arab invasion was just that—an invasion—and historically it created a movement of independence in which many Hispano-Arabs fought to free themselves from the tutelage of their racial ancestors. The religious factor in this struggle corresponds to the period and is less clear than in the struggle of the natives [of Latin America] against Spain. Yet, in both conquests and "reconquests," we can see economic causes which are the basis of all great historic phenomena.

In [Central and South] America, after suffering the inroads of feudalism and mercantilism along with the conquest and Spanish colonization, we now have been suffering the invasion of industrialism or capitalism. . . . It may be that this new invasion will be less extensive in this period, when everything proceeds at a faster pace, but it *is* an invasion with its own particular characteristics, its own particular politics, and with formidable social effects. The question for the future is whether we will undergo further invasions. Underneath these conquering influences from outside, there persists one economic fact—the conqueror always seeks wealth. And the Indian or his descendants, in the great majority, work to create this wealth. It has been calculated by experts that there are more than 75 million Indians in [Latin] America. This means approximately 75 per cent of our total population.* Those Indians,

* The present population of Latin America is more than 200 million—double Haya de la Torre's 1936 estimate.—ED.

with their own traditions, their own languages, their own suffering and aspirations, with their own great problem, constitute in their immense majority a work force, "productivity," the hand that creates the riches. This is the way it has been from the social point of view until now and, relatively speaking, always in [Latin] America. . . .

We in the vanguard, the Apristas, the anti-imperialists of [Latin] America, who are inclined to interpret history economically, have adopted the term Indo-America as a fundamental expression. The invasions of the Anglo-Saxon, Spanish, and Negro races have come to us, are coming to us, and will come to us; they have contributed and continue to contribute to the context of a new [Latin] America. Yet there survives underneath all these the force of the labor of the Indian. If in Cuba he has been wiped out and in Argentina and Costa Rica absorbed, the Indian continues to be the ethnic, social, and economic basis of [Latin] America. This is true both for those who live in the framework of modern civilization and for those who in great number are still grouped in primitive tribal organizations. Many other races are mixed with the Indian race, but this America of ours will find its identity and its course before those 75 million natives have disappeared. Every immigration, every conquest has partially modified the Indo-American race, but the ethnic basis of our people is still definitely native.

Those who live in this period struggle against the Yankee capitalist imperialism just as those who lived 100 years ago struggled against feudal Spanish, French, and Portuguese imperialism. Yankee domination, if it lasts, will also leave its profound traces on us, just as the Spanish domination did. The "Latin American" period, which historically replaced the "Spanish American" period, can be succeeded also by a "Pan-American" stage. We are working against this, especially as regards its imperialist implications. After these three stages, which result from ethnic, political, economic, and spiritual invasions, will come the Indo-America which is to be established and defined. The new revolution in Latin America will be a revolution with an Indian base and orientation, with the native conscience and subconscious expressed in an economic and social renaissance. The Mexican revolution is a symptom of this great movement. The countries where the Indian does not predominate in Latin America cannot withdraw from his influence. . . .

Imperialism in Action

The first stage of industrial capitalism in Central America, as in the majority of our countries, begins with imperialism, which is "the last stage of capitalism" in the typical industrial countries. Capitalism arrives then in these agrarian countries at the height of its expansion, voracious, and developed, without any of the bourgeois virtues that emerged during the historic evolution of European societies in the period of transition from feudalism to industrialism. In Central America, as in most of the Latin American countries, capitalism arrives already imperialist, violent, and piratical, not to construct but only to exploit and withdraw all, leaving almost nothing behind. Vice, corruption, false views of life and of progress are raised up in consequence, and only sorrow and disillusionment are left, a grave danger for those people—their most complicated and serious political, economic, and social problem. . . .

The Struggle of the Two Imperialisms

There are two imperialisms struggling for Latin America, that of Europe and that of North America. But European imperialism is continually losing its influence, while North American imperialism is increasing. Business . . . is one of the aspects and manifestations of imperialism. The commercial struggle between Europe and the United States for Latin American markets is one of the most important consequences of the imperialist struggle between the United States and Europe, a struggle that has other manifestations in the battle for special concessions—linked to the tendencies for political domination of our countries of which Pan-Americanism is an instrument—and to the subjection of the economic life of our countries to the investors. . . .

The Reform of Cordoba

After 1918, from one end to the other of the Latin American continent there arose a new awareness among the youth. From the old University of Cordoba there was the first outcry: "Until now, the universities have been a perennial haven of mediocrities, a source of profit for the ignorant, a secure shelter for the weak, and, what is still worse, a place where all forms of tyranny and stupidity find a source of inspiration. The universities have succeeded in being the faithful reflection of those decadent societies which present a sad spectacle of senile immobility. For this reason, knowledge passes silently by those mute and closed dwellings, or enters mutilated and grotesque into the service of bureaucracy. If in the name of order we are asked to follow along deceitful and docile, we proclaim aloud the sacred right of revolution. Henceforth, the only hope is the heroic destiny of the youth. Sacrifice is our greatest stimulus, the spiritual redemption of the youth of Latin America our only recompense, for we know that our ills are the ills of the entire continent." And the "sacred right of revolution" was exercised in Cordoba, in Buenos Aires, in La Plata, in Lima, in Montevideo, in Santiago de Chile, in Havana, in Bogotá, and in Mexico. The students of the old universities revolted against the past. In that tumultuous and lyrical movement against the old educational systems, there streamed a new spirit of youth which sought to free itself from everything that closed off the past from the future. Henceforth, there was only one [Latin] America. In its broad and fertile lands, a struggle has arisen that will be final. On the one side, the spirit of the past—reactionary and diminishing; on the other side, the revolutionary impulse of youth, which sees its destiny looming up before it. From 1918 to 1925, the conscience of the youth developed and became more precisely defined. At that time, it aimed at the renovation of the educational system and a spiritual confederation of Latin America. Today it seeks a more profound transformation. It struggles for the renovation of the social systems. It aspires to a political confederation of our twenty republics which are divided by artificial nationalism and menaced in common by the conquering imperialism of the United States and the North.

The spirit of [Latin] American youth continually advances to the future. Misunderstood by the old generations of our bourgeois classes, by our bureaucracies, by our oligarchies, it has in them a near and implacable enemy. Young blood, blood of the new liberators of America, has watered our soil. Graves for our new victims have been dug in our land each time that our youth has proclaimed "the sacred right of revolution." But our struggle has hardly begun. Our enemies are powerful and inexorable. They consist in the alliance of Latin American feudalism, the sad remnant of the conquering brutality of Spain, and powerful Yankee imperialism—animating spirit of our new bourgeois class, exalter of our provincialisms, inciter of our tyrannies, creator of our governments, and accomplice in our degenerate internal struggles. . . .

LATIN AMERICA

The Aprista Thesis

For the fulfillment of *Aprista* doctrine, a party has been created which, like the work it hopes to accomplish, is Latin American in character. The base of this party is in the producers, in alliance with the middle classes, also involved in the struggle against imperialism. The party attempts to form an "anti-imperialist consciousness" in the working classes—a consciousness that they are the ones who produce for imperialism, and they alone are those who can place conditions upon it and constitute a force of liberation—without hoping that the proletarians of Europe and the United States will destroy the capitalist system, the origin of imperialism. The alliance with the middle classes reinforces the action of the working classes, especially those which are specifically laborers—new in their role as controlling forces in the state, just as the (economic) system in Latin America which determines their existence as a class is new.

Aprismo already has opened the doors to the future because, following the economic independence of Latin America—an independence that will have to be based on equality in the exchange of raw materials and finished products and the investment of capital according to the principle of progressive nationalization of the sources of production under the control of the state—it will bring about the industrialization of our countries. As a result, a working class will be formed, and favorable conditions will be created for the rapid total direction of the economy and the abolition of the capitalist system. While this revolutionary process is being carried out, *Aprismo* will utilize the anti-imperialist forces of today, not excluding the middle classes, which are threatened with extinction by imperialism. It will seek to defend them through the anti-imperialist state which, by nationalization and progressive socialization of the sources of production, will be definitely oriented in the direction of state capitalism, preventing the middle classes from tending toward large private capitalism, which would mean a return to imperialism.

Aprismo thus presents a complete doctrine and a realistic method of realistic action—that is, an integral economic, social, and political program to secure the economic independence of Latin America.

THIRTY YEARS OF *APRISMO**

The Land of Reflection

Aprismo can demonstrate a particular origin that distinguishes it from the other movements and doctrines of the same type in Indo-America—not only because of its characteristic Bolivarian militancy (it is in Bolivar's glorious name that only the APRA demands the unification of the continent), but also because of the special quality of the numerous movements that preceded it. One can trace their beginning from the active youth movement that between 1918 and 1923 established and propagated the University Reform in all of our republics. From this movement, the founders of APRA have drawn two active inspirational ideals to be translated into moral slogans: to liberate our generation from the "mental colonialism" of Europe, and to unite the intellectual and manual workers to attain together the ambitious goal of a democratic civilization—to establish a confederation of all of our peoples and to attain for them economic justice, without impairment of their liberty. . . . Without these guidelines, it would have been unthinkable, unexpected, and perhaps heretical to conceive or attempt a judgment from *here* and not from *Europe* of our particular historical reality and our special sociological problems. This continent was still the "land of reflection," alluded to by Hegel. In its soil were the buds, offshoots, and seedlings—accidental in all cases—of all the ideas, philosophic sects, literary novelties, and partisan tendencies that could be of use to the Old World. And thus, just as we had countless spokesmen of the utilitarianism of Bentham and Mill, of Saint-Simonianism and of Comte's positivism, of materialism with all its varieties, and of idealism of various kinds, and as there was no lack of monarchists, Jacobins, anarchists, and others, all with their respective heterodoxies and oppositions, by the same process—to pass over a century and move to the world conflagration of the first great war and beyond—Marxism was developed and the Bolshevik echo of Marx-

*Excerpts from Victor Raúl Haya de la Torre, *Treinta Años de Aprismo* (Mexico City: Fonda de Cultura Económica, 1956); translated by the editor, by permission.

ism resounded and then there sprang up the totalitarians, the racists, and the perennial growth of jingoism. But one or the other, those for, and those against, always in imitation—inasmuch as it was obligatory not to go beyond the European models, and not to be separated from their pre-established patterns of thought. . . .

Aprismo *and Communism*

The total separation between *Aprismo* and Communism is obviously fundamental. They start out from divergent historical conceptions. For Communism, the pronouncements of Marx, conceived in one area and one given period (Europe in the nineteenth century), are unimpeachable truths of universal validity. For *Aprismo*, the Marxist conception is an important historical antecedent, but not unchangeable. It is limited and relative to the particular conditions of space and time that make it dialectically opposed to a reality that is different from that of Europe. Marx himself declares in the prologue of *Capital* that the basis of his observation was England—the England of the industrial capitalism of the middle of the nineteenth century—and that from the examination of the English reality, he deduced his "theoretical ideas" as "physics observes the physical phenomenon wherever it occurs." The "classic soil" of the capitalist system is England— that is, the country which, being in the forefront of industrial development at that time, was the prototype of all the others. From here, in a generalization of universal scope, the founder of scientific socialism goes on to say in the same prologue: "The country that is the most industrially developed alone shows the way of the less developed, the image of their own future."

That is the English model. And this was an unfulfilled *European* prediction of world economic development. In the "mirror" (as some translators have figuratively translated the idea of Marx's word "image"), there was hardly the reflection of the future of many countries, and none was reflected as an exact replica. The evolution of capitalism has taken unexpected directions in the last hundred years, and some non-European areas have prospered economically without in any way resembling the special English model. . . .

Then, distinct from the Communist transplantation to Indo-

America of the "party of only one class" and of the European employer, *Aprismo* has put forward arguments that thus far have not been answered: among others, that of the lack of comparability of the proletarian class of the large capitalist countries in a state of advanced industrialization which *produce machinery*, to the producing class of the colonial and semicolonial countries whose infant industrialism, working with raw or half-finished materials, *does not produce machinery*—a fundamental distinction to which I shall return shortly; also the various types of class-consciousness which cannot be confused, that of the long-standing and highly trained proletariats at a high level of civilization, and that of those with a brief history and a much slower and lagging development. *Aprismo* emphasizes the different character—so often referred to by the *Aprista* thesis—of the urban and rural middle classes of Europe and those of Indo-America and the necessity of incorporating our middle classes in the single popular front of *Aprismo*. For these classes are the first ones affected by imperialistic expansion, and from this source have come excellent leaders and vigorous civic movements in defense of the economic emancipation of our peoples. . . .

Between the Communist anti-imperialism in the service of the Soviet empire, and *Aprista* anti-imperialism in defense of our countries, there is the firm separation between two economic and social scenes which cannot be compared—that of the Old World and that of the New World. They should not be confused, despite the way in which the imperialists and their agents and helpers have thoughtlessly claimed to involve us against our will with domestic Communism, which is clearly obedient to foreign ideologies and direction and which attacks us unscrupulously and ceaselessly. . . .

Latin America and the French Revolution

For the discontented colonials of Portuguese and Spanish America, the French Revolution was a great example. Despite the fact that the social and political content of the French movement corresponded to an economic and social stage much more advanced than that which historically was the case among the Indo-American peoples, we adopted the slogans, the precepts, and the formulas of Paris as an infallible recipe that could give us also "liberty, equality, and fraternity." While in France this signified the collapse of feudalism, in Indo-America it represented the affirmation and independence of the feudal colonial power. There the landowning aristocracy was crushed, while here the landholding native aristocrats liberated themselves by revolution from the empire of the mother country and captured the state as an instrument of their class domination.

In these circumstances, the same antifeudal ideology of the French bourgeoisie was used in a revolution of the feudal landowning Spanish- or Portuguese-American class against the economic and political yoke that the Spanish (and Portuguese) crown imposed on it. And from this paradox alone, the result was that, paradoxically, the revolutions of emancipation of Indo-America resulted in political regimes that were democratic in name and corresponded to a later economic and social stage of bourgeois capitalism, but in contradiction to the feudal organization of the dominant system of production in our lands—since independence did not destroy the large plantation but confirmed it. The ideas of the French liberals and radicals lost their subversive effect once the Indo-American republics were established. The slaves were not liberated at once, in spite of the democratic creed. Despite the initial cry of emancipation, the slavery of the Indian continued. Isolation, dear to the landowner, the single class that triumphed from the revolution of independence, brought about the division and subdivision of the ancient viceroyalties of Spain into many republics. All this took place because the economic basis on which society rested was feudal. . . .

Imperialism, the First Stage of Capitalism

Aprista theory recognizes that imperialism, the first stage of capitalism in our countries, brings with it industrialization, although this is unilaterally imposed, and it represents a period of evolution of the economy and of civilization superior to that of colonial feudalism. Modern imperialism, especially North American imperialism, which is so advanced and refined in its methods, only offers advantages and progress at its outset, and produces in our country a progressive movement of the working masses who pass from semislavery and servitude or from the elementary forms of free labor to its specifically proletarian type.

It should be said that as "the *first* stage of capitalism," imperialism brings about the emergence in our countries of the industrial proletarian class, although, for this particular type of industrialism, which is not metalworking, manufacturing, or heavy production, this proletariat is very far from displaying the same characteristics and having the same experience and same class-consciousness as the long-standing and highly trained proletariats of the imperialist countries of developed industrialism. Our industrial working classes in a semicolonial industry of raw materials have a different character.

Thus, imperialism as an economic phenomenon, as the first stage of capitalism in Indo-America—as a stage of ineluctable, progressive industrialization—is both dangerous and necessary. With it, we run the risk of subjection, but without it, there would be inevitable stagnation and retrogression.

Given the preceding propositions, we can conclude that the way for the Indo-American peoples to defy imperialism is to defend themselves from inundation, but without making the water disappear. With this advanced figurative comparison, we mark one of the fundamental *Aprista* declarations, different from those which serve as pretexts for the Communist theses on the phenomenon of imperialism. These tend to direct revolutionary action to stop up the very sources and foundations of the whole system of capitalist production, one of whose huge and widespread effects is imperialism. My book in 1928 has already explained with all exactness that industrial capitalism, which is imported into Indo-America with the imperialist stage, is incipient, young, and colonial or semicolonial in type; that it cannot be compared, as to both its origin and its method of production to the industrial capitalism of the regions of the world in which this economic system has developed. Consequently, this imperialist capitalism has created an industrial proletarian class that is also distinct from the old and organically established industrial proletarian class of Europe. Using their own Marxist teachings as a weapon of argument against the Communist generalizations—according to which the capitalist system can be eliminated only by the revolutionary activity of the industrial proletariats of countries that are highly developed, where class-consciousness and organizational strength have made possible that transformation—my book concludes "that the radical abolition of the capitalist system cannot be accomplished except where capitalism has arrived at the climax of its development, namely in the large countries, which are in the vanguard of world industry. It does not then have to be in the colonial or semicolonial countries—which, recently, are experiencing the first capitalist stage or stages—that capitalism can be destroyed."*

* *El Anti-imperialismo y el* APRA (Mexico City, 1928), p. 22.

On the other hand, the economic capacity of the United States does not permit us to assume that an impending collapse of its power is so near that it would signify our unexpected emancipation. Still, supposing the defeat of the United States in a military conflict with another imperialist power, would this bring liberty to Indo-America or reduce it to submission under a new master? . . .

The Mexican Revolution

This is the first instructive lesson of the agrarian revolution in Mexico upon which APRA draws. This movement and the University Reform are the two particular Latin American developments of this century that are precursors of *Aprismo*. From the latter comes the current of reform leading to our emancipation from mental colonialism through a new interpretation of Indo-American life; and from the former come numerous lessons in iron and steel given by a social revolution that is not socialist, but agrarian, antifeudal, and anti-imperialist.

In my book of 1928, I reiterated these concepts, which I had already published earlier, from 1924 on: The Mexican revolution is the first social movement of our century. It antedates the Russian Revolution and, obviously, that of China, although the imperialist element of the United States press calls it retroactively Bolshevik or Communist, in the same way in which subsequently until today every democratic social movement of the Left in Indo-America has been labeled. But it is not only an agrarian and antifeudal revolution, as it referred to itself in its adopted title, but something more. It is an anti-imperialist revolution and a heroic prelude of revolution. This double character of the Mexican revolution is, as I understand it, indivisible, and this explains many of the frustrations of that particular movement.

Aprismo recognized, then, in the Mexican revolution its particular social, nonsocialist character, although many Latin Americans repeated the European terminology in pompously calling it socialist, and I noted that, as far as that was concerned, "it is not indispensable to be Communist in order to be a revolutionary." But I noted as the principal cause of its "limitations and errors" the isolation of that cruel and heroic popular revolution, and with that assertion I confirmed one of the basic conclusions of our doctrine. No country of Indo-America can liquidate feudalism or emancipate itself economically from imperialism by itself. Both these tasks of general liberation go beyond our nationalist insularity and demand joint action by the countries of Indo-America. Feudalism and imperialism are economic and social systems that are continent-wide and exceed, in their organic field of activity and interdependence of interests, the frontiers of our twenty divided countries. . . .

Aprismo has maintained its premises: Capitalism, or the industrialization of Indo-America, begins in the form of imperialism. Our countries cannot destroy the capitalist system, whose roots and focal points are very far from us. The capitalist system, because of its economic capacity, does not allow us to assume its imminent downfall. Communism, with its dictatorship of the proletariat and its soviets, is unthinkable in Indo-America, whose socioeconomic reality is not Russian. Both Communism and fascism are specifically European phenomena. Our resistance to imperialism is in no form a doctrine of chauvinism against the people of the United States, because imperialism is an economic problem. Our anti-imperialist resistance supposes as the "first step" the political and economic unification of Latin America, and this union will bring us to the end of feudalism by progressive nationalization and cooperativist organization of agricultural production and of other types of wealth and the creation of a new type of state—the anti-imperialist and democratic state of the four powers: legislative, executive, judicial, and economic—based on economic and functional democracy. . . .

The Aprista State

The state proposed by APRA should be, first of all, a state of economic defense that is in opposition to the capitalist system, which generates imperialism—a distinct and special system that results in the abolition of the old oppressive regime. But the new state cannot be capitalist or bourgeois along the lines of France, England, or the United States (countries where capitalism has its origin and its base), nor can it be a feudal state. It is described as the "anti-imperialist state" because it should organize a new economic system, scientifically planned under the form of state capitalism—different from that attempted in Europe during the war, although aimed at directing the national economy and progressively bringing the production and circulation of wealth under state control. In my book of 1928, written more than four years before the election of Franklin D. Roosevelt as President of the United States, I could not use the North American New Deal as an example of that state control of the economy, but there was a clear reference to it as "cases of partial state control of the economy," as in Argentina with petroleum and in Uruguay with the reforms (so little studied in the other countries of Indo-America) introduced by the Colorado Party and its famous statesman Jose Batlle Ordónez. The new state, which would not be based on one class, but would be democratic and representative, involving the three major classes of our country—the peasant, the worker, and the middle class—would efficiently channel and coordinate the effort of the three classes represented in it, and would be the cornerstone of Indo-American unity and the effective emancipation of our peoples. . . .

Nationalization

The "progressive nationalization of wealth" can mean ownership, shared ownership, or control and supervision by the state (according to the situation) of certain sources of wealth—in particular, those which, since they are possessed by foreign businesses, end up in the hands of the governments of those nations of which the owners of the enterprises are citizens. *Aprista* nationalization is inclined to state control through development corporations, in accord with the mechanism of the democratic state of the four powers, and to the stimulation of agricultural and industrial co-operatives, but with respect and guarantees for private property, as in Mexico.

The program does not claim that nationalization without anything more is enough, since we place much emphasis on the scientific magnitude of the problem and the immediate necessity of studying it profoundly in order not to incur the very grave responsibility for having adopted under pressure a nominal and artificial nationalization that would lead to the failure of the business and the loss of the reform itself. In addition—and this ought to be clarified without equivocation—it is necessary to leave a wide field for private initiative, both national and foreign, in its constructive action to promote the ending of feudalism, and the industrialization which is indispensable for the progress of our people. There is a simultaneous, twofold task, to activate and to accelerate the evolution of the backward regions of our economy.

What, then, are those backward regions of the Indo-American economy that need to be activated and transformed in a new type of progress? I have said it already: They are fundamentally our feudal and semipatriarchal systems of primitive production; the reality and the spirit of the *latifundio*, which is still predominant in Indo-America. They are the feudal system that gives us the class of great semibarbarous lords of the lands and mines, slave-holders, masters of the country, and holders of power. They are the allies of imperialism who day by day become its agents and its subordinates. . . .

Relations with the United States

And this essential postulate (essential because on it *Aprismo* bases all its program of the relations between imperialist capital and our countries which require it) is expressed also in the concrete and repeated sentence which is the key to our conception of the problem of imperialism as an economic phenomenon: "The United States is as necessary for us as we are for her." On the basis of this premise, whose reiteration is always timely, the idea and program of the *Apristas* becomes more attainable.

But today, when the doctrine of the Good Neighbor Policy has begun to bear fruit with the detachment of political imperialism from economic imperialism, when North American capitalist investment in Indo-America has lost the unconditional protection of Washington, it is more feasible to demonstrate that imperialism, as the first and necessary stage of capitalism in the underdeveloped countries, has a constructive economic function and fulfills a historic mission of progress with respect to the systems of production which preceded it. Still more, it has also been possible for it to become evident that imperialism, freed from the patronage of the Department of State, could and can meet with the states of Indo-America in conditions of relative equality, and thus negotiate with them, and that this negotiation would bring mutual benefits, because it is based on a principle specifically established beforehand—that foreign capital which seeks areas of investment in our country is driven by an economic necessity as pressing as that which requires us to receive it. By such a reciprocity of interest, it is possible for our states to control investment by a planned and coordinated economy and through appropriate legislation, which guarantees just security to foreign capital. All this depends on us and not on the United States. . . .

Intervention

What is important is to begin by distinguishing good and licit intervention from bad and illicit intervention. . . . Collective intervention can be justified when it is a matter of defending the very existence of a democratic regime based on popular sovereignty —without which the state lacks the institutions of national sovereignty since the government cannot show the real mandate of the people when it has usurped it. It is this case of flagrant usurpation, the most frequent and demoralizing type of attack against democracy in our continent, which should bring about a collective intervention which is fully permissible. Nevertheless, the restrictive propositions of the Inter-American Treaty of Reciprocal Assistance of 1947, of the Charter of the Organization of American States, and of the Pact of Bogotá of 1948 refer exclusively to "external aggression," whether by force or not, of one state against another which can endanger the peace of America from within our hemisphere or outside it, and this is where the weakness of the so-called Inter-American system is evident, the principal objective of which is "to maintain the peace and security of the continent" and not to protect the integrity and security of the democratic order based on pure respect for human and civil rights. For, if indeed it is announced in the Charter of the Organization of American States that "the solidarity of the American states and the high purposes with which it is pursued require the political organization of these states on the basis of the effective exercise of representative democracy," and if they proclaim "the fundamental rights of the human person" and point out what this means for well-being, for work and culture, without any distinctions of any kind, all this is only so much poetry, as beautiful as it is elusive, in the majority of our republics. No democratic principles can be valid and lasting when the fulfillment and implementation of those precepts is confined to governments whose democratic values can be trampled underfoot by any general seizing power and supplanting popular sovereignty with the bayonet.

28. General Juan Velasco

General Juan Velasco, President of Peru, was born in 1910 in Piura, Peru. He joined the army at eighteen, and rose to the post of commander of the Peruvian army and chairman of the Joint Chiefs of Staff at the time of the military coup that removed Fernando Belaúnde Terry from the presidency of Peru in October, 1968. The reason given for the coup was the agreement reached by Belaúnde with the International Petroleum Company concerning the disputed oil fields of La Brea and Pariñas. However the military men were also fearful that the 1969 presidential election would bring to power their archenemy, the Aprista party, led by Haya de la Torre. Haya de la Torre's election had been prevented by a military coup once before, in 1962, but in the face of strong U.S. pressure, the military had agreed to a new election a year later and this had been won by Belaúnde. In 1968, however, the military leaders had no intention of returning power to the civilians, but instead embarked on a course of radical nationalism that departed from the usual conservative pattern of Latin American military men in power. First, the International Petroleum Company was nationalized without compensation (IPC was presented with a bill for "illegal enrichment" over the years). Then, an agrarian reform decree was issued that was far more stringent than the Belaúnde reform of 1965. Banks were nationalized, foreign exchange was strictly controlled, and foreign mining companies were compelled to accelerate their programs or give up their concessions. In 1970, an Industrial Law was adopted which gave workers a share in management, profits, and ownership of the factories, and limited the participation of foreign capital in Peruvian companies.

In its appeal to the Peruvian past, in its pressure for rapid industrialization, in its insistence on ending "dependence" and asserting national control over Peru's resources, and in its attempt to develop a more humane society that is neither capitalist nor Communist, the thinking expressed in the speeches of General Velasco draws on many of the themes that appear elsewhere in this volume.

THE DAY OF THE INDIAN *

Today, the Day of the Indian, the Day of the Peasant, the
Revolutionary Government is making the best of all tributes to
him by giving the whole nation a law which will end forever an
unjust social order. . . . Beginning with this glorious 24th of June,
the peasant in Peru will truly be a free citizen whose right to the
fruit of his labor is finally recognized by his country. . . . Today
Peru has a government determined to achieve the development
of the country by the final destruction of ancient economic and
social structures that have no validity in our epoch. The basic
reforms for which so many of our compatriots have struggled are
now under way. And among them the highest priority must be
given to the reform of the agrarian structure of the country. And
so, faithful to our mission to the country and to history, and to
the explicit goals of the Revolution, the government of the armed
forces today is adopting an agrarian reform law that will mark
the beginning of the true liberation of the Peruvian peasant. . . .

The law is aimed at the destruction of the systems of the
latifundio and *minifundio*† in the Peruvian countryside, replacing
them with a just system of land tenure that will make possible
the spread of small and intermediate landholding in the whole
country. . . . It establishes measures to assure that large landholdings are not fragmented as units of production. It is the system of
landholding that is affected by the law, not the unit of agricultural
or cattle production. Therefore, in the case of agro-industrial
enterprises, the law envisages the establishment of cooperatives
by their agricultural workers but guarantees the functioning of
the new enterprise as a single entity. In this sense, the law considers the land and the plants on it as a single productive unit
subject to the agrarian reform. The industrial plant for the primary processing of the products of the countryside is indissolubly
linked to the land. Therefore, it is impossible to affect one and
leave the other untouched. Thus, just as in the case of petroleum,
where the state expropriated the entire complex including both

* Translated by the editor from *Oiga* (Lima), June 27, 1969.

† *Latifundio* is the term used for an excessively large tract of agricultural
land; *minifundio* for one that is too small to support a peasant and his
family.—ED.

the wells and the refinery as well as all installations and services, so the agrarian reform must necessarily affect the entire business. . . .

A central principle of the law is the emphasis it puts on the reorientation of capital resources toward industry as part of the national effort to put Peru in an advantageous position facing the challenge of the economic integration of Latin America. The new responsibilities that result from the policy of regional and subregional integration demand a vigorous industrial effort and the support of the state for a dynamic and guaranteed policy of industrialization of the internal sector of our economy. Hence, this law also encourages Peruvian industry, the future of which depends on the creation of an expanding internal market of high consumption supported constructively by the state, conscious of the inevitable industrial destiny of our country. From this point of view, it is very important that those who hold capital in this country clearly understand the significance of the agrarian reform law as a way to stimulate the process of industrialization of the country. . . . For this purpose, the agrarian reform law aids in stimulating the dynamism of the industrial sector by reorienting resources toward the promotion of national industry.* . . .

Answering the clamor for justice and the rights of the neediest, the agrarian reform law supports the great mass of peasants who form the Indian communities, which from now on, abandoning an unacceptable racist term, will be called Peasant Communities. The hundreds of thousands of men of the country who belong to them will henceforth have the effective support of the state to receive the credits and technical aid that is indispensable to convert them into dynamic units of cooperative production. We believe that we will thus carry out a duty to make restitution to all those forgotten peasants of Peru who for centuries have suffered all kinds of exploitation and injustice. With this law, their true social redemption is beginning. Never more will they be defenseless victims of the boss's whip. Henceforth with the help of the state, they will share in the responsibility for their own development. Thus, after many centuries, the Peasant Communi-

* The 1969 law provided that bonds issued by the agrarian reform agency might be used to finance new industrial enterprises if they were matched by other capital. For the text of the law, see Paul E. Sigmund (ed.), *Models of Political Change in Latin America* (New York: Praeger Publishers, 1970), pp. 214–20.—Ed.

ties, the ancient *Ayllu*,* symbol of a millenial ideal of justice that was never totally destroyed, will be recognized again as dynamic elements of progress as they once were in the great civilization of our ancestors. . . .

It is not important that some are military men and others civilians. Our country is one and belongs to all of us. What is important is that we carry out the social and economic transformation of our country and make it a free, just, and sovereign nation. From this point of view, we must note the position of the men of the Church. In a recent declaration of the priests of Onis, the imperative urgency of a genuine agrarian reform in Peru was emphasized and it was stated that "in a Christian conception of man and the world the goods of the earth are intended for all men to permit them to realize their vocation and destiny." We are not alone. In the work of the agrarian reform, we will have at our side the peasants, the workers, the students, the immense majority of the intellectuals, priests, industrialists, and professionals of Peru. . . .

This is, I repeat, an historic day the importance of which will increase with the passage of the years. Today the Revolutionary Government feels that it has fulfilled a mission and a duty. Today, on the Day of the Peasant, we look to the citizenry with faith, pride, and hope; and we say to all of Peru that we owe to its people the inspiration of our actions and today we give it a law which will promote greatness and justice in its destiny.

To the man of the land we can now say in the immortal words of Tupac Amaru † "Peasant, the boss will no longer eat from your poverty!" Long live Peru!

* Ayllu was the Inca cooperative unit.—ED.

† Tupac Amaru was a Peruvian Indian who led an unsuccessful peasant revolt against the Spanish landholders in the late eighteenth century. The *Tupamaru* guerrilla movement in Uruguay also draws its inspiration from him.—ED.

THE SECOND ANNIVERSARY
OF THE REVOLUTION *

This is a memorable night. Here we are celebrating the unbreakable union of the people and the armed forces. And that union, an important new element in our history, absolutely guarantees the attainment of the objectives of the Revolution.

While we were separated, a sinister alliance of imperialism and plutocracy was able to prevail in Peru. Now that we are united forever, social justice and the greatness of our country are beginning to take root in the new Peru that we are building. The unity of the people and the armed forces is ending the domination of the oligarchy in Peru. Today, the people have gathered here in free and sovereign fashion to testify to their dedicated support to a Revolution which is their Revolution: to a Revolution which has never used the language of promises because it speaks the language of accomplishments.

The people are now certain that this is an authentic process of national transformation, which is profound and irreversible. The people now cannot be deceived. The reactionary oligarchy should realize that its rule over Peru is ended forever. The union of the people and the armed forces has made this Revolution an indestructible one. . . .

The reactionary newspapers have launched an intense campaign against the government of the armed forces.† What are those newspapers? Are they, as they say, "spokesmen for public opinion"? No. They are solely the property and instrument of the economic circles of the oligarchy that has been driven from power. They represent neither the interests nor the thought nor the desires of the Peruvian people. Who has given them the right to speak in the name of the country? Who has made them the spokesmen for the majority? Who can consider them the defenders of the workers, employees, professionals, and peasants? And who would claim that they are the defenders of Peru?

Those who give them orders to write against the Revolution

* Translated by the editor from a pamphlet published by the Peruvian Ministry of Foreign Affairs, (Lima), 1970. The speech was delivered on October 3, 1970.

† This speech was delivered shortly after the government expropriated *Expreso*, a frequent critic of its policies.—ED.

are the same ones who yesterday commanded them to write
against Peru and in favor of International Petroleum. . . . Those
who pose today as defenders of the workers are the very ones who
always were against the people. Those who call themselves defenders of liberty are the same ones who benefited from all the
dictatorships of the past. Those who today speak of the education
of the people are the same ones who never cared about the misery
and ignorance of millions of peasants. Those who cry for democracy today never did a thing for the little people so that democracy might have a real and valid meaning.

What do those people have to show for having governed the
country since its establishment as a republic? Whose historical
responsibility is it that Peru is an underdeveloped country with
millions of illiterates, of undernourished children, of men and
women condemned eternally to the most unjust poverty. The
oligarchy and its accomplices who governed our country are the
ones responsible for all the great problems and injustices and the
bitter misery of Peru. . . .

Even when some of the representatives of traditional dependent
capitalism declare that they agree on the necessity of making
fundamental changes in the economic and social structure of
Peru, in fact they oppose those changes because they affect their
privileges and interests. From the outset the armed forces declared publically their firm decision to undertake basic reforms,
not merely superficial ones—reforms that affected the traditional
system of economic power in Peru. From the outset, too, the
armed forces expressed their opposition to the economic systems
of capitalism and of Communism. No one then should be surprised that the concrete measures taken by the Revolutionary
Government are different from those of the dependent capitalism
that is responsible for our underdevelopment and our submission
to the imperialistic interests of the great powers. Just as no one
should be surprised that none of the measures of the Revolution
can in conscience be described as Communist-inspired. . . .

The economic order the Revolution is creating is favorable to
workers and to businessmen. Private property will not disappear,
but the exploitative system to which the workers were subjected
in the past will not continue. We are attempting to create a new
type of enterpirse in which the businessman and the worker
participate in the ownership and management of industrial concerns. This new and just economic system offers the businessman

all guarantees and inducements and assures the worker the respect for all his rights. . . .

Today, it is imperative to create the mechanisms and institutions that will make popular participation possible on a permanent and constructive basis. Our Revolution is not interested in the false popular participation defended by the traditional politicians of the old system.* What did the people receive that was permanent or real from the demonstrations in the streets and plazas and their applause for one or another leader full of words and promises but with nothing to show for the exercise of power? This is not the participation the Nationalist Revolution requires. Our Revolution, which has been able to develop its own solutions up to this point, will also solve this crucial problem without borrowing any recipes from anyone else. . . .

The Revolution faces a curious problem in that many of those who support it do so in the erroneous belief that it could be a kind of anteroom for a different revolutionary process, a transition to another type of revolution they consider "real." Perhaps for this reason they believe that they can use this Revolution for their own political purposes, which, however respectable they may be, are not ours. On this point we must repeat what we have declared many times. This is a nationalist and popular Revolution with a deeply humanistic and libertarian orientation. We are building a society that will be neither capitalist nor Communist. We are confronting the problems of Peru on the basis of an analysis of its reality. We are creating new solutions to the problems of our country. We do not need to look elsewhere for the approaches that are necessary for Peru. We are inspired by the history of our people and in constructing our future we seek to recover the imperishable values of the past and vindicate for the present everything that can consitute a real contribution to the new social order in our country.

Likewise we have always proclaimed our deeply Latin American orientation, conscious that the destiny of our continent is one. In this sense we have said that our Revolution represents an historical continuity with the struggles for independence. We must complete the task of those who struggled against foreign oppression one hundred and fifty years ago. Today we fight for

* A reference to the program of *cooperacion popular* sponsored by President Fernando Belaúnde Terry, before his overthrow in 1968.—Ed.

true social justice in Peru and for an authentic economic independence that we never had during the period of the Republic. . . .

This new and authentic Peruvian Revolution in scarcely two years has achieved great social and economic gains. Among them I would cite the following:

The International Petroleum Company no longer exists. The Revolution expelled it forever from Peru. Today the petroleum is ours. We have recovered our dignity and sovereignty.

The peasant has finally begun to own the land that he worked for generations in order to enrich the former masters of Peru. Water is no longer the possession of the powerful. The peasant has regained it.

The factory worker is no longer simply a salaried employee. Through the Industrial Law and the Law of the Industrial Community, the Revolution has given him access to the ownership, the profits, and the management of the companies—which, strengthened by the cooperation of capital and labor, will expand their production for the benefit of all.

The vast mineral resources of Peru will be developed in the future under the conditions prescribed by the new mining legislation, or they will revert to the state. A clear demonstration of this is the fact that the copper mine at Michiquillay has already reverted to the state and will be developed by us for the benefit of all Peruvians.

The marketing of minerals and fishmeal is now a responsibility of the state. This gives Peru a great capacity for external financing and prevents profits and foreign exchange from leaving the country for the benefit of foreign combinations.

We have reformed and strengthened the state bank and bought the Popular, International, and Continental Banks. Now Peru controls the principal sources of credit. The savings of all Peruvians will be put to the service of national development.

Exchange controls now prevent the indiscriminate flight abroad of the wealth that is generated in Peru.

In order to guarantee human rights and dignity and the rule of justice, the Revolution has issued two important legal decrees: the Statute of Freedom of the Press, and the law that reorganizes the judiciary.

The Law of Forced Expropriation of land around urban areas prevents speculation and helps to solve the acute housing problem. . . .

In the international field, our thesis on maritime sovereignty is strongly defended by the Revolutionary Government, gaining the support of many nations of the world in the latest international confrontations.* . . .

Before the statue of the heroic and glorious Tupac Amaru, we promise to be worthy of the new hopes for Peru and the historic meaning of this Revolution—of this Revolution that has a responsibility to achieve social justice and win our Second Independence. To Peru, to its Glory and its People: Long Live the Revolution!

THE INDUSTRIAL LAW †

The alternatives, capitalism or Communism, represent in our judgment a false dilemma. The two great basic problems of our country (underdevelopment and imperialism) developed under the aegis of capitalism and it would therefore be extremely illogical to try to solve them while maintaining the system that produced them. Therefore, this Revolution describes itself as noncapitalist in the sense that the socio-economic order it promotes will not be capitalist. Hence, we consider capitalism as an opposing system.

This in no way means that we accept the Communist alternative. After many years of application in other countries, the concrete reality of Communism as a political, economic, and social system is that it has produced societies that are totalitarian and bureaucratized, entirely incapable of guaranteeing the free development of man in all his dimensions. In the pitiless light of historical experience, intolerance, totalitarianism, and bureaucratization appear as structural faults of Communist societies and not merely nonessential distortions. Therefore, those societies cannot constitute a model for our Revolution. And hence, we consider Communism as an opposing system. . . .

* The Peruvian government claims sovereignty over 200 miles of territorial waters.—Ed.

† Translated by the editor from *Expreso* (Lima), November 16, 1970, (address delivered to the Annual Conference of Businessmen [CADE], in Lima, November 15, 1970).

Seeing that we attack both capitalism and Communism, some have described our movement as socialist, forgetting that due to the enormous variety of meanings that term has acquired, it is no longer capable of expressing fundamental differences in concept and in concrete political practice. In fact, the term "socialist" covers the most varied theoretical formulations and political and social realities in the world today, and this has made any real significance for the word nebulous, since it does not describe a concrete political position except in the most general sense. Others describe us as following a policy of "third world" eclecticism—which adds very little to the understanding of the Peruvian process. Still others place us at some indefinite point in the wide spectrum that goes from some of the traditional political movements in Peru to the formulas of the postwar European Social Democrats or Christian Democrats.

All these analyses contain two fundamental errors. In the first place they attempt to define the Peruvian Revolution not on its own basis but on the basis of external models that vary in accordance with the political sympathies of each observer. And in the second place, they indicate an incapacity to recognize the simple fact that this revolutionary process is an entirely new phenomenon. . . .

We want a social order based on a social morality of solidarity, capable of overcoming the deeply egoistic orientation of individualism but without allowing the concrete being, man, to disappear under the weight of collectivities that coldly manipulate the state bureaucracy of an alienating and dehumanizing system. We are revolutionary humanists and therefore we reject the position of those who, in the name of humanity, despise and submerge man. We wish to vindicate man, not in the sense of exalting an individualism that is socially and ethically sterile but as a member and essential part of a society that is humanized in a combination of values that cannot be those which serve to support capitalism and Communism. In summary, our Revolution aims at a society of solidarity, with full participation, authentic liberty, and social justice, in which the community works for man and for itself and not for the state or for privileged or powerful groups. . . .

We have always been aware of the necessity of promoting the industrialization of Peru at an accelerated rate. In February, 1969, I said that industrial stagnation would make "real economic independence impossible" and I insisted on the need to avoid "a pseudo-industry dependent on foreigners," at the same time that I referred to the industrialists as "the first lines of defense in the war against underdevelopment." . . .

A year ago I maintained that we desired from the industrialists and businessmen of the nation "a vigorous, authentically Peruvian industry not subject to foreign domination or control, capable of satisfying the demands of an expanding internal market and of competing successfully with the industries of other lands. We are disposed to support a protectionist policy that is efficient and genuine, but we believe that it is harmful to the country and to the industry to follow a false policy of protectionism that leads only to stagnation in an industry characterized by high costs, low quality, and excessively rapid and inflated profits." . . .

I want to declare emphatically that there will be no compulsory cooperatives established in small industries, workshops, and enterprises in general. The fact that the Revolutionary Government stimulates cooperatives in all their forms does not mean that we are thinking of imposing it as the sole model of economic organization in the country. Indeed, before today, we have maintained that the government favors a mixed economy within which the state will be a dynamic promotor of development and will stimulate cooperative and participatory forms of industrial and economic organization at the same time that it guarantees the autonomous development of private enterprise in the country. . . . The basic assertion of the Revolution consists of the belief that the apparently irreducible opposition of capital and labor should and must be overcome if we really wish to build an economy equidistant from the schemes of capitalism and Communism. . . . The Revolutionary Government considers that, in the last analysis, the ultimate source of wealth is labor and that, concretely, the economic surplus generated in the process of production should go jointly to the two factors of production. From this point of view, the wage or salary represents not only a payment for a service, a recognition of the right of the working man to the satisfaction of his needs, but also payment for labor as an essential factor of production. In this way, the participation of labor in the wealth the productive process generates should necessarily be a way to provide access not only to immediate additional income but, more fundamentally, to a patrimony capable of producing additional wealth of a permanent character. For this reason, the revolutionary laws in the industrial sector establish the participation of labor in the profits, the management, and the ownership of enterprises. . . .

It should be pointed out that [under the Industrial Law] the workers will not accede to the ownership of 50 per cent of the company as it exists at the time of the establishment of the Industrial Community but as it exists at the end of many years after the annual investment of 15 per cent of the profits before the payment of taxes. When this happens, obviously the company will considerably increase its capital, its plant, and its market. It is possible that at that time it will be for all practical purposes a new company created with the help of the labor and capital of the workers and management. What this means is that no one is taking anything away from anyone but more and more Peruvians will participate in the creation and enjoyment of wealth that is recognized as socially produced. . . .

The Revolutionary Government will respect the interests of the small, medium, and large businesses that respond to the social character of the Revolution. But remember that its historic mission is to the Peruvian nation and that to serve that nation it will never depart from its purpose of carrying out the great changes that are required and that are the essence of the Revolution. . . . The country awaits from you a prompt and constructive response. It cannot be otherwise than an immediate and massive mobilization of the private sector of the economy to promote the industrial development of the country at this stage of the Revolution. You owe it to Peru and to yourselves—and to the generations to come, which will receive the legacy of a country that has realized a high and lasting ideal of justice.

29. José Figueres

José Figueres, current President of Costa Rica, was born in 1906. He was educated at the Universities of Costa Rica and Mexico and at the Massachusetts Institute of Technology. He lived as a coffee planter in Costa Rica until political events drove him into exile in

Mexico in 1942. In 1948, he led a revolution against a corrupt government which had refused to accede to the victory of an opposition candidate. In 1948–49, he served as chief of the revolutionary junta which ruled the country while a democratic constitution was being framed. In 1953, he was elected President, serving until 1958. He has been active in hemispheric affairs, and in 1970 he was once again elected to the Costa Rican presidency.

Figueres identifies himself and his party with the ideology of social democracy. Like the other populist parties of Latin America (e.g., Acción Democrática in Venezuela, APRA in Peru), his Partido de Liberación Nacional (PLN) has been described as socialist; as the selection below indicates, however, Figueres favors a mixed economy combining features of both socialism and capitalism. Figueres is perhaps more ready than other populista leaders in Latin America to view the post–New Deal American economy as a model of this kind of mixture, although he goes further than the Americans in supporting the creation of independent national authorities in such fields as electricity, housing, and land reform.

In the second selection, Figueres analyzes Latin American economic problems and political ideologies in relation to the Alliance for Progress. Christian Democracy is significantly absent from his list of Latin American ideologies, perhaps because its political and economic programs are very similar to those attributed by Figueres to social democracy. However, Christian Democracy differs from populismo in that it is much more directly influenced by the political and economic thinking of European Catholic thinkers and the papal social encyclicals.

SOCIALISM AND CAPITALISM*

In this epoch of Cold War with Soviet Russia, it is fashionable in the United States, among uninformed people, to connect the word "socialism" with undemocratic political doctrines.

On the other hand, in England, the Scandinavian countries, and other places, socialist parties take an active part in present-day politics, enjoying the prestige of being considered democratic.

* From Cartas a un Ciudadano (San José: Imprenta Nacional, 1956); translated by the editor and Ignatius Di Cola.

412   LATIN AMERICA

On its part, the term "capitalism" has a bad reputation in Latin America, where it is frequently considered a synonym for "colonialism" or "imperialism," and in Europe, where it is frequently the equivalent of a "reactionary" attitude, of exploitation of workers.

In this letter, which I address to the common citizen of Costa Rica, I intend to use these words in their original meaning, as terms for two different *economic* systems, which should not be tied to the various *political* systems. . . .

Socialism, as an economic doctrine, has nothing to do with political "totalitarianism," that is to say, with despotism. And the theoretical capitalistic system, of absolute freedom of enterprise, should not be connected with colonial exploitation of one people by another. . . .

As you know, socialism is an economic system inspired by the ideal that "all things belong to all." Of course, it does not refer to things for *personal* use, such as clothing, housing, toothbrushes, but solely to productive properties, such as real estate, factories, buildings, railroads, etc. Socialism recommends that all the means of production belong to the entire nation, and that the state administer them. . . .

For many centuries many well-intentioned thinkers have held that if the system of private property is replaced by public ownership of the means of production, social injustice and misery will cease.

Socialism, basically a noble and generous idea, has much in common with the Christian spirit—that there should be no rich or poor, that we should hold everything in common as brothers in an ideal family. The Mexican Revolution, which was the precursor of all the great revolutions of the twentieth century, put forward one of the best expressions of socialism of all time: "No one has a right to excess when there are those who lack the necessities."

The ideal society will come about, says classical socialism, simply by changing the property system. In our time, socialists who have kept up with the advances in the study of economics are aware that their predecessors overemphasized the role of the property system in producing abundance and prosperity for all. There are other factors, such as productivity, that is, the returns to labor and capital, which were not studied earlier. Nevertheless the old polemic is now taking on a dramatic character. Today a vigorous world movement, Communism, is at its height. It tries to change the property system by force and violence, sacrificing the great human achievements of liberty, respect for personal dignity, morality, and the other spiritual values of our civilization. . . .

Capitalism, in the usual meaning of the word, is an economic system of private ownership of land, industry, and other means of production, which permits everyone to produce what he likes, without any planning or aid, to buy and sell as he wishes, to pay the lowest wages that he can, and to obtain the most advantageous prices which the market will bear, without any sense of responsibility toward his fellow creatures.

Against this economic irresponsibility, the results of which are low production in general and an unjust accumulation for a few, there appeared the idea of socialism, proposing a society diametrically opposed to capitalism.

In practice, neither of the two systems has prevailed in any nation in absolute form, least of all today. The nations that call themselves socialistic have had to leave in private hands at least petty trade, which is difficult to administer through a central organization, and a great part of the land, because the habit of property is deeply ingrained among all the peasants of the world. On the other hand, the great so-called capitalistic nations, and principally the United States, have organized their industry and commerce more in the form of business firms, the capital of which belongs to the public which buys "stocks," or partial titles to property. . . .

The number of stockholders is increasing, so that property is more diffused. At present the firms themselves facilitate the purchase of stocks by their workers. This is a new form of socialization, stimulated precisely by the people who most fear the word "socialism."

There also exist, in those nations, many thousands of small and medium-size businesses, and private farms, and there is a determination to maintain them. However, the state imposes upon them numerous regulations: minimum wages, maximum work day, fixed prices, compulsory insurance, an income tax, etc. The state determines the rates, the scope of operation, the schedules, etc., for transportation and other public service enterprises. With all of this "interference," those businesses are at the service of the community more than at the service of their owners. There is no such thing as "capitalism."

What has happened is that while people in the newspapers were discussing such words and phrases as "directed economy" and "free

enterprise," "inviolable property" and "social necessity," developments have taken, almost independently, the only possible path—
a combination of the two systems, capitalist and socialist, which
endeavors to combine the advantages of both and to minimize the
disadvantages of each. To this synthesis of the two historical trends
the name *mixed economy* is now given. . . .

The Movement of National Liberation has openly decided for a
mixed economy combining private property with state regulation,
individual business with public institutions, because it considers
this convenient for the country, because this is the system which
prevails in the democratic world, and because the majority of our
citizens prefer it although not all of them are able to express their
desires with precision. . . .

In order to orient a large number of enterprises, businesses, and
individual efforts of all types, without intervening in their administration or restricting freedom, the state in a mixed economy
makes use of the system of stimuli and correctives. . . .

When the modern state intervenes judiciously as a stabilizer in
a mixed economy, it forestalls disruptive tendencies, applies rem-
edies in time and with moderation and skill, and avoids much loss
and suffering. . . .

With more or less accuracy (since historic periods are not set off
by a precise line of demarcation), the system of stimuli and correctives has been indelibly associated with the Roosevelt revolution
in the United States. Likewise one can say that the Great Depression was the deathblow to the outdated economic system which we
call "liberal," or, in a more exaggerated fashion, "capitalist." At the
same time it produced the painful birth of a reformist ideology
which has led the United States to a prosperity which could never
have been foreseen.

From 1933 to today, the technique of orienting private enterprise through the organs of the state has been perfected very well
in North America. Not only were further depressions avoided after
World War II and Korea, but for the first time in history the
economy has continued to grow. The figures for the end of 1955
are spectacular.

At this moment in the history of the world, the mixed economy,
in common cause with the whole civilization of the West, is undergoing its greatest test. The Communist prophets announced half a
century ago that the great fluctuations in the capitalist system (depressions) would destroy the whole democratic system. God will-

ing, it is not too early to reply that democracy, by adopting state economic planning which respects freedom and stimulates initiative, has put an end to depressions.

And now what must be done next? Probably an international New Deal. The less developed countries have a right to benefit from the economic knowledge of today. The United States in its pivotal role in the world economy cannot afford the luxury of repeating the mistakes which almost destroyed its domestic economy and its democratic way of life. . . .

The mixed economy, with all its ingenious mechanisms of controls and compensations, does not fully satisfy the socialist mentality, which prefers a simpler formula, such as the fusion of all activities in a single great enterprise, the state. The mixed system gives the impression of being too complicated, insecure, and not very scientific.

Neither does this combination satisfy "liberal" or capitalist thought, which considers it artificial or not very "natural."

Nonetheless, if one takes a good look at it, the system of stimulations cannot be more scientific, nor more natural. What could be more proper than to observe *the natural inclinations*, the tendencies of events, and to place them at the service of man, by means of his intelligence? . . .

Every economic system, every political movement, every social order, has to be judged, in the final analysis, for its spiritual effect upon the men who adopt it; that is to say, for the *human type* which it tends to form, or at least to encourage.

The socialist ideal (which has never been fulfilled, except within small groups) tends to make men less egoistic, more generous, more responsible before society. How? Through an educational process: by making men see that they work in order to serve others, and not merely in order to carry on their own business; by convincing them that the productive effort of each person, his daily contribution to the great economic task, is in reality a *social function*.

In theory, in a completely "free" economy of pure individual initiative, where anyone can form whatever business he wants, or is empowered to form without the state's help or restraint, man must feel like the hunter who goes out to shoot the deer in uninhabited land, shooting big or small, male or female, all that he encounters during every season.

What we are saying is that a totally capitalistic society (which has never existed) would tend to produce a human type who is oblivious of his fellow man, selfish, greedy for goods or self-gratification, without any sense of social responsibility.

It is necessary to note, however, that the possession of goods, and the exercise of property, in a certain way enhances man and makes him more responsible, at least before himself and his family. Accordingly, the capitalist system can also take note of its beneficial effect on the spiritual order. The favorable effects of capitalism emerge plentifully in a mixed economy (such as Costa Rica's, for example), which not only respects property, but also encourages the development of many small farmers. . . .

All businesses and agricultural, industrial, or commercial enterprises, big or small, although they enjoy a large degree of autonomy which their "private" character gives them in accordance with the right of property, nonetheless are subject to a series of laws, controls, inducements, and corrective measures which confer upon them, in reality, a social function. . . .

If the principle that *economic activity is a social function* is adopted, . . . the laws of the nation, the government's orientation, and the public's education can all be directed toward the attainment of a more just and generous society, which will better be able to fulfill the aspirations of those who compose it.

POLITICAL AND ECONOMIC FORCES IN THE HEMISPHERE*

. . . What chance is there of the Alliance's [the Alliance for Progress] realizing its objectives?

To answer this question calls for an analysis of the political forces at work in Latin America. The political situation there is not analogous to that of the United States. Here, granted that many shades and factions exist within the spectrum of the two political parties, it may generally be said that the public mind is either of a conservative bent, anxious to keep things pretty much as they are, or of a liberal bent, desiring to push forward.

* Selections from "Unity and Solidarity in the Hemisphere," in William Manger (ed.), *The Two Americas* (New York: P. J. Kenedy, 1965); by permission of Georgetown University.

In Latin America the ideological picture cannot be thus dichoto-
mized. There are at least three distinct forces at work. There is, of
course, the conservative mind, and it is a brand of extreme conservatism with which most North Americans are not familiar. It is a
mind which wants no reform, fears all change, and wants to freeze
the social reality as presently structured. It has, in fact, managed
to immobilize it for a long time.

Opposed to this conservative mind, we have not one but two
distinct forces. One is, broadly speaking, the world Communist
movement. This certainly is a very important movement of our
time. It is active in Latin America and it does attract many followers. The other force is that of social democratic reform. It rallies
the support of those who, during 175 years of independence, have
been deeply influenced by the ideals of democratic government,
although they have generally been defeated in their efforts to
realize them. This movement seeks to achieve social justice within
the framework of Western-style democratic society. It wishes to
make government an instrument of social justice. Its aim is to
create a democratic welfare state, such as the United States and
every other successful Western democracy today, whether some
people like to admit it or not.

Which of these three forces is likely to prevail? There is little
room for doubt. The kind of conservatism familiar to Latin America has lived its time. It is a thing of the past. Its day is done. The
future in Latin America lies either with the triumph of the Communist world revolution or with the achievement of some form of
the democratic welfare state.

What should be done if we are to achieve social development
along democratic lines? I shall not here discuss what is at the moment being done, or go into the question of what are the immediate possibilities of realizing desired objectives. Instead, let me
simply call attention to the special magnitude of our problem.

It is not simply a matter of raising wages, although indeed in
some areas of the Latin American economy wages must be raised
and raised now. It is not simply a question of land reform in the
sense of a redistribution of land ownership, although this too needs
to be done.

The special nature of our problem is that these, and other
similar or related objectives of social justice, are indeed imperative;
but no less imperative is the need for capital formation. To concentrate social effort either upon the systematized formation of

capital or upon the widest possible distribution of the national income is one thing. It is quite another thing, and incomparably more difficult, to attempt both at the same time.

European çountries and the United States were able to build up capital and lay the foundation of their highly productive societies at a time when social pressures were much less than they are everywhere today. They were able, without much fear of provoking social revolution, to ignore the protests of the poor while they laid the foundations of their prosperity. They were permitted first to achieve the capital formation prerequisite to industrialization and then to turn their attention to the demands of social justice.

In Latin America we do not enjoy the luxury of alternatives. We are obliged to tackle both problems simultaneously. We have to concern ourselves with capital formation at the same time that we concern ourselves with the equitable distribution of national income. This calls for a great deal of wisdom on the part of government and a great deal of understanding on the part of the public and a great deal of effort by everybody. These are objectives not easily accomplished, nor soon. These are goals easier to recommend than achieve.

Another important objective for which we must strive in Latin America is the creation of a common market. Our countries are too small to support, each one severally, a structure of modern industry. A great effort has to be made to integrate our economies, to break down the barriers to commerce, and to foster interregional trade.

Headway is being made. In Central America a common market area is being developed with relative speed. Progress, although slow, is being made toward a free trade zone, including almost all the countries south of Mexico.

These measures are important; but here again we must not overestimate what they can do. By themselves they will not bring about a high production of goods and services and usher in the millennium in Latin America. Mexico and Brazil serve to remind us of this. Each of these two countries, in terms of population and area, is a far larger common market than anything being created in Central America. Yet the per capita income of both is lower than that of some of the Central American countries. This proves that a common market alone, without proper communications, transportation, and many other factors, will not create an economic miracle.

Another aspect of our problem is that Latin American countries must maintain extensive commercial relations with the industrialized world. They need to import many goods and services. Imports have to be paid for, and payment is becoming more and more difficult for Latin America as time goes on.

It is an elementary truth of economics that imports must be paid for by exports. The products which most Latin American countries can export are largely determined by the tropical latitudes in which they lie. These are the traditional products such as coffee, bananas, cocoa, and the like. Perhaps some of our countries will imitate the Japanese and begin to produce interesting gadgets with marketable value abroad; but the time is far off when we shall see them shipping Cadillacs to Detroit.

Now the entire trade relationship between countries which must rely upon selling the kind of products peculiar to Latin America and those which produce industrial goods is out of joint. The advance of technology is in fact forcing it more and more out of kilter and steadily widening the gap between the industrial and the nonindustrial societies. . . .

Will we ever have the mechanisms needed to stop the deepening of this gulf between the industrialized and the nonindustrialized world? Will we ever be able politically to subsidize exports from the industrial nations to the nonindustrial nations? Or to subsidize imports from the poor countries into the rich countries? Will we be able to establish the preferential treatment which, together with certain necessary measures of internal reform, will accelerate the development of the poorer countries? Will the politics of the advanced countries or the politics of the retarded countries, where the problems confront us on every side, prevent us from adopting these bold measures so badly needed in our time? Or will the world continue to be divided between developed and underdeveloped countries facing each other across an ever widening gap? These are difficult questions.

Perhaps nothing will be done and the world will move on to a new catastrophe, either war or another great depression. I do not know which is worse in terms of human suffering. My impression at the moment is that we are justly worried about war, but perhaps not sufficiently worried about the possibility of a world depression.

In some respects the world may be back in the 1920's, heading toward 1929. The markets of the world are not being developed enough to keep abreast of the growth of productivity in industrial countries. There are other serious symptoms, like the problem of balance of payments in the United States, which cause concern. . . .

We need a revolution. I hope it will be a revolution from the top, a revolution of enlightened people who think in terms of such conceptions as the Alliance for Progress, Point Four, the Marshall Plan. We have reached the point where mechanisms must be found to redistribute fairly the world income. This calls for a great conception. I do not know what that conception will be. I do not have the solutions to offer. I do not have the institutions in mind. I do know that they must be found. . . .

. . . As I examine Latin America, country by country, I see a very hard decade ahead. As a consequence of the economic situation, I anticipate setbacks for democracy. We have allowed the situation to deteriorate far too much. It will take a long time to remedy this.

What alternatives to democracy are there? There is dictatorship of the old-fashioned type and dictatorship of the new type, led by young officers, known as Nasserism. Can they bring about the successful transformation of our societies? I am not asking whether they can successfully maintain themselves in power. Almost anybody, given the proper means, can do this. I am asking whether either type of dictatorship, and both have their advocates, can accomplish a rapid development of Latin America in the direction of social justice and in an atmosphere benign to human values. Definitely not.

The military of Latin America may supply the power. Somebody else will have to supply the ideas. In some cases they will turn to the oligarchy for ideas. They have traditionally done so. They are still doing so. This would mean stagnation. In other cases, they will have recourse for ideas—as some are actually doing now although they would be the last to admit it—to the Communist intellectuals. For the Communists do have a plan and they do offer a solution, however ruthless the former and however destructive of spiritual values the latter may be. In this event the future would lie with the Communists.

Can the Communists solve the problems of the next decade, or the next two decades, more successfully than our weak democracies have been able to do? Some people think they can. Many intellectuals, especially in our Latin American universities, maintain that if we would adopt the Communist plan and employ Communist methods, supported by all the authority of a totalitarian state, we could rapidly develop the resources of our countries. I question this on several counts.

First, to carry out their plan, the Communists would have to antagonize the whole managerial class. They would, in fact, have to sacrifice or eliminate the whole owning or managerial class. They would have to improvise a new generation of managers and technicians. They would also inevitably eliminate a great part of the middle class. This would automatically result in a terrific reduction of the national income. This might have only a temporary effect, but meanwhile the people would be starving.

With all of our wants, we do have, relatively speaking, a great deal of administrative machinery, business talent, and enterprise in our Latin American economies. We are doing our best, within our democratic systems, to make use of them, to make use of whatever is valuable. We are not trying to destroy these assets. This is one of the great advantages democracy has over Communism in meeting our problems. Because Communism would be forced, by its very goals and methods, to destroy these assets, it would undoubtedly have to seek outside financial support far more than we do. It would even need to look abroad for food merely to survive.

Can any of the Communist powers supply this kind of aid in the amount needed? I think this is out of the question. From all appearances, supplying Cuba is enough of a burden for the Russian economy. Could they undertake to supply the needs of a single Latin American country the size of Brazil? I doubt it. I sometimes think that, if they could, they would have taken on the task before this.

Again, in assessing the chances of Communist success in developing Latin America, one must take into account the opposition of the United States. This opposition, whether one considers it good or bad, would make it too much of a risk.

What can be done today in the Western Hemisphere, or in the world for that matter, without some kind of coordination with the United States? And what can be done against the will of the United States in an area in which it feels, rightly or wrongly, that its own security is menaced?

Can democracy do the job of development? Can we meet this challenge democratically? No matter what our difficulties are, no matter what the shortcomings of the Alliance for Progress are, this is the system attuned to our way of thinking, the system which we have in our veins. This is the political conception which we share with the United States as common heirs of European culture. . . .

There is something supreme which has brought mankind so far along the path of development, that seems to move us more and more toward world integration under a broad political philosophy of democracy and a wide-embracing ethical system—Christianity or something similar, I hope. Looking back into the centuries and into the millennia and forward into the future, I cannot believe that mankind faces only two alternatives, either universal Communism or universal destruction that would make the earth as barren as the moon. No, I think the earth will go on and that it will be fertile and that people, better than many of us, will continue to enjoy its blessings.

The difficulties facing us are immense. We have to keep faith. We have to keep working, with faith in man, faith in mankind, faith in divine destiny. This alone can keep us going. This alone offers hope for the future.

30. Raúl Prebisch

Raúl Prebisch was born in Tucumán, Argentina, in 1901. He was a member of the faculty of economics at the University of Buenos Aires from 1925 until 1948. Beginning in 1925, he was also a member of the Argentine civil service, filling a variety of administrative and advisory posts. In 1935 he was put in charge of organizing the Central Bank of Argentina and he served as its Director General until he was dismissed by Juan Perón in 1943. Political difficulties with Perón caused him to leave Argentina in 1948 to work for the United Nations Economic Commission for Latin America (ECLA). In 1950, he became the Executive Secretary of ECLA, a position he held until 1962, when he was appointed Director General of the Latin American Institute for Economic and Social Planning. In 1963, he was appointed Secretary General of the United Nations Conference on Trade and Development; when the Conference established a permanent organization at Geneva, Prebisch became its Secretary General.

Although Prebisch is not a political leader, his economic writings have taken on an ideological quality and become a rallying point for those Latin Americans (and, since 1964, Africans and Asians) who demand greater concessions from the developed countries. Prebisch blames Latin America's economic difficulties on both domestic and international factors. Domestically, there is a lack of capital, excessive concentration of power in the hands of the wealthy, an inefficient system of land tenure, and inadequate domestic markets. Internationally, the terms of trade between the developed countries at the "center" and the underdeveloped countries at the "periphery" are increasingly disadvantageous to the latter, because over the long run material and agricultural prices tend to decline while those of manufactured goods remain stable or increase. The Prebisch solution is agrarian and tax reform, planning, and economic integration domestically, combined with international commodity price agreements and preferences for goods from underdeveloped countries. The Prebisch program has now been adopted by the UNCTAD organization and is frequently referred to in writings and speeches by Latin American leaders. (See, for example, the selections by Eduardo Frei and José Figueres.)

TOWARD A DYNAMIC DEVELOPMENT POLICY FOR LATIN AMERICA*

Structural Reforms to Clear the Way for Development

The ills besetting the Latin American economy are not determined by circumstantial or transient factors. They are an expression of the critical state of affairs in our time and of the incapacity of the economic system—owing to structural defects that it has been beyond our ability or our power to remedy—to achieve and maintain a rate of development consonant with the growth of the popu-

---

* Excerpts from a report presented at the meeting of the United Nations Economic Commission for Latin America, Mar del Plata, Argentina, May, 1963.

lation and with its demands for a speedy improvement in its standards.

The increase in the population is certainly phenomenal. At the beginning of the century, there were 63 million inhabitants in Latin America, and the annual rate of demographic growth was 1.8 per cent. Now we number 220 million, and we are multiplying at an annual rate of 2.9 per cent which shows signs of rising even higher.

On the basis of conjectural data, it may be estimated that about half the existing population has a tiny average personal income of $120 a year. And this vast social aggregate accounts for only about one-fifth of total personal consumption in Latin America, showing the highest coefficients of undernourishment, poor clothing, and worse housing, as well as of disease and illiteracy; and, at the same time, the highest rates of reproduction.

It is here that the development effort must be primarily concentrated. The notion, which dies hard, that development takes place spontaneously, without a rational and deliberate effort to achieve it, has proved to be an illusion, both in Latin America and in the other peripheral regions of the world. For a century now our economies have been linked to the international economy, and 50 per cent of the population is still stagnating in pre-capitalist conditions which are incompatible with its growing economic and social aspirations.

Even so, average per capita income in Latin America is appreciably higher than in other peripheral regions, and thus affords an advantageous starting point for the realization of what is no longer a utopian dream: the eradication of poverty and its inherent evils, by virtue of the tremendous potential of contemporary technology and the possibility of assimilating it much more quickly than was the case with the capitalistic evolution of the more advanced countries. However, this rapid penetration of technique demands and brings with it radical changes: changes both in the pattern of production and in the structure of the economy which could not be effectively brought about without a basic reform of the social structure.

The social structure prevalent in Latin America constitutes a serious obstacle to technical progress and, consequently, to economic and social development. The principal manifestations of this fact are three in number:

1. The structure in question considerably hampers social mobility,

that is, the emergence and rise of the dynamic elements in society, men of drive and initiative, capable of taking risks and responsibilities both in technical and economic matters and in the other aspects of community life.

2. The social structure is largely characterized by a situation of privilege in the distribution of wealth and therefore of income; privilege weakens or destroys the incentive to economic activity, to the detriment of the efficient utilization of human resources, land, and machinery.

3. This state of privilege in regard to distribution is not reflected in a rapid rate of net capital formation, but in extravagant patterns of consumption in the upper strata of society, in contrast with the unsatisfactory living conditions of the broad masses of the population.

In these days of zeal for planning there is a great deal of talk about the supreme importance of the role of private enterprise in Latin America and the need to keep it intact. But what is meant by this, in the last analysis? Is it suggested that the present system, under which the energies of individual initiative are cramped by social stratification and privilege, should be kept intact? Or is the way to be cleared for this initiative by the structural reforms referred to, so that the system may acquire the full dynamic force it lacks at present?

Capital Formation and Income Distribution

The test of a system's dynamic strength lies in its ability to accelerate the rate of development and progressively improve the distribution of income. If the annual rate of growth of average per capita income could be raised from the very low figure of 1 per cent registered of late to a minimum of 3 per cent in Latin America as a whole, a rational redistribution policy would enable the personal income of the underprivileged half of the population to be doubled in seventeen years, and the lot of the middle-income groups also to be improved, although at a less rapid rate.

This is where the first step must be taken toward reform of the social structure, since such a rate of growth is not feasible without substantial restriction of the consumption of the higher-income brackets.

The social contrast is striking indeed. While 50 per cent of the population accounts for approximately two-tenths of total personal consumption, at the other end of the scale of distribution 5 per cent of the inhabitants of the region enjoy nearly three-tenths of that total, according to the conjectural estimates referred to above. A policy of austerity mainly affecting this latter social group, and supplemented by the contribution of international resources, would permit an increase in net capital formation and the attainment of the above-mentioned growth target for per capita income, while at the same time redistribution policy would see to it that the income increment thus obtained was passed on to the lower strata of the social aggregate.

Here is essentially what redistribution policy means. It is not a matter of taking income away from the upper minority and simply and solely distributing it among the broad masses of the population, for with per capita personal income in Latin America as a whole barely amounting to $370, the benefits of such a redistribution would not stretch very far. But if, on the other hand, restrictions on the consumption of the privileged groups were reflected in a steady increase in net capital formation, the standard of living of the bulk of the population would rise progressively faster.

Technology has made this dynamic concept of redistribution viable, for the first time in history, for without the immense potential it places at the disposal of developing countries, the effects of the redistribution operation would be very limited in their scope. Thus, the problems of capital formation and income distribution assume very different forms from those they took during the capitalistic evolution of the more advanced countries.

At that time it was capital formation that came first, and the gradual redistribution of income followed. Now, on the other hand, both these requirements present themselves—as they are bound to do—simultaneously, under the increasing political and trade-union pressure exerted by the lower income groups.

The only available means of meeting them is by directly combating one of the anomalies that most affect the development of Latin America, namely, the marked failure of capital formation to reach the levels demanded by contemporary technology, as against the extravagant pattern of consumption of the high-income groups.

Among these upper strata (5 per cent of the population), which account for about three-tenths of Latin America's total consumption, average consumption per household is fifteen times greater than that of the lower strata (50 per cent of the population). If this ratio were reduced 11:1, by the restriction of consumption in favor of increased investment, the annual rate of growth of per capita income could rise from 1 per cent to 3 per cent. And if compression of consumption brought the ratio down to 9:1, the rate of growth might reach 4 per cent or even more, according to the political feasibility of this operation and the capacity of each country to put it into effect.

International Cooperation and the Structure of Trade

This capacity might be seriously handicapped by the external bottleneck in development, which, in conjunction with the limitations of domestic production of capital goods, would mean that not all the additional saving obtained could be invested in such goods. Hence the vital need for international resources, until the structural reforms advocated here enable full advantage to be taken of the increase in savings.

The contribution to be made by international resources is thus of a temporary nature. It would cease to be necessary once the reforms referred to had borne the full crop of results to be expected of them. This is not solely a Latin American concern, since it is also essential to work for the elimination of the external bottleneck by remodeling the existing structure of international trade.

The countries in which industrialization advances most rapidly tend to be affected more and more by the bottleneck in question. Their difficulties do not originate solely in the social structure, but also in the type of trade structure which characterized the epoch of externally geared development that preceded the world depression of the 1930's. Here again, as in other aspects of our development problems, a whole series of out-of-date ideas survives. It is true that the peripheral industrialization of the regions has at last been accepted as an indispensable requisite for economic development. But what is still perpetuated is the anachronistic trade pattern inherent in the peculiar concept of the international division of labor which was prevalent up to a short time ago—the trading of primary commodities against manufactured goods. This is the framework within which the industrialization of our countries has been taking place. And the obstacle to economic development that it represents is now beginning to loom larger at every turn, for whereas the upward trend of demand for the manufactured goods we import is very sharp, primary exports are expanding relatively slowly, largely for reasons over which the Latin American coun-

tries have no control. Thus there is a latent tendency toward disequilibrium which is aggravated as economic development gains
speed.

This is a new phenomenon not experienced by the more advanced countries in the past. Hence it is that its significance is only
now beginning to be understood and recognition accorded to the
vital need to encourage the industrial exports of the peripheral
countries, especially those which have completed the first stage of
the industrialization process.

This encouragement of industrial exports, in addition to exports
of primary commodities, cannot be achieved within the narrow
bounds of the existing markets. It is essential to alter the geographical structure of trade, as well as its composition by products.

Latin America's exports are of course affected by the universal
slowness of the growth of demand for primary commodities, in
contrast with the buoyancy of demand for manufactured goods as
per capita income rises. But this circumstance is combined with
other factors of considerable importance. In the first place, the
moderate rate of economic development of the United States, together with its import restrictions, has exerted an adverse influence
on Latin America's export trade. And, secondly, the protection
and discrimination practiced by the European Common Market
prevent us from taking full advantage of the steady expansion of
demand for primary commodities in the vast economic area it
represents.

Without prejudice to measures aimed at eliminating or reducing
these barriers to trade, it is a matter of urgent necessity to explore
with the utmost diligence the possibilities for trade with other regions of the world, especially those—the socialist economies, for
example—which show a high rate of development.

While it is true that basically the solution of such problems depends upon the great industrial countries and the degree to which
their trade policy favors liberalization, it is no less certain that the
Latin American countries too must put forth a tremendous effort
in the same direction. In this sense, the formation of a common
market is an undertaking that brooks no delay. Its importance has
been realized by the Central American countries, whose determination to establish such a market has been bold and resolute. The
problem of the Latin American Free Trade Association is more
difficult, for the very reason that the development of industrialization in watertight compartments has created vested interests and

prejudices which oppose reciprocal trade without taking account of the serious effects of such an attitude on economic development. This is not a merely technical matter, it is a question of important policy decisions which must follow up the Montevideo Treaty.* The technical groundwork for these decisions is basically complete; all that remains to be done is to study and select the best ways of putting them into practice.

The Closed Type of Development in Latin America

The external bottleneck in development is not due solely to the slow upward trend of exports of primary commodities as against the rapid expansion of industrial imports from the great centers, or to the low level of inter-Latin American trade; it has also largely been determined, in recent years, by the deterioration of the terms of trade and its serious effects on the purchasing power of exports.† The action of all these factors in combination reduced the per capita value of Latin America's exports from $58 in 1930 to $39 in 1960 (at 1950 prices).

The recent decline in the terms of trade is yet another indication of the peripheral countries' congenital incapacity to retain the whole of the benefits accruing from their technical progress. It is not much of a consolation to reflect that when, in the future, the Latin American countries reach more advanced stages of development and their industrialization process is complete, this state of affairs will one day be ended. This is hardly consoling, since it will all take a long time, and in the meanwhile the deterioration of the terms of trade is aggravating the external bottleneck and exerting a marked depressive influence on domestic capacity for capital formation, to the detriment of development itself.

From a different angle, the other notion that still survives in some circles, to the effect that the external bottleneck and the disequilibria in international accounts in which it is reflected are mere matters of monetary operation, has had deplorable consequences, since its practical application—besides adversely affecting economic development—has diverted attention from the basic solutions which this structural phenomenon demands.

This is a point of considerable importance for Latin America, for

* The treaty signed in February, 1960, by seven Latin American countries, establishing the Latin American Free Trade Association.—Ed.

† For Prebisch's argument on the terms of trade, see the next selection.—Ed.

unless such solutions are resolutely sought, our countries will be swept by the force of circumstances toward an increasingly closed type of development, and a steady contraction of their share of trade with the rest of the world, which will add further difficulties to those inherent in this process. In default of sufficient international cooperation in overcoming these difficulties, both in the field of trade and in that of financing, all kinds of authoritarian measures might supervene, with grave consequences for the progressive development of democracy in Latin America.

Internal Bottlenecks

The intensification of development is not simply a question of increasing net capital formation. While this is necessary it is by no means sufficient, since development may be hampered by a variety of factors. Those of an external kind have already been mentioned, but there are also internal bottlenecks that circumscribe or hamper the expansive force of net capital formation.

Furthermore, there is usually a wide margin for the immediate growth of production in our countries because of idle capacity in a number of branches. But the factors in question either rule out this possibility or bring inflationary pressures of a nonmonetary kind in their train if a policy directed toward the full utilization of idle capacity is put into force.

There is no doubt that the most stubborn bottleneck in the whole of Latin America's development process is generally to be found in agricultural production. Several factors are jointly responsible for this: the system of land tenure, which makes it difficult for modern techniques to be assimilated; inadequate state aid in the work of adapting and diffusing these techniques; and the unsatisfactory investment situation. However thoroughly these problems are coped with, unless farmers are given proper incentives, efforts to accelerate development are liable to find their most formidable stumbling block in the agricultural sector. as has been the case in various countries with differing economic systems.

The incentives may be of different kinds, but the most important is that agriculture should reap the benefits of the technical progress it makes, as regards both external aspects and the interplay of internal economic forces. This is the only way in which the wide gap between average income in rural and in urban areas can be gradually narrowed. The fact is that the impoverished sectors of the population are largely to be found in rural areas.

With a little thought, it will be seen that the externally geared growth of earlier periods, based on the characteristic foreign enclaves which did not spread technical progress to the internal economy, broke up the original pre-capitalistic integration of the countryside with the towns. And industrialization tends to accentuate rather than reduce the breach by aggravating the social and economic dichotomy. Steps must now be taken to remedy this.

The widening of the gap was due not only to the structural features of the rural sector, but also to the fact that internal development has not been dynamic enough to raise the farmer's income. What is more, it is the farmer who is usually called upon to bear a considerable part of the cost of import substitution, excessive protection, and unfair marketing practices, as well as social security and other state services from which the rural worker reaps virtually no benefit because he can exert no trade union pressure and has no political contacts. In fact, he continues to play Lazarus to the Dives of urban politics.

No exhaustive examination has yet been made of all the repercussions of these factors on the drift from the countryside to the bigger Latin American towns, which is a disquieting and striking sign of economic and social disequilibrium. There is no doubt that in-migration is bound to take place; nor is there any doubt that the increased technical progress of the rural areas will tend to give it greater momentum. But is it necessary for the displaced population to congregate in the big towns? Why should they not stay in the rural milieu, living in small and medium-sized communities and employed in industries and services that would satisfy some of the requirements of that milieu itself? Why have the bigger towns in Latin America grown, at the expense of the medium and small towns, to an extraordinary extent that is quite disproportionate to the trend of developments in more advanced countries?

These questions cannot be answered satisfactorily except on the basis of careful research. Perhaps the weakness of rural demand or, to put it another way, the concentration of demand in the big towns as a result of the structural and adventitious factors mentioned above may have played an important part in this phenomenon. And, as in the case of other social phenomena, there have been no countervailing reactions but a self-perpetuating spiral,

since the agglomeration of people in big towns concentrates demand there even more, and leads to further population congestion.
It may therefore be concluded that the geographical redistribution
of income is also of great social importance.

Why Should Development Forces Be Deliberately Controlled?

One dominant idea runs through the whole of this paper: Latin
America must quicken its rate of economic development and redistribute income in favor of the broad masses of the population. The
attainment of this objective cannot be postponed indefinitely, nor
are there grounds for expecting that economic development will
take place first and be followed in the natural course of events by
social development. Both must be achieved in measured stages.
This will need the exercise of rational and deliberate action on the
forces of development which cannot take place through the spontaneous interplay of these forces, as happened in the evolution of
capitalism in the advanced countries.

The notion that this type of evolution might be reproduced in
our countries has proved very disturbing. In the advanced countries economic development has been essentially a spontaneous
phenomenon, unlike social development which has largely been
shaped by deliberate policy measures. And the need for this type of
action, the need to plan, is obviously becoming accepted there as
well.

There is one overriding premise to all this: today, when man is
acquiring a power hitherto undreamed of over the forces of nature,
he is not resigned to remaining at the mercy of the spontaneous
play of economic forces with their manifest incapacity to maintain
or achieve a satisfactory rate of growth, while at the same time
reducing cyclical fluctuations, and to bring about equitable income
distribution.

The fact that it is impossible for history to repeat itself in this
matter makes the reasons for finding new paths highly cogent. The
assimilation of an already highly developed technique in a fairly
short space of time is very different from the gradual development
of such a technique since serious incongruities or disparities appear
which have to be dealt with by state action.

Firstly, during the evolution of capitalism, technology was gradually incorporated into the productive process as the necessary cap-

RAÚL PREBISCH

433

ital accumulated. The countries in process of development, on the other hand, have to assimilate a technology that is ready-made. And if they have to climb progressively toward the higher stage already reached by the more advanced countries, their per capita income will have to increase at a swifter pace than the traditional tempo there.

Then, too, this technology and the continual innovations it entails call for substantial capital per head that the advanced countries can easily build up on the strength of their high per capita income. The developing countries, on the other hand, faced with the same highly capital-intensive technology, have an average per capita income that is barely comparable to that of the former countries nearly a century ago. Hence there is no way out but for the state deliberately to reduce the consumption of the higher income groups in the community, whereas there was no necessity for this when capitalism was evolving as a result of the spontaneous and almost automatic saving on the part of those same groups.

These two incongruities bring in their train another, already mentioned. Whereas in the advanced countries net capital formation came first and the redistribution of income later, in our countries the two problems have now to be solved simultaneously, particularly with the ever present temptation of the Soviet method of economic development.

To add to this, there is the rapidity with which techniques for the prevention and cure of disease are spread, and the ensuing sharp fall in the mortality rate, a phenomenon that took place very slowly during the evolutionary stage of the more advanced countries and was accompanied by an equally gradual fall in the birth rate. The increase in income there fostered changes in the psychological attitude to family formation which are not yet in evidence among the broad masses of the Latin American population with their meager resources. This explains the disparity between the exceptionally high rate of population growth in Latin America and the relatively moderate rate prevailing in the course of capitalistic evolution.

The high rate of demographic growth entails a more intensive effort toward net capital formation and enhances the incongruity between the persistent abundance of labor in our countries and the technology we must assimilate, as evolved in the big industrial centers under the spur of an ever increasing labor shortage.

Lastly, mention must be made of the other incongruity or disparity of import and export demand, which was likewise no problem in the past. Thus the big centers, as they grew, did not show that trend toward the formation of external bottlenecks which is characteristic of the Latin American countries.

The task of coping with these incongruities and promoting development entails three forms of state action. First and foremost, changes in the social structure so as to remove the obstacles to development; this consists essentially in making full use of the savings potential, encouraging the intensive utilization of land and capital, and freeing the huge potential of individual initiative now going to waste, thus giving the system its full dynamic force.

These changes in the social structure pave the way for other changes in the production pattern and structure of the economy which are inherent in the spread and absorption of contemporary technology. Lastly, state action is indispensable as a means of progressively remedying the marked disparities in income distribution by virtue of the increase in income accompanying the changes. . . .

. . . It would be a tragedy if in order to free man from want we had to sacrifice other values and subject him to the demands of an arbitrary power. The very idea is fundamentally incompatible with the genius of the Latin American peoples, with their innate urge to free themselves from want in order to liberate the human personality and give full rein, by means of economic development, to democracy and human rights, especially as regards the underprivileged half of the population of Latin America, and to ensure that both there and in all strata of society, social mobility will allow the best elements to move upwards, for the good of economic development and of democracy. The goal must be a social order free from privilege, and not only economic privilege, but also the baneful privilege by which some men usurp dominion over the ideas of the rest, over the creative forces of the spirit, and over the deepest feelings of the heart.

PRIMARY COMMODITY EXPORTS AND THE DETERIORATION IN THE TERMS OF TRADE*

As has been pointed out, the trend toward external imbalance in the developing countries is mainly a manifestation of the disparity between the rate of growth of their primary exports and that of their imports of industrial goods. While primary exports, with certain exceptions, develop fairly slowly, demand for industrial imports tends to accelerate. This is a spontaneous feature of economic development.

The slow growth of primary exports is an inevitable result of technological progress in the industrial centers. On the one hand, there are direct consequences, since technological progress leads to the increasing substitution of synthetics for natural products; and it is also reflected in one way or another in the smaller raw material content of finished goods. On the other hand, there are indirect consequences, since only a small part of the increased per capita income generated by technological progress goes into the demand for foodstuffs and other staple consumer goods, as compared to the demand for industrial goods and services which tends to rise rapidly. It is significant for example, that, in absolute terms, total consumption of wheat in the United States has remained almost constant since the beginning of the century, in spite of the rise in both population and per capita income.

To all these developments must be added the remarkable effects of the propagation of modern agricultural techniques in the advanced countries.

One of the characteristics of technological progress is that it has not permeated all productive activities or all countries evenly, a fact which largely explains the structural differences and consequent contrasts and disparities in the development process. Until fairly recent times, technological progress was confined to industrial production and had not spread to agriculture to any great extent, except for mechanization. Finally, however, the technological revolution reached this lagging sector, first in the United States and then in Europe. Modern farming techniques made rapid head-

* Excerpts from *Proceedings of the United Nations Conference on Trade and Development* (Geneva, March 23–June 16, 1964), Vol. II (Report by the Secretary General) (New York: United Nations, 1964).

way and in fact agriculture is becoming industrialized; thus, new dynamic elements are being introduced into the economic complex, at both the internal and the international levels. The old pattern of trade, under which less developed countries were the suppliers of agricultural exports, is undergoing a change which may become permanent and thus help to develop new forms of the international division of labor.

It so happens, however, that the enormous increase in output that has ensued in some major industrial countries has further weakened the export trade in a number of agricultural products from the temperate zones and also in some tropical or semi-tropical products. And here a very significant fact emerges which is not the inevitable result of technological progress but of political attitudes toward this progress, attitudes that are certainly capable of being changed. In spite of the huge increases in productivity, domestic prices in the industrial countries concerned usually stay higher—and often much higher—than those on the international market. In this way, or through the payment of subsidies to farmers, the adverse effects of technological progress on prices are countered. But this policy also provides an additional incentive to expand production, and the expansion is often carried out on marginal holdings and at excessive costs. In order to guarantee a domestic consumer market for the increased output, imports from other producing countries are restricted or eliminated by various devices. . . . If this encouragement results in exportable surpluses, such surpluses are exported by means of subsidies or other incentives which tend to depress world prices, while other producing countries are unable to follow suit because of the very weakness of their economies. . . .

The easing or elimination of protectionism in the industrial centers could have a far-reaching effect on the prices of the goods benefiting thereby. But it would be idle to believe that this can have any decisive effect on the downward trend of the terms of trade for primary commodities in relation to industrial products, which has again prevailed in the past decade. The factors operating in this direction have deeper roots in the peripheral countries than in the industrial centers. The former suffer from a congenital weakness that makes it extremely difficult, if not impossible, for the deterioration to be checked by a decision on their part and on their part alone. . . .

. . . It should be remembered that, although there are differences from country to country, about 60 per cent, on the average, of the economically active population of the developing countries is still engaged in agriculture and other branches of primary production, working generally at a low rate of productivity, and that to this figure must be added that part of the economically active population engaged in artisan activities and personal services at very low scales of remuneration. All these sectors of the population exert constant pressure on the real level of wages in the developing countries and make it extremely difficult for this level to rise in direct proportion to productivity as the latter improves with technological progress. The increase in income generated by higher productivity in the agricultural sector thus tends to shift to other parts of the domestic market or abroad, as the case may be, provided that the shortage of available land does not absorb the increase in income by raising the rent for the benefit of landowners and provided that the play of market forces is left undisturbed.

In the industrial countries, on the other hand, the relative shortage of labor and strong trade-union organization allow wages not only to rise as productivity increases but even, as often happens, to outstrip the increase.

Thus there is a fundamental disparity in these trends. It is a consequence of the structural differences between industrial centers and peripheral countries and it explains the tendency of the terms of trade to worsen. The protection enjoyed by the primary commodities of the industrial centers obviously encourages this tendency because it accentuates the disparity between demand for primary commodities in the centers and demand for imports of manufactures in the periphery. . . .

With an effort of the imagination it is possible to visualize a situation of dynamic equilibrium in the distant future in which the trend in question disappears as a result of the world-wide process of industrialization. If the advanced centers themselves have not yet succeeded in reaching that stage, the countries on the periphery of the world economy can hardly be expected to do so within a short space of time. The readjustment will come about in the end when the structural change is completed, but the period of transition will be very long. In the meantime, it is precisely through this period of transition that the present and successive generations are destined to live, and it is those generations which will have to bring about the change. The change will also require capital formation on a vast scale, to say nothing of time. In the developed economies, capital formation, intrinsically very strong, is facilitated by the very increase in productivity which accompanies technological progress, whereas in the developing countries, owing to the transfer abroad of income caused by the deterioration in the terms of trade, the capacity for capital formation, intrinsically very feeble, will be further diminished. . . .

. . . Ought we to face up to this phenomenon with a great sense of foresight?

There are various ways in which this can be done: by means of commodity agreements, which not only improve prices but also facilitate access to the markets of the industrial countries, or by compensatory financing. These are in fact convergent measures, the nature of which will be analysed in the appropriate part of this report. Suffice it to say here that there are difficulties but that they can be solved. However, for the technical discussion to be profitable, it must be preceded by a political decision of the first importance, namely, a decision to transfer, in one way or another, to the countries exporting primary commodities the extra income accruing to the industrial countries as a result of the deterioration in the terms of trade.

From a pragmatic point of view this means recognizing that countries experiencing a deterioration in the terms of trade have a *prima facie* claim upon additional international resources—resources over and above those which they would have received in the normal course of events. . . .

31. *Osvaldo Sunkel*

Osvaldo Sunkel was born in Santiago, Chile, in 1929. He studied at the University of Chile and the London School of Economics. From 1955 to 1962, he was a member of the group of brilliant young economists (which also included Celso Furtado) who were working with Raúl Prebisch at the U.N. Economic Commission for Latin America (ECLA) in Santiago. Since leaving ECLA, Sunkel has been teaching at the University of Chile and (until 1968) at the Latin American Institute of Economic and Social Planning. He is also Senior Research Fellow at the Institute of

International Studies of the University of Chile. An article Sunkel published in the journal of the Institute is included here because it is one of the best expressions of the theory of depen-dencia *that has, in a few years, become the most common method for Latin American social scientists to analyze their history, eco-nomics, politics, and social structure.* Since this article was written, the solutions for* dependencia *suggested by Sunkel— economic integration on a basis that discriminates against non-Latin American companies, greater state control of investment and foreign trade, increased specialization and socially planned production—have been influential in the policies of the Andean Subregional Group and of the Allende government in Chile.*

NATIONAL DEVELOPMENT POLICY AND EXTERNAL DEPENDENCE †

National development policy to be effective must promote struc-tural and institutional changes that are considered to be essential to achieve specific social objectives. This necessarily implies the alteration of traditionally accepted situations and, consequently, a challenge to the established interests related to those situations both nationally and internationally. Thus we can say that the development policy of our countries—both as to its objective, intensity, means, and effectiveness—is situated within certain limits of flexibility. Its "freedom of maneuver" will depend principally on the internal situation and the international ties of the country.

As to the internal situation, this will be affected in the course of time by changes the development process itself produces; in-dustrialization, urbanization, occupational differentiation, changes

---

* For a revised and updated version of his theory, see Sunkel's article "Capitalismo transnacional y desintegración nacional en la América latina," *El Trimestre Economico*, vol. XXXVIII, no. 150, pp. 571–628. See also Fernando Henrique Cardoso and Enzo Faletto, *Dependencia y Desarrollo en América Latina* (Mexico: Siglo XXI, 1969), and Theotonio Dos Santos, *Dependencia y Cambio Social* (Santiago: CESO, 1970), and the attack on "dependentismo" in J. Hodava, "La dependencia de la dependencia" *Aportes*, no. 21 (July 1971), pp. 7–15.

† Translated by the editor from *Estudios Internacionales* (Santiago), Año 1, No. 1 (April, 1967), by permission of the publisher.

in the social structure, the alteration of attitudes and values, modifications in the patterns of political participation, transformation in the social function of women, technological changes in the means of communication and information available to the mass of the people, changes in the magnitude and functions of state activity, etc.

As for the foreign ties of our countries, the influence these exert on national development policy results from the fact we are situated in the system of international relations of the capitalist world. This is characterized by the presence of one dominant power, a series of intermediate powers, and the underdeveloped countries which are members of the capitalist bloc. The system of international relations of which we form a part is—like the internal situation—essentially dynamic. It experiences significant alterations, both because of internal changes in the countries concerned, and because of the alternatives made available in its constant confrontation with the other principal system of international relations—that of the socialist world, headed also by one dominant power. . . .

If we look at what economists, sociologists, and political scientists are writing in Latin America, the subject of external dependence is significant by its absence. It seems that sociology, economics, and political science since the war have not been concerned with the question, and I wonder if this strange phenomenon is not already a first manifestation of our dependence. The fact is, we do not dare to discuss the topic either because of its connotations and political risks, or because it has not been approved as part of the antiseptic and formalistic approach that now serves as the model for our social scientists. To find serious analyses of the topic it is necessary to go back to the classical theories of imperialism in their Marxist or non-Marxist versions. But it is clear that those theories, developed, written, and published almost entirely in the first three decades of this century, have to a large extent been rendered obsolete by the profound internal changes in the countries involved and by the radical transformation in the relations among them.

Another set of writings related to the subject of dependence, which is more recent but partial, is contained in the critical analysis of the classical theory of international trade. I am speaking of the writings of Prebisch, Singer, Myrdal, and others represented institutionally in the work of the Economic Commission for Latin America (ECLA) and, more recently, in the Secretariat of the United Nations Conference on Trade and Development (UNCTAD). Nevertheless, they treat only one aspect of external dependence. . . . Increasing attention has also been given to the massive transmission of attitudes, values, forms of consumption and life-styles, forms of artistic expression, of social organization, of research and technological development that has accelerated substantially in recent years. . . .

If we look at the development programs, especially in their political versions, of many countries in Latin America, we can see that one of their fundamental objectives is self-determination, independence, a reduction in the degree of external dependence. Still more, if we analyze the programs and policies of development and industrialization in Latin America—and in other underdeveloped areas of the world as well—we can observe that one of their essential elements is precisely the desire to overcome situations of external dependence. I will begin therefore from the premise that this is one of the fundamental objectives of economic development policy in many Latin American countries.

The question which then can be asked is this: Will any development policy whatever lead to that objective? At the outset we can say, no. There are examples of policies of development—in the sense of economic growth—that have been successful from that unilateral point of view but that have involved not only the emigration of an important part of the population but also the denationalization of those countries and their absorption into other cultures and civilizations; in short, which has resulted in the establishment of what someone accurately has called "a branch-plant country" (pais succursal).* I believe that this is certainly not the ideal model of development to which Latin Americans aspire. In fact our view of such a model is revealed by the fact that one of the objectives of national development policy is, on the contrary, the affirmation of the national personality. It is necessary therefore to examine the development policies that are being carried out in Latin America to see if indeed they are leading to one of the essential objectives of national development or whether on the contrary they are leading toward a greater dependence on the exterior. . . .

Our analysis has revealed contradictory tendencies as to the pos-

* Sunkel is thinking of Puerto Rico.—ED.

sibility of carrying out national development. On the one hand, basic changes are taking place in the social structure: massification, an increase and a differentiation among the intermediate groups, and a broadening of the process and mechanisms of political participation. On the other hand, there are the interest groups and sectors associated with external activities, as well as a process of cultural and ideological alienation particularly among the intermediate groups, at least those who are achieving their objectives through the present process of development. Consequently, if this analysis is correct, we do not seem to have here any inevitable laws or historical tendencies in one direction or another, but rather contradictions that create the possibilities for choice and alternatives in terms of the changes that can take place among exogenous variables and of the manipulation of the variables which are subject to direct influence. . . .

The historical evolution of our economies has imprinted certain characteristics on our economic structure, which we should list in our consideration of the problem of dependence and national development policy: In the first place, the traditional economic structure has been partly retained, which has seriously limited modernization and the introduction of technology in rural productive activity. . . . In the second place, we have inherited a structure of foreign trade that in open contradiction to the political declarations repeated for at least twenty to twenty-five years, remains a specialized structure of the export of one or a few primary products. . . . In the third place, the industrialization stage has not produced all the benefits that were hoped for from that process. In particular, it has failed to achieve one of its basic objectives—the reduction of external dependence. Indeed, while industrialization has permitted us to reduce expenditure upon imports in relation to the domestic economy—the import coefficient—it has also meant an important change in the structure of imports. If, in earlier decades, a large proportion of our foreign exchange was spent on nonessential consumer goods, today at least the most industrialized economies in the region import almost exclusively essential goods—machines, equipment, and tools for maintenance purposes and to increase productive capacity; raw materials and semifinished products to assure a normal level of economic activity; and, often, basic foodstuffs to maintain popular consumption. Thus we have arrived at a situation of external vulnerability in which any change in foreign prices and any problem of external financing causes serious difficulties. . . .

Finally, another inherited characteristic of this stage of industrialization is the establishment of a large and active state, which has carried out three functions since 1930. On the basis of an increasing share of the financial proceeds from export, which was the only sector of the economy where, because of its increasing productivity, an abundant surplus was being generated, the state began to carry out three activities. It acted as a *mechanism to transfer financial resources* and subsidize the development of private industrial activity, generally through development institutions; as a *mechanism for the redistribution of income*, through directing resources to welfare purposes through social security, insurance programs, and the expansion of education, housing, and health services; and as a *mechanism for state investment*, in order to establish and expand the economic infrastructure of transport, communications, and power, and to create basic industrial enterprises, generally in steel. . . .

As a result of the processes I have just outlined, our countries are, from the point of view of the structure and functioning of their economy—entirely dependent. The serious problem, which is not always recognized, is that this extreme dependence of our economies is rooted in the vulnerability and tendency to deficit of our foreign trade; in the fact that the type of industrialization and the form of exploitation of the export sector has not permitted our countries, with certain exceptions, to acquire their own capacity for adaptation and technological invention; in the fact that an important and probably increasing part of the industry and export activity belongs to foreigners or depends on licenses or external technical assistance—all of which puts a heavy burden on foreign exchange; in the fact that the public sector and foreign accounts have a persistent tendency, with certain exceptions, to deficit, which leads to external financing. In certain conditions, this external financing can mean the accumulation of external debts so considerable and with such a structure of repayment that debt service obliges us to recur in a really vicious circle to further external financing. . . .

In spite of the efforts to industrialize and to develop a welfare policy, we can observe that an increasingly large mass of the population continues to be segregated from the benefits of the socio-economic system, constituting large sectors that have not succeeded in integrating themselves in the economic, social, cultural, and political life of our countries or have been integrated in an exploitative way. Hence, while a revolutionary course has been prevented for the present, to persist in the "developmentism" of the last decades, now that its positive stage has been completed, will lead to frustration. . . .

Integration could be a basic instrument for the national realization of Latin America. But it could also lead to the establishment of further "branch-plant" economies in Latin America. Present integration policies seem to favor the latter tendency since, at the outset, the subsidiary enterprises of a large non-Latin American multinational main company located in many countries in the region are the ones that are in the best situation to plan their activities to take advantage of a free trade zone and to replace national enterprises even on the domestic market. . . . An integration which will lead to the objective of Latin American fulfillment and less external dependence of the region as a whole and of each country in particular will require multinational initiatives to develop, at least in the first stage, basic productive sectors—steel, petrochemicals, electronics, mechanics, etc.—under Latin American control. . . . The immediate efforts for integration should concentrate on achieving productive agreements, particularly with relation to the increase of productive capacity in the area of basic productive goods, and through enterprises, consortia, or state or mixed Latin American multinational trusts—that is to say, in the multinational planning of basic and expanded industrial activities. . . .

It is evident that there is a conflict of interest between the desire of the exporting country to maximize its export income and that of the international oligopoly to maximize its worldwide profits. This conflict can only be overcome by direct intervention in the enterprise and in its policies of production, refinement, sales, markets, and prices—either through nationalization, the association of the private enterprise and the state, state supervision, or some other form of effective control. . . .

Classical private foreign investment or its domestic imitation through licenses or trademarks has other serious inconveniences. For one thing, it inhibits technological development in domestic manufacturing. Note that a world war was necessary for the American automobile industry to produce a vehicle, the jeep, suited to the needs of rural life in underdeveloped countries. It also promotes the incorporation in the national productive structure of those patterns of production of conspicuous consumption goods that are the result of the "demonstration effect" and that the policy of limitation of the importation of superfluous consumer goods was supposed to prevent. A further problem in many countries, which can be extremely serious, is the amount represented in the balance of payments by financial agreements concerning profit remission, dividends, interest, royalties, payment for administrative services and for technical assistance.

The moment has arrived to find a mechanism that can replace or modify the traditional form of absorption of modern technology and external savings. Very interesting experiments along these lines are the investment, trade, and loan agreements the socialist countries have just concluded with the European capitalist countries— e.g. the agreement between the Fiat company and the U.S.S.R. . . . The point is to replace the traditional mechanism of orientation and decision in international trade and investment, which is lodged principally in the great vertically-integrated international oligopolies, by direct agreements between a decision-making center, which is authentically national, and those multinational enterprises or other decision-making centers located in other nations. . . .

One alternative is to oblige the foreign companies to reinvest their profits within the country. But this would lead to a process of "denationalization" of the existing national industries or to a rapid and considerable expansion of new foreign industries relative to those that are domestically owned. In any event, this would produce a considerable loss of resources once the foreign company reached the limit of its expansion in the domestic market. . . .

We must try to produce manufactured goods that are attainable and appropriate for a great potential market consisting of persons of low income, mostly in rural areas. In place of an indiscriminate open door policy, unrestricted stimulation of substitution industries, and external technological absorption, we should move to a restrictive policy that prohibits new activities where there is unused existing capacity and encourages industrial concentration in large specialized productive units in place of the small units producing everything, which are customary today. . . .

The purpose of this work is only to point out by way of illustration some of the basic reorientations that are required by a national development policy, to show the technical viability of such policies, to suggest that the adoption of such policies is possible for us and does not depend solely or principally on foreigners, and to show that it is possible to translate a national development policy into concrete strategies that will gain the political support of broad intermediate and popular sectors both in the city and in rural areas. . . .

32. Salvador Allende

Salvador Allende, elected president of Chile in 1970, is a committed Marxist and one of the founders of the Socialist Party in Chile. Allende was born in Valparaiso in 1908 of a family that can trace its ancestry to the Spanish colonial period. Active in radical politics from his days as a medical student, he was elected to the Chilean Congress in 1937. In 1940, he was appointed Minister of Health in the Popular Front Government of Pedro Aguirre Cerda and from 1945 until his election as President, he was a member of the Chilean Senate. One of the architects of the agreement between the Socialist and Communist Parties that established the Popular Action Front (FRAP) in 1956, he has been a perennial presidential candidate of the left. He first ran with little success in 1952, but, in 1958, he came within 34,000 votes of defeating the right-wing candidate, Jorge Alessandri. In 1964, he was soundly defeated by Eduardo Frei of the Christian Democrats, but, in 1970, a three-way split between himself, Alessandri, and the Christian Democratic candidate enabled him to win the presidency with 36.3 per cent of the vote. The Popular Unity coalition that supported him included, in addition to the Communists and Socialists, a major portion of the centrist Radical Party and a left-wing splinter group from the Christian Democrats. In the speech that follows, Allende asserts that his regime is pursuing a democratic, pluralist, nonviolent course in achieving a Marxist socialist state—an alternative model, "anticipated by the classics of Marxism," to the dictatorship of the proletariat employed in the Soviet Union and China. Promising to use constitutional methods to change Chile's economic and political institutions, he seeks the socialization of the economy and a "revolutionary" break with the past, while, at the same time, maintaining industrial and agricultural production, respect for law, and friendly relations with all nations.

THE CHILEAN WAY TO SOCIALISM *

The Chilean government today has a new political force whose social function is to support not the traditional dominant class but the overwhelming majority of the people. This change in the structure of power must necessarily be accompanied by a profound transformation in the socio-economic order that Parliament will be called upon to institutionalize. We will be compelled to take more decisive steps in our progress toward the liberation of Chilean energies for the rebuilding of the nation. To the Agrarian Reform already under way and the nationalization of copper which only awaits final approval of a plenary session of both houses of Congress, we must now add new reforms—whether they be by the initiative of the Parliament or by a proposal from the executive, or by a joint initiative of the two houses, or by way of a legal appeal as expressed in a plebiscite. . . .

Although the circumstances in Russia in 1917 and in Chile today are very different, the historical challenge is similar. Russia in 1917 made decisions which had a great effect on contemporary history. There it was demonstrated not only that backward parts of Europe could move ahead of the more advanced countries, but that the first socialist revolution need not necessarily be under the control of the industrial powers. The challenge was accepted, and one of the forms of socialist society—the dictatorship of the proletariat—was established. Today there is no doubt that in this way nations with a large population can break with backwardness and achieve the advances of contemporary civilization in a ralatively short time. The U.S.S.R. and the People's Republic of China are eloquent demonstrations of this.

As in the case of Russia, Chile has now found it necessary to develop a new means of constructing a socialist society—our revolutionary way, the pluralist way, anticipated by the classics of Marx-

---

* Translated by the editor from *La Via Chilena* (First Message of President Allende to the Plenary Session of Congress, May 21, 1971, Santiago, Chile).

ism, but never before given concrete expression. Social thinkers have thought that the first countries to travel this road would be more developed nations, perhaps Italy and France with their large Marxist-oriented workers' parties. Nevertheless, history again has shown that one can break with the past and construct a new model of society not only where this was predictable in theory, but where more favorable conditions were created for its establishment. Chile is the first nation to follow the second model of transition to a socialist society.

... I am sure that we have the energy and the necessary capacity to carry out our great effort—the establishment of the first socialist society that is built along democratic, pluralist, and libertarian lines. The skeptics and predictors of catastrophe will say this is not possible. They will say that a Parliament that has served the dominant classes so well is incapable of transforming itself into a Parliament of the Chilean people. They have stated even more emphatically that the police and armed forces who, up to this time, were the supporters of the institutions that we are superseding, would not accept the role of guarantors of the popular will that has decided to built socialism in our country. . . . For my part I declare, Honorable Members of the National Congress, that since this institution is based on the popular vote, nothing in its very nature prevents it from converting itself *de facto* into a Parliament of the People. And I affirm that the Chilean police and armed forces, faithful to their tradition and duty of noninterference with the political process, will support a social order that corresponds to the popular will as expressed in the terms that the constitution establishes—an order which is more just, more humane, and more generous for all, but especially for the workers who, until this time, have given so much and received almost nothing. . . .

The causes of our backwardness have been and still are the combination of the traditional ruling classes with external subordination and internal class exploitation. The ruling classes profited from their association with foreign interests and the appropriation of the surpluses produced by the workers, leaving them only the minimum indispensable to maintaining their working capacity. Our primary task is to dismantle this confining structure which only produced a distorted development, and build a new economy that will follow the other without retaining its characteristics. This new order will maximally preserve the productive and technical capacity which we have achieved despite the vicissitudes of underdevelopment, and avoid artificial crises created by those whose archaic privileges are being taken away. . . .

We are treading a new path; traveling without a guide through unknown terrain, holding fast to our fidelity to the humanism of all ages—especially to Marxist humanism—and keeping before us the aim that we desire, inspired by the most profound goals of the Chilean society. . . . In more direct terms, our task is to define and put into practice, as the Chilean way to socialism, a new model of the state, economy, and society, that is centered on the needs and aspirations of man. . . .

THE PRINCIPLE OF LEGALITY

The principle of legality rules today in Chile. It has developed as a result of the effort of many generations against absolutism and the arbitrary exercise of the power of the state. It is an irreversible conquest as long as there is a difference between rulers and ruled. The popular movements are not opposed to the principle of legality. We protest against a legal order whose postulates reflect an oppressive social regime. The juridical norms that order the social relations among Chileans correspond today to the exigencies of the capitalist system. In a regime of transition to socialism, the juridical norms will accord with the needs of a people attempting to construct a new society. But legality will remain.

Our legal system must be changed. This is the great responsibility of the houses of Congress at the present time: to see to it that the transformation of our juridical system is not impeded.*. . .

INSTITUTIONAL DEVELOPMENT

The struggle of the popular movements and parties that are in the government today has contributed substantially to one of the most promising characteristics of the country: We have an open institutional system that has resisted anyone who has tried to contravene the will of the people. The flexibility of our institutional system permits us to hope that, like our legal system, it will adapt itself to the new requirements in order to produce, through constitutional channels, the new institutions that are required to over-

* This is a reference to Allende's proposal for Neighborhood Tribunals blocked by the opposition-controlled Congress.—ED.

come capitalism. The new institutions will respond to the goal that legitimates and guides all our actions—the transfer of political and economic power to the workers and the people, as a whole. To make this possible, first priority must be given to the social ownership of the basic means of production.

At the same time, it is necessary to adjust the political institutions to the new reality. For this reason, at an appropriate time, we will propose to the sovereign will of the people, the replacement of the present liberal constitution and bicameral system with a constitution of a socialist orientation and a single chamber. . . .

POLITICAL LIBERTY

In the same way, it is important to recall that for us, as representatives of the popular forces, our political liberties are a conquest of the people in the painful passage toward their emancipation. They are part of what is positive in the historical period which we are leaving behind. And furthermore, they must continue. Therefore, we respect liberty of conscience and of all beliefs. . . . But we would not be revolutionaries if we limited ourselves to maintaining political liberty. The Popular Unity government will reinforce political liberty. It is not enough to proclaim it in theory and frustrate it in practice. We will make it real, tangible, and concrete—possible to the extent that we have achieved economic liberty. And, therefore, the Popular Government is inspired in its policy by a premise that is artifically denied by some—the existence of classes and social sectors with antagonistic and opposing interests and the existence of unequal political power within the same class or sector. . . .

VIOLENCE

The people of Chile are achieving political power without being obliged to use force. Without having to combat a despotic or dictatorial regime, they are advancing toward social liberation with only the limitations of liberal democracy to contend with. Our people hope to carry out the stage of transition to socialism without recourse to authoritarian forms of government. . . . Our people have risen up against the institutionalized violence imposed on them by the present system of capitalism. . . . Nevertheless, it is my obligation to point out that one danger can threaten the course marked out by present conditions and our collective conscience. That danger is violence against the decision of the people. If internal or external violence in any of its forms, whether physical, economic, social, or political, threatens our normal development and the achievements of the workers, this would create a serious danger for the continuity of our institutions, our legal order, political liberty, and pluralism. . . .

SOCIALIZATION OF THE MEANS OF PRODUCTION

Chile has begun to recover its principal source of wealth—copper. The nationalization of our copper mines is not an act of vengeance or a symptom of hatred for any group, government, or nation. On the contrary, we are exercising the inalienable right of a sovereign people—the full use of our national resources developed with our national work and effort. To recover copper is a decision of Chile, and we ask the respect of all countries and governments for the unanimous decision of a free people. We will pay for the copper mines if it is fair to pay for them, or we will not pay for them if it is unfair to do so. We will look out for our own interests, and we will be implacable if we find out that the negligence or prejudicial actions of persons or corporations are harmful to the country.

We have nationalized another of the basic riches of the country —iron. A short time ago, we completed negotiations with Bethlehem Steel, in accordance with which the iron mines will be transferred in their entirety to the area of social ownership. At the present time, we are studying the establishment of a national steel complex that will join six enterprises with the Pacific Steel Company. The agreement with the American industry has shown once again that the government can offer equitable treatment to foreign capital without surrendering the basic interests of our nation. But we will not tolerate the disregard for our laws and the lack of respect for the authorities that we have found in some foreign companies. We have recovered coal for collective ownership and nitrate is also ours. . . .

In accelerating agrarian reform, we have carried out an important part of the goal established for this year—the expropriation of 1000 large estates (*latifundios*). The process is being conducted with respect for existing legislation and protection for the interests of the small and medium-sized farmer. We wish to establish a new agriculture that will be more vigorous and solid in its organization as well as much more productive. We wish Chile to become self-sufficient in food production. We wish the men who live from the land to benefit equitably from the fruits of their labor.

The establishment of state ownership of the banks has been a decisive step. With complete respect for the rights of the small stockholder, we have taken over nine banks and are about to obtain majority control of others. On the basis of what has taken place so far, we expect to achieve a reasonable agreement with the foreign banks. We seek in this way to achieve control of the financial apparatus, and to widen the social area in the production of material goods. We seek to place the new banking system in the service of the socialized area and in the reach of small and medium-sized industrialists, businessmen, and farmers, who have been discriminated against in the past. . . .

The occupations of housing settlements, the indiscriminate occupations of agricultural areas are unnecessary and harmful.* According to our actions and attitude, we have the authority to be believed. Therefore, the plans fixed by the government and the process for carrying them out must be respected. . . .

OUR FOREIGN POLICY

Our first decision corresponding to the majority will of the Chilean people was to re-establish relations with Cuba which had been the subject of unjust sanctions. We also established diplomatic and commercial relations with China, Nigeria, and the German Democratic Republic. We have established commercial relations with the Democratic Republic of Korea and the Democratic Republic of Vietnam. . . .

Our struggle against backwardness and dependence on foreign hegemonic powers means that Chile has common interests with other peoples in Asia and Africa. This is why the Popular Government has decided to participate actively in the deliberations and agreements of the group of "nonaligned" nations. . . .

My government wishes to maintain friendly and cooperative relations with the United States of America. We have tried to create conditions for understanding our situation that will prevent the generation of conflicts, and not allow nonessential questions

---

* After Allende's election, a wave of occupations led by left-extremists swept the country, adversely affecting food production and housing construction.—ED.

to prejudice that aim or impede the negotiated and friendly resolution of the problems that may be presented. . . .

Those who live from their labor now have in their hands the political direction of the state. The creation of a new social regime has the people as both actor and judge. The state will orient, organize, and direct, but in no way replace the will of the workers. In both economics and politics, the workers themselves must have the power to decide. To achieve this will be the triumph of the revolution. For this the people struggle—with the legitimacy given by respect for democratic values, with the certainty given by a program, with the strength that comes from being the majority, with the passion of the revolutionary. *Venceremos!*

33. *Eduardo Frei*

Eduardo Frei, the President of Chile, was born in Santiago in 1911. He took a law degree at the Catholic University of Chile, where he was active in national and international student organizations. After finishing his studies, Frei went to edit a newspaper in Iquique (in the provinces), where he wrote his first book, Chile Desconocido (The Unknown Chile). *In 1938, he was one of the group of young Catholic leaders who withdrew from the Conservative Party to form the National Falange, which stood for a reformist policy very different from that of its counterpart in Spain. Frei was President of the Falangist Party three times, and, in 1949, was elected to the Chilean Senate. In 1957, the Falangist Party changed its name to the Christian Democratic Party of Chile, and a year later nominated Frei as its candidate for the presidency. He was unsuccessful in that election, but in 1964, he was elected President with the largest plurality in Chilean history. Forbidden by the Chilean constitution to succeed himself, he did not participate in the 1970 presidential election, which was narrowly won by Salvador Allende. With the defeat of the Christian Democratic candidate, Radomiro Tomic, Frei continued to be the leading figure in the party and the most likely candidate to oppose the left in the 1976 presidential elections.*

In the first selection below, written before he became President, Frei attacks the evils of Communism and capitalism, and develops the Christian Democratic conception of a "middle way" which consists of the involvement of the worker in management and ownership, the promotion of intermediate groupings between the individual and the state, and government action to limit the power of large economic concentrations.

CHRISTIAN DEMOCRACY
IN THEORY AND PRACTICE*

Capitalism and Communism

If we compare the proposals of *Quadragesimo Anno* with the realities of the present, we can observe that they are still perfectly valid. The world of economics is still oscillating between the extremes of liberalism and collectivism, capitalism and Communism, free enterprise and statism. In the face of these, the encyclical proposed a system of moral ideas that can produce a different formula. The task that was presented to Christians was precisely to construct this formula. Can we say that they have constructed it?

If we continue our observation, we can assert that the formulas presented at the two extremes are simple, effective, and, from their point of view, efficient. Are we able to offer a formula that is characterized by equal efficiency and clarity? This is the problem. . . .

There is something that we should understand. Capitalism as a system dehumanizes the economy, although, in its first stage, it meant an enormous expansion of economic development and the creation of wealth. Yet there is no doubt that it tended to concentrate economic power in a few hands, to allow the great monopolistic powers to control the market so that, by a fierce dialectical process within its own structure, it led to the disappearance of economic freedom. In the productive process, it separated

---

* Excerpts from *Pensamiento y Acción* (Santiago de Chile; Editorial del Pacífico, 1958); translated by the editor, by permission.

labor from management and, more than that, from the concept of property and the exercise of that right.

With regard to [the evils of] capitalism, we note that there are two well-defined plans of action: the reformist and the revolutionary. The revolutionary aims at the destruction of the regime in a sudden, violent, and total manner. In fact [in revolutionary regimes], private capitalism has been replaced by that of the state, the property holder who controls capital by the bureaucrat who controls the power of the state, the business manager delegated by the stockholding property owner, by the managerial bureaucrat delegated by the government which administers the state, and the more and more concentrated powerful monopoly capitalists by the powerful supermonopoly of the state.

Basically, we could say of the two systems that Communism is a continuation of capitalism, drawing the latent tendencies in its structure to their logical conclusions. The two differ not in technique, but in purpose. Technically, there is no difference if the administrative group is made up of private stockholders or of bureaucrats representing state ownership. The difference is that the first is directed by various groups that exercise control for their own interests, and the second is directed by those who administer the state for the purpose of collective goals. This could be a greater justification of the second system, but if we analyze what has happened more profoundly, we will see that this advantageous result is more apparent than real.

On the theoretical level, this seems very clear, but at the practical level, it does not occur with the simplicity that the scheme appears to offer. When capitalism is a monopoly under the sole control of the state, there results as a consequence a concentration of power in the bureaucracy that is as merciless or more merciless in its operation than the private businessman. According to the classic example of the textbooks of sociology, a worker, representing labor, alone and isolated, appeared before the employer burdened by a triple inferiority—psychological, economic, and legal. But the condition of the worker who confronts the bureaucrat-employer suffers from the same inferiority and adds a fourth—political inferiority. The private employer wielded the weight of his economic power, while the state employer wields the weight of his economic and political power, since he also has behind him the purposes of the state. Hence, for the worker, his real juridical condition has not changed, only the name of his employer. . . .

But Christians refuse to accept the alternatives of capitalism or Communism, because they know how closely the two are linked in their basic development. It is curious that some have appropriated the idea of capital as if capital and capitalism were synonymous, although there is also a statist and Communist capitalism. Similarly, there are those who think that private initiative and personal liberty are synonymous with individualistic liberalism. The goals of liberty and initiative can only be conceived and realized in a new system of values. If they could be attained in the past century, in a limited class and social type, present historical conditions demand that they be indicated in a different social situation and with a different purpose and meaning. Freedom today depends on a decent standard of living, and initiative cannot be a matter of appetite and interest, but must be integrated into the collective common good.

It is a fact that capitalism and philosophic and social liberalism have not succeeded in giving expression to the desires of the common man. They have brought the world to an increasing proletarianization, which is the reverse of what is affirmed by some superficial arguments concerning the distribution of small property or corporation stocks. In economics, secondary facts are of no importance, and the terms are essentially relative. It is a question of power. Today someone who has a piece of land exercises his property right, but economic power resides in high finance, in the cartels, and in the concentrated holdings of the large corporations.

In this, everything is subject to change. A century ago, the one who dominated the textile industry controlled industrial power. Twenty years ago, a nation with a heavy steel industry led in economic and political domination. Today power resides in nuclear energy, and in time the possession of a steel industry will be no more important than the production of textile fabrics.

Production has become technically complex. It requires an immense effort of scientific creativity. It means the domination of vast markets, variable and delicate in their reactions, which are aimed at satisfying human necessities, but which do this by periodically destroying the man who produces the goods in order to serve the same man when he tries to satisfy himself as consumer. There is the latent danger of a machine system that is so fearful, moving at such a continually increasing velocity (it is enough to look at the production figures in the European countries which, seven years after being devastated by war, surpassed all the prewar levels, without citing the American figures, which can only be expressed in billions) that it can only be managed by concentrated and absolute power, because the uncontrolled expression of its demands cannot be resisted by a normal democratic state. On the other hand, to leave this machine system uncontrolled in a fundamentally weak state which does not have the active specific mission of defense of the common good would be even more fatal and impossible. The system of counterbalances of which Donoso Cortés spoke a century ago would be operative here: no internal control on man; propaganda that arouses an unlimited appetite for goods; economies that are incapable of satisfying the desire for these goods, arousing the multitude to desperation when it considers its misery. What is the only state which is able to discipline and contain this?

Thus it is that capitalism leads inevitably finally to Communism. Thus it is naïve to find the remedy in a system of partial improvement—a house and a salary. The problem of the economic system is much more profound and concerns the whole structure, the motivations, the fundamental conceptions of the economy and its purpose, and of man as a moral being.

A Third Alternative

But here there arises a new problem with regard to this productive mechanism whose technique dominates the world and whose moving force appears to subjugate it. The extremes present formulas that fasten on us like claws. Do we possess a way, a method, that offers something other than aspirations, intentions, or principles? . . .

We are going to outline our position not only to those who accept Christian thought, but also to the groups called humanistic socialists, who have had practical experience with the program of Marxist socialism, but who also recognize the essential principles that have been maintained by Catholic philosophy on the sociological plane. The great task of Christians consists in being able to explain this method, which can be perceived only uncertainly and inexactly. Its principal elements have, as a matter of fact, been demonstrated to be valid.

The action of the state cannot be an absorbing and paralyzing intervention, but must respect intermediate organisms—the family, the city, the region, the trade union, the business enterprise. It must exert an effective authority for orientation, planning, and leadership. It ought to be strong enough to prevent the creation beyond its regulatory authority of economic powers which can oppress and control the market for products and for work. It cannot be the impotent witness of what goes on in the market, because it would mean the end of liberty if each citizen were left to act according to his interest and his influence.

For this purpose, it is necessary to have higher controls, to create new conditions and to coordinate but not to constrain them. It is necessary to have planning, because this represents the common good of the whole nation and because all isolated efforts represent only a part of the interest of the whole. We know today that the income of a nation is distributed among labor, capitalization, and profit. The state should know which part can be used for consumption and which should be utilized for capital, which proportion can go to the public sector and which to the private sector. It can and ought to maintain a monetary flow according to the volume of economic activity. No one today can believe that this must be subjected to a freedom that would be a fiction, destroying itself by the very mechanism of economic factors.

But this action for the common good can better develop and perhaps can only be developed when it is not thought that a progressive statism is being established when colossal bureaucratic powers are created, which, by their very ineffective existence, consume the resources they are administering so that the mechanism created by man destroys man rather than serving him.

We think, for example, that the government of the United States, when it created the Paley Mission to study raw-material resources, reserves, and conditions in the world, fulfills its task of watching over the destiny of the nation better than when an improvising government of ours thinks that it has made progress by its improvisation in creating new supervisory groups. . . . The same thing happened in Italy, where the government faced the problem of housing by establishing construction areas and factories for prefabricated materials, substituting for direct construction a national effort with the cooperation and initiative of all citizens. Thus the state served man better than by creating institutions which, whether for financial or technical reasons, have demonstrated themselves incapable of resolving this difficult problem. But this is hardly a mention of a fundamental theme whose concrete application must be worked out and defined. Nevertheless, there remains the fundamental question—namely, that of the economic structure itself, the functioning of the productive unit, and the harmonization of the factors that compose it. On this subject, it has been difficult to make progress. Some try communitarian forms, which are attractive without as yet having any experimental validity. The experiences of codetermination are thus far varied, but one cannot say that they are conclusive.

Today a new era is opening up. The business enterprise is composed of the investor who provides the capital, the manager, and the worker. If we could imagine a vast process of universal extension of property through the organized acquisition of shares by the worker, not in the limited context of the old worker-stockholder, but a planned and large-scale access of labor to capital, we could imagine a social organization in which man would participate in the economic process in two ways—as worker, by his salary, and as owner of capital, through profit. This process ought not to be thought of solely as limited to the enterprise in which the worker is employed, but applied to any enterprise, since the important thing would be to give the worker property and, more than that, to involve him in the process of capitalization, which is the foundation of the economic process, the condition of stability for the worker himself, and the sole form that offers the possibility of raising his standard of living.

This would require action that would make it easy for organized savings to go into investment, something that could not occur without a more equitable distribution, the present goal of the worker movement and of the employees. This type of investigation requires an effort of creative imagination, but it is an especially difficult problem that must be resolved, like all those which aim at transforming structures and institutions in which very diverse factors enter, which cannot be foreseen. Their difficulty cannot be appreciated except at the time when they are carried out, and no effort of logic is capable of anticipating it. It is for this purpose that I make these observations, to arouse others to the study of those possibilities which are open to reflection and action. . . .

The foundations of a humanistic economy should be the result of an encounter between our philosophy and the scientific experience that emerges from the economy—the vivid comprehension of the reality in which we live and the will for presence by the Christian as a constructive element in the society to which he belongs. . . .

34. Jaime Castillo

Jaime Castillo is the principal ideologist of Latin American Christian Democracy by virtue of the very large number of books and articles he has written on the subject. The selection below is taken from a speech delivered at a seminar organized by the Institute of Political Studies, a Christian Democratic research group of which Castillo is the director. In the article, Castillo tries to define the goal of communitarianism, the term now being used by Latin American Christian Democrats to describe their alternative to the extremes of both individualism and collectivism, represented by the United States and the Soviet Union. In common with most writers on Catholic social thought, Castillo analyzes the property right in terms of the ethical requirements of the natural law, but he also finds it necessary to defend the notion of natural law itself from the increasing criticism which has been leveled at it by Catholic writers since the Second Vatican Council. The refusal of Castillo to give specific details on the structure of communitarian society reflects the bitter dispute within the Christian Democratic Party over whether communitarianism is to remain only an ideal vision of a future society or become the basis for an immediate and radical restructuring of property relationships in industry, agriculture, and society. In 1969, the party split on this issue, and several of its more radical members formed the Movement for United Popular Action (MAPU), which later became part of the electoral and government coalition of Salvador Allende.

PROPERTY AND THE
COMMUNITARIAN SOCIETY*

Individualism—Its Essential Insight and Historical Development

Individualism developed as the assertion of the rights of the individual against a tyrannical society, not against a just society, for that would make no sense. The virtue of individualism, then, was that it defended certain rights which had been ignored. It asserted the existential reality of the individual against those who would deny the value of the individual, [and] it demonstrated that the individual had a role in history, or, rather, that society could not be explained by reducing it to social factors. . . .

In our view, this position is open to criticism when we see its ideological implications and when its essential intuition is distorted as it is applied to reality.

On the first point individualism is based on an illegitimate abstraction because it sets the individual and society in opposition to one another. We believe, and in this we agree with Marx, that society is not an abstraction which exists above the individual. The individual is a social being. Individuals do not exist in the way that individualism conceives of them. Only the social individual exists. Hence the individual and society are not opposed to one another; they harmonize with one another and require each other.

On the second point, that of historical reality, individualism in the modern age produced a capitalism which is based on an individualistic concept of property and a nonsocial view of man. It also developed the system of government known as liberal democracy, which was a necessary prerequisite for an economic order which is now socially and morally passé, and for a society which rejected the idea of community and impeded its development. Thus, this democracy became a regime which destroyed the possibility of true human community life and lost its original meaning.

Individualism holds an erroneous conception of human rights—

* Excerpt from *Propriedad y Sociedad Comunitaria*, presented at the International Seminar on Property, organized by the Instituto de Estudios Políticos, Santiago, Chile, in February, 1966; translated by the editor.

they are considered as rights of man against society, in circumstances which require that they be oriented toward the community. Marx said this in criticizing the human rights which were proclaimed by the French Revolution. Liberty is not the right to oppose or remove oneself from the life of a community but is a condition of its progress. To understand differently is to encourage disassociation from society, which is basically nothing but monstrous egoism.

Collectivism—Its Essential Insight and Historical Development

Applying the same scheme, the essential insight of collectivism seems to us to be a reassertion of the rights of society against an individualistic system which had been carried to its logical conclusion. Historically it was a reaction, but at the same time a fundamental value was involved—the reassertion of the fact that the individual cannot realize himself except in the community. . . . The social sphere has a value, as is demonstrated by social science, and it cannot be ignored in the explanation of the process of history. . . .

In its historical development, collectivism takes on the character of a kind of absolutism. In the field of economics, a collectivist economy implies the forcible suppression of all forms of private property. In politics, it has meant a totalitarian system in which dictatorship appears to be essential. In this way, the possibility of a rich, organic, natural life of human association is prevented, for, when the individual is suppressed, what is essentially human also disappears.

Communitarianism as a Synthesis

As we have seen, a false opposition of the individual and the group presents the problem in a unilateral form and leads to individualism or collectivism. As we understand it, communitarianism results from the realization that by applying proper categories of analysis we can succeed in harmonizing the two extremes. In this way, communitarianism is the assertion of the individual *and* the community. It prevents us from falling into the error of conceptual alienation by virtue of which, as Marx says, we create fetishes which hypnotize and capture us under the spell of unilateral views of reality.

The synthesis is based on conceptions of the person and the community which basically point to the same thing. The person is a social individual. This is the only reality because man always exists in society and is a social being. This means that reality has two aspects, the person and the community, both of them inseparable. Consequently, when we think about the problem we must take account of the two aspects. Hence we reject the definition of society which individualism offers us because it makes it appear that society is composed of atomized individuals, unrelated to one another. This is to falsify reality, not to describe society.

These ideas can be expressed with some precision in two formulas. One is that of Maritain,* "the community of free men." This sums up our ideological goal—a community, or rather a spiritual community, of many individuals, of free men in a community with the highest degree of freedom. The second formula is that of Toniolo,† "a community of communities." Here one can see what the political and social organization of the communitarian society would be. There would be a multiplicity of organizations which implies a greater possibility of realizing freedom than if the society were simply reduced to a single social segment. . . .

Individualism put into action fails because the egoistic instinct which inspires it leads to injustice and abuse. Collectivism also fails due to a spiritual inadequacy which fatally leads it to reproduce the situation which it claims to avoid. Communitarianism on the other hand, for the reasons pointed out, opens the way to an infinity of approximations of truly human forms of community life. . . .

Property and Natural Law

. . . In response to those who claim that private property is a matter of natural law, we hold that that system is not required by natural law but only conforms to it when at a given time it is the best method to regulate and permit the most efficient use of all the goods of the earth. . . .

What is a matter of natural law is what we call the right of common use, that the enjoyment of goods is a demand of human

---

* Jacques Maritain, a French Catholic philosopher whose political works are a major source of Christian Democratic ideology.—ED.

† Giuseppe Toniolo (1845–1918), an Italian social thinker whose writings influenced the founders of the Italian Christian Democratic Party.—ED.

nature because man should satisfy his needs with the goods which have been placed at his disposal.

Nevertheless, there are those who, without denying that the right of common use is essential and permanent and that systems of appropriation are mutable, would deny the existence of natural law itself. In my opinion to deny the theory of natural law is as absurd as claiming to deny the theory of being. It is an impossible claim. And if we deny the existence of the natural law we will of necessity develop the same solution under a different name. Ultimately it seems to me that discussion on this matter is a dispute over terms rather than over concepts.

What is meant by natural law has to be conceived, it seems to me, as that minimum of rational terminology which is necessary to explain an obvious fact—that there exists in human nature a certain need to use and dispose of things in a way which accords with the ethical and social character of every human act. The formula, natural law, therefore expresses something very minimal and perhaps excessively vague—that man proceeds in accordance with the integrity of his being. To concretize a theoretical system to reflect this exigency is inevitable from the point of view of logic, but it runs the risk of seeming to set down in precise terms what is a complex of visions. These then become for some a substitute for reality, abstractions in the bad sense of the word. The polemics of those who in their turn develop another set of abstractions or ideological fetishes exaggerate the problem and prevent simple and authentic reflection. . . .

The Communitarian Society

First, in a communitarian society there will be the full realization of community in the sense which we explained above. There will be a plenitude of human life in common. It will be a fraternal society [in which] the highest human values will prevail. This is the same as saying that the full human life of each man will be realized in its plenitude.

Second, the communitarian society will give preference to social values over those of the individual. On this point I must also refer to something which we have debated elsewhere—the opposition of communitarianism and socialism. I have said it already—I think that both terms point to the same thing. At least their relation is very intimate. Nevertheless, I personally think that the term communitarianism is an expression which is more vivid, more vigorous, and more expressive of our thinking. In addition, the term social-ism implies certain doctrinal principles which are questionable as far as we are concerned and which are also linked to the experi-ences of totalitarian collectivism. Therefore, I prefer to use the term communitarianism. In any case the idea is the same, but to use the term communitarian socialism is to involve oneself in an unnecessary redundancy and at the same time to create certain doubts on our part.*

The communitarian society will possess a structure which is in accordance with what has been said above. Its decisive characteris-tic will be a communitarian type of property holding (by com-munities of workers, cooperatives, and other social forms), but it will allow for personal property when it has a social function as well as for the retention of some property by the national com-munity. The dichotomy between capital and labor will be super-seded by communitarian relationships, that is, by uniting labor and capital in the hands of the workers themselves. This will take place gradually and in different ways which it would be useless to try to describe in detail at this time.

Third, the driving motivation of the communitarian society will be the interest of all its members in its establishment, a solidarity derived from a common effort to reach a goal which benefits everyone. On this point we can recall the "organic solidarity" which Durkheim† describes as characterizing developed societies. In addition, the stimulus of material interest will also be present, combined not with an individualist spirit of monetary gain (for that will tend to disappear as repugnant to the ideal of commu-nity) but with a spiritual interest in the construction of a fraternal society. These two interests, intimately linked to one another, are human, living, vital, real interests and this will tend to assure that they will be satisfied. . . .

* This is a reference to the increasing use of the term communitarian socialism by the left wing and the youth organization of the Chilean Christian Democratic Party in order to indicate their opposition to the continued existence of "capitalist" property relationships in Chile.—ED.

† Emile Durkheim (1858–1917), a French sociologist.—ED.

35. Golconda Group

Colombia's Golconda Group derives its name from a rural retreat house in the diocese of Buenaventura where a group of forty-nine Colombian priests met with the Bishop of Buenaventura to discuss the problems of their country and of Latin America. Stimulated by the meeting of the Latin American Bishops Conference (CELAM) at Medellin in 1968 and by the visit of Pope Paul VI, the group drew up a document that blames the problems of Latin America on the oligarchy and foreign "dependence." The Golconda Group describes the present situation as one of "institutionalized violence" and calls for establishment of a socialist society. Their Marxist-influenced thinking reflects the increasing radicalization of a sector of the Catholic Church in Latin America, typified by the participation of Father Camilo Torres with the Colombian guerrillas (during which he was killed, in February, 1966) and by similar declarations and actions by churchmen in Brazil, Uruguay, Argentina, and Chile.

THE GOLCONDA GROUP:
FINAL DOCUMENT *

We declare that, contrary to certain distorted interpretations, the tragically underdeveloped condition of our country is the historical product of economic, political, cultural, and social dependence on foreign centers of power that operate through our ruling classes. The principal characteristic of underdevelopment in Colombia, as in all of Latin America, is the domination of our society by a minority class, the privileges of which extend back to the colonial period. Indeed the struggles for Independence, far from limiting its power, served to strengthen it still more. In reality, there was no popular revolution at that time but a mere changing of the guard—the first of an indefinite series of such changes, which continued to the present day in all of Latin America—the

* Translated by the editor from, *El Libro Rojo de los Curas Rebeldes* (Bogota: MUNIPROC, 1969); issued in Buenaventura, December 13, 1968.

passing of the colonial government into the hands of the native-born aristocracy.

The armies that were hastily improvised at that time were maintained later, and continue down to the present day, to protect that established "order." Political power arose as the protector and promoter of a system of privileges that the national constitution justified. The Church, for its part, sanctified it as if it were the undoubted expression of the will of God.

This ruling class appears now as the absolute owner of the lands that once belonged to the Indians and uses them to its own exclusive advantage. Meanwhile, the overwhelming majority of the population, after shedding their blood on the battlefields, have found it impossible to live as citizens in their own country. Behind the monuments and buildings, the luxurious airports and super-highways, lies a suffering and humiliated people silenced by its own lack of consciousness and repressed by the force of the violence exercised by those in power.

What can we do to liberate these people, the baptized sons of God, from this real servitude and slavery—to use the expression of our bishops? There is much talk of genuine agrarian reform, but is such reform possible without a prior change in the structure of foreign dependence? It is precisely this dependent situation that produces the present distorted structure, which is usually described by the ambiguous term "underdevelopment"—ambiguous because it leads us to think in purely quantitative terms, as if underdevelopment could be overcome by a simple increase in effort without any necessity of structural changes. It fails to recognize that the industrial revolution is the cause and motivating force of development.

Conversely, we can describe as the cause and motivating force of *under*development (a) our lack of heavy industry, which produces an industrial dependence with respect to means of production—machines and equipment; and (b) the existence of industrial production that does not produce foreign exchange, since it lacks a market in the centers of power, so that the country is deprived of the possibility of direct self-financing and is obliged to support itself with a product like coffee, which has no necessary relation to industrial development.

There is no doubt that it is impossible to change this situation without a genuine revolution that will expel the ruling classes in this country through whom the dependence on foreigners is exercised. The same is true for a genuine agrarian reform that will give the people real access to the fruits of the earth and to participation in production, in the basic decision-making in the country, and in its greatness. . . . We must also mention urban reform. We believe that this will necessarily be one of the first steps to be taken once the country has embarked upon a radical change in its structures. . . .

In summary, we can say that, due to the present situation of exploitation and institutionalized violence and in spite of efforts that are now being carried out, hungar and misery are joined with sickness on a massive scale, with infant mortality, illiteracy, marginality,* profound inequalities in income and tensions between the social classes, outbreaks of violence, and little participation of the people in the common good. . . .

In theology there has been some progress in overcoming the old exaggerated and misunderstood opposition between the temporal and the eternal, the natural and the supernatural, the earthly and the celestial. The distinction that was not supposed to imply a separation ended up as such and degenerated into an opposition— while reality is one in itself and in the design of God (Genesis, 1–2) where the material, the human, the cosmic, distinct from God, possesses a value in itself and at the same time is the result of the will of God and not a degeneration on the plane of being and value . . .

In the social, economic, and political areas, we note the following objectives:

1. To insist that good will is not enough and that it is necessary to know objective reality.

2. To develop a scientific method of investigation and work that nonetheless avoids empiricism and practicalism (practicismo).

3. To involve ourselves more and more in the various forms of revolutionary action against imperialism and the neocolonial bourgeoisie, avoiding the temptation to succumb to attitudes of passive observation, which result in the justification of the status quo.

4. To avoid limiting ourselves narrowly to community work thus losing sight of the national and international context.

5. To struggle unceasingly for the reform of Church structures, both in its internal organization and in the elimination of pre-

---

* Marginality—a term coined by DESAL, a Catholic research organization in Chile, to describe the situation of peasants and slumdwellers living on the margin of modern society.—Ed.

conciliar * vestiges such as the union of Church and state, the separation of which is demanded by the different aspects of the person and of society in which the action of the Church and that of civil government are carried out. . . .

6. Our emphatic rejection of neocolonial capitalism, which is incapable of solving the acute problems afflicting our people, leads us to orient our efforts with a view to the establishment of a socialist type of society that will permit the elimination of all forms of exploitation of man by man and that will respond to the historic tendencies of our time and the special characteristics of Colombians.

7. Our conviction of the necessity of a profound and urgent change in the socio-economic structures of the country leads us to declare our unreserved solidarity with all who struggle for the change. . . .

8. We reject as divisionist maneuvers the so-called traditional political parties that divide our people into two large groups, each one led by sectors that exploit the masses of the people in the same way and are equally submissive to, and colonized by, foreign monopolies. . . .

9. We likewise reject the immense military budget that is devoted to the maintenance of armed forces that are not oriented to the defense of our sovereignty but to the violent repression of the popular demands of the workers, peasants, and students, in defense of structures that favor the minorities who exercise political and economic power. . . .

All our actions of service must be guaranteed by personal and community activity, to which we must dedicate ourselves completely and in poverty. . . . We believe that it is contrary to that spirit of poverty to charge fees for the administration of the sacraments and religious services since the monetary element prevents one from seeing the freedom of the grace conferred and signified by the sacrament. We do not believe that foreign organisms should be used as distribution agents for agricultural surpluses † that disguise as supposed aid the exploitation that is taking place through the progressive deterioration of trade, cloaking it with an aura of generosity and considering the recipients as beggars.

---

* A reference to the Second Vatican Council (1962–65).—Ed.

† A reference to the distribution of surplus food by Caritas, the Catholic charity organization.—Ed.

36. Carlos Marighela

Carlos Marighela was born in 1911. At twenty-three, he joined the Brazilian Communist Party and later became a member of its Executive Committee. During the brief period after World War II when the party was legal in Brazil, he was a prominent spokesman for the party in the Brazilian Congress. In 1966, he broke with the party because of its policy of discouraging armed resistance to the military government, and in 1967 attended the Latin American Solidarity Conference in Cuba. An urban guerrilla organization, formed under Marighela's direction in 1968, engaged in more than 100 bank robberies and killed an American army captain as a spy. In November, 1969, Marighela was himself ambushed and killed by the Brazilian police in Saõ Paulo. Six months before his death, he completed a pamphlet on the strategy and tactics of urban guerrilla warfare. It has been translated and distributed by Cuban propaganda organizations and is one of many indications of the shift from the countryside to the city as the primary area of revolutionary activity in Latin America. Along with the example of the Algerian revolution and the writings of Frantz Fanon, it has also influenced student and black revolutionaries (e.g., the Black Panthers) in the United States and Europe.

MINIMANUAL OF THE URBAN GUERRILLA *

A DEFINITION OF THE URBAN GUERRILLA

The chronic structural crisis characteristic of Brazil today, and its resultant political instability, are what have brought about the upsurge of revolutionary war in the country. The revolutionary war manifests itself in the form of urban guerrilla warfare, psychological warfare, or rural guerrilla warfare. Urban guerrilla warfare or psychological warfare in the city depends on the urban guerrilla.

* From *Tricontinental* (English edition) Havana, no. 16 (Jan.-Feb., 1970).

The urban guerrilla is a man who fights the military dictatorship with arms, using unconventional methods. A political revolutionary and an ardent patriot, he is a fighter for his country's liberation, a friend of the people and of freedom. The area in which the urban guerrilla acts is in the large Brazilian cities. There are also bandits, commonly known as outlaws, who work in the big cities. Many times assaults by outlaws are taken as actions by urban guerrillas.

The urban guerrilla, however, differs radically from the outlaw. The outlaw benefits personally from the action, and attacks indiscriminately without distinguishing between the exploited and the exploiters, which is why there are so many ordinary men and women among his victims. The urban guerrilla follows a political goal and only attacks the government, the big capitalists, and the foreign imperialists, particularly North Americans.

Another element just as prejudicial as the outlaw and also operating in the urban area is the right-wing counterrevolutionary who creates confusion, assaults banks, hurls bombs, kidnaps, assassinates, and commits the worst imaginable crimes against the urban guerrillas, revolutionary priests, students, and citizens who oppose fascism and seek liberty.

The urban guerrilla is an implacable enemy of the government and systematically inflicts damage on the authorities and on the men who dominate the country and exercise power. The principal task of the urban guerrilla is to distract, to wear out, to demoralize the militarists, the military dictatorship and its repressive forces, and also to attack and destroy the wealth and property of the North Americans, the foreign managers, and the Brazilian upper class.

The urban guerrilla is not afraid of dismantling and destroying the present Brazilian economic, political, and social system, for his aim is to help the rural guerrilla and to collaborate in the creation of a totally new and revolutionary social and political structure, with the armed people in power. . . .

The urban guerrilla has a certain advantage over the conventional military or the police. It is that, while the military and the police act on behalf of the enemy, whom the people hate, the urban guerrilla defends a just cause, which is the people's cause.

The urban guerrilla's arms are inferior to the enemy's, but from a moral point of view, the urban guerrilla has an undeniable superiority. . . .

Within the framework of the class struggle, as it inevitably and necessarily sharpens, the armed struggle of the urban guerrilla points toward two essential objectives:

(A) the physical liquidation of the chiefs and assistants of the armed forces and of the police;

(B) the expropriation of government resources and those belonging to the big capitalists, *latifundists*, and imperialists, with small expropriations used for the maintenance of individual urban guerrillas and large ones for the sustenance of the revolution itself.

It is clear that the armed struggle of the urban guerrilla also has other objectives. But here we are referring to the two basic objectives, above all expropriation. It is necessary for every urban guerrilla to keep in mind always that he can only maintain his existence if he is disposed to kill the police and those dedicated to repression and if he is determined—truly determined—to expropriate the wealth of the big capitalists, the *latifundists*, and the imperialists.

One of the fundamental characteristics of the Brazilian revolution is that from the beginning it developed around the expropriation of the wealth of the major bourgeois, imperialist, and *latifundist* interests, without excluding the richest and most powerful commercial elements engaged in the import-export business.

And by expropriating the wealth of the principal enemies of the people, the Brazilian revolution was able to hit them at their vital center, with preferential and systematic attacks on the banking network—that is to say, the most telling blows were leveled against capitalism's nerve system. . . .

Men of the government, agents of the dictatorship and of North American imperialism principally must pay with their lives for the crimes committed against the Brazilian people.

In Brazil, the number of violent actions carried out by urban guerrillas, including deaths, explosions, seizures of arms, ammunition, and explosives, assaults on banks and prisons, etc., is significant enough to leave no room for doubt as to the actual aims of the revolutionaries. The execution of the CIA spy Charles Chandler, a member of the U.S. Army who came from the war in Vietnam to infiltrate the Brazilian student movement, the military henchmen killed in bloody encounters with urban guerrillas, all are witness to the fact that we are in full revolutionary war and that the war can be waged only by violent means.

This is the reason why the urban guerrilla uses armed struggle and why he continues to concentrate his activity on the physical extermination of the agents of repression and to dedicate twenty-four hours a day to expropriation from the people's exploiters. . . .

OBJECTIVES OF THE URBAN GUERRILLA'S ACTIONS

With his technique developed and established, the urban guerrilla bases himself on models of action leading to attack and, in Brazil, with the following objectives:

(A) to threaten the triangle in which the Brazilian state system and North American domination are maintained in Brazil, a triangle whose points are Rio, Saõ Paulo, and Belo Horizonte and whose base is the axle Rio–Saõ Paulo, where the giant in-dustrial-financial-economic-political-cultural-military-police complex that holds the entire decisive power of the country is located;

(B) to weaken the local guards of the security system of the dictatorship, given the fact that we are attacking and the guerillas defending, which means catching the government in a defensive position with its troops immobilized in defense of the entire complex of national maintenance, with its ever present fears of an attack on its strategic nerve centers, and without ever knowing where, how, and when that attack will come;

(C) to attack on every side with many different armed groups, few in number, each self-contained and operating separately, to disperse the government forces in their pursuit of a thor-oughly fragmented organization instead of offering the dicta-torship the opportunity to concentrate its forces of repression on the destruction of one tightly organized system operating throughout the country;

(D) to give proof of its combativeness, decision, firmness, determination, and persistence in the attack on the military dic-tatorship in order to permit all malcontents to follow our example and fight with urban guerrilla tactics. Meanwhile, the government, with all its problems, incapable of halting guerrilla operations in the city, will lose time and suffer endless attrition and will finally be forced to pull back its repressive troops in order to mount guard over the banks, industries, armories, military barracks, prisons, public offices, radio and television stations, North American firms, gas storage tanks, oil refineries, ships, airplanes, ports, airports, hospitals, health centers, blood banks, stores, garages, embassies, residences of outstanding members of the regime such as ministers and generals, police stations, and official organizations, etc;

(E) to increase urban guerrilla disturbances gradually in an endless ascendancy of unforeseen actions such that the government troops cannot leave the urban area to pursue the guerrillas in the interior without running the risk of abandoning the cities and permitting rebellion to increase on the coast as well as in the interior of the country;

(F) to oblige the army and the police, with the commanders and their assistants, to exchange the relative comfort and tranquillity of their barracks and their usual rest, for a state of alarm and growing tension in the expectation of attack or in search of tracks, which vanish without a trace;

(G) to avoid open battle and decisive combat with the government, limiting the struggle to brief and rapid attacks with lightning results;

(H) to assure for the urban guerrilla a maximum freedom of maneuvers and of action without ever relinquishing the use of armed violence, remaining firmly oriented toward helping the beginning of rural guerrilla warfare and supporting the construction of the revolutionary army for national liberation. . . .

The Bank Assault as Popular Model

The most popular assault model is the bank assault. In Brazil, the urban guerrilla has begun a type of organized assault on the banks as a guerrilla operation. Today this type of assault is widely used and has served as a sort of preliminary examination for the urban guerrilla in his apprenticeship for the techniques of revolutionary warfare. . . .

The bank assault is a typical expropriation. But, as is true in any kind of armed expropriatory action, the revolutionary is handicapped by a two-fold competition: (a) competition from the outlaw; and (b) competition from the right-wing counterrevolutionary.

This competition produces confusion, which is reflected in the people's uncertainty. It is up to the urban guerrilla to prevent this from happening, and to accomplish this he must use two methods: (a) he must avoid the outlaw's technique, which is one of unnecessary violence and appropriation of goods and possessions belonging to the people; and (b) he must use the assault for propaganda purposes, at the very moment it is taking place, and later distribute material, leaflets, every possible means of explaining the objectives and the principles of the urban guerrilla as expropriator of the government, the ruling classes, and imperialism. . . .

KIDNAPPING

Kidnapping is capturing and holding in a secret spot a police agent, a North American spy, a political personality, or a notorious and dangerous enemy of the revolutionary movement.

Kidnapping is used to exchange or liberate imprisoned revolutionary comrades, or to force suspension of torture in the jail cells of the military dictatorship.

The kidnapping of personalities who are known artists, sports figures, or are outstanding in some other field, but who have evidenced no political interest, can be a useful form of propaganda for the revolutionary and patriotic principles of the urban guerrilla provided it occurs under special circumstances and the kidnapping is handled so that the public sympathizes with it and accepts it.

The kidnapping of North American residents or visitors in Brazil constitutes a form of protest against the penetration and domination by United States imperialism of our country. . . .

TERRORISM

Terrorism is an action, usually involving the placement of a bomb or fire explosion of great destructive power, which is capable of effecting irreparable loss against the enemy.

Terrorism requires that the urban guerrilla should have an adequate theoretical and practical knowledge of how to make explosives.

The terroristic act, apart from the apparent facility with which it can be carried out, is no different from other urban guerrilla acts and actions whose success depends on the planning and determination of the revolutionary organization. It is an action the urban guerrilla must execute with the greatest cold bloodedness, calmness, and decision.

Although terrorism generally involves an explosion, there are cases in which it may also be carried out by execution and the systematic burning of installations, properties, and North American depots, plantations, etc. It is essential to point out the importance of fires and the construction of incendiary bombs such as gasoline bombs in the technique of revolutionary terrorism. Another thing is the importance of the material the urban guerrilla can persuade the people to expropriate in moments of hunger and scarcity resulting from the greed of the big commercial interests.

Terrorism is an arm the revolutionary can never relinquish.

POPULAR SUPPORT

One of the permanent concerns of the urban guerrilla is his identification with popular causes to win public support.

Where government actions become inept and corrupt, the urban guerrilla should not hesitate to step in to show that he opposes the government and to gain mass sympathy. The present government, for example, imposes heavy financial burdens and excessively high taxes on the people. It is up to the urban guerrilla to attack the dictatorship's tax collection system and to obstruct its financial activity, throwing all the weight of violent revolutionary action against it.

The urban guerrilla fights not only to upset the tax and collection system; the arm of revolutionary violence must also be directed against those government organs that raise prices and those who direct them, as well as against the wealthiest of the national and foreign profiteers and the important property owners; in short, against all those who accumulate huge fortunes out of the high cost of living, the wages of hunger, excessive prices and rents.

Foreign trusts, such as refrigeration and other North American plants that monopolize the market and the manufacture of general food supplies, must be systematically attacked by the urban guerrilla.

The rebellion of the urban guerrilla and his persistence in intervening in public questions is the best way of insuring public support of the cause we defend. We repeat and insist on repeating: *It is the best way of insuring public support.* As soon as a reasonable section of the population begins to take seriously the action of the urban guerrilla, his success is guaranteed.

The government has no alternative except to intensify repression. The police networks, house searches, arrests of innocent people and of suspects, closing off streets—all make life in the city unbearable. The military dictatorship embarks on massive political persecution. Political assassinations and police terror become routine.

In spite of all this, the police systematically fail. The armed forces, the navy, and the air force are mobilized and undertake routine police functions. Even so they find no way to halt guerrilla operations, nor to wipe out the revolutionary organization with its fragmented groups that move around and operate throughout the national territory persistently and contagiously.

The people refuse to collaborate with the authorities, and the general sentiment is that the government is unjust, incapable of solving problems, and resorts purely and simply to the physical liquidation of its opponents.

The political situation in the country is transformed into a military situation in which the gorillas appear more and more to be the ones responsible for errors and violence, while the problems in the lives of the people become truly catastrophic.

When they see the militarists and the dictatorship on the brink of the abyss, and fearing the consequences of a revolutionary war that is already at a fairly advanced and irreversible level, the pacifiers, always to be found within the ruling classes, and the right-wing opportunists, partisans of nonviolent struggle, join hands and circulate rumors behind the scenes, begging the hangmen for elections, "redemocratization," constitutional reforms, and other tripe designed to fool the masses and make them stop the revolutionary rebellion in the cities and the rural areas of the country.

But, watching the revolutionaries, the people now understand that it is a farce to vote in elections that have as their sole objective guaranteeing the continuation of the military dictatorship and covering up its crimes.

Attacking wholeheartedly this election farce and the so-called political solution so appealing to the opportunists, the urban guerrilla must become more aggressive and violent, resorting without letup to sabotage, terrorism, expropriations, assaults, kidnappings, executions, etc.

This answers any attempt to fool the masses with the opening of Congress and the reorganization of political parties—parties of the government and of the opposition it allows *—when all the time the parliament and the so-called parties function thanks to the license of the military dictatorship in a true spectacle of marionettes and dogs on a leash.

The role of the urban guerrilla, in order to win the support of the people, is to continue fighting, keeping in mind the interests of the masses and heightening the disastrous situation in which the government must act. These are the circumstances, disastrous for the dictatorship, which permit the revolutionaries to open rural guerrilla warfare in the midst of the uncontrollable expansion of urban rebellion.

---

* The Brazilian government permits only two political parties to function: the pro-government ARENA and the officially tolerated opposition MDB. —ED.

Selected Bibliography

For background and further reading related to the themes treated in this book, the following works are recommended:

Introduction

ALMOND, GABRIEL and JAMES M. COLEMAN. *The Politics of the Developing Areas.* Princeton, N.J.: Princeton University Press, 1960.

ALMOND, GABRIEL. *Political Development.* Boston: Little, Brown, 1970.

ANDERSON, CHARLES W., FRED VON DER MEHDEN, and CRAWFORD YOUNG. *Issues of Political Development.* Englewood Cliffs, N.J.: Prentice-Hall, 1967.

APTER, DAVID (ed.). *Ideology and Discontent.* New York: The Free Press, 1964.

BAYLEY, DAVID H. *Public Liberties in the New States.* Chicago: Rand-McNally, 1964.

BIENEN, HENRY (ed.). *The Military and Modernization.* Chicago: Aldine-Atherton, 1971.

BLACK, CYRIL E. *The Dynamics of Modernization.* New York: Harper & Row, 1966.

COX, RICHARD (ed.). *Ideology, Politics and Political Theory.* Belmont, Cal.: Wadsworth, 1969.

EMERSON, RUPERT. *From Empire to Nation.* Boston: Beacon Press, 1962.

HUNTINGTON, SAMUEL P. and CLEMENT H. MOORE (eds.). *Authoritarian Politics in Modern Society.* New York: Basic Books, 1970.

HUNTINGTON, SAMUEL P. *Political Order in Changing Societies.* New Haven: Yale University Press, 1968.

JANOWITZ, MORRIS. *The Military in the Political Development of New Nations.* Chicago: University of Chicago Press, 1964.

JOHNSON, JOHN H. (ed.). *The Role of the Military in Underdeveloped Countries,* Princeton, N.J.: Princeton University Press, 1962.

KAUTSKY, JOHN H. (ed.). *Political Change in Underdeveloped Countries.* New York: John Wiley, 1962.

KAUTSKY, JOHN H. *Communism and the Politics of Development.* New York: John Wiley, 1968.

McCORD, WILLIAM. *The Springtime of Freedom.* London and New York: Oxford University Press, 1965.

MOORE, BARRINGTON. *The Social Origins of Democracy and Dictatorship.* Boston: Beacon Press, 1966.

ORGANSKI, A. F. K. *The Stages of Political Development.* New York: Alfred A. Knopf, 1965.

PENNOCK, J. ROLAND (ed.). *Self-Government in Modernizing Nations.* Englewood Cliffs, N.J.: Prentice-Hall, 1964.

PYE, LUCIAN W. *Aspects of Political Development.* Boston: Little, Brown, 1966.

VON DER MEHDEN, FRED. *The Politics of the Developing Nations.* 2d ed. Englewood Cliffs, N.J.: Prentice-Hall, 1969.

WEINER, MYRON. *Modernization.* New York: Basic Books, 1966.

Part I: Asia

BARNETT, A. DOAK. *China After Mao.* Princeton, N.J.: Princeton University Press, 1967.

BRECHER, MICHAEL. *Nehru: A Political Biography.* London and New York: Oxford University Press, 1959.

EBON, MARTIN. *Lin Piao.* New York: Stein & Day, 1970.

ERICKSON, ERIC. *Gandhi's Truth.* New York: W. W. Norton, 1969.

FAN, K. H. *The Chinese Cultural Revolution: Selected Documents.* New York: Grove Press, 1968.

JACK, HOMER (ed.). *The Gandhi Reader.* New York: Grove Press, 1961.

MINTZ, JEANNE. *Mohammed, Marx, and Marhaen: The Roots of Indonesian Socialism.* New York: Praeger Publishers, 1965.

SCHRAM, STUART. *The Political Thought of Mao Tse-tung.* Rev. ed. New York: Praeger Publishers, 1969.

SHAW, BRUNO (ed.). *Selected Works of Mao Tse-tung.* New York: Harper Colophon, 1970.

Part II: The Islamic World

ABDEL-MALEK, ANOUAR. *Egypt: Military Society.* New York: Random House, 1968.

ABU JABER, KEMAL. *The Arab Ba'th Socialist Party.* Syracuse, N.Y.: University of Syracuse Press, 1966.

BINDER, LEONARD. *The Ideological Revolution in the Middle East.* New York: John Wiley, 1964.

HAIM, SYLVIA H. (ed.). *Arab Nationalism.* Berkeley, Cal.: University of California Press, 1962.

HALPERN, MANFRED. *The Politics of Social Change in the Middle East and North Africa.* Princeton, N.J.: Princeton University Press, 1965.

KARPAT, KEMAL H. (ed.). *Political and Social Thought in the Middle East.* New York: Praeger Publishers, 1968.

KERR, MALCOLM. *The Arab Cold War, 1958–64.* London and New York: Oxford University Press, 1965.

MANSFIELD, PETER. *Nasser's Egypt.* Rev. ed. Baltimore, Md.: Penguin Books, 1969.

MOORE, CLEMENT H. *Tunisia Since Independence: The Dynamics of One-Party Government.* Berkeley, Cal.: University of California Press, 1965.

RIVLIN, BENJAMIN and JOSEPH S. SZYLIOWICS (eds.). *The Contemporary Middle East.* New York: Random House, 1965.

SHIRABI, HISHAM. *Nationalism and Revolution in the Arab World.* Princeton, N.J.: D. Van Nostrand, 1966.

VATIKIOTIS, P. J. *The Egyptian Army in Politics.* Bloomington, Ind.: Indiana University Press, 1961.

VATIKIOTIS, P. J. (ed.). *Egypt Since the Revolution.* New York: Praeger Publishers, 1968.

Part III: Africa

ABRAHAM, WILLIE. *The Mind of Africa.* Chicago: The University of Chicago Press, 1963.

AUSTIN, DENNIS. *Politics in Ghana, 1946–60.* London and New York: Oxford University Press, 1964.

BRETTON, HENRY. *The Rise and Fall of Kwame Nkrumah.* New York: Praeger Publishers, 1966.

CARTER, GWENDOLEN M. (ed.). *African One-Party States.* Ithaca, N.Y.: Cornell University Press, 1964.

CERVENKA, ZDENEK. *The Organization of African Unity and Its Charter.* New York: Praeger Publishers, 1969.

COLEMAN, JAMES S. and CARL ROSBERG, JR. (eds.). *Political Parties and National Integration in Tropical Africa.* Berkeley, Cal.: University of California Press, 1964.

DUMONT, RENE. *False Start in Africa.* 2d ed. New York: Praeger Publishers, 1969.

FRIEDLAND, WILLIAM A. and CARL ROSBERG, JR. (eds.). *African Socialism.* Stanford, Cal.: Stanford University Press, 1964.

GUTTERIDGE, WILLIAM. *The Military in African Politics.* New York: Barnes and Noble, 1969.

HODGKIN, THOMAS. *African Political Parties.* Baltimore, Md.: Penguin Books, 1961.

JULY, ROBERT. *The Origins of Modern African Thought*. New York: Praeger Publishers, 1967.

LEE, J. M. *African Armies and Civil Order*. New York: Praeger Publishers, 1969.

LEGUM, COLIN. *Pan-Africanism, A Short Political Guide*. New York: Praeger Publishers, 1965.

LEWIS, W. ARTHUR. *Politics in West Africa*. London and New York: Oxford University Press, 1965.

MAHIOU, AHMED. *L'Avènement du Parti Unique en Afrique Noire*. Paris: Librairie Generale de Droit, 1969.

MARKOVITZ, IRVING L. *Leopold Cedar Senghor and the Politics of Negritude*. New York: Atheneum Press, 1969.

MAZRUI, ALI. *On Heroes and Uhuru Worship*. New York: Humanities, 1967.

MBOYA, TOM. *The Challenge of Nationhood*. New York: Praeger Publishers, 1970.

MORGENTHAU, RUTH SCHACHTER. *Political Parties in French-Speaking Africa*. London and New York: Oxford University Press, 1964.

MPHAHLELE, EZEKIEL. *The African Image*. New York: Praeger Publishers, 1962.

NKRUMAH, KWAME. *Africa Must Unite*. New York: Praeger Publishers, 1963.

NYE, JOSEPH. *Pan-Africanism and East African Federation*. Cambridge, Mass.: Harvard University Press, 1965.

ODINGA, OGINGA. *Not Yet Uhuru*. New York: Hill and Wang, 1967.

ROTBERG, R. and ALI MAZRUI (eds.). *Protest and Power in Black Africa*. London and New York: Oxford University Press, 1970.

SENGHOR, LEOPOLD SEDAR. *On African Socialism*. New York: Frederick A. Praeger, 1964.

SKURNIK, W. A. E. *African Political Thought: Lumumba, Nkrumah, and Toure*. Denver, Colo.: University of Denver Press, 1968.

THIAM, DOUDOU. *The Foreign Policy of African States*. New York: Phoenix House; New York: Praeger Publishers, 1965.

WALLERSTEIN, IMMANUEL. *Africa: The Politics of Unity*. New York: Random House, 1967.

ZARTMAN, I. WILLIAM. *International Relations in the New Africa*. Englewood Cliffs, N.J.: Prentice-Hall, 1966.

ZOLBERG, ARISTIDE. *Creating Political Order: The Party-States of West Africa*. Chicago: Rand-McNally, 1966.

Part IV: Latin America

BONACHEA, ROLANDO and VALDES, NELSON D. (eds.). *Che: Selected Works of Ernesto Guevara*. Cambridge, Mass.: M.I.T. Press, 1969.

DAVIS, HAROLD E. *Latin American Social Thought Since Independence.* 2d. ed. Seattle: University of Washington Press, 1966.

DENTON, CHARLES F. *Patterns of Costa Rican Politics.* Boston: Allyn & Bacon, 1971.

DUNCAN, W. RAYMOND and JAMES NELSON GOODSELL (eds.). *The Quest for Change in Latin America.* New York: Oxford University Press, 1970.

GIL, FEDERICO G. *The Political System of Chile.* Boston: Houghton, Mifflin, 1966.

GOTT, RICHARD. *Guerrilla Movements in Latin America.* New York: Doubleday, 1971.

HALPERIN, ERNST. *Nationalism and Communism in Chile.* Cambridge, Mass.: M.I.T. Press, 1965.

HILLIKER, GRANT. *The Politics of Reform in Peru.* Baltimore, Md.: The Johns Hopkins Press, 1971.

HIRSCHMAN, ALBERT O. (ed.). *Latin American Issues: Essays and Comments.* New York: The Twentieth Century Fund, 1961.

JORRIN, MIGUEL and JOHN MARTZ. *Latin American Political Thought and Ideology.* Chapel Hill, N.C.: University of North Carolina Press, 1970.

KAROL, K. S. *Guerrillas in Power: The Course of the Cuban Revolution.* New York: Hill and Wang, 1970.

SIGMUND, PAUL E. (ed.). *Models of Political Change in Latin America.* New York: Praeger Publishers, 1970.

SKIDMORE, THOMAS. *Politics in Brazil.* New York: Oxford University Press, 1967.

STEPAN, ALFRED. *The Military in Politics: Changing Patterns in Brazil.* Princeton, N.J.: Princeton University Press, 1971.

SUAREZ, ANDRES. *Cuba, Castroism, and Communism, 1959–1966.* Cambridge, Mass.: M.I.T. Press, 1967.

VELIZ, CLAUDIO (ed.). *Obstacles to Change in Latin America.* London and New York: Oxford University Press, 1965.

WILLIAMS, EDWARD J. *Latin American Christian Democratic Parties.* Knoxville, Tenn.: University of Tennessee Press, 1967.